Niebuhr's Lectures On Roman History

Vol. II

by

Barthold Georg Niebuhr

Double 9 BOOKS

Niebuhr's Lectures On Roman History

Vol. II

by Barthold Georg Niebuhr

ISBN: 978-93-71462-69-3

Published by

DOUBLE 9 BOOKS

2/13-B, Ansari Road
Daryaganj, New Delhi – 110002
info@double9books.com
www.double9books.com
Tel. 011-40042856

ABOUT THE AUTHOR

Barthold Georg Niebuhr was born on August 27, 1776, in Copenhagen, Denmark, to Carsten Niebuhr, a renowned geographer and explorer. Raised in an intellectually rich environment, he developed a deep interest in classical antiquity from a young age. He studied at the University of Kiel and later pursued a career that bridged finance, statecraft, and scholarship. After working as a banker and holding various public offices, he turned to academia, where he significantly influenced the field of historical research. Niebuhr became a pioneering figure in the modern study of Roman history, advocating for critical methods of source analysis and emphasizing the need to distinguish myth from fact in ancient narratives. He delivered influential lectures in Bonn, shaping a generation of historians with his rigorous, analytical approach to historiography. Niebuhr's work laid the groundwork for viewing history as a discipline grounded in evidence and interpretation rather than legend. He passed away on January 2, 1831, in Bonn, Germany. His daughter, Amalia Francke, survived him. Throughout his life, Niebuhr sought to elevate the standards of historical inquiry, making a lasting contribution to both classical studies and modern historical methodology.

CONTENTS

THE FIRST PUNIC WAR

Every body knows that Carthage is a colony of Tyre, founded seventy-two years before the received date of the building of Rome. This statement is quite historical. It rests upon those highly important notices in Josephus' work against Apion, from Phœnician chronicles which he read in a Greek version of Menander of Ephesus. They are fully as genuine as Berosus and Sanchoniathon, and closely tally with the history of the Jewish kings: fraud on the part of Josephus is not to be thought of. The Romans knew of the historical books of the Phœnicians: after the destruction of Carthage, they presented them to the library of the Numidian kings. If we wish for a true and authentic account of the earliest history, we should be very thankful to have such dates as these. The assertion also of Timæus that Rome was built about the same time as Carthage, is not wide of the mark; that is to say, if we reckon the Sæcula at a hundred and ten years. Utica (Athika אָקִיתָע) is an older colony of Tyre than Carthage: its foundation belongs to the age in which the power of the Phœnicians was at its height, and they had settlements in Cyprus, and were establishing themselves in every quarter. Those of Cythera, Thasos, and elsewhere, are of much later date; but it is likely that Cadiz (Gades) already existed when Carthage was built.

Carthage was originally founded under the name of Bozra (in Greek Βύρσα, whence the legend of the bullock's hide). By the side of this Bozra, that is to say, city, there arose, even as Naples did at the side of Parthenope, a new town, אָתְדַח הָתְרַק *Kartha chadtha,* (by contraction Karchadta, from which the Greeks made out Καρχηδών). The town, for perhaps two hundred years, increased but slowly; it paid tribute to the Libyan peoples, and was for a long time in a state of dependence upon Tyre. Towards this, her mother-city, Carthage was never wanting in filial piety, not even when its relations to her had completely changed, which is one of the fine traits in her history. Of the time when Carthage began to extend its sway, we know nothing: placed as it was in the midst of barbarous nations, which were not able to amalgamate with it, it could not have risen into prosperity as quickly as the Greek colonies on the Asiatic coasts, where races of men were dwelling between which and the Pelasgian stock there was affinity, although not in language, yet in that spirit of refined humanity which distinguished them;

as, for instance, the Lycians, and Carians, who, even before they were hellenized, had already attained to a considerable degree of civilization, as we see from their monuments and institutions. The Carthaginians did not betake themselves to husbandry, and therefore they could not multiply as fast as families which spread out; the Libyans were hard, oppressive neighbours, barbarians (*Berbers* as they are called to this very day) who only gradually mingled with the Phœnician settlers. It was not until the middle of the third century of Rome, more than three hundred years after her own foundation, that Carthage made her appearance as a power. The earlier times are shrouded in impenetrable darkness. Justin gives some notices from Trogus, but most carelessly; so does also Diodorus, who in all likelihood borrowed from Timæus: the former has an account of a civil war, and of a conquest of Carthage by Malcus, one of its generals. Certain it is, that Carthage for a long time paid tribute to the Libyans; and the first sign of its vigour, is the throwing off of this yoke in a hard-fought struggle. Particularly favourable to Carthage seem to have been the fortunes of the mother country Phœnicia, which, after having long and painfully striven against Egypt, yielded itself to Persian protection; for though indeed its condition was thus tolerable enough, yet at times a foreign yoke was felt to be galling, and many may have then emigrated to the free colony, which was made to thrive the more, as Tyre, owing to its connexion with Persia, now became the port for the whole of Asia, even as far as India. The treaty with Rome in the year of the city 245, shows that the Carthaginians were then already masters of part of Sicily, of Sardinia, and of Libya, so that they were a great people for that age. About the year 272, they are said to have come over with an army of 300,000 men into Sicily, against Gelon of Syracuse and Theron of Agrigentum: this, however, is not real history. Pindar and Simonides sang the achievements of Gelon and Theron; but history was not yet written. It is not that such an expedition has never taken place; what is doubtful, is the assertion that it happened at the same time as the invasion of Xerxes. The battle of Himera is said to have been fought on the very day that he was defeated at Salamis; but, on the other hand, the better chronological statements which rest upon the authority of Timæus, show that Gelon, who is supposed to have conquered at Himera, came to the throne at a later date than that of the battle of Salamis. The expedition of the Carthaginians must have happened in the 76th, or 77th Olympiad, and it must have been insignificant. They were beaten, and did not for a long time think again of undertaking anything against Sicily: they now strengthened themselves in other quarters. When the Athenians engaged in their enterprise against Sicily, we hear little or nothing of the Carthaginians; they were confined to Motye, Panormus, and Solois, the first of which three places is a Phœnician settlement. Yet when the expedition had come to such an unhappy end, the implacable revenge wreaked against Segesta and the other cities which had welcomed the Athenians, now brought on the ruin of Sicily. These cities applied to Carthage, which sent a considerable army over (350): all the Greek towns were involved in the greatest danger; Selinus, Agrigentum, Camarina, Gela, and other places were destroyed. Dionysius the elder concluded a disadvantageous peace, but was afterwards more successful. In the reign of Dionysius the second, the Carthaginians renewed the contest. Timoleon defeated them, and drove them back to Motye and Lilybæum; yet in the peace the old *status quo* was re-established, and the western part of Sicily remained in their hands: the rivers Nimera and Halycus continued to be the boundaries which thenceforth were looked upon as the normal ones, and were generally restored when a peace was made. In the days of Agathocles, the Carthaginians besieged Syracuse; but in a second campaign, during which Motye was destroyed, and they were for some time confined to Lilybæum, they were compelled to restore the boundary of the Himera. Then followed the events of the times of Pyrrhus, who carried out the plans of Agathocles still further. After his departure, the Carthaginians spread themselves again, and afterwards got possession once more of Agrigentum.

At the beginning of the first Punic war, Carthage was mistress of the whole of the western half of Sicily, and of the northern coast as far as Messana. In Africa, her rule extended to the corner of the great Syrtis; nearly the whole of the territory of Tunis was subject to her. Along a great part of the African coast, there was a number of Carthaginian colonial towns. There were likewise several of them in the interior; for the Libyans had adopted Punic civilization: even St. Augustine says that the Punic language was his mother tongue. When two hundred years afterwards the Arabs conquered these regions, they were able in some degree to converse with the inhabitants; and the present Tunisian dialect, as well as the Maltese, without doubt has still retained some Punic elements. The coast of Algiers, as far as the straits of Gibraltar, was occupied by their factories only, the mountains there approaching too near the sea to leave room for colonies. In Sardinia, the Carthaginians ruled over the whole of that gloomy but fruitful isle, with the exception of the inner highlands; and these were inhabited by savage tribes, which to this day have not changed their way of living, but, for instance, even now wear those sheep skins which Cicero calls *mastrucæ*. In Corsica, they had a few settlements, probably the excellent harbours there: the Balearic isles were also subject to them. The coasts of Granada and Murcia were likewise in their possession; and Cadiz, although a sister town, was treated as a dependent.

As to the constitution of Carthage, we are utterly in the dark. What has been written on it, is but insignificant; nor have my researches led me to any important results. They had, according to Aristotle, a δῆμος, that is to say, a mixed commonalty which had come together (συνήλυδες) of colonial citizens and Libyans (Amazirgh, Schilha's, Maxyes, Massesyles). The Libyans, in their whole physical constitution, do not in the least differ from the nations of Southern Europe; and thus likewise ancient Egypt, before it was conquered by the Æthiopians, had a white population: the whole of the Mediterranean therefore was inhabited around by whites. These Libyans could very easily have amalgamated with the *Pœni* in a δῆμος, even as at Rome the plebeians did with the patricians; yet there would be this distinction, that these last were of the same stock, whereas the Libyans and the *Pœni* were altogether different, and particularly so in their language. The relation between the Libyans and the *Pœni* is analogous to that of the Lettish and Lithuanian tribes to the German settlers, or of the Slavonic population near Lübeck and the Germans, the former of whom also became completely Germanized. We know moreover that Carthage had a senate; this is still the governing body in the first Punic war. According to Aristotle, the δῆμος at Carthage had but little to say, not much more than at Sparta, where only those who were in authority might speak in the assembly, and not the people, who were merely to assent or to reject; at Carthage, any one of the people was at least free to stand up and make a speech. Those whom Aristotle calls the βασιλεῖς, even the Suffetes or *Schofetim,* were no doubt in earlier times the commanders of the army likewise: afterwards, when the civil and military power were jealously kept distinct, their office was merely an administrative one. We also find that there was a powerful corporation called the Hundred, which cannot but be the same as the Hundred and Four in Aristotle: these I have long ago referred to the fifty weeks of the year. Moreover, he speaks of another kind of magistracy, of which we merely know that it was a πενταρχία (if the reading be correct, as the text of Aristotle's Politics is derived from a single Parisian MS. of the fourteenth century), and that its members were chosen by the Hundred and Four. Of what nature it was, we do not know.

The Hundred and Four are no doubt the *centum senatores,* before whom, says Justin, the kings and generals had to undergo their εὐθύναι; they may have been a court of control to check the administration of the senate, very much like the Ephors in Sparta (παραπλήσιοι ἐφόροις). Aristotle points out, that, properly speaking, the power of government lay with the senate; single cases only were brought before the people: there was therefore no magistracy which could agitate the δῆμος, like the tribunes at Rome. The chief offices were given ἀριστίνδην and πλουτίνδην: in a later passage, Aristotle says positively that the highest places were ὠνηταί, and Polybius confirms it. People were not in the least ashamed to take money from the candidates: things were managed as in the small cantons in Switzerland, where the office of bailiff (*Landvogt*) was sold in the most shameless manner, or as in Venice. There the places were not quite bought in due form; but it was well understood, that one had to pay for them: the great offices of state were sought after as a *provvigione*, as a means of restoring embarrassed fortunes. The rich were never punished, not even for murder; but they paid damages, and there was a regular sale of *cartes blanches* for manslaughter. This was also the case with the Carthaginians. They were a commercial people, but this should by no means have bereft them of the feeling of honour: we do not find it to be so in England, for instance. Among the trading communities of the United States, similar sentiments are said to prevail as in Carthage. Such a disposition as this cannot but lead to utter ruin. The Carthaginians, owing to their rapacity, were grievously hateful to their subjects: the Libyans had to pay a fourth part of their produce, and in some extraordinary cases even half; besides which, there was whatever the governors might squeeze out of them on their own account; and these, as Aristotle already tells us, were positively sent down to suck the blood of those who were under their rule. This plan was adopted to keep individuals among the citizens in good humour. The contrast between the Carthaginians and the Romans in their better times, is very striking. Some great men, of course, were exceptions, as they were able to act freely, like kings: when Hamilcar commanded in Spain, the Carthaginians were quite popular there. The nation was unwarlike; they kept mercenaries, and had only a cavalry of their own: the mercenaries were faithless in a countless number of instances. The Carthaginians not unseldom left the same generals for many years in possession of their command; but the separation of it from the civil magistracy had this disadvantage, that they often rebelled. The generals, however, became very familiarly acquainted with their armies, and a good captain was thus enabled to achieve quite incredible things, whilst a bad one might also do great mischief. Among the Romans, it was, of course, quite different. With them, there was a constant change; men were in office for one year, and then, at most, one more as proconsuls.

If we would understand the first Punic war, we ought to have in our mind's eye an outline of the natural features of Sicily. As every body knows, the core and frame-work of the whole island is Ætna, from which a chain of mountains stretches close along the sea, and is continued on the opposite shore as far as Hipponium in Bruttium. For the mountain ranges in the South of Italy belong geologically to Sicily, whilst the hills of the Northern Apennines are a different ridge. The *Apenninus* so ends that the two sets of mountains are connected together by low hills, on the spot where the Greeks had more than once the intention of making a canal. The mountain ridge, therefore, runs north from Ætna as far as Messina on the eastern coast; to the south, it leaves a considerable plain near Leontini towards the sea; between Syracuse and the western country, there is only a low range of hills. West of Ætna, it continues under the names of the Heræan and Nebrodian mountains. From Pelorus to Himera, it is quite close to the sea, which washes its foot; so that sometimes there is not even a road between. From Himera onward, there is a small strip of coast, and the mountains fall off in height: at some distance from Palermo, the country becomes quite flat; the only eminence is the hill in which is the cavern of St. Rosalia (the ancient Hercta).[1] The range of mountains then goes further to the west, and rises again: Eryx (Monte San Giuliano) is the largest mountain after Ætna; it towers in a quite extraordinary way from among the lower groups. The country round Enna is flat. The southern coast to Agrigentum is a large plain, by Gela and Camarina also it is flat; south of a line drawn from Agrigentum to Catana, there is either nothing but hillocks, or a dead level.—According therefore to this nature of the ground, campaigns had to be managed. Otherwise it would be incomprehensible why the Romans did not march from Messina to Palermo by the northern coast, but went to the southern part, where they could have had no other base but Syracuse to rest upon. To this, my attention was directed by the campaigns of the English in 1812, in which likewise the troops could not go by land from Messina to Palermo.

The first Punic war may be divided into five periods:—

1. From 488 to 491, when the Romans carry on the war without a fleet. The Carthaginians are masters of the sea; the Romans have the greatest difficulty in crossing, and can only get at them in Sicily by land.

2. From 492 to 496, to the landing of Regulus in Africa.

3. From 496 to 497, the campaign of Regulus in Africa.

4. From the destruction of the army of Regulus to the victory of L. Cæcilius Metellus near Panormus. Fortune is nearly equally balanced; the Romans lose two fleets by storms, the Carthaginians have the upperhand in Sicily: nevertheless the Romans are victorious at last.

5. From the beginning of the year 502 to 511; from the contest for Lilibæum and Drepana, to the victory near the Ægatian isles. The ten years' struggle is confined to an exceedingly narrow space, being important rather in a military than in an historical point of view. The diversion

> of Hamilcar Barcas, of which, unfortunately, we know so little, is, owing to the taking of Hercta and Eryx, one of the most remarkable in the military history of any age; it shows a great man, who creates new resources for himself, and avails himself of them. Yet for the history of nations this period is not so important.

The Carthaginian system of warfare is quite unknown to us; we can only say, that, where the Carthaginians themselves were in arms, they were drawn up in a phalanx just like the Greeks. The Spaniards very likely stood in *catervæ*, and fought with small swords, and *in cetris*, that is to say, linen coats of mail. The Gauls, no doubt, fought in great masses.

In the year 490, the third of the war, the Romans undertook to besiege Agrigentum with two armies. This town was of great extent; yet, as a city it was but a mere shadow of what it had been a hundred and forty years earlier, before its first destruction by the Carthaginians. Within its high and strong walls, a considerable army of the enemy had now thrown itself. The name of the Punic general was Hannibal. The Carthaginians were called by their first-names only, and one might be easily led to think that they were all related to each other, as there were so few of these names, Hannibal, Hanno, Hamilcar, and some others. These correspond to our christian names, to the Roman *prænomina*, as Gaius, &c. They certainly had, all of them, family names also, which, however, at that time were not yet made use of to designate individuals: they had even bye-names, but these have been partly lost to us. The generals who bear the name of Hannibal, are in the whole of Carthaginian history so insignificant, when set beside that great man who gave the name its renown, that little mention only is made of them. Hannibal had posted himself with fifty thousand men within the wide and waste precincts of Agrigentum; the two consular armies advanced on the south against the town, entrenched themselves in two camps, and constructed two lines against the city, and against any one who might attempt to relieve it. The Carthaginian generals were very bad in the beginning of the war; they either made no use at all of the elephants, or only a limited one, and they were very loth to give battle to the Romans. Hannibal had now imprudently allowed himself to be thus hemmed in, and as Agrigentum does not lie close to the sea, he could not get any succours from thence: yet he succeeded in conveying to the Carthaginians, by single messengers and letters, his entreaties for relief. They indeed, when he had been besieged five months, sent Hanno with a large army and fifty elephants. This general pitched a strong camp near Heraclea; took Erbessus, the arsenal of the Romans; and by means of barricades of felled trees, &c., so shut them in, that they were much distressed for want of supplies, and on account of the state of health of their troops: for the Carthaginians were masters of the sea, and the Numidian horsemen, the Cossacks of the ancients, made it exceedingly difficult for them to forage. It seemed as if they would be obliged to give up the siege, and to retreat; yet they could not bring themselves to do so, showing in this instance also their perseverance, and on the contrary, they kept up the blockade so strictly, that Hannibal found no means of bettering the condition of his troops. When under these circumstances two months had gone by, Hanno may have had reasons to attack; yet the Romans gained a complete victory, and set themselves up again by the booty which they got in his camp. All this time, Hiero had given them every possible help: without him they would have perished. Hannibal, who had been brought to extremities, took advantage of the moment when the Romans were enjoying themselves the night after their victory, to make preparations for a sally. The soldiers filled the ditches of the Roman lines with fascines and sacks of straw, climbed over the ramparts, drove back the outposts, and thus fought their way through: all that the Romans could do, was to annoy them in the rear. Whoever was able to bear arms, got off in this way; but the inhabitants of the town were for the most part left behind, as well as the sick and the weak. Agrigentum was, on the following morning, sacked and pillaged, like a town taken by storm. Here the Romans made up for all their privations: the whole of the unfortunate population was swept away.

After this frightful event, a year passed by without any remarkable occurrence. The Carthaginians strongly provisioned and fortified their other stations in the west; yet they also acted on the offensive. Their fleet cruised off the coasts of Italy, which it laid waste; the northern coasts of Sicily likewise surrendered to their power from fear, whilst the Romans kept the inner island and the eastern coast. The conquest of Agrigentum gave the latter quite different ideas with regard to the war. Formerly, they merely wanted to have Messana and Syracuse as dependent allies; but now their object was to drive the Carthaginians altogether from the island, as Dionysius, Agathocles, and Pyrrhus had done: they saw, however, that this could not be done without a fleet. It was the same difficulty as at Athens, where, in the Peloponnesian war, and in the times immediately following it, they had no other ships but penteconters, *lembi*, and triremes (with from 200 to 220 men, who were partly rowers and partly marines, and with a deck; the penteconters, which had 50 men,[2] were open, and the benches for the rowers in both were placed across, before and above each other); these vessels had been outdone long since, and larger ones were needed. In Syracuse, the cradle of mechanical art, quadriremes, and soon afterwards quinqueremes, were first mounted, ships of a larger class, which were not round, and which might properly be called ships of the line; for, the difference of the triremes and quinqueremes cannot have consisted merely in the number of the benches and the rowers, but it must really have been in the build itself, otherwise no great skill would have been required to construct them. These quinqueremes had already for a long time been in use, especially in the Macedonian, Sicelian, and Punic fleets; but neither the Romans, nor the Antiates had them. The Romans had also triremes, and wherever the Antiate vessels are mentioned, they are triremes.—The oars had the same effect as our steam boats, being independent of wind and tide: the ancients could, however, sail very well besides.

A quinquereme had three hundred rowers and a hundred and twenty marines; to these rowers the triremes could oppose but a hundred and twenty, who therefore were able to do as little against them, as a frigate or a brigantine would against a ship of the line. This accounts for the statement, that the Romans had had no fleet at all; and yet they had built triremes for the passage to Sicily. They wanted therefore a model, from which the ships might be built on correct principles, so that they could be worked with ease; and they might certainly have sent for a shipbuilder to Greece, or to Egypt, to Ptolemy Philadelphus, with whom they were already allied, and have fetched a model thence; for the ancients indeed built from models. But it so happened that a Carthaginian ship of war was driven ashore, and from it they built a hundred and twenty quinqueremes.[3] These were indeed very unwieldy, and the Romans had not the number of sailors which they wanted, that is to say, more than 30,000. They were therefore obliged to man them with levies from the inland districts, and with slaves, as the Russian ships are by conscription in the interior of the empire;—for, the seamen from Etruria and the Greek towns were by no means sufficient (Polybius goes too far, in stating that they had had no able seamen at all): these were trained to ply the oars upon scaffoldings on dry ground. This drilling, as it is told to us, seems to be utterly ridiculous; and the Carthaginians must have been altogether unlike our nations, if on this occasion a whole crowd of caricatures were not published among them. There was in those times the same contrast between a Roman and a Carthaginian ship, which there is now-a-days between a Russian and an English or American man of war. But the Romans, being great in this as they were in all things, devised the means of overcoming this disadvantage. Their fleet was unable to make head against the Carthaginians in the ordinary tactics; and it was very likely at that very time, and not at a later one, that the idea was conceived of ridding the sea-fight of all artificial evolutions, and rather making ship fight against ship. For it required the greatest skill to manage and steer the ships against wind and tide in the same way as a rider manages his horse, so as to shatter the enemy's vessel by means of the *rostrum*, and to tear off the benches of the rowers; this was more than the Romans dared to think of. Wherever an enemy is to be met who is greatly superior in skill, the only way of conquering is by employing masses, or some unexpected invention. Thus Carnot gained the victory for the French, by opposing masses to the thin lines of the enemy; the battle of Wattignies (15, 16 Oct. 1793) is the turning point of the modern history of warfare, the end of the old, and the beginning of the new tactics. General Hoche had recourse to the same system in Lorraine; by masses the Americans also beat the English ships, which, otherwise, they would have never succeeded in doing. The Romans invented boarding-bridges made of wood, which were wide enough for two men to run upon abreast, and protected on both sides by railings; on the prow of every ship a large mast was set up, resting on which the bridge was drawn up aloft, the upturned end having an iron ring through which a hawser was passed: the bridge was raised or lowered by a windlass, and it fastened itself to the hostile vessel by means of a grappling-iron. Thus the advantage of superior skill which the Carthaginian rowers possessed, was done away with. The Romans, moreover, had their best legions on board, and in all likelihood the Carthaginians had only middling or bad marine soldiers, as these were not picked. This was in the year 492, according to Cato; in 494, according to Varro. The first attempt was not, however, successful, or in the beginning all the ships were not yet armed in this manner. A squadron was caught at a great disadvantage near the Liparian isles, owing to the bad look-out of the Roman commander Cn. Cornelius, and many ships were lost; but the Carthaginians also, some time afterwards, got right into the midst of the Roman squadron, and several of their ships were taken. But the decisive affair was the naval victory of the consul C. Duilius off Mylæ. The Carthaginians engaged in the battle with a feeling of great contempt for their enemy, having 130 vessels against 100 Roman ones; but they soon found how much they were mistaken, when the Romans began to board, and the sea-fight was changed into the nature of a land one. Fifty Carthaginian ships were taken; then the Romans, quite intoxicated with their victory, landed in Sicily, and relieved Segesta (which, like Rome, boasted of its descent from Troy). Duilius was the first who led forth a naval triumph at Rome. He got the right of being lighted by a torch carried before him, when returning home of an evening from a feast, and of being accompanied by a flute player; moreover, as is generally known, the *columna rostrata* was erected to him. What this really was, we do not exactly know; perhaps it was a brazen pillar, cast from the beaks of the ships which had been taken: a pillar from which brazen beaks stick out, as it is generally represented, is quite a modern, and altogether ungrounded conceit. On the column there was an inscription, in which the victory and the booty won by Duilius were set forth. A small remnant of it is still in existence; yet the present tablet has not been put up in the time of Duilius himself, as some of the Roman antiquaries have also perceived. It is built of Greek marble, which in those days was not yet known in Rome. According to Tacitus, it was struck by lightning in the reign of the emperor Tiberius, and restored by Germanicus; but the old language and spelling were still faithfully kept. With that age, the form of the letters also agrees: those on the tombs of the Scipios are altogether different.

After this victory, the hopes of the Romans were unbounded: the war in Sicily was pursued with redoubled vigour. In the following year, the Roman fleet went to Sardinia. The conquest of this island was difficult, as on the coasts the Punic language and manners had spread; yet as all the subjects there had been kept in an unwarlike condition owing to the jealousy of the mother state, the attack was somewhat facilitated. But for all that, it had no important result.

The two following years were spent in making conquests in Sicily, besides this expedition to Sardinia. In this war, A. Atilius Calatinus got into an impassable part of the country; and a tribune, whose name is stated differently, M. Calpurnius Flamma, or Q. Cæditius Laberius, sacrificed himself with a small band for the sake of the army, as Decius did in Samnium. According to Cato, in the *Origines*, he was found after the battle, dangerously wounded and still scarcely breathing, among the dead; but he afterwards recovered.

In the third year after the victory of Duilius, the Romans appeared with a considerable naval force before Sicily; and a drawn battle was fought off Tyndaris on the northern coast, of which the Carthaginians were masters, from Lilybæum nearly to Mylæ. But as the war in Sicily was not decided, and year by year a few small places only were taken, while the Carthaginians still held all the important possessions in their province, the Romans in 496 resolved upon transporting the war to Africa, as there was no hope of its being ended without some great blow being struck. The example of Agathocles had shown how vulnerable the Carthaginians were in Africa. They therefore intended to force the Carthaginians to make peace; at that time they would indeed have contented themselves with Sicily. They now doubled their armaments, and built an immense fleet; the Carthaginians likewise, when they heard of it, built a very great number of ships. Such huge masses do not give one much pleasure in history, as even barbarians are able to get them up: the superiority of talent and skill over physical force has no chance on such occasions. The victory also of Duilius by means of boarding-bridges, is, when closely looked at, only the result of a clumsy device by which the true science of the Carthaginian navy was baffled. In the seven years' war, when line-tactics were in vogue, the art of war, as an art, was of a far higher order than it is, now that armies fight in masses: the masses likewise of artillery mark the evident decline of the intellectual spirit and of humanity in warfare. The Romans put to sea with three hundred and thirty ships, most of which were quinqueremes, and the Carthaginians with three hundred and fifty. Polybius himself is amazed at these huge masses, and remarks in his preface, how even the great battles of the Macedonian kings, of Demetrius, Ptolemy, and others, and in later times, those of the Rhodians, shrink to nothing in comparison. They also outvied each other from henceforth in the size of their ships, some of which had even as many as nine banks of oars, like the one which was built by Archimedes for Hiero, who sent it to Alexandria. These preposterous monsters surpassed in bulk our ships of the line. Men afterwards came back to the use of the very lightest vessels, such as *liburnæ* and *lembi*; of these we are unable to give a clear idea. In the most brilliant days of the Byzantines and Venetians, battles were fought with very small ships. The Romans were 140,000 rowers and marines, the land forces alone amounting to 40,000: they had also a number of transports, especially for the cavalry (ἱππηγοί). It is not unlikely that the Romans built so many ships, merely to carry over their large army to Africa in one voyage; and that the Carthaginians did so, on the other hand, in order to resist them. The expectations of every one were riveted upon this undertaking, just as in the times of the Spanish Armada.

As the most important points on the northern coast of Sicily were still in the possession of the Carthaginians, and provisions had to be taken in at Syracuse, the Romans did not venture to sail round Lilybæum; but they preferred the way round Pachynus. Between that headland and Agrigentum, the Carthaginians met them with the whole of their fleet. The Roman ships being still unwieldy, the result depended, as before, on the use of the boarding-bridges. They had hit upon a strange disposition: their ships were divided into four squadrons, each of which had one legion with its brigade of allies, and a number of transports. The two first squadrons sailed so as to form two sides of a triangle, or an angle, the two admirals being placed side by side, and therefore with their *rostra* standing out towards the sea. The base of the triangle was formed by the third squadron, which advanced straight forwards, and had the transports in tow. Behind these sailed the fourth squadron, which was to cover the rear. The two first were each commanded by a consul, the third and fourth by other leaders, of whom we do not know any thing further. They therefore formed an ἔμβολον, in which the attack of the enemy is a manœuvre for the execution of which a great many favourable circumstances are requisite; and the ships which at other times used to sail on in a straight line, diverged and made a wedge.

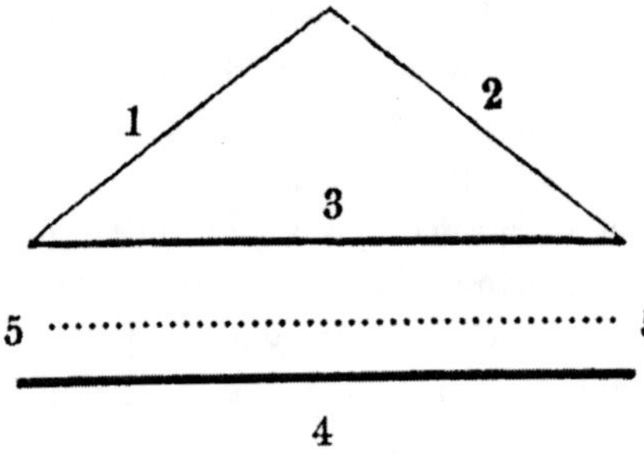

1, 2, 3, 4, the numbers of the squadrons. 5, the transports.

The Carthaginians, who fell in with them near Ecnomus, had a more judicious arrangement. Their left wing, being about the fourth part of the whole of their fleet, sailed in a long line along the coast; and joining it at a right angle was the main body of their large armament, which, ship by ship, stood out far into the sea. The Romans passed by the line along the coast, and attacked the salient line. It was not the plan of the Carthaginian admiral, that this should withstand the end of the wedge which was forcing itself in; they therefore set sail, and seemed to flee, so as to separate the Romans from their third and fourth lines, and the Romans pursued them. But two parts of the long line formed again, and fell upon the Romans, who had detached themselves from the third squadron; the third part, which was sailing in the open sea, returned and attacked the fourth Roman squadron; and in the meanwhile, the line which was off the coast, came up and engaged the third squadron, which now abandoned the transports to their fate. Thus arose three distinct sea-fights: the first and second Roman squadrons conquered easily; the fourth had a doubtful victory; and the third was hard pressed, but the centre turned back to defend it. The boarding-bridges were also employed in this action with great effect. The result was the complete rout of the Carthaginians: thirty ships were sunk, part of them being driven ashore and wrecked, and sixty-four taken; from thirty to forty thousand men fell into the power of the Romans.

After this defeat, the beaten fleet made its escape to Africa, and went to protect Carthage against an attack; the men had lost all strength and spirit. The Romans had the sea clear before them to carry their plan into execution, and the two consular armies, that of Manlius and that of Regulus, proceeded to Africa. They landed on the south side of the headland of Hermæum, over-against Carthage, at the mouth of the gulf of Tunis, near a town which the Romans call Clupea, the Greeks Aspis, (the Punic name we do not know,) a place, which they took after a creditable defence. They now made it their arsenal, and spread from thence into the heart of the country. The really efficient armies of the enemy were stationed in Sicily; the Carthaginians had made sure of baffling the undertaking, and were therefore quite unprepared in Africa. They had fortified colonies on the coast only; as for the interior, with the exception of a few *municipia*, they had the same policy as the Vandals, who, fearing rebellions, pulled down all the walls of the towns, just as the Lombards did afterwards in Italy. Wherever therefore the Romans came, they marched in: a foreign conqueror was looked upon by the Libyans as a deliverer; for, although the Carthaginians were no barbarians, yet they were very hard masters. For they followed the system, which is found throughout the East, that the sovereign is the owner of the soil, and the possessor has the enjoyment of it only so long as it pleases the lord and master. They also wanted immense sums of money for their Celtic and Iberian mercenaries, and were therefore obliged to squeeze them out of their subjects. In the war of Agathocles, the consequences of this system had already been seen. Indeed the spirit of the Africans had been crushed, so that they did not break out in open rebellion, as they did in his time; for the Carthaginians had taken a fell revenge after his departure. Yet they did not aid Carthage in any way. A most inconceivable order now came from Rome, that one of the consuls, L. Manlius, should return home, it being perhaps believed, that the force of Regulus was sufficient by itself: Manlius therefore sailed back with almost the whole of the fleet, and brought over the booty. The Carthaginians retreated into inaccessible parts of the country: Regulus nevertheless defeated them near Adis. Their militia troops were exceedingly timid; it was easy for the Romans to drive them out of their strongholds. Regulus stationed himself not far from Carthage: he took the fortified town of Tunes, and encamped near the river Bagradas: the Carthaginians were pressed most closely. In this camp, as the ancients generally relate, (Livy also has it,) a serpent, which was a hundred and twenty ells in length, is said to have made its appearance, and to have torn to pieces a great many Romans, until the soldiers battered it with catapults and *ballistæ*. This tale, in the midst of an account which is quite historical, is most surprising. That earth and sea may contain creatures which occur so rarely, that one is inclined to take them for fabulous, cannot indeed be positively denied; it may have been a giant serpent. But in all likelihood, this story, like so many others, has its origin in Nævius' *Bellum Punicum*, which poet himself served as a soldier in that war. At all events, it would be wonderful if the size of the dragon had amounted in ells to exactly that number which is so often met with in Roman measurements, namely, 12 × 10.

The Carthaginians had utterly lost courage, and they could not withdraw their army from Sicily without giving up that island altogether:

they therefore sent an embassy to Regulus, and sued for peace. Regulus' fame has been very much exaggerated by apophthegmatical histories; he is undeservedly represented as a martyr: in the heyday of his good fortune, he showed himself ruthless, intoxicated with victory, and ungenerous. We have a story of him, that he had then asked the senate for his recall, that he might attend to his farm; but we know on the contrary from Polybius, that he had particularly set his heart upon bringing the war to a brilliant end, before a successor arrived. So much the more senseless was it in him to ask of the Carthaginians impossibilities, and to offer them much worse terms than they really obtained at the conclusion of the war, just as if he had meant to drive them to despair. Had he stipulated for the evacuation of Sicily and the payment of a contribution, the Carthaginians would have been quite willing; but he had the preposterous idea of crushing Carthage with one blow. His conditions were quite insane: even had they been besieged, the Carthaginians could not have fared worse. They were to acknowledge the supremacy of Rome; to make an offensive and defensive alliance with the Romans; to enter into no treaty without the permission of the Romans; to yield up all their ships of war but one, and to have nothing but triremes; to give up Sicily, Sardinia, Corsica, and the Lipari isles; to abandon their Italian allies; to deliver up the prisoners and deserters; to ransom their own captives; to pay all the expenses of the war, and a contribution besides. The Carthaginians declared that they would rather perish; and luckily for them the Romans carried on the war badly. Instead of establishing themselves within the gulf of Tunis, opposite Carthage, as they ought to have done, they had now sent off their fleet; the Carthaginians therefore could make use of their ships to hire troops everywhere. Among these, there were also many from Greece; one of them, the celebrated Xanthippus, who was not, as Diodorus says, a Spartan, but as we learn from Polybius, a Neodamode who in his education had been subjected to the laws of the Spartans (τῆς Λακωνικῆς ἀγωγῆς μετεσχηκώς), and had thereby acquired an inferior right of citizenship. In the case of a Spartan, this would have been quite a matter of course; but, besides these, Lacedæmonians also (περίοικοι), and Neodamodes, even the children of foreign πρόξενοι, might subject themselves to the laws of Lycurgus, which is a position not yet clearly explained. Xanthippus was one of the greatest men of his age; and he furnishes us with a case in point, which shows how much Sparta must have been stunted, owing to her not making the Lacedæmonians equal to the Spartans. He came to Carthage as a mercenary, but as an officer: he had certainly been recruiting at Tænarus. When he saw the preparations of the Carthaginians, he openly declared that it was no wonder that Carthage was going to ruin; and on this he was called before the senate,—in this case, it was an advantage that the military and the civil administrations were distinct,—and he was asked for his opinion.

He explained to them, that as indeed they had plenty of elephants[4] and Numidian cavalry, which was a formidable force against such a small army as that of the Romans in the midst of an enemy's country, (about 16,000 men, according to Polybius; with all the reinforcements, perhaps 20,000, among whom there were 15 or 1,600 cavalry) they ought to seek the plains, whilst the advantage of the Romans was in the mountains. The elephants had hardly been employed in any battle by land at all, unless perhaps in the little skirmish near Tunis. Xanthippus was listened to: he was intrusted with the charge of the mercenaries. His arrangements excited astonishment: the soldiers believed that under his guidance they were sure to conquer; the whole of the camp demanded him for their leader, and the Carthaginian general, who very likely had got his instructions in this matter from the city, yielded the command to him. This is a great resolve. When Xanthippus had now well drilled the Carthaginians, he went out against the Romans into the open field, and thereby filled them with great wonder and dismay. He compelled them to fight, and made a masterly disposition: the Roman army had no centre; but the Greeks had three divisions, and he drew up his army in the following manner. The Carthaginians occupied the centre as a phalanx; for being townsmen, they could only be usefully employed in masses:[5] on the two wings, he placed the mercenaries, and joined to them the cavalry on the flanks. The Romans likewise put their cavalry on the flanks; but in placing the infantry they departed from their general custom, as before the centre of the Carthaginians a hundred elephants had been stationed: they formed themselves against these in an order of battle of great depth. Yet the shock was irresistible: the left wing of the Romans indeed conquered the mercenaries; but in the meanwhile, the cavalry of the Carthaginians had thrown itself upon the right wing, and the elephants trampled down everything before them: then the phalanx rushed on, and the whole of the Roman army was annihilated. Only two thousand men of the left wing made their escape in the rear of the Carthaginians to Clupea. Regulus retreated with five hundred Romans to a hill, and was obliged to surrender. Xanthippus was now the universal hero: they wished him to stay at Carthage; but he was wise enough to return home with the rich presents which he received, lest he should become an eyesore to an envious and heartless people, as the Carthaginians were. Polybius tells us that there was also another account, even that the Carthaginians had given him a bad ship, that he might perish on the passage; and that according to some, he had really become a victim, and according to others, he had saved himself by getting into another vessel. The Romans sent out the fleet, which had been still preserved, to take up the garrison of the besieged town of Clupea; the Carthaginians went against them, and were defeated. The number of ships which, according to Polybius, were captured on this occasion, is very likely to have been changed from 114 to 14.

The Romans now evacuated Africa, taking with them the garrison of Clupea; and they sailed back for Syracuse, to make their passage through the straits of Messina to Rome. As it was the time of the summer-solstice, the pilots warned them against the possibility of a storm, as the Sirocco at that season of the year sometimes increases into the most dreadful hurricane, and the coast in those parts is destitute of harbours. But the commanders scorned them, most likely because they were foreigners; and thus a terrible shipwreck between Agrigentum and Pachynus utterly destroyed nearly three hundred vessels out of three hundred and sixty, which was the most dreadful disaster that had occurred until then (497). Not long afterwards, Seleucus Callinicus also suffered a similar shipwreck. The Carthaginians might now believe that the Romans would grant a peace on fair terms. For this reason, it is said, they sent Regulus to Rome with offers of peace: if he could not get them accepted, he was to obtain at least an exchange of prisoners; yet Regulus advised against both of these things, returned to Carthage, and was there put to death by torture. The first who, with great independence of spirit, proved the groundlessness of this story, was the excellent French philologist Paulmier de Grentemesnil (Palmerius). He lived in the times of the brothers Henry and Adrian Valesius (Valois); he was particularly well read in Polybius, and he pointed out, how incomprehensible it was, that Polybius, although he told the achievements of Regulus at such length, should not have mentioned a word of this story. The further arguments have been put forth by Beaufort. From a fragment of Diodorus, it appears that the Roman senate gave as a pledge for Regulus, into the hands of his wife and family, two Carthaginian prisoners of rank; and that these were most frightfully tortured, so that the tribunes of the people called together the senate, and compelled the monsters to liberate one of the prisoners whom they had shut up in an exceedingly narrow chest with the other, who was already dead. Now, both of these learned critics say very rightly, that even if the Carthaginians had really tortured Regulus, this had merely been done in retaliation; and that moreover the accounts of his death are so very different. According to some, he was blinded; according to others, tortured to death in a chest stuck full of iron spikes; and again, according to others, he was exposed to the sun and the insects. Some writers of the middle ages, like the authors of the spurious *Acta Martyrum*, felt quite a particular pleasure in devising the most horrible and complicated tortures: this is also the case with the story of Regulus. It is altogether a forgery; and Palmerius and Beaufort have just grounds for their conclusion, that it was only invented to wash out the foul stain of the tortures of the Carthaginian prisoners. I believe that it has been borrowed from Nævius; for Diodorus does not know of it, as is evident from his fragments: he had but a very imperfect knowledge of Roman history, and only from the earlier, and almost contemporary writers, Philinus of Agrigentum, Timæus, and Fabius Pictor; the poet Nævius, he had not read. Thus it was very likely that the latest Roman historians brought that tale into circulation from Nævius. Cicero already is acquainted with the legend; it must have therefore been either in Cato's *Origines* or in Nævius.[6] If it originated with the later historians, it has arisen at least a hundred, or a hundred and twenty years after the time of Regulus.

The Romans did not conclude the peace; in spite of their ill luck, they were resolved upon going on with the war. The Carthaginians now armed themselves with redoubled courage: they sent considerable reinforcements to Sicily, and learnt how to make a right use of their elephants; the Romans, on the other hand, became daunted, and withdrew into the mountains. The Carthaginians wished to carry on the war either by sea or by land: to do both at the same time, was more than they could manage. The Romans then built a new fleet, took Panormus (Palermo), and went again to Africa, and wasted the country between Carthage and Tripolis; hereupon they returned to Sicily, the fleet having had a wonderful escape in the small Syrtis. When bound for Italy, they were again overtaken on the passage by a storm, and hardly a vessel was saved.

The southern gales, every one of them from south-east to south-west, are always in the Mediterranean the most dangerous storm-winds; and they are the more destructive, as the Italian coast is almost without any harbours, and full of breakers: the storms which blow from the north are harmless. Yet when the currents from the Adriatic and the Pontus meet, ships during a north easterly wind are irresistibly drawn into the Syrtes (from σύϱειν), so that they are in them before their reckonings would lead one to suppose it.

This was now a second blow for the Romans, and one from which they did not recover: they did not think of making peace, yet they tried to carry on the war at less expense. The Carthaginians were masters of the sea, and they made use of their superiority to lay waste the Italian coasts; but they managed the war in a wretched manner. The Romans remained unshaken in Sicily, and thus, although indeed they shunned a general engagement, they took several strong places under the very eyes of the enemy, and reduced the Carthaginians to the possession of the north-western part of Sicily. In the year 501 (according to Cato), fortune turned her back upon the Carthaginians: L. Cæcilius Metellus defeated Hasdrubal near Palermo. Hasdrubal had tried to take advantage of the great fear which the Romans had of the African cavalry, and to recover Palermo, very likely with the connivance of the inhabitants: he encamped in its beautiful plain about half a (German) mile from the town, and ravaged the fields. Metellus kept himself in his fortified camp ready to fight: he showed himself here to be a great general, and made it his particular object to render the elephants harmless. The Carthaginians advanced to attack the camp: Metellus drew up all his light troops on the edge of the ditch, with a good supply of missiles; the legions manœuvred on the flanks. The light infantry now sallied forth against the enemy, enticed them on, and then threw themselves into the ditch, and hurled an immense number of javelins and burning arrows against the Carthaginians and their elephants: the camp-followers were constantly bringing them fresh ammunition from the town, and at the same time, the soldiers from behind the breast-works discharged their *pila*. The Carthaginians now wished to sweep them down with one mighty onset; but the elephants were wounded, and thus became wild, and several of them plunged into the trenches, from whence the light-armed soldiers of the Romans jumped behind the fortified lines, and the maddened beasts turned against their own masters. This was the moment for which Metellus had waited all along: from the sidegates of the lines, the legions burst forth, routed the Carthaginian infantry, and put their whole army to flight. More than a hundred elephants were captured. These were brought to Rome on rafts built for the purpose, and killed by missiles in the circus, perhaps to give the people a representation of the battle in which they had been taken.

This victory restored the courage of the Romans; yet the conclusion of the war was extremely hard to bring about, as they did not again venture over to Africa, and the Carthaginians made no attempts to recover what they had lost in Sicily. The latter were now pent up quite at the western end of the island; all that they had still left were the towns of Lilybæum, Drepana, and Eryx. The year after (502), the Romans therefore began the siege of Lilybæum, which lasted till the close of the war, yet not as a siege in form, but as a blockade. The part of the war which follows, might with great propriety be called the Lilybæan one. This last act is the finest on the side of the Carthaginians; the Romans distinguish themselves in it only by their perseverance.

The victory of Metellus in the fourteenth year of the war, was the first pitched battle, with the exception of that near Adin in Africa, in which the Romans had conquered. The siege of Lilybæum was undertaken by them under very unfavourable circumstances. The Carthaginians were in fact masters of the sea; but owing to the tremendous expenses of the war, they had retrenched their naval armaments as much as they possibly could: the

Romans had again a fleet off Lilybæum, which was likewise of limited force, and not intended for sea-fights, yet sufficient to make the communication difficult with that town. Lilybæum is a Punic name; it means, according to Bochart, the place which lies towards Libya (לְלִבְיָ); it was without doubt a mixed Punico-Libyan colony, and at that time the only Punic town in Sicily, having been founded by the inhabitants of Motye, which had been destroyed by Dionysius. As Lilybæum was the residence of the Carthaginian general, it had grown into a considerable town just as did Carthagena in Spain; Palermo, on the contrary, was a thoroughly Greek city, peopled by Greeks and Hellenized Siculians and Sicanians, although it had long been under the Punic rule. Lilybæum had a good harbour, which was yet safer from its being so difficult to get into it. The sand which the south winds bring thither from the Syrtes, had already accumulated there, and formed a sort of lagune; owing to this very cause, the whole harbour of Marsala is now no longer in existence. The fortifications of the place were very strong.

Besides Lilybæum, three German miles from it, the Carthaginians had Drepana (the present Trapani) with its noble harbour, which even now, in spite of the attempts of Charles V. to fill it up, is excellent; and besides Drepana, the town of Eryx with the mountain of that name. Within this district the war was concentrated for nine years; this gave rise to the utter wretchedness of the island, which was quite ruined by it.

The Romans blockaded Lilybæum on the land side, and at the same time cruised before the harbour: they battered the wall, and pulled down part of it; but Himilco, the commander of the Carthaginians, withstood them with the most unflinching steadfastness. A disposition to treachery often showed itself among the troops of the Carthaginians; for they scarcely ever employed their citizens as soldiers, but only as officers, and some also in the cavalry; the main body therefore consisted of mercenaries, so that it is the more to be wondered at that the Carthaginians had distinguished generals. For this reason, they had now much trouble to secure the attachment of these soldiers, who were gathered together from all quarters, most of them being Greeks, Gauls and Spaniards; they could scarcely manage them by any other means than by the hope of gain. Hamilcar and Hannibal alone knew how to bind to themselves even these mixed masses by their own personal qualities; at all other times, these men were ready to commit every sort of treachery for money. Into a plot of this kind some of them now entered with the Roman consul; but an Achæan, Alexo, discovered it, and tried to counteract it; and so the rest were gained over by promises and sacrifices, and the traitors cast out. The Romans here, for the first time, betook themselves to the Greek method of besieging: before the Punic wars, there is nothing like a real siege, but only blockading and storming.[7] They made great progress, and threw down six towers (unless Polybius dates this circumstance too early). The Carthaginians communicated with the besieged by means of a bold seaman, who in a swift ship ventured to pass through the midst of the Roman fleet, and repeated the same feat several times. They ascertained that without speedy assistance, the town must be lost; and so they determined to send ten thousand men to its relief, who, to the great dismay of the Romans, made their way through their guardships. Just at first, the Carthaginians made a sally, which indeed led to no advantage; but soon afterwards, during a dreadful hurricane, they ventured upon a new and successful attack with every possible sort of contrivance for setting fire: as all the Roman machines were made of wood, they were every one of them burnt. It was high time, as six towers had already fallen (for to this period of the siege the notice in Polybius seems in fact to belong). The Romans must have felt convinced that after the loss of their battering engines, they could no longer do any harm to the town by merely blockading it; they tried therefore to throw up a mole across the entrance of the harbour. In this, however, they only succeeded so far, as in some measure to obstruct the communication of the Carthaginians with the town, which had hitherto been too free.

In the course of so long a war as this, some distinguished Carthaginian generals had already been formed; but not a single one among the Romans, whose advantage lay only in their troops. In 503, the Romans, without the enemy's being aware of it, received reinforcements under the command of the consul P. Claudius, the son[8] of Ap. Claudius Cæcus, who had all the faults of his father, but none of his great qualities. He was a reckless, unprincipled man. On account of the great expense, Rome seems to have confined herself to one army. It is uncertain, whether Claudius had already come out as consul to Sicily before the sally of Himilco, or only after it. The Roman fleet was lying near Lilybæum, most of the vessels being drawn up on the strand, while only single ships rode out at sea to keep up the blockade; the sailors had been armed, and made to fight on shore. But infectious diseases had broken out to some extent, as might be expected, the small island of Sicily being quite exhausted by the war; many also had perished in the engagements, so that seamen were scarce. To remedy this defect, sailors were enlisted at Rome; they were, however, people of the lowest rank, whose property was under four hundred *asses*, and who had certainly never been at sea. Claudius now proposed in a council of war, to make an attempt to surprise by sea the port of Drepana, where the enemy's fleet was stationed. The council, according to Polybius, seems to have approved of it. This writer indeed is himself of opinion that the undertaking was practicable; yet we can hardly believe it, when we see that it was so easily foiled. Claudius then set sail about midnight with the newly manned fleet; at the dawn of day, the Carthaginians beheld from their watch-towers that part of the Roman ships were already in the harbour. The fleet was sailing in a single line along the coast. The Carthaginian general Adherbal knew that, if he confined himself to the defence of the town, his ships in the harbour would be in great danger of being taken; he therefore ordered the ships to be quickly manned, and to sail out on the other side of the haven. His object was, to drive the Romans quite into the harbour along the coast, which was lined by the Carthaginian soldiers. The Roman consul now gave the signal for retreat; but this, owing to the narrow entrance of the harbour, occasioned the greatest confusion: the thronging of the ships which turned back, and of those, which, having received no counter order, were still coming in, was very great, and they were severely damaged. Outside the harbour, they found the Carthaginian fleet, which had better ships and better crews, already drawn up; and these now advanced to attack the Romans. The consul then placed his ships along the coast, with the πρύμνα towards the land, in a long line; the Carthaginians, having behind them the open sea, had the advantage of being able freely to manœuvre: it seems that the Romans made no more use of the boarding-bridges. Ninety-three Roman ships were taken, many were destroyed, not more than about thirty reached Lilybæum: with them was the consul Claudius. He was recalled: fierce reproaches were made against him that he was the cause of the disaster; that he had impiously scorned the auspices; that the birds of the augurs had refused to eat, and that thereupon he had ordered them to be thrown into the sea. He had to appoint a dictator: in mockery he named the son of a freedman, a client of his, one M. Claudius Glycia: the name of the grandfather is not mentioned in the Fasti. Since the curies had lost their power, it had become the right of the consul to appoint a dictator; whereas formerly he merely proclaimed him. P. Claudius was put on his trial: according to Polybius, and to judge from an expression of Cicero's, he was condemned to a severe punishment; according to others, the *comitia* were dispersed by a thunderstorm, whereupon the matter was dropped, which seems to betoken the influence of a powerful party. When he was already dead, his sister likewise brought upon herself a severe punishment by her genuine Claudian insolence. Annoyed by the crowd in a procession, in which she took a part as a Vestal, she loudly exclaimed, it was a pity that her brother was no more alive to get rid of some of the rabble at sea. This also proves, that at that time the sailors were levied from the *capite censi*. She was prosecuted for a *crimen majestatis* before the plebeian ædiles, and condemned to pay a heavy fine. The dictator Claudius Glycia was of course induced by the senate and the people to resign his dignity. The conduct of Claudius is quite in keeping with the many acts of wanton insolence which were displayed by all his family; they may be traced from the middle of the fourth century down to the emperor Tiberius: the character for insolence is nearly hereditary in them. Immediately afterwards, another misfortune befalls the Romans. They had still kept up their spirits; for they already sent again eight hundred ships with provisions to Lilybæum, without doubt escorted by a considerable fleet, a proof of the importance of the commerce in the Mediterranean; but the ships of war were not sufficient to protect them. With this fleet the consul L. Junius sailed again through the straits of Messina to Syracuse, as the commissariat was chiefly dependent on the latter town; he there took in his full cargo, and very imprudently sent part of the fleet with some ships of war in advance. The Carthaginians under Carthalo put to sea to meet them, and so frightened them, that they laid to in a very bad roadsted among breakers, off the southern coast (between Agrigentum and Camarina), so that even Carthalo shrank from attacking them. L. Junius was very late before he set out from Syracuse, and when he found that Carthalo was lying between him and the other convoy, he likewise went to a bad roadsted. Then arose one of those terrific gales, which in Italy are always southerly winds. The Carthaginians, experienced seamen as they were, had the foresight to double Pachynus in time, and there they got into a safe harbour; the Romans, on the contrary, were driven by the Scirocco on the breakers off the coast, and were so completely wrecked that not a plank of their ships remained serviceable; out of the whole fleet, two ships only were saved. A great number of lives also were lost; the consul escaped, and retreated with the survivors by land towards Lilybæum. An opportunity now offered itself to him of doing something after all, even of surprising Eryx, a town, which lay on the slope of the mountain of the same name, at the top of which was the temple of Venus as an Acropolis. He made himself master of the town by means of bribery. This was the only advantage which the Romans gained this year.

The Romans now gave up the sea, with the exception of a few ships, and the war was hopeless for them: it required Roman perseverance, not to despair altogether. No doubt it was also somewhat earlier than this that the Carthaginians tried to get a loan from Ptolemy, 15,000,000 dollars, I believe; but he declared to them, that he would thus break his neutrality. The Romans helped themselves in every possible way by war-taxes; yet this struggle ate away their strength as well as that of the Carthaginians.

Now appeared the great Hamilcar Barcas. Whether he sprang from a high family, is unknown to us. Barcas, Barak (קרב), seems to mean lightning, even as the Scipios in Lucretius are called *fulmina belli*: *Barka* is the Syriac form. He enters upon the stage at once. His undertakings are not dazzling, he makes no conquests; but he retrieved the affairs of Carthage in Sicily by his indefatigable activity (*unus illis restituit rem*). Hamilcar, to my mind, is almost greater than his son; the whole of history does not know another instance of a father and son who were so eminently great in an art, as these two were: one must be born a general as well as a painter, or indeed any other kind of artist. Had Hamilcar guided the councils of the senate of Carthage earlier, the war would have ended to the disadvantage of Rome. Hamilcar began his career with an undertaking, which in boldness surpasses everything that we know. Near Palermo is Hercte, a mountain of considerable extent; from its name, there must have been there a state-prison; by its side is a harbour which was quite sufficient for the wants of the ships of war of those times. Here Hamilcar landed unexpectedly with a squadron; gained possession of the height by surprise or treachery; established himself in it, and remained in connexion with the fleet, which, at every opportunity, devastated from thence the coast of Italy as far as Cumæ, perhaps also with the intention of driving the allies into defection. He was himself just returned from a foray into Bruttium when he took up his position there, and he maintained himself, as in a fortress; he got reinforcements from time to time, but as for provisions, he had often barely enough to keep body and soul together. By his appearance in the field, the attention of the Romans was turned from the siege of Lilybæum. Battles were of daily occurrence; men fought from sheer exasperation. At the end of three years, he managed to get into communication with the town of Eryx, and made himself master of it quite unexpectedly. The Romans, however, still held the *arx* on the top of the mountain; and he now encamped between it and the town below, that by blockading the citadel, he might always give the Romans plenty to do, and thus draw them away from Lilybæum and Drepana, and wear them out. He fully attained his object; and so he remained four years in this position, without the Romans making any progress. This struggle shows what dogged resolution can do; and therefore Polybius himself, who had much experience in war, expresses the highest admiration for it. The communication with the sea was more difficult here, than even at Hercte. Hamilcar found himself there with an army of mercenary soldiers, hundreds of whom would certainly have sold their father and mother for a hundred pieces of gold; but such was the awe with which he inspired them, that not an attempt was made to practise any treachery against him. He now carried on the war in the most simple manner; Polybius says that it was not possible to relate its history, on account of the sameness of the incidents;

we therefore know but very little of it. The engagements were often most bloody; yet they never afforded any decisive advantage to the Romans, not even when the Carthaginians were beaten. The newly discovered fragments of Diodorus contain an interesting anecdote. The year before the war was brought to a close, C. Fundanius, an obscure general, was fighting against Hamilcar, whose troops suffered a defeat, owing to the fault of Vodostor, a commander of the infantry. Hamilcar sought for a truce, that he might fetch the dead bodies and bury them; but the consul answered, that he ought rather to take care of the living, and to capitulate to him. A very short time afterwards, the Romans in their turn were soundly beaten; but Hamilcar told them, that as far as he was concerned, they might freely take away their dead, as he made war against the living only. This story, like others of the same kind, is no doubt from Philinus, who always represents the Carthaginians as generous.

The peculiar character of the war in Sicily impressed the Romans with the conviction, that without an immense effort they would not be able to bring it to an end. They therefore resolved upon building a third fleet, and had recourse to a very remarkable way of raising a loan. The property-tax, which had hitherto defrayed the expense of building the fleet,—it was so much per thousand,—could no more be levied, because the poor could not now pay it: it must until then have been a dreadful burthen upon the people. The state may have in the meanwhile sold much of the *ager publicus*; the cost besides of the administration of the republic was almost nothing, and indeed the allies also may have contributed much to the building of the former fleets. Of permanent loans the ancients had no idea: once, in the second Punic war, we meet with one which was more in the style of our own. The wealthy Romans now undertook to build two hundred ships at their own expense, on condition that the money was to be repaid to them should matters turn out well. This implies that in the event of a failure they renounced their claims. The fleet was built quite on a different plan from the former ones; for the Romans had got hold near Lilybæum of a very fine Carthaginian galley, and all the quinqueremes were constructed after its model. These were manned with particular care from the best sailors of all Italy; as marines, the best soldiers of the legions were employed. This time also, the Romans made no more use of the boarding-bridges. It is possible that the ships were better built owing to the very circumstance of their having been taken in hand by private individuals: all the public works were done by contract, and of course the censor could not always have his eye upon the way in which they were executed.

Upon the Carthaginians, the news of this building came quite unexpectedly. They too had broken up their fleet on account of the expense, and had confined themselves merely to what was strictly necessary; nor had they at Carthage any notion of making extraordinary sacrifices, as was done at Rome. They therefore equipped in all haste what ships they had, in order to convey reinforcements and provisions to Lilybæum, Drepana, and Eryx. These vessels, even those which were ships of war, laden with corn, and manned with marines who were by no means picked, arrived at the Ægatian islands, from whence they were to cross over to the coast, along which the Roman fleet was then cruising. The plan of the Carthaginians was, after having landed, to take in the best troops of Hamilcar as marines, and then to risk a sea-fight. The Roman fleet was under the command of the consul C. Lutatius Catulus, and of the prætor Q. Valerius Falto. They also had their doubts. A battle could not be avoided; it was therefore best to attack at once, while the Carthaginian ships were still heavily laden. Corn, when it is only pitched in loosely, and not put into sacks, is a very bad cargo, as it shifts with every wind. If then these were allowed to land, they would return with lightened ships, and with marines from Hamilcar's army who were not afraid of fighting the Romans; yet the true advantage of the latter was indeed in the lightness of their galleys and the excellence of their troops. There was only this objection, that the Carthaginians had the wind in their favour, whilst the Romans would have with great difficulty to bear up against them with their oars,—a circumstance which among the ancients was very unfavourable in a sea-fight, as a ship which was going against the wind, offered a much greater surface to the stroke of the enemy. Hanno, the Carthaginian general, tried to cross over with full sails, and perhaps also with oars (the ancients had latteen sails); thus they came upon the Romans with double force, and it seemed a great risk for the latter to accept the battle. Nevertheless they did not shrink from it. The Carthaginians were hardly able to move their ships, and the bad condition of their troops gave the Romans such an advantage, that they won a complete victory. Both had played their last stake, so that the Carthaginians were ruined. The Romans took seventy of their ships, sank a number of them, and scattered the rest.

It was impossible for the Carthaginians to provision their distressed garrison, and still less could they quickly fit out a new fleet. They therefore resolved to make peace, and, according to Polybius, chose Hamilcar to negociate it. Sicily, of course, was to be ceded; two thousand two hundred talents (3,300,000 dollars) were to be paid, and all the Roman prisoners and deserters to be given up, while they should have to ransom their own prisoners: the assent of the Roman people was reserved. The demand that Hamilcar and his troops should lay down their arms, and march out as prisoners of war, was indignantly rejected. The Roman people insisted on an additional charge of a thousand talents, these to be paid at once, and the two thousand two hundred by instalments within ten years; and likewise on the cession of all the islands between Sicily and Carthage, which shows that the Carthaginians still held the Lipari isles. This was necessary, if a lasting peace was to be concluded.

Thus ended this war of twenty-four years, which indeed gained Sicily for the Romans, but turned it into a wilderness: the whole of the western part of the island especially was laid desolate, and from that time it has never recovered. There was yet, it is true, some civilization left; Greek art still lingered there. The work of devastation was completed in the second Punic war; in the Servile war, the island was nothing but a dreary waste, and however wretched its state is now,—the modern Sicilians, next to the Portuguese, rank the lowest among the nations of Europe,—yet it was still more lonely and desolate in the times of Verres. Under the Roman emperors, there was no amendment: hence in the itineraries we find that the roads do not pass by towns,—for these had perished,—but by farms. Thus dissolved into large estates Sicily continues until the days of Gregory the Great, when we may again have an insight into its condition from the letters of that pontiff. The present population, in spite of its miserable government, has risen nearly to the double of what it was: under Verres it was below a million. It is as if the soil had lost all its heart and fruitfulness. The small kingdom of Syracuse was an exception, owing to the great wisdom with which it was ruled by Hiero.

SICILY A ROMAN PROVINCE. PRÆTOR PEREGRINUS. WAR WITH THE FALISCANS. MUTINY OF THE MERCENARIES IN CARTHAGE. THE FIRST ILLYRIAN WAR. THE LEX FLAMINIA FOR THE DIVISION OF THE AGER GALLICUS PICENUS. WAR AGAINST THE CISALPINE GAULS. THE SECOND ILLYRIAN WAR. THE CARTHAGINIANS FOUND AN EMPIRE IN SPAIN

After the peace, the Romans formed Sicily into a province. In a province, a Roman commander, either still holding a curule office or with a prolonged *imperium*, carried on the government, and had the same power over the country as in times of war, by virtue of the *lex de imperio*. It is a false notion, that in the provinces the inhabitants had no right of ownership; they had indeed, though not according to Roman, but according to provincial law. There were in the provinces *civitates liberæ, civitates foederatæ*, and subjects. The confederate states were treated like the Italian allies: some of them had the land as their own, and paid taxes on it, sometimes in proportion to the produce, and sometimes at a fixed rate; others indeed lost their ownership in it, so that it might be disposed of by the Roman republic; but retained the enjoyment of it on paying a rent. This was done when the provinces rebelled again and again, and were reconquered; and thus it came to pass that in several states the land was almost entirely forfeited to the Roman republic, whilst in others it was not so at all. This was not understood by the later writers, as Theophilus, and even Gaius himself already. From that time, there was generally a prætor and a quæstor in the province of Sicily. Hiero remained independent as did the free cities in Italy, and likewise the state of the Mamertines, Tauromenium, Centoripa, and other towns in the interior.

The war was ruinous to the Romans, whom it impoverished, and consequently to their morals also; for wounds like these do not always heal after the return of peace. During a struggle of this kind, contractors and the very dregs of the rabble grow rich, and the old citizens become poor: the first Punic war is therefore one of the first causes of the degeneracy of the Roman people. In the course of this war, there must have been many changes of which we have few or no records; we only know of some small matters. In the year of the city 506, as we have now been able to learn from Lydus *de Magistratibus*, a second prætor was appointed, who was to administer the laws to the *peregrini*. A great change had therefore taken place, that foreigners were to have a *persona* in Rome, instead of being obliged to be represented by a citizen as formerly: in this we acknowledge an important diminution of the spirit of faction. Suetonius says of a Claudius, who without doubt belongs to the beginning of the first Punic war, that he had resolved upon ruling Italy by means of the clients: this is one of the proofs which show that the clientship had a dangerous character, and how beneficial it was to dissolve that connexion. Yet the prætor was not restricted to his civil jurisdiction; Q. Valerius commanded the fleet besides, and another prætor we meet with at a later period in Etruria. We also find in Livy by no means in every year a prætor for the *peregrini*. The phrase *prætor peregrinus* is a barbarism; Livy, in the fourth decade, always uses a circumlocution instead of it.[9]

Another great change from an accidental cause, is little noticed. Dionysius says, that until the Φοινικὸς πόλεμος, the state had yearly given fifty thousand drachmas for the public festivals. This was now changed, and the Greek system of Liturgies was introduced, by which rich men had to defray the cost of the festivals as a public burthen. As the ædileship was the stepping-stone to higher offices, this measure gave rise to an important political revolution. Polybius has not remarked this. He finds fault with the Carthaginians for their practice of selling offices, and sets the custom of the Romans in direct contrast with theirs; yet it was then just the same at Rome. Fabricius, and men like him, could now no longer have worked their way to high office, without having to encounter the greatest difficulties.

In the nature of the senate, there was likewise a great change effected shortly before the first Punic war. The senate had at first been a representation of the people, and then of the curies; afterwards the will of the censors was paramount in its selection, and this was a blessing for the state. The composition of the Roman senate may perhaps have been best about this time: on the other hand, this power was in truth anomalous and dangerous, as the example of Ap. Claudius had shown. But now the senate was indirectly chosen by the people for life. The quæstors, of whom there had originally been two, then four, and now eight, became the *seminarium senatus*: he who had been quæstor had already the right *sententiam dicendi in senatu*, and might in case of a vacancy at the next census, if there was no particular charge brought against him, reckon with certainty upon getting into the senate. In this way, the senate was then changed into a sort of elective council; only the expulsion of unworthy members still belonged to the province of the censor. Still more completely was the senate chosen by the people in the seventh century, when the tribunes of the people also got into it.

As may be well imagined, it was with much difficulty that the Romans recovered from so exhausting a struggle. Their losses had been immense; besides other things, there were seven hundred ships of war: of the arrangements and measures which they adopted after the restoration of peace, we know but little. Soon afterwards, a war broke out against the Faliscans, which was ended in six days. It is almost incomprehensible, when the whole of Italy, with the exception of some little troubles in Samnium, had remained in obedience all the time of the Punic War, that after its conclusion such a dwarf could now have risen against the giant. This can only be accounted for in this way, that perhaps at that period a truce had expired, and the Romans did not wish to renew the former conditions. The town was destroyed, in order to strike terror into the Italians by the example.

Yet the Carthaginians were in a still worse plight than the Romans. Their distress was the same; they had also been beaten, and had every year to pay a portion of the heavy contribution; and the Romans moreover were no indulgent creditors. They had likewise to pay off their mercenaries who had returned from Sicily; but they had no money. Besides all this, the state was badly governed, and Hamilcar, the greatest man of his age, was thwarted by a whole faction. The friends of Hamilcar are likewise called *factio*; yet this means nothing else but people from all ranks, the best part of the nation, who sided with the distinguished man whom the majority attempted to cry down. Such was the condition of Carthage, that the great resources which Providence gave her in Hamilcar and Hannibal, led to nothing but her ruin; had she followed the advice of Hamilcar, and not spared her rich citizens, but made another mighty effort, she might have paid off the mercenaries, and have raised a new army. Instead of this, the Carthaginians foolishly tried to bargain with these barbarians, and with this view brought together the whole army. The consequence was, that it threw off its obedience to them, and a dreadful war broke out, which became a national one for Africa, as the Libyans, even with enthusiasm, rushed into the arms of the troops: the women gave their trinkets for the support of the war. Even old Phœnician colonies, such as Utica, Hippo, Clupea, rose against Carthage, so that the power of the city was often driven back almost within its own walls. The Roman deserters, who were afraid of being given up to their own government, placed themselves at the head of the insurrection, especially a slave from Campania of the name of Spendius: Carthage was brought to the brink of destruction. The Romans, during this war, at first behaved in a high-minded manner; and here we meet with the first traces of navigation laws, and of those claims on neutrals which have caused so many quarrels in modern history. The Romans in fact decreed, that no ships of the rebels should be allowed to come to Italy; and that, on the other hand, none should sail from thence to the harbours of the rebels in Africa. The Italian ship-masters did not observe this; but they went whithersoever their interest called them: the Carthaginians had therefore a right to seize all the Roman ships which were bound for such a harbour, to confiscate the cargo, and to detain the crews as prisoners; and for this they might appeal to the Roman proclamation. The Romans had even let the Carthaginians levy troops in Italy; they also negociated with them for the liberation of the prisoners: the Carthaginians gave them up, and the Romans, on their side, released those whom they had still kept since the war. They likewise facilitated the traffic with Carthage. The war lasted three years and four months; it was waged with a cruelty which is beyond all conception, very much like the thirty years' war, which was a war of fiends. At last, owing to the generalship of the great Hamilcar Barcas, and the horrors committed by the mercenaries themselves, it was put down, and revenge was taken.

Then the envy of the Romans was aroused. The mercenaries in Sardinia had likewise risen against the Carthaginians, and had murdered many of those who were settlers there, though probably only the officers and magistrates; for as late as Cicero's times, the population of the sea-port towns of Sardinia was Punic. Against the mercenaries, the Sards now rose in their turn, and drove them out of the island, renouncing also their allegiance to the Carthaginians. After the war in Africa was ended, Carthage wished to reconquer Sardinia; but the rebels placed themselves under the Romans, who, with shameful hypocrisy, declared themselves bound not to abandon those who had committed themselves to their protection, and, when the Carthaginians fitted out a fleet against Sardinia, asserted that this would be a war against themselves. It was therefore impossible for the Carthaginians to carry on this war; and Hamilcar, who like all men of sterling mind, was for letting go what could not be kept, without giving way to maudlin sorrow, advised them to yield in this matter until better times: on this, the Carthaginians swore to have their revenge, but for the present not to make war. They made a new peace, in which they gave up Corsica and Sardinia, and had besides to pay twelve hundred talents. This conduct is one of the most detestable misdeeds in the Roman history.

To the east of Italy, since the Peloponnesian war, an empire had arisen in a country where formerly there were only single tribes. This was the Illyrian kingdom. How it rose, we cannot exactly tell: it did not spring from the Taulantians. Since the days of Philip especially, larger states had formed themselves out of the small ones; and perhaps it was created by Bardylis, who in the times of that king founded an empire in those parts. Nor do we know anything for certain about the royal city: it was probably in the neighbourhood of Ragusa; the worst pirates must have dwelt in northern Dalmatia. For some time (about the year 520), in the then broken state of Greece, they, like the Albanians of the present day, roamed everywhere by land and by sea; and wasting the coasts, particularly the unfortunate Cyclades, they dragged away the full-grown inhabitants, and cut off all traffic. Perhaps only the Macedonians and Rhodians opposed to them any resistance; yet they were very likely not sorry to see piracy carried on against others, as is also the case with modern nations, which rule the seas. The Illyrians, however, meddled also with the Romans; and the more so as their boldness increased, when under Agron, their king, the gain from their piracy grew greater, and having a run of luck, they made prizes on the coast of Epirus and Acarnania. The Romans dispatched an embassy thither. Agron had died in the meanwhile, and his son Pinnes was under the guardianship of his mother, queen Teuta, who held the regency. She answered, that on the part of the state no wrong would be done to the Romans; but that it was an ancient right and custom of the Illyrians, for every single captain to take whatever fell in his way. One of the Roman envoys, probably a son of the great Ti. Coruncanius, now replied that it was the custom of the Romans to amend the bad customs of other nations. For this she had the ambassadors murdered, whereupon the Romans sent a fleet and army over to Illyria. The Illyrians, who now began to spread their rule, were just besieging Corcyra, which before the Peloponnesian war was a paradise guarded by a fleet of several hundred galleys, but owing to incessant wars, was now all but a desert. The island was obliged to surrender before the Romans arrived. These however landed from Brundusium before Dyrrhachium near Apollonia, and rescued it, as they also did Epidamnus and Dyrrhachium. The neighbouring tribes submitted; and the governor of Corcyra, Demetrius Pharius, a scoundrel, who in all likelihood was bribed, gave up to them the island. Issa also the Romans delivered, and they advanced through Upper Albania along the Dalmatian coast. They met with no resistance of any consequence: only one strong place held out, all the rest surrendered; so that the queen was obliged to come to terms and make peace. The Illyrians now renounced their dominion over part of the Dalmatian isles and over Upper Albania; and they bound themselves not to sail to the south beyond the Drin, a river which flows from the lake of Scutari, and with no more than two unarmed vessels. This was an immense benefit for the Greeks. What was the fate of the tribes between Epirus and Scutari, cannot be told with certainty; but most likely, they, as well as Epidamnus and Apollonia, remained absolutely dependent on the Romans, although these had no garrison and no prætor there. The latter may perhaps have levied a moderate tribute from them.

As benefactors of the Greeks, and attracted by the irresistible charm which the praises of that people had for so many nations, the Romans sent ambassadors to Greece, to make known there the conditions of the treaty with the Illyrians. At that time, the Ætolians and Achæans were united against Demetrius of Macedon, which gave a moment of relief to this unfortunate country: to both of these peoples the Romans dispatched the embassy on political grounds. But the one to Athens had no other object than to earn Greek praises; it was an homage paid to the intellectual power of that city. For though the poor Athenians had in those days fallen to the very lowest ebb, yet the memory of their ancestors was still alive, and honours bestowed by them were still of value.[10] The motive for a special embassy to Corinth, although it belonged to the Achæan league, is evident, as Corcyra, Apollonia, and Epidamnus, were Corinthian colonies. The Corinthians rewarded the Romans by giving them the right of taking part in the Isthmian games; the Athenians granted them isopolity, and admission to the Eleusinian mysteries.

Once before already,—soon after the Punic war, or even while it yet lasted,—the Romans had meddled in the affairs of Greece. The Acarnanians and Ætolians were then at war. The Ætolians and Alexander of Epirus had divided Acarnania between them; but the Acarnanians had recovered their freedom, and were defending it against the Ætolians. They now betook themselves to Rome, on the strength of their forefathers not having fought against Troy; in proof of which they referred to the Catalogue of Ships in the Iliad. Patron too, who piloted the ships of Æneas, was an Acarnanian. The Romans also alleged this as the motive of their protection; but their embassy was treated by the Ætolians with utter scorn, and it led to nothing. Justin, not without a certain feeling of enjoyment, tells this from Trogus Pompeius; for Trogus was no Roman by birth, but was sprung from a Ligurian or Gallic tribe.[11] They now, in the year 524, had better success, and obtained from the Greeks the honours which have been mentioned.

It is by no means true that history has the effect of weakening one's belief in an overruling Providence: in it we see realized what Herodotus so often says, ἔδεε γὰρ αὐτὸν ἀπολέσθαι; one may say just as often, ἔδεε γὰρ αὐτὸν σώζεσθαι. Had the Gauls, for instance, burst upon Italy during the first Punic war, they alone would have been sufficient to interrupt its course, and the Romans could not have thrown themselves with all their might on Sicily. If Alexander, son of Pyrrhus, had tried to avenge the misfortunes of his father in Italy, there can be no doubt but what he might at that time have still broken up the leagues in that country, and have destroyed the power of the Romans. Yet everything combined in their favour: the Carthaginians got a good general only at the end of the war; Alexander of Epirus contented himself with small conquests; the Gauls were quiet. The Romans indeed were in dread of an attack from the east; they seem to have been prepared for whatever might happen, and for this reason they still kept a garrison in Tarentum. Even before the first Punic war, they had made a friendly alliance with Ptolemy Philadelphus; after the peace they concluded another with Seleucus Callinicus. Thus far did they now already stretch out their arms.

The Gauls had lost the Romagna, and had not stirred for fifty years: they were perhaps themselves glad that the Romans seemed to have forgotten them. The Senonian territory had come into the hands of the Romans as a wilderness; but it is a fine country: here, according to the provisions of the agrarian law, a great number might settle and occupy land. About the year 522, the tribune C. Flaminius, in spite of the violent opposition of the senate, carried a bill in the assembly of the people for the division of this *ager Gallicus Picenus*. The *ager* of the Senonians is part of the Romagna, of Urbino, and the March of Ancona; the colony of Ariminum was already established there. Polybius, in a most unaccountable manner, calls this motion of Flaminius an attempt at rebellion; an example of how even a sensible man may err in judging of some particular circumstance, or follow others, without thinking himself on the subject. As none of the other tribunes would interfere, those who were in power got the father of Flaminius to make his son desist; and the old man ascended the *rostra*, and led him off. Here we behold the change which had taken place in the state of things: the father, a plebeian like his son, opposes the division of the *ager*. And again, we see in this an instance in which, as might be done by virtue of the *Lex Hortensia*, a measure of this kind was carried against the wishes of the senate, by a *plebiscitum* which emanated from a single body; and in this meaning perhaps is the expression of Polybius to be understood (ἀρχηγὸς τῆς ἐπὶ τὸ χεῖρον διαστροφῆς τῆς Ῥωμαίων πολιτείας). In this assignation of the *ager publicus*, the point in dispute was no longer whether the plebeians were to have any share in it. On the contrary, the leading men of both orders had divided the possession between them, and had thus enriched themselves; and now the population which had since grown up, laid claim to its assignation, so as to establish a new and free peasantry in the room of those who had died off, or had been bought up, and to give fresh life to what was left of the old yeomanry, which had thus dwindled away.

It is, however, quite a different question, whether an extensive settlement in those parts was prudent at such a time, when a war with the neighbouring Gauls was to be dreaded. Yet after all, this war must one day or other have broken out. The Gauls could not long dwell quietly in Lombardy, and it was all one, whether it came on a little sooner. Certain it is, that this settlement alarmed the Boians in what are now the districts of Modena and Bologna, probably also in that of Parma: the population in fact had recovered from its losses, and was thirsting for revenge. They were also afraid that the great men at Rome, who had lost their large estates in the Romagna, might seek for new ones in their own country. The Romans, however, did not yet think of war with the Gauls: they had cast their eyes on Spain, and they had no hope of being able to drive the Gauls out of Lombardy. It is said that at that time the Romans carried on wars against the Ligurians; but we should be sadly mistaken if we fancied that they had already invaded Liguria proper, the territory of Genoa. It was, on the contrary, the Ligurians who had spread in the Apennines as far as Casentino and Arezzo, after the might of the Etruscans and Gauls had been broken at the Vadimo; and it could have been none other than these. It was a hard struggle. The Ligurians defended every single mountain, and each of the small tribes was only mastered after having been almost entirely crushed.

Of the Gauls, there were in the north of Italy the Boians and Insubrians; the former, south of the Po in the Romagna; the latter, in the territory of Milan, and in the plain between Bergamo and Brescia; yet these two cantons were not Gallic, but probably Rhætian, of Etruscan extraction. Between the Insubrians and Venetians dwelt the Cenomanians, between Milan and Mantua; these had placed themselves under the protection of the Romans. On the other side of the Alps, there was a great movement, and the Boians could now induce Transalpine volunteers to come over: these negociations caused the Romans great alarm. Several years now passed away: at length, eight years after the Flaminian law, a countless horde made its appearance, and the war broke out in 527. This war is memorable in history for the immense preparations of the Romans; it was a swarm which they had to deal with, very much as in the time of the Cimbrians. Among the tribes which were in arms, there were also Tauriscans. These, on other occasions, we meet with only in Carniola: whether in those days they were also in Helvetia, we must leave undecided. The Romans called forth a general levy throughout all Italy: the allies obeyed very readily, as they looked forward with dismay to an invasion of the Gauls. The Romans opposed to the enemy an army on the common road of the Gauls near Rimini, which was under the consul L. Æmilius, and another, a prætorian one, in Etruria. At the same time, the consul C. Atilius had gone with a fleet and army to Sardinia, as the Sards had revolted. In the neighbourhood of Rome, there was a reserve: all the Italian nations were in marching order. Polybius here gives a list, from which we find that he had not a clear insight into the subject. The numbers are wrongly written, and all attempts to sum them up are fruitless: several peoples are not named at all. I believe that Fabius wrote in a hurry, when he stated the numbers at 800,000 foot and 80,000 horse. In short, this list is of no use; and at any rate, one ought never to draw from this census such conclusions with regard to the population of the ancient world, as was done in the dispute between Hume and Wallace; for although Hume keeps on the side of common sense, yet he takes the matter too lightly. Perhaps something has slipped out in Polybius.

The Romans evidently looked forward to this war with far greater fear than they did to that of Hannibal. Such is human nature! The Apennines north of Tuscany were then quite impassable, and there were only two ways there by which Italy could be invaded: the one was by Fæsulæ, and the other through the territory of Lucca, down by Pisa, where the whole valley at that time was a great marsh. By one of these two roads the Gauls must have passed, probably by the latter; but whilst Hannibal's march through these swamps has become famous, history is silent with regard to that of the Gauls. They left the Roman consul in his position near Ariminum, and fifty thousand of them burst into Etruria. Probably the army of the Romans was stationed near Florence, so as to block up the road to Rome; and thus one can understand that they were late in knowing of the invasion of the Gauls, and of their march as far as Clusium. Thither the Gauls had arrived, within three days' march from Rome. The Romans now broke up, that they might either cut off from them the way to Rome, or at least follow after them: the Gauls were apprised of this, and retreated. They marched from Clusium through the Siennese territory to the sea: here we find them in the neighbourhood of Piombino, over-against Elba. Polybius says that they now fell in with the Romans near a place called Φαίσολα. This the commentators preposterously mistook for Fæsulæ above Florence; yet it must have been between Chiusi and the sea-coast, not far from Aquapendente.[12] Here they laid a trap for the Romans. They broke up with their infantry, and withdrew to a good position; the cavalry remained behind, and was to provoke the Romans, and then, slowly falling back, to entice them to the spot whither they wished to bring them. The Romans suffered there a great defeat: a part only of them retreated to a strong height among the Apennines, where they defended themselves against the Gauls. Luckily, the consul Æmilius, who had left his station near Ariminum, had now advanced through the Apennines to reinforce the army; and when he did not find it in its former place, he proceeded by forced marches along the road to Rome, and came up the night after the disastrous battle. He did not know that the Romans were surrounded on the mountains; but the Gauls halted when they saw his watch-fires, and the hard-pressed Romans sent messengers to him, and acquainted him with their situation. The next morning, he now wanted to attack the Gauls; these, however, had chosen to retire. As they had gotten a vast deal of booty during the campaign, they did not wish with such an *agmen impeditum* to enter into battle, and so they resolved to return home, and advance again afterwards. Such a resolution can only be made by a barbarous people. They marched slowly along the sea-coast, laying everything waste: the consular army followed, to keep them in check, but was afraid of them. The Gauls would thus have returned unhurt, had not Atilius in the meanwhile brought his undertaking in Sardinia to a successful close. The Sardinian army having been recalled, was driven by contrary winds to land at Pisa, not far from the very spot where the Gauls just happened to be. Atilius had the intention of joining the other army; but when he heard of the invasion of the Gauls, he left his baggage behind at Pisa, and began his march to Rome along the coast: as for the defeat of the Romans, he knew nothing of it. Near a place, called Telamon, his light troops fell in with some of the Gauls. Some of these, who were made prisoners, let out how matters really stood; that the Gauls were close at hand, and that the consul Æmilius was following them. Æmilius had heard of the march of Atilius; but he was not aware how near he was. Now as the battle of Telamon was fought in the neighbourhood of Populonia, it is evident also from this, that Φαίσολα could not possibly have been Fæsulæ near Florence. The Gauls, who were now in a dreadful plight, first got their baggage out of the way, and then tried to occupy an eminence hard by the road: thither Atilius sent his cavalry, and the fight began. The Gauls opposed one front to Atilius, and another to Æmilius. Atilius was slain, and his head cut off, and brought to the prince of the Gauls; but his troops avenged his death, and the cavalry became masters of the hillock. The warriors who were arrayed against Æmilius, fought stark naked with all the wildness of savages; the rest of the Gauls also were without coats of mail, and they had narrow shields, and large Celtic mantles. Polybius speaks in this battle of *Gæsati*; these can hardly have been mercenaries, as he supposes, but javelin bearers,—from *gæsum*, a javelin, inasmuch as Virgil in his magnificent description of the Gauls uses this word in contradistinction to the swordbearers: they were Allobroges; for they came from the Rhone.

These Gæsatians all of them made a stand against Æmilius; the light troops, armed likewise with missiles, were sent to attack them, and after a fierce struggle they fled. The rest of the Gauls having collected on both sides into immense masses, the day ended in the death of 40,000, and the captivity of 10,000 of them, so that scarcely any one escaped. Thus, by the most lucky combination of circumstances, the danger was warded off. The war was not, however, decided before the fourth year.

In the following year, the Romans crossed over the Apennines into the country of the Boians, who immediately submitted. In 529 and 530, the war was in the Milanese territory, the land of the Insubrians. These were supported by the Transalpine Gauls, and they offered a stout resistance: that such an open country, which had but one stronghold, was defended in this manner, does honour to the bravery of these tribes. The Romans were forced at the confluence of the Po and the Adda to retreat. The Cenomanians, between the Adda and the Lago di Garda; the Venetians, whose capital was Patavium; and the Euganeans, were friendly to the Romans: the Venetians were a people of quite a different race from the Tuscans, being probably of Liburno-Pelasgian descent; they possessed the country between the Adige and the four eastern rivers, and were highly civilized. The Insubrians afterwards sued in vain for peace: the Romans did not trust them, and wished for their destruction. In 529, C. Flaminius gained a great battle against the Insubrians, north of the Po, in which he is unjustly reproached with bad generalship. In the fourth year of the war, the Romans reduced their only fortified place, Acerræ, and utterly routed them near Clastidium. The great captain M. Claudius Marcellus slew with his own hand the Gallic chief Virodomarus. After this campaign, Milan was taken, and the Insubrians made their unconditional submission, having been all but exterminated.

In the Capitoline Fasti, we find that Marcellus had triumphed *De Gallis Insubribus et* Germanis. I cannot say positively whether the piece of stone on which the *er* stands, has been put in at a later period or not, often as I have examined that monument. The stone is broken at the *r*, thus much is certain: but whether the restoration is new, or whether the piece which was broken off, was again fastened in, I do not venture to decide. It cannot be *Cenomanis*, the *G* being distinct; *Gonomanis* does not occur among the Romans. The thing is not quite impossible. This would then be the earliest mention of our national name. In the age of Julius Cæsar, the Germans in all likelihood dwelt only as far as the Main, or the Neckar at most; but in earlier times, they lived further to the south, and were pushed back by the Gauls. Those Germans in the Valais who were known to Livy,[13] are remnants of that migration.

After the victory at Clastidium, between Piacenza and Alessandria, the Romans immediately founded two colonies, Placentia and Cremona, on both banks of the Po: the boundary was pushed on to the Ticinus. There is every reason to think that Modena also was fortified; but it was afterwards lost again for some time, during a fresh insurrection of the Boians. The Ligurian tribes in Piedmont were still independent by rights, though not in reality.

In the first Illyrian war, the Romans owed their speedy success to a Greek, Demetrius of Pharus. As governor of Corcyra, having in all probability been bribed, he had surrendered the island to them; and by their influence he had been appointed guardian of the king who was a minor. His was a character in keeping with that age of infamy; he was a traitor to all parties. He now conspired against the Romans, and during the Gallic war he excited the Illyrians to rebellion, which shows that these peoples paid tribute to Rome. Besides this, with a fleet of fifty *Lembi*, he dared to commit piracy in the Archipelago against the defenceless Cyclades. The Romans sent over a consular army under L. Æmilius Paulus; the hopes of the rebels were quickly blighted, and their capital Dimalus was taken (a name which proves, that the modern Albanian language is like the ancient Illyrian, for *dimal* in Albanian means a double mountain). The seat of Demetrius was his native island Pharus, which the Romans took by a stratagem: he himself made his escape to Macedon, where the last Philip had just begun his reign, and he became his evil genius. Thus the second Illyrian war was very soon ended. The Romans on the whole at that time enlarged their dominion. We have nothing to inform us when the Venetians became dependent: in the great Gallic war we find them as allies. The Istrians, however, were subjected even before the war of Hannibal, and the Venetians must then have been already conquered; so that the acquisition of the supremacy over them probably dates from this period.

While all this was taking place, events were brooding, of the fearful nature of which the Romans were far from having the least conception. Hamilcar Barcas had turned his eyes towards Spain, thus showing that he was a truly great man in not allowing himself to be discouraged by his former ill successes, and in not repining against fate. The Carthaginians had until then placed all their hopes on Sicily; and there were fellows indeed at Carthage (like Hanno, by whose speeches Livy spoils his fine description of the war of Hannibal), who partly from envy and bad feeling, and partly from miserable cowardice, were of opinion, that after the loss of Sicily and Sardinia, one ought now to yield altogether. Just as Pitt, after the American war, when it was believed in foreign countries that the peace of Paris had broken the power of England, with redoubled courage undertook the task of infusing new strength into his country; thus also did Hamilcar. At an early period already, the Phœnicians had settled in Spain. Gades is said to have been older than Carthage, and that place was indeed very important as the centre of the trade with the Cassiterides. Tin was of the greatest value to the ancients for making the copper, of which they had plenty, fusible: the use of calamine in the manufacture of brass, is of much later invention. Very likely, neither the Phœnicians nor Carthaginians had any settlements on the western coast besides Gades; but they certainly had some on the southern coast, in Granada, Malaga, and Abdera, and a mixed nation (Μιξοφοίνικες) had sprung up there, namely the Bastulans. But into the interior the Carthaginians had not yet penetrated, although they seem to have had connexions there. The yoke of Carthage was deeply hated in Africa, as was shown in the insurrection of the mercenaries; now, on the contrary the great tact of Hamilcar and Hasdrubal shines forth in the foundation of a Carthaginian empire in Spain: they laid upon the Spaniards a very easy yoke. Hannibal was married to a Spanish woman of Castulo, and these alliances between Carthaginians and native women must have been of very frequent occurrence: among the Romans, such marriages were regarded only as concubinage. Hamilcar had devised the plan of creating in Spain a province, which was to make up to Carthage for Sicily and Sardinia, and from which it might also derive what it could never have got from those isles: neither Sicily nor Sardinia were able to give Carthage any considerable military strength. The weakness of Carthage lay in this, that it had no army of its own; and that great man now conceived the idea of forming a national Carthaginian army out of Spaniards, who were partly to be subjected, and partly to be gained over and made Punic. Southern Spain has immense natural advantages; its silver mines are of extraordinary richness. The Carthaginians had known of these before; but it was Hamilcar who first introduced a regular system of working them, and thus he, or his son-in-law Hasdrubal, was led to found the town of New Carthage (Carthagena). The stores which had been furnished by Sicily and Sardinia, were just as well supplied by Spain. They now got a population of millions, from which they no more took faithless mercenaries; but there they made levies as in their own country. The Romans no doubt looked with jealousy at the progress they were making; yet they could not hinder it, so long as the Cisalpine Gauls stood on their frontier, prepared to avenge the defeat of the Senonians and Boians.

The whole of Spain consisted of a number of petty tribes without any connexion whatever between them; whilst in Gaul, at least some one nation or other, the Æduans, the Arvernians, held the supremacy. The Spaniards were of various kinds: whether the Turdetanians and the northern peoples, the Cantabrians, were of a different race, as the ancients say; or whether all the Iberians were sprung from the same stock, as is maintained by that great etymologist, Humboldt, we cannot decide. Not being acquainted with the language myself, I must abstain from giving an opinion; yet surely, notwithstanding the great weight of Humboldt's authority, the statements of the ancients ought also to be taken in consideration. Certain it is, that the tribes south of the Sierra Morena, the inhabitants of Bœtica, had quite a different character from those of the northern part of the country. They were highly civilized; they had a literature of their own, written laws, and books; of their alphabet, which is altogether peculiar to themselves, and not derived from that of the Phœnicians, there are remnants still existing on inscriptions and coins. The letters have quite a primitive form. Yet these peoples were quite as warlike as those of the north: they were not, however, good for attack, but merely for defence. In earlier times only, they succeeded in driving the Celts across the Pyrenees into Aquitain; afterwards, we always find them confined to their boundaries, within which they made a desperate stand; so that what an Arab general said of them is true, that behind walls they were more than men, and in the field more cowardly than women, which has also been borne out in the latest wars. An exception to this, however, were the Celtiberians; and the others also showed themselves brave, when they were trained by great generals like Hannibal and Sertorius, and likewise in the fifteenth and sixteenth centuries. Otherwise, they confine themselves to desperate resistance, even behind wretched fortifications; they kill their women and children, and defend themselves to their last drop of blood. Now Hamilcar, and after him Hasdrubal, spread further and further, drawing one people after the other into the Carthaginian league, and training soldiers.

Hamilcar had hardly finished his war against the mercenaries, when he founded the Carthaginian empire in Spain. He staid there eight years, of which he made an incomparable use. He died in Spain, and left the command to his son-in-law Hasdrubal, which was quite different from the Roman custom. The Carthaginian general not only keeps his office for life, but he also bequeaths it at his death to his son-in-law, like an heirloom. It is true that this required a great deal of influence at Carthage, and this is what Livy calls *factio Barcina*.

THE SECOND PUNIC WAR

Livy begins his account of the war of Hannibal with the remark, which several others had made before him, that it was the greatest war which had ever been waged by the greatest and most powerful states, when in the height of their greatest vigour. Yet now that two thousand years are passed, we can no longer say the same. The seven years' war, especially the campaign of 1757, exhibits a greater accumulation of achievements than any part of the war of Hannibal; nor is it inferior in the greatness of the generals. But thus much we may say, that no war in the whole of ancient history is to be compared to this. Nor is there, on the whole, any general to be placed above Hannibal, and of the ancients none can stand at his side. Whilst in the first Punic war, only one great general makes his appearance upon the stage, we see in this, besides Hannibal, Scipio likewise, who, as a general, is indeed not fully his equal, but has claims notwithstanding to be ranked among the very first; and after him, Fabius and Marcellus, who in any war would have gained a high renown, and could have only been eclipsed by men of such extraordinary greatness; and besides these, many other stars of the second magnitude.

The war of Hannibal has been described by several of the ancients. It formed the substance of the works of Fabius and Cincius: in those of the latter it was treated exclusively. He wrote it, as far as he himself lived to see it, very explicitly, merely prefixing an introduction on the earlier history. Fabius had a more extensive plan; he took in both wars. Of Fabius we may say with certainty, that his account to a great extent forms the groundwork of that of Appian: Dionysius left him at the beginning of the first Punic war, and he is there without any guide. I am able to show, that statements of a marked character in Appian and in Zonaras are taken from Fabius; for Dio Cassius also acknowledged that he could find no better source. Very nearly about the same time, Chæreas and Sosilus wrote: of both of these Polybius speaks with censure; he denounces them as fabulists, although Sosilus had staid in the camp with Hannibal. It is strange that Livy did not think of making any use of Hannibal's short memoirs, and of a letter of Scipio to Philip of Macedon in which he recounted his achievements. Polybius has made use of an authentic document of Hannibal, on a brass tablet in the temple of Juno in Lacinia,[14] in which the numbers especially were given with great accuracy. As far as Polybius goes, we have nothing left to desire: the third book is the masterpiece of what has been preserved to us of his history; unfortunately we have but the first years of his. He too certainly had before him the excellent work of L. Cincius, who described this war as an eye-witness. There was also an account of it in Latin, about the middle of the seventh century, by L. Cœlius Antipater, probably a Greek freedman. He wrote with rhetorical pretension, and I think that many things in Livy are to be traced to him, particularly where the latter goes off into the romantic. For Cœlius had wished to write history for effect, and it may not have been without justice, that Cicero speaks slightingly of him.

In Livy's work we may clearly distinguish the different sources. In the beginning, the description of the siege of Saguntum is taken beyond a doubt from Cœlius Antipater; other parts follow most closely in the footsteps of Polybius; elsewhere he has either made use of the *Annales Pontificum*, or of those annalists who had embodied them in their histories. The whole of the third decade is written with evident fondness for the subject; yet he is wanting in the knowledge of facts, in experience of real life, and in the power of taking a general view: he never gets away from the *umbracula* of the school. Wherever he deviates from Polybius, he is altogether unworthy of belief; and however beautifully his history of the war is written, it is still quite plain that he was unable to bring before his mind one single event, as it really happened: his account of the battle of Cannæ, for instance, is untrue and impossible; whilst, on the other hand, that of Polybius is so excellent, that one may get a most distinct idea of the locality, and even draw a map from his statements, and the better one knows the nature of the spot, the clearer becomes his description. The work of General Vaudoncourt, published some years ago at Milan under the title of *Campagnes d'Annibal*, which, merely because its author is such an able man, has been praised by every body, is an utterly worthless production. The maps are good for nothing, and the plans are drawn from fancy; he did not understand how to read an author critically, he had no knowledge of Greek, and he has not given anything new: there is only one point of ancient tactics about which I have learned anything from him. He is especially mistaken in the notion which he has formed of the battle array of the Carthaginians; he believes them to have been drawn up in phalanx, which they were not. They were just as moveable as the Romans, and the sword alone was the weapon which they relied on: lances they very likely had none, but javelins in abundance. Ulric Becker's treatise on the history of the war of Hannibal (in Dahlmann's "Researches in the Field of History"),[15] although not a mature work, is really valuable, and should not be overlooked.

Hamilcar was succeeded by his son-in-law Hasdrubal, who, after an administration of nine years, was murdered by an Iberian whose chieftain he had caused to be put to death. This personal attachment to their princes prevailed among the Iberians: no one durst leave the death of his chief unavenged,—nay, if possible, he was not to survive him. Hasdrubal had with him for his education young Hannibal, who soon became the favourite of the army. The oath of Hannibal rests on his own authority; the circumstances of it, however, are told in different ways. He is said to have been nine years old when his father went over to Spain (516 according to Cato), and this seems to be historical: if so, he was born about 507, which would make him twenty-seven years old when he marched to Italy. This is the very age, at which several generals have shown themselves greatest. Frederic the Great was twenty-eight years old when he conquered Silesia; Napoleon twenty-seven, or twenty-eight, when he undertook the Italian campaign. The whole conduct of Hannibal during this war bears the character of a very young man; and he was by no means an old one when he died, being nearer his fiftieth than his sixtieth year. Very likely, he was born just before Hamilcar went to Sicily. His brothers were Hasdrubal and Mago. Whether Hasdrubal was his elder, is doubtful; Mago was considerably younger.

The opinions of the ancients as to Hannibal's personal character might very easily have been divided. In the Roman writers, he appears throughout only as a terrific being. Livy's delineation of him is in some parts quite excellent,—no one could gainsay his extraordinary qualities as a general: yet when Livy says that these were darkened by *vitia* of equal magnitude, he is in direct opposition to Polybius. The latter expressly disputes the fact of Hannibal's cruelty, and says that whenever anything of the kind did happen, it was through the fault of some subordinate commander, especially of another Hannibal. He also flatly contradicts the statements about his bad faith (*plus quam Punica fides*). Atrocities may have been committed,—there are stories of these in Appian which are borrowed from Fabius,—nor will I doubt in the least that the war was conducted with cruelty on the side of the Carthaginians; but so it was likewise by the Romans. This is the general character of the ancient wars, which we are far from representing to ourselves as so horrible as they really were. Sometimes also there are cases in which a general cannot help himself.[16] Of the bad faith of Hannibal, not an instance can be brought forward; on the contrary, as far as we have any positive evidence, he must have kept his word; otherwise he would have been taxed with it, especially in capitulations, and then indeed people would not have capitulated to him. The Romans are awful liars when they want to lay the blame upon their enemies. Such stories as the murder of the senate of Nuceria, and the extermination of that of Acerræ,[17] are unauthenticated. In peace, he is quite a different man from Scipio. The latter forgot himself after his victory; he did not find himself at home in the free constitution of his native city, and as a peaceful citizen he never was of any use to the commonwealth; the example which he set of contempt for an impeachment was perhaps highly perilous and baneful. It was great in him, that he did not make an ill use of the popular enthusiasm in his behalf: but he was conscious of his own greatness; he displayed from the very first, when he stood for the ædileship and the consulship, an overbearing pride; he wished to raise himself with impunity above the laws wherever he could harmlessly do it. With the influence which he had, he might have become the source of the greatest blessings to the state; but this was not the case. Not a law, not a beneficial measure is to be traced to him. The neglect of the Roman constitution after the Punic wars, was a principal cause of the decay of the republic: with regard to this, it was in his power to have done much good. Hannibal, on the contrary, comes forth after the Punic war as a public benefactor likewise, as a reformer of the law, of the administration and finances of his country. Scipio and Hannibal were both of them well acquainted with Greek literature. Hannibal had Greeks for his companions, and though indeed they were not the most distinguished men of their day, this shows that in his leisure hours he enjoyed a literary conversation. [18] There was something irresistible about him, which he seems to have inherited from his father. For sixteen years, he commanded an army which at last, like that of Gustavus Adolphus, had not a man of the old soldiers left; but consisted only of a herd of abandoned adventurers. Though he was placed in the most difficult circumstances, no Gaul ever attempted anything against him; the ruthless, reckless Numidians never dared to raise a hand against him. He demanded of the Italians the most gigantic efforts; he wore them out, was not able to protect them; and still he so fascinated them also, that they never wavered in their fidelity. A man, like him, who achieved such things as the settlement and subjugation of Spain, the march across the Alps, the victories over the Romans, the shaking of Italy to its centre, we may call the first and greatest of his age,—indeed we might almost call him the first and greatest in all history. How little in comparison has Alexander done! He had no difficulties whatever to overcome. As for Scipio, he entered the lists against his rival under the most favourable circumstances: if he had not conquered, Hannibal must have been more than man. But Hannibal worked for the sole purpose of delivering his country; and when he returned thither, it was his only object to restore it. Even when banished, he did not seek for protection anywhere; but wherever he was, he commanded, he stood forth as a superior, and never bowed before any one, nor ever sinned against truth. Such a man I admire and love, almost without any qualification. That he let Decius Magius go from Capua, was not policy: it was a greatness of mind of which very few only would have been capable. Scipio could have done it.

The third general of this war, Q. Fabius Maximus, had gained some reputation already in the former obscure contest: the surname of Maximus, however, is inherited from his grandfather, or great-grandfather, Q. Fabius Rullianus in the days of the Samnite wars, who received it when he separated the four city tribes from the country ones. He acted in what seemed to him the fittest way, and was net afraid of doing what might be mistaken in him for cowardice. *Unus homo nobis cunctando restituit rem*, says Ennius. He was a very good general; he had coolness, circumspection, and quickness of eye: but he has been much overrated notwithstanding. Daun has been compared to him, and there were many who thought that this was doing too much honour to the Austrian commander; but Daun was by no means inferior to him as a general. The only important achievement of Fabius is the recovering of Tarentum; yet, after all, what was it? What is certainly true, is his opposition to Scipio. All the speeches of Hanno and others in Livy, are perhaps rhetorical trifles from Cœlius Antipater; but this opposition bears the impress of history. One sees distinctly that he was of an envious mind. He could not bear the great rising star; he would rather have had Hannibal unconquered, than that Scipio should gain a glory which outvied his own. He did not rejoice at the freshness of the new generation; he wished Hannibal to be worn out by the power of time alone.

The fourth character of this war is M. Claudius Marcellus, a dashing, able general, the opposite to Fabius in his daring, distinguished as a commander, and at the same time a brave soldier.

We also divide this war into periods. To the introduction belongs all that happened previously in Spain from the taking of Saguntum to the march over the Alps 534. The first period of the war itself contains the first three years, and a part of 537, during which was the irresistible progress of Hannibal. The second extends from 537 to the taking of Capua 541, when his star was already on the wane, while the Romans once more gained ground, and their prospects became brighter. The third is from 541 to 545, when Hannibal set his hopes on Spain, and on being reinforced by his brother Hasdrubal. He maintains himself in Apulia, Bruttium, and Lucania, until Hasdrubal's defeat on the Metaurus. The fourth period is from 545 to 550, when Hannibal was obliged to evacuate Italy. The last, from his arrival in Africa to the end of the war.

The years 535 to 546, or 547, are those of the wars of the Romans in Spain, which were waged with various success until the taking of New Carthage. The time from 548 to the end, may be called the African war of

Scipio. The Sicilian war and the conquest of Sardinia, from 535 to 540, come in like episodes. In 540, the Macedonian war begins, which lasts until 547.

Hannibal had taken upon himself the command after Hasdrubal's death, and he forthwith displayed increased activity. The Romans, probably after the outbreak of the Cisalpine war, had made a treaty with Hasdrubal, not with the Carthaginian state, by which both parties with regard to Spain fixed upon the Ebro as the boundary between their respective possessions. Owing to the great gap which here occurs in our history, we cannot make out at what time the Romans settled in those parts; yet at the beginning of the second Punic war, they were masters of Tarraco and of the coast of Catalonia. Livy adds, that the Saguntines were to be left as a free state between both. Polybius, notwithstanding his general excellence, is sometimes mistaken in details. He had first edited his work down to the war of Perseus, a second edition went as far as the taking of Corinth; yet it may clearly be shown that he did not revise the first books in the second edition, and it is plain that he had not at that time the least knowledge of the geography of Spain: very likely he fancied, as Livy evidently did, that Saguntum lay east of the Ebro. Moreover, he knows nothing of the fact that Saguntum was to remain independent, and yet he had all the documents before him. Were it not so, there would then indeed have been a breach of faith on the side of Hannibal. Perhaps the Romans did not mean at any rate to abandon the people of Saguntum, with whom they were in alliance; and yet it may not have been expressedly stipulated, that an attack on Saguntum would be a violation of the peace. Now it is generally thought from the treaty between Rome and Carthage, that the Carthaginians had then under their rule the whole of Spain as far as the sources of the Ebro; but this is by no means the case. Under Hamilcar, they seem to have acquired the whole of Andalusia, and the greater part of Valencia; but beyond the Sierra Morena, they in all likelihood only first spread under Hasdrubal: their sway never extended further than New Castile and Estremadura; Lusitania, Old Castile, and Leon, never belonged to them. The farthest point to which Hannibal reached in the campaign against the Vaccæans, described by Polybius, was Salamanca, where, however, he did not found any lasting dominion: the tribes in the interior, and the Celtiberians, seem never to have acknowledged the supremacy of Carthage. The other peoples were under its protectorate: they retained their own form of government, and though not bound to serve, were ready to enlist under the banners of the Carthaginians, who gave good pay. Polybius himself remarks very justly, that the Romans kept silent at the progress of the Carthaginians, because they were greatly afraid of offending them now that the Gauls had stirred. Had Hamilcar been alive, he would perhaps have taken a share in that war. It is strange that once during this period a Carthaginian fleet makes its appearance off the coast of Etruria.

Hannibal carried on the war in Spain only as a preparatory one: his real object was the war in Italy, which he now tried to kindle. The Carthaginians stood in the same position to him, as the Romans did to Cæsar; commanding as he did an army entirely devoted to him, in a country subjected by him, he was not to be controlled by the senate. Carthage, according to the natural march of development in republics, was then already on the decline: the chief power had passed from the senate to the popular assembly. Now, although the people might have idolized Hannibal, yet the senate was hardly friendly towards him; and notwithstanding the general hatred against the Romans, the majority at that time were not perhaps of opinion, that a war would bring relief, and they could not see in what way Rome was to be attacked. The higher classes were also afraid of Hannibal at the head of a victorious army.

The siege of Saguntum is placed by Livy in the year 534; yet he sees himself that it took place in 533. Polybius blames Hannibal for having tried to kindle the war by all kinds of artifices, and for this he has been reproached with having been too much the partisan of the Romans; but even as he is to be acquitted of this charge, so must Hannibal of his. Polybius would have had him at once demand Sardinia; but that he could not do. Had Hannibal been a king, he would perhaps have done it; but as it was, he was obliged to draw the Carthaginians into the war by degrees, whether they liked it or not. With this view, he intrigued in Saguntum, and got up a quarrel between the Saguntines and the Turdetanians, (but very likely we ought to read, instead of Turdetanians, *Edetanians*, who were inhabitants of Valencia, as the former lived too far off). Saguntum may not have been a purely Iberian town: it is said that colonists from Ardea had settled there, in which case it would be Tyrrhenian; and this is not unlikely, although afterwards perhaps the Iberian population outnumbered them. The derivation from Zacynthus has probably originated only from its name. Some years before, there had been troubles there; (several of these Spanish towns were republics; one must not fancy that their inhabitants were barbarians like the Celts;) and the Romans had come forward as mediators, and the victorious party had wreaked its vengeance upon the conquered. Hannibal took advantage of this, and stirred up the latter: at the same time, he complained at Carthage that the Saguntines, relying upon Rome, had been guilty of acts of violence against Carthaginian subjects. This is certainly craftiness; but he could hardly have behaved otherwise if he wanted to kindle the war. The Romans were exceedingly afraid of a Carthaginian war: the manner in which the city had risen again, could not but make an impression upon them. They did not know how it was to be carried on. They could only remove it to Africa by means of a fleet, of which the cost was enormous, not to speak of the many disasters which they had already had to suffer from it. To Spain also they had to transport the war by sea; and in that country, they had no base for their operations, and only insignificant allies. There, on the other hand, Carthage had at her disposal the whole of a subjugated population, and all the troops which were wanted in readiness; whilst Rome had to fight her battles with her own men, and these she had to bring over at an immense expense. The Romans therefore let Hannibal widen his rule, without themselves undertaking anything; nay, even when he began the siege of Saguntum, they merely negociated, and took no measures for sending assistance thither; so that Hannibal besieged the town for eight months, whilst they were engaged in the Illyrian war. The full description in Livy of the siege of Saguntum is certainly from Cœlius Antipater: according to him, the inhabitants themselves destroyed their town from despair; this is a repetition of what is told of so many Spanish towns. Another account is given by Polybius, which is really historical. Hannibal besieged the town, which lay one mile from the sea-coast, on the last ridges of the mountains which, rising from thence, separate Arragon from Castile. At the end of eight months, it was taken, but by no means destroyed: on the contrary, Hannibal found in the booty the means for fresh undertakings, and for rich presents to Carthage; and thus he was able to strengthen and encourage his own army. This is a complete refutation of Livy's story, which also betrays itself by its empty prolixity. Hannibal himself had been wounded at this siege. So little is it to be placed in the year 534, that Hannibal afterwards put his army into winter-quarters, where he completed his preparations for his great expedition. The Romans had sent an embassy to him in behalf of their injured allies, but he referred them to Carthage: there they made their complaints, and demanded the giving up of Hannibal, and of the commissaries (σύνεδροι) who were with him, which throws some light on the state of things at Carthage, which is otherwise so obscure. The Carthaginians, instead of going into the complaint, tried to prove to the Romans that Hannibal had done no wrong; that Carthage could not be restricted by its treaties with Rome with regard to its acquisitions in Spain. Polybius justly remarks, that they argued beside the point, without entering into the question which was really before them. The Roman ambassadors now made a *sinus* of their toga, and declared to the Carthaginians, that they might choose between peace and war; the Carthaginians answered that they would follow the choice of the Romans; and when these cried out "war," a loud shout of joy was raised.

One would now have thought that the Romans had already made great preparations; yet this was not the case. They had at that time only a small fleet, which moreover we afterwards hear of but seldom, and even then, little is said about it. The consuls, since the Ides of March, were P. Cornelius Scipio and Ti. Sempronius Longus. The Romans had the intention of sending the consul Scipio with two legions and ten thousand allies to Spain, and Sempronius with the same number of troops to Africa. The Carthaginians had no fleet of any importance; this was the first fault committed by them in this war. It may be that the rich who were in the government made niggardly retrenchments, that they might cut down the expenses of the war as much as possible. The plan of the Romans was not badly devised; only it is plain that they were quite mistaken in their estimate of their antagonist. Had Scipio arrived in Spain, before Hannibal had passed the Ebro, his army would have been driven by Hannibal into the sea, or annihilated within the first weeks, and the invasion of Italy would have become far more easy. And yet, if Hannibal had not carried on the war with such very great speed, the season of the year might have come on, in which he could no longer have crossed the Alps. The Romans show themselves unskilful at the beginning of every great war; their troops were not thoroughly trained, they had no standing army like Hannibal, nor did it even occur to them that they ought to place the very best of their generals in command. Hannibal took the wisest precautions: he sent the chief men of the conquered tribes over to Carthage, or kept them with him; and he despatched besides some picked Spanish troops for the defence of Africa, and a body of Libyans trained by himself, who were to garrison Carthage. Into Spain, on the other hand, he drew over a great many Libyans.

The Roman consul Sempronius went with a hundred and sixty quinqueremes to Africa, and already dreamed of a siege of Carthage; but before he reached it, events of quite a different kind had come to pass. Hannibal, who had rested himself during the winter, now crossed the Ebro with ninety thousand infantry and twelve thousand horse (according to Polybius, who took it from the tablet of Hannibal,—a number which the writer certainly meant to be correct; yet one ought perhaps to suppose it to be a slip of the pen, so as to read seventy thousand instead of ninety). The tribes beyond the Ebro were allies of the Romans, though not subject to them, and were therefore hostile to the Carthaginians: they made a stout resistance; but Hannibal quickly hastened on and took their strongholds, at the cost, however, of many men's lives. He in all likelihood set out in May, as from Polybius it is pretty certain that he reached Italy in the middle of October. There is no doubt but that, if he could have started a month sooner, his expedition would have been far from being as dangerous as it was; yet the obstacles which had given rise to this delay, must have been insurmountable. He was leagued with those Gauls in Lombardy, who four years before had been subjected and cruelly treated by the Romans: they had promised him to put the whole of their force at his disposal. The Romans, however, had now seen through his plan. A year before, they had begun to build Placentia and Cremona; colonists were sent thither in great haste, and the fortifications completed before the beginning of the campaign; so that neither Hannibal nor the Gauls were able to take these places. Polybius rebukes the writers of his day, who spoke of Hannibal's undertaking as of a thing that had never happened before, but had sprung from a desire of doing some thing which was unheard of, and never could be carried through without the co-operation of unearthly powers. The story that a demon had showed Hannibal the way, is in Livy changed into a dream of surpassing beauty, as if a being more than human were directing Hannibal not to look backward, but only forward; but the writers of those times gave it as an actual part of their narrative.

Hannibal crossed the Pyrenees with fifty thousand infantry and nine thousand horse, numbers which Polybius has likewise evidently taken from the monumental tablet of Hannibal. The passage was effected near Figueras and Rosas towards Roussillon, where it is easiest. He had previously sent envoys to the Gallic tribes from the Pyrenees to the Rhone, to ask them for a free passage through their countries, and had tried to move them to peace by presents of money; so that he reached the Rhone without meeting with any hostility worth mentioning. After the passage over the Pyrenees, signs of a dangerous mutiny began to show themselves; three thousand Carpetanians returned home, and Hannibal also of his own accord sent back other Spaniards whom he suspected. His army seems to have suffered from desertion besides: otherwise it could not have lessened so much as Polybius states. He advanced with the utmost speed. From Carthagena to the Po, Polybius reckons two hundred German miles, which is indeed somewhat exaggerated; but, even then, what difficulties were to be overcome! Until Hannibal came to Cisalpine Gaul, he had to pass through nothing but tribes to whom his march was as a curse. Having gone through the beautiful province of Lower Languedoc, he came to the Rhone in the neighbourhood of Pont St. Esprit. As for the inhabitants of Languedoc, they had been obliged to send their women and children into the Cevennes; but things were now quite different. The Gauls of the Dauphiné, Provence, and those parts, had the rapid river in front of them, and could therefore more readily venture upon resistance; perhaps they had heard moreover that a Roman army was already in Catalonia, nay, even, on the Gallic coast. However much they at other times had scorned the Romans, they now looked to them with eager confidence. P. Scipio had on his voyage to Spain put in at Marseilles, as he had learned that Hannibal, whom he supposed still at the Ebro, was already near the Rhone. He could not but have found it hazardous to take the field against an army of such superior numbers; but in conjunction with the Gauls on the left bank of the Rhone, he could have hindered the enemy's passage over the river. Hannibal, even without this, had already immense difficulties in his way: the building of a bridge of boats was no easy task. He therefore bought from the people who lived along the bank on which he was, every kind of boat that he could get, and he had canoes made of trees; then he ordered a division to make a night-march higher up the river, so as to cross over on rafts at a spot which was some way off, and threaten the Gauls in the rear. This plan succeeded; yet one cannot understand how the Gauls were not up to it. When the detachment had made its appearance, Hannibal embarked all his forces in the boats, and crossed the stream whilst this division attacked the Gauls. Thus, after inflicting great loss upon the Gauls, he landed on the other side: he got the elephants over with a great deal of trouble. His victory over Nature, which seemed here herself to have set bounds to his advance, made a decisive impression on the neighbouring tribes. Had he delayed eight days longer, Scipio would have barred his way, and hindered him from crossing. He had only thirty-eight thousand infantry, and eight thousand cavalry left; the latter were most of them Numidians, and on the whole were only good for foraging and skirmishing, but not for regular fighting: he had still nearly all his elephants. He now sent some Numidians on to the road to Marseilles, and these fell in with some of the Roman horse: on both sides they were astonished at the meeting. Scipio, who had but just heard of Hannibal's passing over the Pyrenees, could not have thought that he had already crossed the Rhone. An insignificant skirmish took place, in which the Romans had the advantage. Hannibal, however, did not mind the Roman general, but continued his march.

Here we begin to have most discrepant accounts of Hannibal's expedition. Had he gone in the direction which Livy makes him take,—up the valley of the Durance by Briançon, Mont Genèvre, and Susa, and coming out near Turin,—he could not have done a better service to the Romans; Scipio would have fallen upon his rear, and on the other side, from the mountains, the Gauls would have laid wait for him, with barricades of felled trees, and the like. There was even among the ancients already some uncertainty as to the road by which Hannibal crossed the Alps; Polybius says nothing about it, because in his time it may have been a thing generally known. Some thought that he had gone over the Little, others, over the Great St. Bernard; others again were even for the Simplon: in times of old, there was no road over Mont Cenis. In these days, opinions are also divided. And yet, after General Melville's masterly researches, edited by the younger De Luc,[19] which are based on a more accurate survey of the places themselves, there can be no more doubt on the subject: that Letronne, who truly deserves to be spoken of with respect, does not see this, is passing strange. No other road can be meant, but that over the little St. Bernard. In the beginning of October, Hannibal was on the last mountains. The little St. Bernard has no glaciers at all, nor is it much higher than the Brenner; in summer it is even a green Alp, and though indeed for a pretty long time it is covered with snow, this always melts away; at the very top, the soil is still so fertile that rye grows there: on the great St. Bernard, on the contrary, there is everlasting snow. On the mountain over which Hannibal went, was a frequented road, and there he found new-fallen snow. Particularly decisive, however, is the following circumstance: before Hannibal reached the top of the mountain, he had a sharp fight with the Alpine tribes, on which, as Polybius says, he stationed himself with his reserve near a white rock. Now, there is in the whole of that part of the country only one rock of gypsum, which lies near the old road in the Tarantaise; the inhabitants still call it *la roche blanche*: De Luc remarks that whoever has once passed that way, must needs remember the cliff for ever. The Alps in Polybius mean the whole mountain range from Savoy and Aosta; there are several ridges of them, running one behind the other, to be crossed.

Hannibal had to go higher up the Rhone, that he might get further away from Scipio. Had Scipio dared to follow him, he would have been just as well pleased; for he was sure to have beaten him, and Scipio would have been lost, if defeated. He marched as far as Vienne, a place which was the capital of the Allobroges, which Livy does not mention; that it is Vienne, has also been shown by Melville. Here a civil war was going on. Hannibal took the part of one of the pretenders to the throne, led him on to victory, and got great supplies from him. The Allobroges had at that time the country between the Rhone, the Saone, the Isère, and the west of Savoy. Near Vienne, he left the Rhone, and turned towards Yenne and Chambéry, where Melville has discovered an old Roman road from Chambéry by the great Carthusian monastery: it was used during the whole of the middle ages, and was abandoned only as late as in the seventeenth century. From Chambéry, he came into the Tarantaise, and followed the Isère up to its source. To the Alpine tribes which dwelt in the small valleys, Hannibal's expedition was a real calamity; it was like a swarm of locusts which eat up all that they had. Hannibal did everything he could to make them friends; yet they all of them withstood him. They did not indeed venture upon open resistance; but they had recourse to cunning, which is the characteristic of weak nations. They brought provisions, and even hostages; and then fell upon the Carthaginians as they were marching through the defiles. But Hannibal had never trusted them, as on the whole he never let himself be deceived: his plan had been to send his baggage in advance, to follow cautiously, and strongly to cover his rear; and thus he managed to beat them off. Yet the Carthaginians suffered a dreadful loss. Melville has shown, that the onward march, although very toilsome, and through unfriendly tribes, was by no means over fields of ice and snow, but across a thickly-peopled, beautiful country: the road winds between the hills through rich and well cultivated mountain valleys, through woods of walnut trees, and corn fields. But when from thence it mounts up higher into the Alps, it becomes exceedingly narrow and difficult, being in most places nothing but a path for beasts of burthen, by which not more than two can barely pass each other; and it runs along the brink of deep mountain steeps, over most of which torrents rush: it is only within the present century that a carriage road has been made. Fifteen days were spent by Hannibal on his march through these mountains; yet for the greater part of that time, his way led through those fine valleys, full of cultivation and wealth, the inhabitants of which one must not deem to have been more savage than the Tyrolese were in the fifteenth century. [20] Thus he came as far as the Little St. Bernard. Had he reached it a month sooner, in August or the beginning of September, no snow would yet have fallen, and he might every where have found fodder for his cattle. The chief difficulty was the carrying of provisions for thirty or forty thousand men, eight thousand horses, and certainly as many as four thousand mules and pack-horses, which were laden with the bread; for, if the snow fell, it was impossible to get fresh grass for the beasts. A great part of the baggage had been taken by the mountaineers. Until he came to the heights of the Little St. Bernard, Hannibal had not much suffered from the cold; want of food and the enmity of the neighbouring tribes were his worst hardships: but now, when he reached the top of the mountain, he was overtaken by a fall of snow, which made the roads quite impassable. Only think, what a dead stop this must have been for Africans! The greatness of the snowdrifts, by which many deep clefts in the rocks were covered over, soon gave rise to accidents; the feet of the horses slipped, and the animals tumbled down the steeps; fodder was scarce, and many elephants died of cold. The army also suffered from hunger, like the French on their retreat from Russia; in those few days, thousands met with their death. The story of Livy, that Hannibal softened the rocks by fire, and split them by means of vinegar, and thus made a way for himself, is a fable. This is only sometimes possible, when there are cliffs of limestone; but to imagine it in the case of a whole army, and with a mountain like the Alps, is one of those things of which one cannot understand how a man of sense can write them down. Particularly dangerous was the descent: with a great deal of trouble they reached a spot, of which Livy speaks just as incomprehensibly as Polybius does clearly. The roads, in fact, were in some places carried round the mountains, so that on one side there was often an abrupt precipice; now it not unseldom happens that torrents undermine a way like this from beneath, and it falls in; or that avalanches bury it. This had happened here. A bit of the road had fallen in a year before, and it had not yet been mended, as Polybius tells us in the most natural manner. Livy, who takes it for granted that Hannibal had altogether made the road for the first time, says that he had now been stopped all at once by a precipice; and that on this he had ordered trees to be felled, and had had them piled up below against the steep, so as to go down by them as on ladders. But according to Polybius, the landslip went down a stadium and a half, that is to say, a thousand feet in depth, to the bed of the river Dora at the mouth of the valley of Aosta. Hannibal tried to go by a new way, having heard perhaps that some huntsmen of the Alps had already struck out several other tracks. It did not answer; and so he had to encamp for three days and three nights in the midst of the snow, that at the spot where the road was broken down, he might make with timber a new one broad enough for the beasts of burthen to pass. This is the place where indeed the distress of the army was overpowering, and it suffered such immense loss, especially in beasts. This difficulty being overcome, they came by and by to the valley of Aosta, where the Salassians dwelt, a cultivated and rather civilized country. The story of Hannibal's having shown to his army, from the top of the mountain, the blooming land of Italy, is likewise an impossible one, and a rhetorical flourish: from the summit of St. Bernard, one sees nothing but mountains.

Hannibal was now in the valley of Aosta. A great part of his elephants were dead, and his army now consisted of no more than twenty thousand foot (twelve thousand Africans, and eight thousand Spaniards), and six thousand horse, most of them Numidians. It is wonderful how strong the horses here showed themselves to have been; the Numidians must have treated them with great care.

The whole management of the war on the side of the Romans, is a remarkable counterpart of that want of design, and that sluggishness, which in the wars of the revolution so often let the victory fall into the hands of the French. When the Romans heard that Hannibal was going to cross the Alps, they most certainly must have thought him a madman: this supposition alone can account for the slackness of their movements. Scipio, who had advanced as far as Avignon, ought, as he had a fleet, to have been in Lombardy, long before Hannibal reached the St. Bernard. He very likely thought, that there would still be always plenty of time whenever he came; and thus, when he arrived at the Po, Hannibal was already descending the Alps. The reports also of the losses of the Carthaginians, one may fancy to oneself from that logic of absurdity of which we have heard so many examples during the revolution. His condition was now indeed a very bad one for an ordinary general; yet Hannibal, without stopping, hastened on with his army in which typhus fever must necessarily have raged, and which must have looked like a horde of gipsies. Scipio had only two legions, a corresponding number of allies, and a few horse. The Romans were in many respects the slaves of established usage, from which they frequently did not know how to free themselves in an emergency. Thus from ancient times downward, such an army was looked upon as quite large enough, and therefore they did not send more. Part of the Gauls were already in open rebellion; the Boians, the summer before, had beaten a Roman legion, and kept the survivors shut up in Modena,—they dwelt from Parma and Placentia to the frontier of the Romagna,—and by treachery they seized three Romans of rank who had been sent as triumvirs to found Placentia, that they might exchange them for their own hostages. They sent ambassadors to meet Hannibal at the Rhone, and invited him to their country. The Insubrian Gauls beyond the Po were likewise ripe for rebellion; but they did not yet venture upon any open movement. Hannibal marched against the Taurinians, and conquered Turin; and whilst he was engaged there, Scipio had arrived at Genoa, and had crossed the Apennines and the Po, to take up his position in the country of the Insubrians. Here Hannibal turned round to face him. They encountered, for the first time, at the Ticinus, probably in the neighbourhood of Pavia, and to the dismay of the Romans, Hannibal had still a very large army. A cavalry skirmish took place: the Romans were defeated by the Spaniards and the Numidians; Scipio himself was wounded, and only with great difficulty got out of the affray, as some have it, by his son, who was afterwards so famous as P. Cornelius Scipio Africanus. This result of a fight which in itself was insignificant, convinced the Romans how much they had been mistaken as to the condition of Hannibal's army, and that they should have to keep on the defensive. Scipio abandoned the northern bank of the Po. He had thrown a bridge of rafts over the river, and in the consternation it was broken up too soon: part of the troops, which were to cover the bridge on the left bank, were taken prisoners by the Carthaginians.

The consul Sempronius had effected a landing at Malta, conquered some places on the Italian coast, and taken some booty; he now returned, and went to join Scipio. Here the discipline of the Romans truly shows itself. They knew that nothing is more fatiguing for the soldier, than to march in columns on the road, and they therefore avoided it as much as they could. But now they did a thing which only seems possible under circumstances of extraordinary enthusiasm. The army was not kept together, to march to the place of its destination; but every one was to take his oath on such and such a day to make his appearance at a given place, severe punishment being denounced against the breach of the oath. Sempronius mustered his troops at Puteoli,[21] and there dismissed them with orders to meet him again near Ariminum. From thence they marched to the Trebia, and joined Scipio. What we cannot now understand, is how the consuls could have united; Sempronius must have marched through Liguria by Genoa.[22] Here the two consuls take the command by turns. The accounts of the fight on the Trebia are not even now quite correct. Vaudoncourt has not turned to account his position as a chief officer on the staff: his notions with regard to this battle are quite incomprehensible. As the Romans ford the Trebia in order to engage, and one wing, which is cut off, falls back upon Placentia without recrossing the river, we must necessarily presume that Hannibal was on the right, on the eastern bank of the river, and had crossed the Po below Placentia. It is quite in the style of Hannibal's tactics to go round the enemy and cut off his retreat, as he was certain of his superiority; just as Napoleon in 1800 passed the Po between Pavia and Piacenza, and placed himself between the bungling, stupid general Melas and his base, so as to bring him to battle at Marengo, and Melas was obliged to conclude the convention. The Romans therefore passed the Po near Piacenza, and Hannibal below this town. This is manifest from the whole position; Major-General Von Schütz of Magdeburg, who is a distinguished tactician, assures us that it could not have been otherwise. This explains also why the Roman camp was removed. The Romans, after they had crossed, had the Trebia behind them (on the west), which made their position a hazardous one, as in case of defeat they would have been driven into the river: for this reason, they placed the Trebia between themselves and Hannibal, as a protection; and they pitched their camp in a strong ground at the foot of the Apennines, where they were nearer to Sempronius. Their object, which was to effect a junction with the army of Sempronius, they had attained, as we have already mentioned; but they were cut off from Rome, and pushed towards Piedmont. If Providence has once decreed that a campaign must come to a hapless end, all kinds of untoward circumstances will crowd upon each other. The wound of Scipio was slow in healing, and he was not able to appear at the head of the army; and thus the Romans were paralysed, whilst Hannibal for two months and a half, ever since his march over the St. Bernard, had made use of his time to strengthen his position, and to restore his army, especially as to horses. He also took from the Romans their magazines, so that they became very hard pressed. Sempronius, when the two armies had joined, looked upon this state of things as highly disgraceful, and insisted upon giving battle; he said that one ought to fight as soon as possible, and not let the Carthaginians seem formidable: Scipio, on the other hand, was cautious, and would not give his consent to this. Hannibal, who knew all that was passing, was very much bent on bringing them to an engagement; for so long as they lay where they were, he could not go into winter-quarters; and he also wished to get the Romans out of the way, that the Gauls might thus be encouraged to declare themselves. He was about two (German) miles south of Piacenza, on the right bank of the Trebia, and the Romans on the other side: he now enticed them on by small skirmishes, in which he let them gain seeming advantages. The river Trebia, in the year 1799, became noted for the battle which Macdonald lost against Suwarow: on that occasion, I gathered exact information concerning it. The locality is very remarkable, and quite tallies with the description of Polybius. It is a mountain torrent with many arms, very broad, and straggling through thickets and heaps of gravel: there are many islets in it in summer; in winter, when the snow melts, or after heavy rain, these are quite flooded over. It is not deep, so that it can always be forded: the banks are overgrown some way up with shrubs. In these, Hannibal placed troops in ambush, and Sempronius thought that he was afraid; but it was Hannibal's plan to get the Romans to cross the river. It was about Christmas tide, and so he did not wish his soldiers to wade through the river, which was cold as ice: that he wanted the Romans to do. They fell into the snare. Hannibal, on the other hand, had large fires lighted in his camp the evening before, (brandy there was none at that time, except in Egypt, where certainly they knew how to distil, as the whole process is depicted on the walls at Thebes); he also made the men take a good meal of warm food, and rub themselves before the fire with oil; thus they became quite warm and brisk. There was a sharp snow-storm,—the cold is in Lombardy not less severe than in Germany,—the Romans had now the madness to wade during the night through the river, which was so swollen by the snow, that they were up to the chin in water: they got quite benumbed, and they had the pelting storm right in their faces. The fight was a fierce one, as indeed there were thirty thousand Romans against twenty thousand of the enemy; but the Carthaginian cavalry quickly routed that of the Romans, and the Roman infantry also was too tired out to effect any thing. They did what they could; but they were fighting as militia against veterans, besides which they had the elements against them, and when they had passed the river, the men in ambush arose and fell upon their flank. The loss was very great: some were driven into the river, and perished; the left wing—about ten thousand men—escaped to Placentia. The snow-storm was so fearful, and the troops were likewise so much in want of rest, that Hannibal was unable to pursue the enemy, though otherwise he always made the very most of his victories. The Romans therefore, one and all, threw themselves into Placentia, where they had their magazines, and there they remained some time. At first, the consul deceived the senate by false reports; but the truth was soon known. Hannibal took up his quarters on both banks of the Po, and lived in plenty on the stores of the Romans; he wished his troops to have their full rest, and did not care for Placentia. The Insubrians also now declared for him. The Romans, on the other hand, embarked on the Po, and went to Ariminum, where the new consul Flaminius brought them reinforcements.

According to Livy Hannibal tried that very winter to break through the Apennines into Etruria. This is possible, but hardly likely; Polybius does not mention it: it may have been a movement of no consequence, perhaps a reconnoitring. Livy's description, however, of the locality, and of the struggle which Hannibal had to sustain with the elements, is, as I myself know from experience, a very happy one.

The unlucky honour of the consulship devolved, the next year, on C. Flaminius, a man, whose name has come down to us with disgrace, though, as far as we can judge from his actions, unjustly. He had, when a tribune, carried through the assignment of the *Ager Gallicus Picenus*, for which the nobles never forgave him; he now, as consul, supported a tribunician law which also gave high offence, and was a remarkable instance of the hypocrisy of the nobility. The aristocracy always rail against trade, business, and so forth, and talk of noble feeling and high-mindedness; and yet, they will not let an advantage slip out of their hands. The new law decreed, that no senator, and no one, whose father had a seat in the senate, should own a sea-going ship of more than a certain tonnage, nor for any other purpose than to convey corn from his estates to Rome; and it therefore debarred the nobility from making money by traffic, and restricted them to what they got from their landed property. Commerce, shipping, and such things, were to be left to the trading class which had now risen, the *equites*, and the senators were not to interfere with them. Nothing indeed could have been more in the spirit of the Venetian aristocracy in the best times, than such a law; but the grasping nobility of Rome felt so much aggrieved by its operation, that Flaminius was spoken of as a turbulent fellow. Flaminius may have been a rash and hot-headed man; yet I am convinced that he was any thing but a revolutionist. In the same spirit, he was also now decried for having made too much haste, because he had set out for Ariminum, without waiting for the Feriæ Latinæ! Such an accusation is quite unbearable; for it is plain that Hannibal had not waited for the end of the Latin holidays. Flaminius in fact still came too late.

The prospects of the Romans were very gloomy, the enemy being in Italy with a superior force. And when they raised new legions, a great disadvantage now shewed itself; for the veterans were lost, and the Roman system of tactics was the very worst when the troops were not well trained, (hence the defeat at Cannæ,) as, on the other hand, it was the best with practised soldiers: they ought now to have formed in phalanx only, so as to keep their ground by means of masses. Hannibal had three roads before him, two of them through Tuscany, and one along the Adriatic to Rimini; there lay the army of Sempronius, reinforced by the fresh draughts which the new consul had brought with him. In Tuscany, the Romans must have expected no attack whatever, nor does any army seem to have been stationed there, unless perhaps an Etrurian levy at most; for Hannibal met with no resistance at all when he had resolved to go through the marshes. One of the roads was through the Apennines, by Prato to Florence; the other, from Bologna by Pietramala and Barberino, where the Apennines are broadest and wildest. The latter of these must at that time have been impassable, having perhaps been left to grow wild as a protection against the Gauls; it also passed too close by the Apennines,[23] and Flaminius might have arrived before its difficulties were overcome. He therefore chose the other road. With regard to this, much dispute has unaccountably arisen, and even the judicious and excellent Strabo is mistaken in thinking of the marshes near Parma: in Tuscany, no one now has a doubt about it. The road in question led by Lucca and Pisa. It is a very pleasant one now; but formerly the outlet of the Arno was a shallow gulf running up into the land as far as Sendi,[24] and this had been filled up from time immemorial, and had become a marsh like the Pontine, only it was not quite so unhealthy. Even now, on the northern side, one still sees a succession of lakes, six German miles long; the marshes drained by canals may everywhere be traced. This extends as far as Pisa, which lies somewhat higher, and is connected with the fruitful country of Lucca. Here, by Lucca where in spring all is a vast lake, we must presume the march of Hannibal to have been. He had learned that it was not a morass, but that it could be passed, although the whole way was under water: the Romans, however, did not expect any inroad from thence. Hannibal very likely went first to Modena, in order to deceive the Romans, and then turned off to the right. The difficulties of the march may have been somewhat exaggerated; but on the whole, there is a correct notion at bottom. Hannibal lost very many men and horses, and all his remaining elephants but one: he himself lost an eye. After three days and a half, he got out near Fiesole, and marched behind Florence into the upper valley of the Arno, which even as early as that time was drained; and he allowed his soldiers, among whom there were now already many Gauls, to console themselves for the toils which they had gone through.[25] The Romans under Flaminius were encamped near Arezzo. He believed that Hannibal would now burst upon Ariminum, and so he wished to go across the Romagna to the assistance of the Romans there. But Hannibal now suddenly appeared in the heart of Etruria, on which Flaminius broke up in all haste, that he might get the start of him in reaching the road to Rome. Hannibal advanced to Chiusi, wasting the country on his way; Flaminius followed with his utmost speed. Among the hypocritical reproaches made against him was also this, that he had not stopped his march when a standard stuck fast in the ground,—a superstition which, to use the remark of Polybius, is beyond all conception. Hannibal went on from the upper valley of the Arno below Cortona, having the lake of Perugia (Trasimenus) on his left, still on the road to Rome. He had got ahead of Flaminius by some days' marches; the latter with hurried speed pressed on from Cortona. Hannibal could now already discern the goal, and he wished for a decisive battle. When the Romans reached the pass on the south side, they found it beset. On that very morning, there was an impenetrable fog, so that they saw neither the hills nor the lake: the troops in front kept pushing on, in order to find room. When these were already attacked at the defile, the men behind, as they were marching in a long column, did not perceive any thing of it; and now the rear itself was charged by the troops which had been posted on the hills. Then the Carthaginians wheeled to the right, until they outflanked the Romans, and thus drove them towards the lake; and these, in order to force their way, again and again assailed the intrenchments of the defile, without effecting anything. The battle had a great resemblance to the unfortunate affair of Auerstedt, where continual assaults were likewise made in vain, and one division sacrificed after another. At last, about six thousand men made an assault upon the hills, broke through, and thus made their escape: the rest were either driven into the lake, or taken prisoners. In *Dutens Manuel du Voyageur*, and other books, it is stated that the names of two spots of that neighbourhood, *la Ossaja* and *Ponte di Sanguinetto*, referred to the battle on the Trasimene lake; yet at the latter place a battle cannot possibly have been fought, and *la Ossaja* was as late as in the sixteenth century called *Orsaria*, that is, bear's-garden, because the lords of Perugia kept there the bears and wild beasts for their sports.

Just as Shakspeare connects awful natural phenomena with frightful moral ones, and as Thucydides in the Peloponnesian war always mentions such phenomena, thus also during the war of Hannibal the earth was convulsed with throes. The year of the battle at the Trasimenus was, as Pliny says, richer in earthquakes than had ever been known in the memory of man: fifty-seven of them were observed. We shall not discuss whether these were all on different days, or whether it was always the same one on different points. Many places lay in ruins, as Cannæ in Apulia; others lost their walls. But we cannot believe what Livy relates, that during the battle such a dreadful earthquake had happened, that the walls of many Italian towns fell down, and yet that the contending armies were not aware of it.

It is possible that the thick fog was connected with this earthquake. Fogs are, however, very frequent there at that time of the year: I have myself seen a very thick one in the same neighbourhood, which very strongly reminded me of the battle at the Trasimene lake. Flaminius himself fell bravely fighting. Although his guilt is infinitely small when compared with the charges which have been laid upon him, yet, according to my views of the battle, he is not quite to be acquitted of carelessness; but in great events which are to change the destinies of the world, a fatality rules, which blinds the eyes even of the very shrewdest.

After this battle, Hannibal exchanged, even as he had already begun to do so after that of the Trebia, the arms of his Libyans for those of the Romans, a proof how, even in the midst of war, he still trained his troops. The practice of the *pilum* was not so easy to learn: in fact, to use the Roman arms with success, he was obliged to adopt their drill in all its parts. To the Spaniards he left their original mode of fighting. As early as after the battle of the Trebia, he had made a difference between his prisoners. He had treated the Italians with kindness, having often given them presents, taken care of their wounded, and then sent them home, probably under a promise of serving no longer against him; he now did the same on a larger scale, and announced himself to the inhabitants of Italy as their deliverer from the Roman yoke. A man like Hannibal was far from intending, with the troops which he had brought with him, and the Cisalpine Gauls who had joined him, to sweep down like a torrent upon Italy, and without fresh forces to scale the walls of Rome: he must have founded all his hopes on rousing the south of Italy, by the remembrance of the old struggles with Rome, to cast off the Roman rule, and unite with him, and thus to shake down Rome in the course of a few years. Pyrrhus had the power, to run down Rome; Hannibal had first to create one for himself. He must have started immediately after the battle, as in Umbria he fell in with a reinforcement of four thousand men, which the consul Servilius sent to Flaminius, and which consisted chiefly of cavalry: it was surrounded by Hannibal, and almost entirely destroyed. Such is the account of Polybius, which has every appearance of truth; Livy, on the contrary, says that Centenius had formed an army by order of the senate, when tidings had been heard of the defeat at the Trasimene lake, a thing which is not likely, as the news could not yet have reached Rome.

Hannibal now turned to Spoleto, which he could hope to overawe; yet the town, which belonged to the third line of the Roman colonies, remained faithful, and held out. Hannibal, like many great generals, Frederic the Great, for instance, had an aversion to sieges, and he never undertook any in person. He first tried to intimidate Spoleto; and when he did not succeed in it he withdrew. The gates were everywhere shut against him, wherever the earthquake had not opened them. He strove therefore to spread terror far and wide. Why did he not march close up to Rome? why did he not entrench himself before its walls? and why, if he could not take it by storm, did he not at least try and blockade it? But for a siege like this, very great machines were indeed requisite, and as he had none whatever with him, he could only have burned down the suburbs. When one knows the extent of ancient Rome, one understands the difficulties of a siege. The Capitoline hill was a scarped rock; the side of the Quirinal to the *Porta Collina* was very much like it; then came the wall of Servius Tullius: it would have needed an immense army to invest Rome. Hannibal's men were suffering from sickness, especially from diseases of the skin; the horses also had suffered much; he had therefore to put them into quarters. The unhealthy air of the neighbourhood of Rome in summer is another reason. The battle at the Trasimene lake may have taken place in May, or in the beginning of June, and already before the festival of St. Peter and St. Paul, the malaria at Rome begins; so that the army would have been swept away by disease. He therefore stationed himself in Picenum and the March of Ancona, a fruitful country, with a very temperate climate, and exceedingly healthy. There he had his summer-quarters, which in Italy are just as necessary as winter-quarters are elsewhere. The earthquakes had been his battering rams, and the walls of not an inconsiderable number of Italian towns had been thrown down: he was thus able to enter into them without hindrance, and to appropriate to himself their resources.

Whilst he was allowing his soldiers this necessary relaxation, the Romans made every exertion in their power, and appointed Q. Fabius Cunctator dictator. The flower of the Roman troops were destroyed, and Fabius had to bring together a new army: this was now a medley of all sorts of people; even the prisoners were already taken as volunteers. With such troops he was to make head against Hannibal, whose power could not but increase with his success; whilst, on the other hand, the Romans had the consciousness of having been beaten, and dared not risk an engagement, although Hannibal, like all great generals, was not willing to give battle when there was no necessity for it. Fabius perceived that he had to train his troops, and that it was very fortunate for him that the allies remained faithful: this he was to turn to advantage. He also hoped that the consequences which might be expected from such a motley composition of Hannibal's army would show themselves; and yet this was not the case. That army was indeed swept together from all nations,—Gauls especially there were in it, though these were so exasperated against the Romans, that he might safely rely upon them,—but his choice troops consisted of Africans, and in a lesser proportion, of Spaniards, which last were most likely the best of all. Moreover, he had many slingers; his infantry did not yet on the whole amount to more than forty thousand men; and with this army, he was in a country in which not one town had hitherto opened to him its gates of its own free will. The country especially which he had last marched through, was firmly attached to the Romans; in Apulia, perhaps, the feeling was already different.

Hannibal, however, started in autumn, and marched along the Adriatic through the Abruzzi, the country of the Marrucinians and Pelignians. Here Fabius withstood him, and tried to cut off his supplies, in which he also partly succeeded. But Hannibal, when hard pressed, eluded his vigilance, and quietly breaking up his camp, appeared all at once in Campania. It was his design to make himself master of Casinum and the Latin road, and by confining the communication between Rome and Campania to the Appian road alone, to try and see whether the Italians would declare for him. Here we may see an example of the disadvantage of the want of maps, although on the whole it is wonderful how well they managed in ancient times without them. Hannibal meant to give the order to lead the army to Casinum; but the guide, either misunderstanding him, or from downright dishonesty, led him through Upper Samnium, along the banks of the Vulturnus, down to Casilinum; and here Hannibal perceived that he was in quite a different neighbourhood from where he had wished to be. In the meanwhile, Fabius had been beforehand with him, and had left the Latin road, and strongly posted himself in Samnium. Hannibal, after having visited the country of the Falernians and Campania with devastation, and made an immense booty, owing to which the men of rank at Rome were already sufferers, now wanted to begin his retreat through Samnium to Apulia, a very mild, sunny district, where he meant to take up his winter-quarters, and to establish a communication with Tarentum and other towns of lower Italy, and also with the king of Macedon. Here Fabius cut off his retreat near Mount Callicula, blocking up with his troops the Caudine road, while another body of Romans beset the passes of Casinum, which led to Rome. Then Hannibal availed himself of his famous stratagem: he had encamped near the mountains which Fabius occupied. Livy's account of this stratagem makes out rather a silly story for the Romans. He says that Hannibal tied faggots to the horns of oxen, and setting these on fire, had them driven up into the mountains between the Roman posts; and that on this, the Romans, believing them to be spectres, had betaken themselves to flight. But the real truth is what Polybius tells. Nothing was more common among the ancients than to march by torch light. Now, when the Romans saw lights between their stations in the space which was left unoccupied, they thought that the Carthaginians were breaking through; and they quickly made for what they supposed to be the endangered spot, that they might stop their further progress. In the meanwhile, the rest of the Carthaginians had advanced close to the defiles, and had stormed the abandoned posts; and thus the whole of the army got off without any loss: the Roman camp was burnt. Hannibal encamped on the borders between Apulia and the country of the Frentanians. Fabius followed him; and here the Master of the Horse, Minucius, in Fabius' absence, and contrary to his orders, engaged in a successful battle with Hannibal. This raised the pride of the Romans so much, that they took it into their heads, that all their former mishaps had only befallen them by chance, and that now they were able to make up for it all; and Minucius got an equal command with Fabius. Hannibal enticed him out, and gave him such a defeat, that he would have been annihilated, had not Fabius and a faithful band of Samnites come up at the very nick of time. Fabius brought the campaign to an honourable conclusion, as he did not lose anything against Hannibal, and not to lose anything, was a great deal indeed. Minucius resigned his power. Hannibal passed the winter in a state of actual distress: he was badly off for provisions, and as yet, not a single people had declared for him.

In the year 536, L. Æmilius Paullus and C. Terentius Varro were consuls. For the first, and perhaps, the only time in Roman history, symptoms now manifest themselves, like those to which we are so well accustomed in the times of Cleon and Hyperbolus, namely, that we meet with tradesmen holding the first offices of the state. C. Terentius Varro is said to have been the son of a butcher, which is so much at variance with everything before and after, that we can hardly believe it. Yet if this were so, the notion of plebeity must already have been quite changed, and such trades were carried on, not only by foreigners, Metics, and freedmen, but also by born citizens. Terentius Varro is made out to have been a demagogue who had a decided influence with the people, and used it in a spirit the very fellow to that of Cleon at Athens. But if we look to facts, we might entertain some doubts with regard to the sentence of condemnation, which our historians pronounce against him. If the overthrow at Cannæ had really been owing to his fault, and his fault alone, how would the senate—although, *ominis causa*, he was no more chosen consul—have over and over again, during a long series of years, entrusted him with an army, and after the battle have gone out to meet him, and to thank him for not having despaired? This shows that the judgment formed of Varro, as handed down to us, cannot be relied on; and that the pride of the great men was arrayed against him, as it was in former times against Cn. Flavius. That the learned M. Terentius Varro was his descendant, seems to be beyond a doubt: the latter, who lived not a hundred and fifty years later, belonged to the aristocratical party,—so much, and so quickly will the state of things change. L. Æmilius Paullus was μισόδημος, very likely from just causes; he had, after his Illyrian campaign, been wrongfully accused, and had a narrow escape from being condemned.

It was the rule that each consul had to command a consular army of two legions, each of four thousand two hundred foot and two hundred horse, with a corresponding number of allies: the latter furnished five thousand men and six hundred horse. If this force was to be strengthened, four legions and a proportionate number of allies took the field, in all, 16,800 Romans, 20,000 allies, and 3,200 horse; if one wanted to increase it still more, then, instead of four thousand two hundred Romans, there were five thousand levied for each legion, and three hundred horse instead of two hundred. The Romans now raised such an army of eight legions; and besides the consuls of the year, those of the year before were also placed at its head as proconsuls. This army collected in Apulia. Q. Fabius most earnestly recommended that his plan should be faithfully kept to, and such was likewise the conviction of the consul L. Æmilius Paullus; but the feeling at Rome was quite different.

The description of the battle of Cannæ in Appian, is taken from Fabius Pictor; the very same is likewise to be found in Zonaras. According to this version, Terentius Varro was far from being so blameable as Livy, and also Polybius make out. In fact, it is said that at the departure of the consuls from Rome, the whole people had raised an outcry against the sluggishness of Fabius, and had demanded a battle, because the long war pressed heavily upon them. This story is likely in itself, and it accounts for Paullus having yielded against his own conviction. The two consuls joined each other in Apulia, and embarrassed Hannibal by their superior numbers: he took up his position near Cannæ. This town had been destroyed by the earthquake; but the *arx* was yet standing, and he took it by treachery. The statement in Gellius[26] that the battle was fought on the second of August, is hard to understand: if it be correct, the two armies must have faced each other for months. But it would seem from Polybius' account, that the season was not yet so far advanced; though this is by no means clear: the harvest there is at the end of May, and it must at all events have been already over. Both armies were encamped on the banks of the Aufidus, in the midst of the plains of Apulia, where the soil throughout is calcareous, as in Champagne, and there are therefore but few springs in it; so that they were obliged to keep near the river. Hannibal is said to have been so hard put to it for provisions, that, if the battle had been at all delayed, he must needs have decamped. Yet he enticed the Romans into fighting; for in a petty skirmish, whilst foraging, they got the best of it, as he did not come to the support of his men, but feigned to be afraid. The Romans still had a camp on either side of the river; their base was Canusium, their magazines at Cannæ: Hannibal took these before their eyes, they being not yet strong enough to hinder it. Even later than this, Paullus was very loth to give battle, and it would also have perhaps been best to wait quietly: the longer Hannibal kept himself inactive, the more favourable matters became for the Romans; if once the day was lost, all would be lost. Yet, on the other hand, much might be said in behalf of the expediency of a battle. If the Romans could not gain the victory with such superior numbers, they gave the allies, who, as it was, were already troublesome, the opportunity of falling off; and if, in their rear, the Samnites, or Capua proved faithless, their situation would have been desperate. The Romans therefore passed the river.

The first who has given a satisfactory and clear description of the ground of the battle of Cannæ, was the traveller Swinburne. From his account, the battle may easily be made out. The Aufidus near Cannæ makes a bend within which the two armies took their position: the Romans stood on the chord of the arc which is formed by the river; Hannibal likewise passed over, and rested his two flanks on the curve of the river, so that the numerical superiority of the Romans was of no avail.

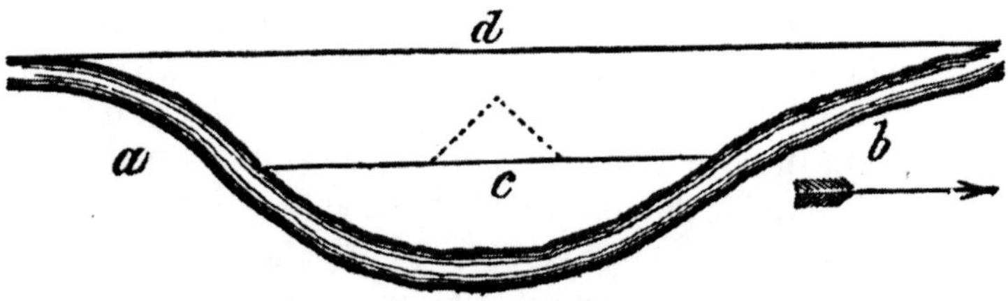

a. Place where the Romans crossed.

b. Place where the Carthaginians crossed.

c. Line of battle of the Carthaginians.

d. Line of battle of the Romans.

The Romans therefore had the land behind them. Hannibal placed himself in such a dangerous position, because anyhow he was lost, if he did not win this battle. The Romans had 80,000 foot, and from 6 to 8,000 horse; among the latter, about 2,500 were Romans. The Carthaginians had 40,000 foot, and also about 8,000 horse, most of which, however, were Numidians; these were excellent for foraging, reconnoitering, and harassing the enemy, but by no means fitted to stand the shock of a battle, and of no use at all against heavy cavalry: if they were worth anything, it was against light infantry. The Romans left ten thousand men behind in the camp, and thus advanced against the enemy with only 70,000, from whom we are besides to deduct a large number for those who at all times, and especially in a summer campaign, are either sick, or remain behind from other causes. On their right wing, they had the Roman cavalry; on the left, was that of the allies. Hannibal had no elephants in this battle: he placed his best cavalry on his left wing, over-against the right one of the Romans; on his own right, he had the Numidians. Besides these, there were on the left wing the Libyans, and on the right, the Celts and Spaniards, but part of the Libyans and Celts were also in the centre. The Romans had not room enough for the whole of their army; so that they were drawn up unusually deep, many maniples being one behind the other, which in their system of warfare was of no advantage. The battle was opened by the cavalry on the left wing of the Carthaginians making an attack upon the Roman horse, who, although they fought with great bravery, were soon routed, as the whole battle lasted only a short time: it began two hours after sunrise, and was ended two hours before sunset. In the meanwhile, the Numidians on the right wing were engaged with the cavalry of the allies. Hannibal now divided his line in the middle, and ordered one half to advance with the right, and the other with the left shoulders forward; so that they advanced in the form of a wedge against the Roman centre. This was an employment of what is called the oblique line of battle, which in the seven years' war was so fatal at Collin, wherein one of the two extreme points stands still, while the rest of the line moves forward: he did this here with two lines. The Romans advanced to meet them, and the fight was very bloody. The Carthaginian troops could not break through, so they retreated by the wings; and these, when the Romans were pressing on, wheeled half round and attacked them in the flanks. At the same time, the cavalry of the Carthaginian left wing had gone round that of the Romans, and having been joined by the Numidians, it had routed the cavalry on the Roman left: it could now freely fall upon the Roman infantry from the rear. Æmilius Paullus was mortally wounded, and in the dreadful confusion there was no longer any command; so that two hours before sunset the whole army was annihilated. The loss is not stated with precision. Polybius, contrary to his custom, gives the largest numbers: according to him, out of 80,000 men, 50,000 were killed, and 30,000 taken prisoners: but in this instance, we must deem Livy's statement to be the more correct one. Not to speak of those who were saved by having remained behind in the fortified camp, there also escaped at least ten thousand men from the field of battle; the Romans consequently lost about forty thousand men. In Zonaras and Appian, we meet with the following story, borrowed in all likelihood from Fabius, which is characteristic, as it shows how the Romans tried to throw a vail over their disasters. It is said that in Apulia a breeze rises every afternoon from the east, that is to say, from the sea, which lifts up clouds of dust from the chalky soil; and that Hannibal on this had not only placed himself in such a position that the Romans had the dust blown into their faces, but also on the day before had caused the ground to be ploughed, so as to increase these clouds. That he took advantage of the wind, we may believe; the rest sounds somewhat unlikely. There is another idle tale of his having allowed Spaniards, with daggers hidden about them, to go over as deserters to the enemy, and that these, being stationed by the Romans in the rear of their army, had afterwards suddenly fallen upon them. This is quite a childish and pitiful fable. The day after the battle, the Romans in the camp surrendered, on condition that if the Roman people would ransom them, they should regain their liberty. Varro escaped with seventy men to Canusium, whither all those now collected, who had got away safe; and with these he betook himself to Venusia. Here Hannibal again shows how much he disliked sieges; for he let Canusium alone with its Roman garrison, and hastened to Capua, with which he had already before entered into negotiations.

Cato has told us that Maharbal, the commander of the Carthaginian cavalry, called upon Hannibal to follow him, saying that on the fifth day he would hold a feast as conqueror on the Capitol. Hannibal smiled, and said that it was a fine idea, but that it could not be carried out. Then Maharbal had answered, "Thou art able then to gain a victory, but not to make use of it!"—There is no saying indeed what impression it would have made in Rome, if, instead of any tidings from the field of battle, the Carthaginian cavalry had been seen on the Latin road. But even cavalry could hardly have done it: the distance in a straight line is from fifty to sixty German miles; so that they must have had relays of horses: for infantry, the thing was quite impossible. Against cavalry, the gates might have been shut. Nor would the Romans have felt so utterly defenceless as they did after the battle at the Alia. There were recruits in Rome, who were drilled, and in training for the naval service; nothing would have been achieved, and the Carthaginians would in the most pestilential time of the year have been lying before the walls of Rome. To burn the country round the city, would not have been of any use to Hannibal; whilst, on the other hand, it could not but have made the worst impression upon the Italians, had he returned with the cavalry without having done anything.

How soon Hannibal arrived at Capua, is more than we can tell, as, generally speaking, in such matters we have no precise dates given us by the ancients; yet in the same year he was master of Capua, much earlier than it would seem from Livy's account. This town enjoyed isopolity with the Romans, and was under its own government; its nobility held itself equal to that of Rome, and was connected by marriage with the very highest Roman families, even with the Claudii. During its long alliance with the Romans, it had gotten great wealth and many demesnes, and it was therefore in a very prosperous condition. But owing to their riches and their luxury, its citizens had become utterly effeminate; so that they formed the strongest contrast to the moral and political energy of Rome. If such a town had dreamed of acquiring the leading rule over Italy after the downfall of that city, it was an inconceivable delusion. Were the nations indeed to shake off the yoke of Rome, only that they might put themselves under that of Capua! But the Campanians flattered themselves with the hope of getting this hegemony with the help of Hannibal, who fostered their day-dreams, but without promising them anything for certain. They therefore separated from Rome, formed a league with Hannibal, and received him into their city, which he forthwith made his arsenal. The terms of their alliance, taken literally, were very favourable. They were granted perfect independence; and it was stipulated that no single Campanian should be charged with any burden whatever; that they should not have to furnish any soldiers; and that, in short, they should be free from everything which had been irksome to the Tarentines in their alliance with Pyrrhus. The Romans had no garrison at Capua; but three hundred horsemen from that town served in Sicily, and as hostages for these, Hannibal gave them as many Roman prisoners. They seem to have been exchanged: Rome, at that time, was by no means so haughty. The description in Livy of the way in which Hannibal established himself in the town, of the banquet and the attempt to murder Hannibal, is wonderfully beautiful, but certainly a romance. The story of Decius Magus, the only man in Capua who raised his voice for remaining true to the Romans, may alone have some foundation, however much it be embellished: there is no reason for us to doubt, that Hannibal banished him as a friend of the Romans. On the part of Capua, it was indeed a foul ingratitude to fall off from Rome, and therefore the frightful vengeance of the Romans is very much to be excused. The Campanians had derived from their alliance with Rome nothing but benefit; and now they did not only show themselves ungrateful, but they also committed an act of useless barbarity. They put the Romans who were staying with them, to death in overheated bath rooms. Nothing is more sickening than the arrogance of the unworthy, when they array themselves against worth.

Whether it be true that the winter-quarters in luxurious Capua made the troops of Hannibal effeminate and dissolute, or whether this be a mere rhetorical flourish, cannot now be decided any longer; but it is evident that the Romans made a better use of the winter. When after long and extraordinary exertions, men come into an easy life, they often fall into a state of lassitude; they are then very apt to lose the proper tone of mind, and the power of finding their way back to their former condition, and it returns no more. This is a rock on which many great characters have split. What, however, has not been taken into account, is that Hannibal was not able to recruit his army from Spaniards and Libyans. Every one of his battles cost him many men; little skirmishes, and diseases in foreign climate, swept away a great number; and he was only able to make up his losses from the Italians, which we know with certainty as for the Bruttians. This circumstance is quite enough to account for the demoralised state of his troops. The Prussian army of 1762 was much inferior to that of 1757, and likewise the French one of 1812, which fought in the Russian campaign, was not so good as that of 1807. Another difficulty for him was that the Romans, after the battle of Cannæ, had not let their courage droop: they would not even receive Carthalo, the Carthaginian ambassador. He found himself in the same plight as Napoleon was in Russia, after the battle of Borodino, when the peace was not accepted. It is true that part of southern Italy declared for him, and that he might have reinforced himself from thence; but all the Latin colonies throughout its whole extent remained faithful, and were not to be conquered. He was master of the country, but with a number of hostile fortresses in it. If he wanted to advance by Campania, he was obliged to subdue the whole chain of fortified colonies, or to break through them, and reduce the Latin and Hernican towns in the neighbourhood of the city. These places were entirely in the interest of Rome, and indignant at the faithlessness of Capua. It was especially Cales, Fregellæ, Interamnium, Casinum, Beneventum, Luceria, Venusia, Brundisium, Pæstum, Æsernia, and others, which paralysed the peoples there; these could not fairly gather their forces, because they had to fear the sallies of the Romans. They therefore in most instances blockaded those towns, and were no increase of strength to Hannibal. Thus his position was far from being an easy one. He reckoned upon support from Carthage and Spain; the former he got, as Livy states in a few lines (probably from Cœlius Antipater), although in his view of the matter, it is always as if the Carthaginians had deemed the whole undertaking of Hannibal to be madness. According to Zonaras (from Dio Cassius), the reinforcement was considerable; but it only came in the following year, or even later: from Spain he received none at all. If dearth of money had exercised as decisive an influence among the ancients, as it does with us, the Romans indeed could no more have done anything. But they made every possible sacrifice; and thus it happened that by the battle of Cannæ they only lost those districts which yielded themselves to the enemy, whilst they had no danger to fear with regard to the rest. The Marsians, Marrucinians, Sabines, Umbrians, Etruscans, Picentines, and others, remained faithful to them.

In the list of the peoples which fell off after the battle of Cannæ, as given by Livy and Polybius, no distinction is made between what took place at different times: the course of defection was but gradual, and there was no general rising,—so strong was the belief in the unshaken might of Rome. Immediately after the battle, a part only of the Apulians, Samnites, and Lucanians, fell away; so did afterwards the Bruttians, and at a much later period, the Sallentines; but none of the Greek towns as yet. It seems that the Ferentines, Hirpinians, and Caudines declared for Hannibal, whilst he was still on his march to Capua: Acerræ was taken after a long siege. Hannibal's object, while he was abiding in Campania, was now to gain a sea-port; so that he might keep up a direct communication with Carthage. He found himself in the strangest position; for though the general of a first-rate power, which was mistress of the seas, he did not possess one single harbour. An attempt against Cumæ and Naples was repulsed. Near Nola, for the first time, the current of his victories was checked; Marcellus threw himself into this important town, put down the party which wanted to go over to the Carthaginians, and drove Hannibal back; which is described by the Romans as a victory, but was not so by any means, although it was now something great, even to have delayed the progress of Hannibal. Marcellus showed here considerable talent as a general, and once more inspired the Romans with confidence.

The Bruttians, after having themselves fallen off, now succeeded in gaining over Locri, the first Greek town, which declared for Hannibal. Croton was taken by force of arms; and this completed the ruin of that place, which, though once so great and prosperous, was still inhabited only about the centre, as Leyden is now, and still more so, Pisa; so that the deserted walls could easily be stormed. Every attempt on the part of the inhabitants to defend the town was impossible; for after the different devastations by Dionysius, Agathocles, and the Romans under Rufinus, in the war of Pyrrhus, their number had become very small. Thus Hannibal had now seaports; and he received by Locri that reinforcement of troops and elephants from Carthage, which was the only one which he ever had from thence in a large mass: its amount is unknown to us.

With the taking of Capua, ends the first period of the war of Hannibal, which here reaches its culminating point. From 537 to 541, five years elapse to the fall of Capua, which is the second period. The Romans make now already the most astonishing efforts. Their legions were continually increased. Allies we hear no more about: the bravest had most of them fallen away; Etruscans, Umbrians, &c., are not even spoken of. Perhaps they incorporated the allies for the time of that war with the legions, so as not to let them stand isolated. Instead of confining themselves to the lowest scale, the Romans conceived the grand idea, of redoubling their exertions everywhere, and of raising an entirely new army. They refused to ransom the prisoners, and therefore Hannibal sold these for slaves, and they were scattered all over the world: many of them may have been butchered. This conduct of the Romans must not be judged of too severely. One should bear in mind, that in the first moment of dismay, after the battle of Cannæ, they were completely stunned: in such moments, those who belong to a mass, will act quite without any will of their own. It may also be well imagined that Hannibal demanded ready money, and that the Romans were not able to pay it. This may have been a principal motive. Those also who had escaped from the battle of Cannæ, were treated with undeserved severity; just as the unfortunate Admiral Byng was shot by the English. The whole of the young men were enlisted; nevertheless there was a scarcity of freemen able to bear arms. Many, from utter despondency, tried to shun the service. All who had not been able to pay a *delictum*, and likewise all the *addicti*, were discharged on the bail of the state, that they might serve; eight thousand slaves were bought on credit from their masters, and two regiments formed of them; even gladiators and their weapons were taken, as there was also a want of arms. Of the warlike races, there still remained on the side of the Romans only the Marsians, Marrucinians, Vestinians, Frentanians, Pelignians, and Picentines. Their greatest strength lay in the many Latin colonies, which extended from Bruttium to the Po. Such were the resources of Rome, and notwithstanding Livy's account, there is no denying that the danger was very great. He describes the rich individuals who advanced money to the state, as excellent patriots, although we know for certain that they were guilty of the most infamous fraud: they had the supplies for Spain ensured against danger at sea, and had then caused ships laden with the worst articles, to be wrecked. The price of corn had risen to ten times its ordinary rate. The town of Petelia alone among the Lucanians kept true to the Romans, for which it was destroyed by the Carthaginians and the rest of the Lucanians; Bruttium, the greater part of Samnium, and many Greek towns went over to the enemy; the Romans had the ground shaking under their feet. It is surprising that, under these circumstances, not only had Hannibal no lasting success, but the Romans also raised their head more and more. Their troops gradually became well trained, as their foes did not fight any great battles, which of course gave them time for practice; and thus they got an army which was certainly better than the one they had before the battle of Cannæ. Hannibal left Capua, and stayed in Apulia and Lucania, where he marched backwards and forwards, and made little conquests, so as to keep the Romans in constant excitement: we cannot quite trace his designs. In the following year, he made two unsuccessful attempts upon the Roman camp near Nola. Marcellus and Fabius were here opposed to him; the operations of the latter were slow, but highly felicitous. Hannibal is stated to have said, that he considered Fabius as his tutor, and Marcellus as his rival; that Fabius was teaching him to guard against blunders, and Marcellus how to develope his good ideas. This saying is certainly authentic; it displays Hannibal's great soul.

As early as in 539, the Romans again established themselves in Campania with a decided superiority. The Campanians showed themselves to be pitiful cowards. They appeared in the field but once, near Cumæ, and were beaten; then they allowed themselves to be pent up like sheep, and Hannibal made several attempts to relieve them. One Hanno is routed near Beneventum by Tib. Sempronius Gracchus, which is the first decisive victory of the Romans; it was chiefly gained by the slaves (*volones*), and these had their freedom given them for it. In the following year, Arpi returned to the side of the Romans, and in this way they gradually got many a little town. These small undertakings, which led to encounters of which the success was various, fill up the time until 540, when Tarentum delivered itself over to Hannibal; the secession of Metapontum and Thurii followed shortly afterwards, and it was perfectly justifiable in a moral point of view. When the hostages which these places had given to the Romans had made their escape, and had been retaken, the latter caused them to be indiscriminately put to death; and therefore, as so many had lost a son or a brother, and the very first families in these towns had been thus deeply wronged, they naturally sought for revenge, and gave themselves up to Hannibal. Yet the citadel of Tarentum remained to the Romans, and into it the garrison of Metapontum also threw itself. The negotiations with Philip of Macedon, which took place at this time, may have detained Hannibal in the east of Italy. Whilst he was waiting till matters improved, he reduced the Sallentine towns, and tried to keep the allies which he still had true to him; for the Lucanians and the neighbouring peoples changed, like weathercocks, with every wind. The Romans now set to work in good earnest to take Capua. Hanno was still carrying on operations in that neighbourhood; but they had already for two years established themselves near Suessula, and had been laying waste the whole country, so that famine had raged for a good while in Capua. I cannot understand, why Hannibal, who now had got reinforcements, did not make every exertion to relieve Capua which the Romans had invested with a double entrenchment. He ought to have attacked them in their entrenchments, and driven them out. At the urgent request of the Campanians, he made in 541 an attempt, the meaning of which, however, is not to be accounted for by our history, and there are many contradictions in this undertaking. If we follow the most unpretending account, Hannibal attacked the Romans, but was not able to break through their lines: a few Numidians only got through, and opened a communication with the town. But this could not be followed up, and so he determined to make a diversion.

Of the two conflicting statements as to which road he took, we are to consider that of Cœlius as the most improbable. The point in dispute is, whether he came before the Porta Collina from the north, through the country of the Pelignians, and on his retreat started from the Capena, or the reverse. The former account is the more worthy of belief; the other line would be too great a way round. This determination of his seems to have taken the Romans by surprise; so that there was hardly time enough for half of the troops from Capua to reach Rome by the Appian road before him,—he was some days march in advance,—although he moved along the arc of that chord by which they went, namely, across the Vulturnus, through the district of Cales towards Fregellæ, which was a very strong place. The people of Fregellæ, like brave men, had broken down the bridges over the Liris, and while he had to wait there till they were rebuilt, he wasted their country: he then marched by the Latin road, and through Tusculum, to the gates of Rome. But before his arrival, the consul Fulvius had come up by the Appian road, and was at the Porta Capena. Whilst Hannibal was already on the Esquiline, the former marched through the city by the Carinæ at the very nick of time, and by a sudden attack hindered the Carthaginian general from surprising the city on that spot. This was also what Hannibal had wished; but he had hoped that both the armies would be called away from Capua: the general, whom he had ordered either to relieve the place, or else carry off its population, must not have been able to do it. Hannibal encamped before the Porta Collina, on the Monte Pincio, beyond the low grounds of the gardens of Sallust. Here history again appears poetical. Twice did Hannibal march forth to offer battle to the Romans, who also went out against him; but both times a thunderstorm is said to have broken out just then, and when the two armies withdrew, the brightness of the sky returned. These *portenta*, we are told, convinced Hannibal that he could do nothing against Rome. Other stories sound very fine; but they likewise are idle tales. The Romans, it is said, at the very moment that Hannibal was encamped before their city, were sending out reinforcements to the army in Spain; and the field which was occupied by the enemy, was sold at just as good a price as in the height of peace. It was not advisable for Hannibal to accept a battle: he had no stronghold whatever in his rear, while the Romans had behind them the unscaleable walls of the city. When he had stayed eight days before the town, and the Roman allies far and wide had not stirred, he broke up again, and retired by Antrodoco and Sulmo to Samnium and Apulia, going through the midst of hostile countries in which all the towns were shut against him, like a lion chased by the hunters, but unhurt. The object of his undertaking had been baffled; he was in that dismal plight, that with great objects and great means, he still wanted the very thing, however trifling it might have been, which could have brought about the result of those objects and means.

In Capua, the distress had risen to the highest pitch, and the town wanted to capitulate; but the Romans demanded, that it should surrender unconditionally, on which the heads of the hostile party, Vibius Virrius and twenty-seven other senators, resolved to die. And indeed the result showed that they were right; for the Romans behaved with the most frightful cruelty. The whole senate of Capua, without any exception, were led in chains to Teanum, and the proconsul Q. Fulvius Flaccus wished not even to leave the decision to the Roman senate. But the proconsul Appius Claudius, to whom, as well as the other, the city had been yielded up, wished to save as many as he could, and he wrote to the senate, requesting them to institute a *causæ cognitio*. Flaccus however, foreseeing this, went to Teanum, and leaving unopened the letters received from the senate, ordered all the senators of Capua to be put to death. Jubellius Taurea, the bravest of the Campanians, whose heroism was acknowledged even by the Romans, killed his wife and children, and himself awaited his execution by the Romans. When the gates of Capua were opened, there is no doubt but that the inhabitants suffered all that the citizens of a town taken by storm have to suffer from the fury of the soldiers. Destroyed it was not; but all Campanians of rank were banished, most of them to Etruria; a great number of them were still executed as guilty, and even without any direct charge against them, they lost their property; the whole of the *ager Campanus*, all the houses and landed estates were confiscated; so that there remained nothing but the common, nameless rabble, and not a magistrate, besides foreigners and freedmen. The city was afterwards filled again with a new population of Roman citizens and others; a Roman præfect was sent thither to administer the law. Atella and Acerræ, the periœcians of Capua, had a like fate. From one of the Campanian towns, the whole of the population went over to Hannibal.

During this period, in the year of the battle of Cannæ, or in the following one, old Hiero died at the age of ninety. His son Gelon, who bore the same character for mildness as his father, but had been long dead, had two or three daughters, and a son, Hieronymus. Hiero's authority was as well established as if his family had sat on the throne for centuries. Hieronymus, who succeeded his grandfather, was a contemptible, effeminate fellow; his father Gelon would have followed quite a different policy from his. That the Syracusans did not like to have the Romans as their real masters, was but natural; yet they were obliged to acknowledge either the Carthaginians or the Romans as such, and the latter, after all, had, on the whole, treated them well. But there was a general fatality, which made all the nations fall away from Rome. Hannibal had behaved in the same way towards Sicily, as he had done in Italy after the battle on the Trasimene lake: he had dismissed the Syracusan prisoners with presents, and after the battle of Cannæ, he sent envoys to Syracuse to entice the king into an alliance. Among these emissaries there were Hippocrates and Epicydes, two grandsons of a Syracusan, who, when banished from his native city, had settled in Carthage; a proof that such metics in Carthage did not cease to be Greeks, although they had even Carthaginian names, as we may see from monuments. These two were readily listened to by Hieronymus. Their first proposition was to divide Sicily between Carthage and Syracuse, with the Himera as a boundary, as in the days of Timoleon; but Hieronymus in his day-dreams was not yet content with this: he would not promise his alliance for anything less than the possession of the whole island. Hannibal, who was far from being much in earnest in this discussion, granted him his demand; for he hoped that afterwards indeed he would be able to put him down, if he could only get him for the present to declare himself against Rome. The Syracusans, who under Hiero's rule had never thought of a revolution, were disgusted with his grandson's ridiculous aping of eastern kings, and also with his outrages and those of his companions; so that a party was formed which wanted to restore the republic, and of course it was joined by all who were for the Romans, and likewise by all those men of sense who looked upon the rule of the Carthaginians as more ruinous than that of the Romans. The conspiracy was discovered, and one of the accomplices punished with death; yet those who had been found out would not betray the rest, and thus Hieronymus was off his guard when a great number of conspirators carried out their design, and he was murdered on the road from Syracuse to Leontini, one of the most considerable places of his petty kingdom. After his death, the republic was proclaimed, and a number of generals appointed, very likely, one for every tribe (φυλή). We find that a βουλά had always, even under the kings, a share in the administration, as in all the republics governed by tyrants: that council was allowed to continue. The question now was, who were to be generals? There were also the brothers-in-law of the king elected among them; so that the revolution cannot have been a root and branch one. Nor indeed did they yet know after all whether they ought to uphold the league with the Carthaginians. The Roman prætor Appius Claudius negotiated with them, wishing to keep up the Roman alliance, and the Syracusan citizens felt great hesitation to break it; but these two envoys of Hannibal managed to get themselves chosen generals, and they now did all they could to disturb the negotiation. The whole history of those events is exceedingly perplexed. Livy has it from Polybius; his account therefore is authentic. After there had been several times an appearance of peace being concluded, the Carthaginian party brought about a revolution with the help of the mercenaries, by which the chief power was placed in the grasp of Hippocrates and Epicydes, and the whole family of Hiero was murdered on the threshold of the altar. After this horrible event, all was wild confusion: there was a republic indeed in name; but these two fellows ruled by means of the mercenaries; the unfortunate Syracusans were mere tools in their hands. Yet it must not be forgotten, that it was also the unjustifiable cruelty of the Romans which had irritated men's minds. The community of Enna, called together under a false pretext, was slaughtered for a sham insurrection; so that far and near, every one fell away to the Carthaginians. These now sent a considerable fleet under Himilco to Sicily, which was indeed quite right and welcome to Hannibal himself, for the purpose of maintaining the island, and dividing the Roman forces. The fleet, for some time, kept the communication open between Carthage and Syracuse; but the generals showed themselves to be most wretchedly incompetent. Marcellus, who had gained glory by his contest against Viridomarus, and near Nola, now got the command of a Roman army in Sicily, and invested Syracuse. The town was quite easy to blockade on the landside; but the sea remained nearly always open. The war lasted for two years (538-540). It is represented to us as the siege of Syracuse; but it rather consisted in the Romans carrying on war from two very strong camps against the surrounding country. Himilco had made himself master of Agrigentum, and from thence of a great part of the Sicilian cities. Only the western towns of Lilybæum and Panormus, and Messana and Catana in the north, remained always with the Romans; but the whole semicircle round Agrigentum, even beyond Heraclea, became subject to the Carthaginians. The Carthaginians tried to relieve Syracuse, and they encamped in its neighbourhood; but the unwholesome air, which had prevailed there ever since the foundation of the city, and had more than once proved its salvation, destroyed the whole of their army, and the general himself, and Hippocrates, who had joined him, died. Marcellus made several attempts against Syracuse; but when from the sea-side he attacked the Achradina, all his endeavours were baffled by the mechanical skill of Archimedes. As is well known, there are many accounts of this matter: the best authenticated confines itself to this, that Archimedes foiled all the attempts of the Romans to sap the walls; that he smashed the sheds which protected the assailants, and destroyed the battering engines on their ships by his superior machinery. It seems less true that he set fire to the Roman fleet with burning-glasses: the silence of Livy, and consequently of Polybius, from whom he borrowed his description, bears witness against it. Marcellus never could have taken the town, had he not by chance perceived that part of the wall, which adjoined the sea, was but badly fortified, and had he not heard at the same time from deserters that the citizens were quite heedlessly keeping a festival. This day he availed himself of to scale that weak place; and thus the Romans became masters of two parts of the town, Tycha and Neapolis, and soon afterwards of the Epipolæ, that is to say, the town on the heights: the greater portion was still to be taken, namely, the old town (Νᾶσος), and the most flourishing part, namely, the Achradina; for Tycha and Neapolis were only suburbs, which were not even connected with the city. The Syracusans now began to treat. They were much inclined to surrender, and Marcellus wished for nothing better; but the Roman deserters, in their rage and despair, wanted to hold out to the last gasp, and they managed to mislead the mercenaries, and to inspire them with their own fury. Thus in a massacre the most eminent citizens were butchered, and these barbarians usurped the government; so that there was now at Syracuse the same terrible state of things which we read of in Josephus of the besieged city of Jerusalem. If the Romans ever could have openly departed from their principles, and have allowed the deserters to go out free, Syracuse would not have been destroyed: but they would not deviate from them ostensibly, although they did so in other ways; for they had recourse in this war to bribery and corruption of every kind, means which they had formerly scouted. Marcellus bribed Mericus, a Spanish general among the mercenaries, to give up to him part of the Achradina; and this treachery was planned with such fiendish cleverness that it was completely successful. The garrison of the Νᾶσος was enticed out under the pretence of repelling the enemy, and the Νᾶσος as well as Achradina were taken. Syracuse was at that time the most magnificent of all the Greek cities, Athens having long since lost its splendour. Timæus, who had lived in the latter city, and must needs have had a distinct remembrance of it, acknowledged Syracuse as the first and greatest of all.

The humanity of Marcellus after the conquest of the town, is by the ancients generally set forth as quite exemplary; but the Ἐκλογαὶ περὶ γνωμῶν now show us what a sort of forbearance it was. The town was not burned, but completely sacked; and the inhabitants were driven out, and had to tear up the grass from the earth, to appease their hunger. The slaves were sold, a fate, which was so much envied by those who were free, that many gave themselves out to be slaves, and let themselves be sold, only to keep soul and body together. All that was in the town, became the prize of the soldiers or of the state; Marcellus carried away the highest works of Grecian art in a mass to Rome. Livy's remark is a true one, that this melancholy gain was avenged upon him, inasmuch as the temple of *Virtus* and *Honor*, which he thus bedecked, was already thoroughly stripped by others in his (Livy's) times. After the fall of Syracuse, the war in Sicily lasted yet two years, and it ended with the taking of Agrigentum, which was still more terribly dealt with, as the Romans sold all the freemen as slaves. Thus Agrigentum was thrice laid waste:—once under Dionysius; then, a hundred and fifty years later, in the first Punic war; and now once more, after another fifty years. It was the most splendid town in the island next to Syracuse, and it became at that time the insignificant place which it is still to this day. M. Valerius Lævinus, a Roman of humane disposition, afterwards gathered together a new community therein (549). This victory over the Carthaginian army was also brought about by treachery; for a Numidian captain named Mutines went over with his soldiers to the Romans, and, like Mericus, was liberally rewarded by them. Thus, in the sixth year after the defection of Hieronymus, Sicily was again quite under the rule of the Romans.

The taking of Syracuse is of the same date as that of Capua (541), and both of these events may show us, how little the wars of the ancients are to be deemed like those of our own days. Since the end of the seventeenth century especially, quite a different notion of waging war has come into vogue. The last war of horrors, was the devastation of the Palatinate under Louis XIV.

The period from 541 to 545 is enlivened by a number of battles, in which Hannibal almost always had the best of it. From the tenth year of the struggle, he was in possession of the greatest part of Apulia, Samnium, and Lucania, and of the whole of Bruttium: here was the seat of the war in the tenth, eleventh and twelfth years. He defeated the proconsul Cn. Fulvius near Herdonia with considerable slaughter; from an ambush, he surprised the consuls, M. Claudius Marcellus, and T. Quinctius Crispinus: both of them died; the first, in the fight; the second afterwards, of his wounds. He took Arpi and Salapia (likewise an Apulian town); but the Romans recovered them again. Tarentum he gained after a three years' siege, in which he displayed all the superiority of his genius. Every one of the Greek towns of Lower Italy had now gone over to him. Tarentum, which had fallen into his hands owing to the treachery of the inhabitants, was afterwards again betrayed to the Romans by the commander of the Bruttian garrison. The city was treated like one which had been taken by the sword: all its treasures were carried to Rome, and thenceforward Tarentum appears desolate, until C. Gracchus sent a colony thither.

The Romans might have expected from the very beginning, that the Carthaginians, after the great successes of Hannibal, would send from Spain army upon army. It was not therefore on account of their small settlements there, but to prevent these from sending out new troops, that with incredible exertions they dispatched an army to Spain under the command of P. and Cn. Scipio (in the second year of the war, 535). These at first established themselves in Tarragona, and from thence they harassed the Carthaginians. After the battle of Cannæ already, it was intended that Hasdrubal, Hannibal's brother, should set out for Italy with an army to support him; but the Scipios hindered this, and although in the beginning the rule of Carthage had been really popular, the fickleness of the Spaniards led them to join the Romans, when they saw that they were only used by the Carthaginians as tools to furnish numbers of men and supplies of money for the war. How these wars were conducted, is not to be clearly made out from Livy's narration. It is surprising, but there seems to be no doubt of it, that the Romans advanced as far as Cordova; (for Illiturgis is surely the place of that name near Cordova, and not the other). This war is not worth a detailed description, as from the great distance of the scene of operations, according to Livy's own opinion, who is here our only authority, all the accounts of it are anything but trustworthy.[27] We cannot even say for certain how long the two Scipios (*duo fulmina belli* in Lucretius and others) carried it on. Livy mentions the eighth year; but if this were reckoned from the arrival of the Scipios in Spain, it would not tally with the one in which he places their death. But I am very much inclined to believe that they were not killed before 542: otherwise there is a gap, and the date of Hasdrubal's departure from Spain is too early.

The Carthaginians had increased the number of their troops, and had raised a considerable host, which was to march under Hasdrubal to Italy. They had divided it into three bodies, which by skilful movements separated the armies of the two Scipios, and won two battles against them. In the first of these, P. Scipio was slain, owing to the faithlessness of the Celtiberians, a plain proof of the barbarous condition of that people. Faithlessness is a leading feature in the character of barbarians: good-faith is not the growth of the savage state, but of a higher civilization; the savage follows the impulse of his passions. The ancient Goths, and still more so the Vandals, were just as faithless as the Albanians of the present day. Thirty days after his brother, Cn. Scipio also fell: the Romans lost all the country beyond the Ebro, and their rule in Spain was almost wholly destroyed. Yet, if we trust the accounts which Livy repeats without quite believing in them, they soon retrieved all their losses; a Roman knight, L. Marcius, gathered together all that had been left of his countrymen, and with these, in his turn, he utterly routed the Carthaginians. The senator Acilius, who described this victory in Greek, has said that the Carthaginians lost by it thirty-eight thousand men, and the whole of their camp; but Livy himself seems rather to agree with Piso, that Marcius had only collected what remained of the Romans, and beaten off the attacks of the Carthaginians upon their entrenchments. The difficulty at Rome was now what to do, as the army was nearly destroyed, all but the remnant at Taraco. A reinforcement was sent out under C. Claudius Nero;

but he did not succeed in doing anything beyond occupying a somewhat larger space along the sea coast on this side of the Ebro, and hindering the march of Hasdrubal. It was determined therefore, as both the consuls were engaged in Italy, that the people should elect a general with proconsular power to go to Spain. *Comitia centuriata* were held, as at the election of a consul; but no one offered himself as a candidate. On this, P. Scipio, the son of the Publius Scipio who had lately fallen, a young man in his twenty-fourth year, stepped forth, and proposed himself for that dignity. To him the Roman people had, even at an early period, directed its attention. He is said to have saved his father from a deadly stroke at the battle on the Ticinus already; and after the rout at Cannæ, to have compelled the young Roman nobles who in their despair would have left the city to its fate, and have emigrated to Macedon, to take an oath on his sword not to go away. But if he was really not more than twenty-four years old when he went to Spain, he could hardly have saved his father at the Ticinus. As no one else applied for it, the place was given to him in spite of the opposition, made by many on the ground of his being still so young, and *ex domo funestata,* in which even the year of mourning was not yet over.

Scipio was called among his contemporaries the Great, a surname which has unjustly fallen into disuse; for no man in the Roman history ought to be set above him. His personal qualities everywhere turned the scales. He was not only a great general, but also a well educated man; he possessed Greek learning, and understood the Greek language, so that he composed his memoirs in it. It was the opinion of the people that there was some mysterious influence upon him, and he fostered it by his own belief that he was leagued with the powers above. If he gave advice in the assembly or in the army, he always gave it as if it had been inspired by the gods, and all his counsels succeeded. He also went every morning to the temple of Jupiter on the Capitol, and would stay there for a while by himself. At one time, he gave out that he had heard a voice which prophesied victory to him; at another, he told his soldiers that in three days he would take the enemy's camp with its rich stores; and it turned out as he had said. This wonderfully strengthened the confidence which the soldiers had in him. We must therefore either deem him to have been an inspired enthusiast, or a crafty impostor, just like Mohammed. The latter hypothesis is not to be thought of. It is a great question to this day, whether Cromwell until his last years was an honest fanatic or an impostor. There is in such characters a remarkable mixture, which is scarcely to be distinguished.

Scipio was at that time highly popular in Rome, even in the senate, and he was furnished with all the means for carrying on the war. The first period which he passed in Spain, was taken up by preparations at Tarragona; it very likely lasted longer than what Livy states. The latter himself tells us that some writers dated the taking of Carthago Nova later than he did; and this is probably correct, as it surely is to be placed one year later, in 546; for otherwise the conduct of the Carthaginians would be unaccountable, nor could it be understood how Scipio could have marched from Tarragona to Carthagena in spite of three hostile armies. Very likely the writers thought that it had been inglorious for Scipio to have rested for so long a time. Hasdrubal had gained over the Celtiberians as free allies, and had raised among them an army which he was to lead to Italy. Besides Hasdrubal, Hannibal's brother, there were also Hasdrubal, Gisgo's son, and Mago, another brother of Hannibal, in Spain. But Scipio led his army to New Carthage, without the Carthaginians having expected it. With regard to the details of this campaign, and the time which it lasted, it is impossible to arrive at any positive result. New Carthage, for a city, was but small, as indeed most of the towns in southern France, Italy, and even in Spain, were smaller in the days of old than they are now. It was scarcely more than a military station; but during the short time since it had been founded, it had already become of great consequence: it was well-peopled with a numerous Punic community; it was an important place of arms; there were arsenals and dockyards in it; and it was strongly fortified with high and new built walls. To take this place, was one of those all but impracticable undertakings, which are only possible from their being quite unlooked for. The town lay on a peninsula. Scipio, who must have had intelligence of its weakness, first made an attack on the wall which was on the peninsula; but his men were repulsed with great loss. That part of the bay which washes the north side of the town, is a shallow pool, and does not belong to the harbour; there is still a tide there, though not so strong a one as on the open sea, and it may be forded at low water, as a firm bed of gravel runs along the wall: these shallows Scipio had caused to be examined by fishing boats. He renewed the attack from the land side, and whilst the ebb was at its lowest, he had soldiers brought to the shore, who scaled the low wall by means of ladders, and made themselves masters of a gate; and thus the town was taken by storm. This loss was a death-blow to the Carthaginians. Hasdrubal must at that time have already been in the country near the Pyrenees, and he must have reckoned on the place being able to defend itself.

How many troops Hasdrubal carried over to Italy, is not exactly known to us, as we are left here without Polybius.[28] He did not march with a large army from Spain; but, with the skill of his father and brother, he increased it in Gaul. Many a messenger, as Livy expressly tells us, had in those days stolen across the Alps over to Hannibal in Apulia; so that the Alpine tribes had already become acquainted with the Carthaginians. Moreover, by a twelve years' intercourse the people there were convinced, that the passage through their country was only a secondary object, and that therefore it was their interest to grant it under fair conditions. Hasdrubal avoided the blunder made by his brother in starting too late; in the autumn his preparations were ended, and he now set out, going a great way round. It is evident, on a careful collation of the different statements, that after a short engagement with Scipio, he marched from the country of the Celtiberians, not through Catalonia, but through Biscay, by what is now Bayonne, along the north side of the Pyrenees; so as to elude the Romans, and not be stopped by them. In the south of Gaul, he took up his winter-quarters somewhere in modern Roussillon, and was able to start from thence by the first beginning of spring. We learn from Livy, that at that time the Arvernians had the *principatus Galliæ*, and that they allowed him a free passage. He now reached Italy without any mischance, because he had started early enough. When it is said that he had gone over the ground which had taken Hannibal five months, in two, this applies only to his march from the Pyrenees to Placentia, whereas Hannibal had set out from New Carthage.

The Romans heard with great dismay of Hasdrubal's departure, and they made immense exertions. Hannibal was well apprised of everything; but he expected his brother later. There is no doubt but that in the course of the preceding years he had received more reinforcements than Livy tells us; yet his old troops were indeed almost gone, and he had nothing but Italians, whom, however, he had completely under his control and command: he was therefore now obliged to carry on the war according to the Roman system. It was his endeavour, by continual marchings and counter-marchings in Apulia, Lucania, and Bruttium, to move the Romans from one place to the other, like a clever chess-player; and in this he was perfectly successful. Had Hasdrubal been like Hannibal, he would not have loitered. But he wished first to take Piacenza, which, wonderful to say, had held out until then in the midst of the Gallic tribes; for thus he would remove this thorn from the side of those Gauls, and at the same time gain a safe place of arms. In this he wasted a good deal of time in vain, which perhaps was one of the causes of his bad success. His messengers to Hannibal were intercepted, and his letters read. The Romans kept Hannibal hemmed in within three armies, none of which, however, had the courage to give battle: their main force they had sent against Gaul. Hasdrubal's plan was to march, not through Tuscany, but along the Adriatic to the frontier of Apulia, where Hannibal was stationed. He was opposed by C. Claudius Nero as commander-in-chief; to Ariminum, M. Livius Salinator had been sent with the *volones* and two legions of allies, six legions altogether. But Livius fell back before Hasdrubal as far as Sena

Gallica, and would have retreated even to the Aternus in Picenum, had not Nero risked an expedition which is one of the boldest and most romantic ever made, but which was nevertheless successful. Hannibal was certainly not informed of the approach of his brother; this is proved beyond dispute by his march to Larinum: yet as he was not in a condition to take the Roman camp by storm, Claudius picked out the flower of his troops, and went with these by forced marches to the aid of his colleague. Hasdrubal, who had got ready to attack Livius, perceived from a careful observation of the Romans as they were turning out, that the state of their horses, arms, and accoutrements, which was quite different from what had been seen in Livius' troops hitherto, betrayed their having made a long march; from this he concluded that the latter had received reinforcements. In the night his attention was still more aroused: he heard the trumpets and bugles blow twice, from which he inferred that there were two consuls, although the Romans had in other respects taken every care to deceive him, and had not enlarged their camps. When Hasdrubal was sure of this, he wished to go a long way round, whereas until then he had evidently advanced by the straight road along the Adriatic. He had crossed the Metaurus, but now he wished to recross the river; and he marched higher up on its opposite bank, so as to approach the Apennines, and thus turn the Romans, or else to keep himself on the defensive behind the Metaurus. Here he had the misfortune of his guide deserting him; and he went along the river, under the very eyes of the Romans, without being able to find the ford. It is not unlikely that heavy rains had lately fallen; for otherwise the Metaurus may be forded anywhere. When he had been wearing himself out during the greatest part of the day, and he was now wavering, now trying to cross over, the Romans fell upon him. The battle was set in array in a manner worthy of a son of Hamilcar and brother of Hannibal; the Iberians and Libyans fought like lions: but the star of Rome decreed a requital for the day of Cannæ, and almost all the army, though not the whole of it, as Livy says, together with the general himself, was destroyed. Those who escaped, only got off because the Romans were too tired to follow after them any farther. According to Appian (whose account is from Polybius or Fabius), part of the Celtiberians cut their way through, and reached Hannibal; and in this there is an air of truth, as it does not redound to the glory of the Romans, and is not therefore likely to have been invented by them: the Gauls who were not slain, retired into their own land. Thus the whole undertaking ended in discomfiture. The Roman army now quickly returned, without Hannibal's having ventured in the meanwhile to strike a blow. Claudius caused the head of the hero-warrior of the house of Barcas to be taken to the outposts of Hannibal, who in this way received the first tidings of his brother's overthrow. Here ends the third period of the war.

After Hasdrubal had led his troops into Italy, there still remained in Spain the two armies of Hasdrubal Gisgo and of Mago, which had been driven back to the Atlantic. Against these, Scipio carried on the war the rest of that year, and in the following one; but all the spirit of it had fled with the Barcine Hasdrubal. Mago tried only to keep Gades; Hasdrubal after a series of battles went over to Africa. In Gades, a city which wanted to be equal with Carthage, and yet was subject to her, treachery was brewing; they were engaged in a plan to give up Mago to the Romans. It was discovered and defeated: the magistrates were enticed out, and put to death. Mago, however, now received orders to withdraw from the place. He was to go to the Balearic isles, which seem to have revolted against Carthage; and from thence to Liguria, there to collect a force with which he was to support Hannibal in Italy, and also, at the same time, to raise troubles in Etruria. When the Spanish peoples saw that the Carthaginians had given them up, and that they were employing the last means in their power to squeeze out of them supplies for other wars, they refused to obey them any longer. To the inhabitants of Gades also, the severity which had been shown towards them, was only an additional motive for an everlasting separation; and they made an alliance with the Romans, to which some writers give an earlier date than we can possibly assume from the very connected account of Livy. This is a political falsification of history; the Gaditanians in fact pretended out of vanity to have concluded it immediately after Scipio's arrival in the country. Scipio was still remaining in Spain in 545 and 546; the Carthaginians were quite driven out of it.

Yet the Romans had no firm footing in that country; for they only offered to its people, who had reckoned upon having freedom, a rule which perhaps was still more oppressive than that of the Carthaginians, with whom they had an opportunity of getting pay, as these employed mercenaries, whilst the Romans only occasionally took small bodies of Celtiberian troops into their service. The Romans also now revenged themselves on some towns which had behaved with particular fury against them. There happened at this period some horrible events, the outbursts of a fanaticism of bravery which is turned into madness. Such was the defence of Illiturgis and of Astapa. From the latter of these, all who were able to bear arms sallied forth, and fought to the last man; and at the same time, those who remained behind killed the women and children, and set fire to the town, laying hands on themselves also while it was burning.

While Scipio was now putting the province in order, which was still limited to Catalonia, Valencia, and Andalusia, an insurrection was planned among the Spaniards. Few of the Spanish states were republics; most of them were governed by princes, two of whom, Mandonius and Indibilis, after a long alliance with the Romans, had imbibed a furious hatred against them. Here also that nationality of the Spaniards which one meets with in all ages, displays itself in the wrath which all at once breaks out against the foreigners, whom they had wished from the beginning only to use as tools. These events are also remarkable for another reason, being the first traces of a state of things which long afterwards showed itself in a more decided shape, the tendency of the Italian allies towards equality with the Romans. Yet our accounts of them are incomplete, and do not hit the main point. Scipio was very ill; and a report got abroad of his death, at a time when there was stationed near Sucro an army of eight thousand men, consisting of Italian allies, and not, as Livy says, of Romans. These resolved to make themselves masters of Spain, and to found an independent state. The first pretext of this insurrection was the arrears of their pay, which, although it was taken from their own treasuries, they received much more irregularly than the Romans: on the whole, they felt that they were neglected, and yet they well knew, that there was no doing without them. They chose two from among themselves, an Umbrian, and a Latin from Cales, to be their generals, and even invested them with the consular insignia, which Zonaras mentions, though Livy says nothing about it: these took the command, and were entering into an understanding with the two Spanish princes. The crisis seemed most highly dangerous; but when the tidings of Scipio's recovery reached the camp, they at once lost courage, and his personal character had such influence, that they abandoned every idea of an insurrection, and thought of nothing but making their peace. Scipio came down to Carthagena; he behaved as if he deemed them to be in the right, and intimated to them, that they might atone for their offence by serving against the Spanish princes; and that they were to go to Carthagena to receive their pay, either singly, or in a body. They determined upon coming in a body, as this seemed to be the safer plan, and they believed that everything had been forgiven them. And their minds were set quite at ease, when on the day before their entry into Carthagena, they met with a quartermaster, who told them that the Roman army was to march to Catalonia: thus they arrived in the evening, and were quartered in the suburbs, the officers in the town itself. The latter were invited to the houses of the most respectable Romans, and arrested during the night. The next morning, the Roman army, on which he could implicitly rely, made a show of marching out of the gates, and the mutineers were summoned to the *forum* to get their pay: these had their suspicions completely lulled, and they came unarmed. But at the gates, the columns were ordered to halt; they occupied all the streets, and hemmed in the mutineers. Scipio now addressed these last, and told them what punishment they had deserved; yet he contented himself with having only the ringleaders, thirty-five in number, seized and put to death: the rest received their pay, and were let off. After this, the war against the Spaniards was easy. The two princes were pardoned on their oath to keep quiet.

Before Scipio had yet left Spain, he achieved a feat of romantic daring in going over to Africa to visit Syphax, the king of the Massæsylians, who lived in eastern and part of western Algeria, and whose capital was Cirta: the geography of those countries at the time of the Carthaginian rule, is one of the most obscure. Syphax was not tributary to the Carthaginians, but in that sort of dependence in which the prince of a barbarous people must be upon a very powerful and civilized state: he served them for pay, and felt altogether subordinate; sometimes he was quite at their disposition, at others, he fell away from them, after which, he would make peace again. Just then, he was at peace with them; but he had previously, when at war, made overtures to the Romans, and on his demand for Roman officers to train his troops, Scipio had sent over envoys with full powers. This, however, led to no results; for in the meanwhile peace had been concluded, and Syphax kept neutral. Scipio now ventured to cross over at his invitation, in the hope of forming an alliance with him, as he had, from the very first, entertained the just notion of attacking Carthage on her own ground. Here he actually met with Hasdrubal, son of Gisgo, at the same banquet. The object of the conduct of Syphax towards the Romans, was not to allow the Carthaginians to become too powerful, and to draw money out of them: that he let Scipio escape, is really to be wondered at.

In Spain, all was now ended, and Scipio returned to Italy, where, however, he was not granted a triumph, because while conducting this war, he had not held any curule office: every other mark of honour was shown him. He was still proconsul; before that, he had been ædile; he had not yet been prætor; nevertheless he now stood for the consulship, though he had not yet reached the age prescribed by law: the *leges annales*, by a very wise enactment, had been set aside for so long as the war should last. He was unanimously chosen by all the centuries; the nation longed to see the end of the war, and every one expected it from him. As far as we can see, this was nothing but one of those silly notions, by which the public are so easily taken in; the great men, it was said, were right glad that the war with Hannibal should drag on, as thus they could so much the oftener get for themselves the highest dignities. Scipio, who was the idol of the people, was withstood by the party of the grandees, of which Fabius is to be deemed the mainspring,—a party just like the one which Livy describes as having existed in Carthage against Hannibal. Yet one ought to be fair, even to that party. Old Fabius Maximus, perhaps already in his eightieth year, was at its head for more reasons than one; perhaps, even because, like every old man who sees his own brightness fading away, he was inclined to look upon the rising young men with unfavourable eyes. Scipio also, from the very circumstance of his being no common man, may have seemed to the Romans a very incomprehensible character; many may have been afraid that his good luck would make him reckless, as it did Regulus; others, that it might tempt him to overthrow the constitution. That this suspicion was utterly groundless, as far as it was founded upon Scipio's personal disposition, may safely be asserted; yet we find it mentioned here and there,[29] that it was intended to make him consul or censor for life: had this been done, he would have been king, although, as things then were, this could not possibly have been brought about without bloodshed: yet it shows, that the mistrust, after all, was not without reason. Hence it was that a determined opposition manifested itself in the senate, to whose department belonged grants of men and money. Scipio tried to get Africa for his province; but they gave him Sicily, without allowing him any other troops but those which were there already: he, however, got leave to try his chance in an expedition with those who might voluntarily offer themselves. This conduct of the senate towards Scipio is an acknowledged fact, and by it Rome was very nearly on the point of losing again all the advantages of the war. This behaviour of the senate ought to be borne in mind, when its stedfastness in the war with Hannibal is spoken of.

The influence of Scipio's personal qualities was now seen. In Italy there was famine and disease, and yet part of the Etruscan and Umbrian states, which were not obliged to bear any burthens whatever, and therefore, owing to the regard which the Romans then had for every sort of privilege, had remained in full vigour, whilst Rome had worn herself out, exerted themselves for Scipio, as much as if they had themselves to undertake a war. They built a fleet for him, and equipped it; Arretium gave him arms for thirty thousand men, and likewise money and provisions; from the Sabines, Picentines, Marsians, and other neighbouring peoples, a great number of veterans and young discharged soldiers volunteered to serve under him. Thus he got a considerable fleet and a large army, quite against the wishes of the senate. He crossed over to Sicily, made from thence an attempt upon Locri, and took that town from Hannibal; yet, on the whole, the year of his consulship passed off without any thing remarkable. Why he waited so long in Sicily, has not been fully accounted for; it seems that he took matters easy, and willingly lingered in these Sicilian regions, being particularly delighted with Syracuse. Men's expectations were most signally disappointed: it had been believed, that as soon as his preparations were at all complete, he would pass over to Africa; and now it was understood that he was living quite in the Greek style at Syracuse. Commissioners thereupon were sent to inquire into the matter, and if the charge were true, to depose him; but he so overawed them, that they reported that he was by no means wasting his time, but was finishing his preparations.

Hannibal, after the battle of Sena, had already foreseen the issue of the war; but he did not yet lose courage. On the contrary, he deemed it his duty to struggle to the last moment, that the Romans might not be sure of their own country; yet, as he could not defend such extensive provinces, he evacuated Apulia, Messapia, the country of the Hirpinians, and the greater part of Lucania, so that he only kept the south-eastern part of it, and Bruttium. Here he remained for three campaigns, with a perseverance which Livy himself admires; like a lion, he made whoever dared to touch him, pay heavily for it. Within this narrow tract of country, he had to recruit and provision his army, and to detain the Romans, so as to keep them away from Africa, living the whole time in the midst of peoples whom he drove to despair by the most exorbitant demands. And he succeeded in all this, without a thought either of rebellion or of violence being awakened against him; yet he was neither able to pay nor to feed his army, and he suffered from plague and hunger. His headquarters and arsenal was Croton. Thus the war went on, until the Carthaginians called him to Africa, the Romans narrowing his district more and more by wresting from him one place after the other.

It was not till the year after his consulship, 548, when his proconsular *imperium* was prolonged, that Scipio with four hundred transports, protected by forty quinqueremes, crossed over to Africa. If the Carthaginians had had their ships of war assembled, they must have baffled Scipio's undertaking; but this could hardly have been the case, or else their inactivity would have been quite unaccountable. How many troops he carried over, was unknown, even to the ancients themselves; as an average number, we may assume sixteen thousand men foot, several thousand horse, and a considerable fleet: when these departed, there were great tremblings of heart in the timid party among the Romans, who thought of nothing but the fate of Regulus. Scipio's arrangements were admirable. In three days he made the passage, and landed north of Carthage, not far from Utica, near a headland at the mouth of the river Bagradas, which, like almost all the rivers which fall into the Mediterranean, has formed another mouth farther on, its old one having been choked up with sand; Shaw, however, in his travels, fixes the point with admirable precision. Its memory was kept up as long as the Roman empire lasted, by the name of *Castra Cornelia*; it was a headland with an offing, a gradually sloping beach of gravel, on which the ships had to be drawn up. Here Scipio entrenched himself, and from thence made excursions. In the meanwhile, Syphax had been entirely gained over to the Carthaginians, having married Sophonis (in Hebrew Zephaniah), or, as Livy has it, Sophonisbe, the daughter of Hasdrubal, the son of Gisgo. When Scipio had landed, a Carthaginian army under Hasdrubal, a great Numidian one under Syphax, and a smaller Numidian one under Masinissa, went out to meet him. Masinissa was hereditary prince of the Massylians, a people on the frontier of what is now Tunis, which dwelt at the foot of the mountains. He was a vassal of the Carthaginians, had served under their standards in Spain, and in that country already had entered into some correspondence with the Romans. He is known to have been the guest-friend of Scipio; in the *Somnium Scipionis*, he makes his appearance as a venerable old man; he was brought up in Carthage, and, at least in his later years, understood Greek or Latin. These African princes were all of them thoroughly faithless. That his truth to the Romans ever became so renowned, was merely owing to the fact that it was his object to enrich himself at the expense of Carthage, in which he was aided by the Romans; but his son, who already stood in a different relation to them, in the third Punic war certainly did them a great deal of mischief. A romance has been got up, in which Masinissa is in love with Sophonisbe, and therefore jealous of Syphax; with the latter, he is said to have been involved in a war, and afterwards reconciled. He now came, it would seem, as an ally of the Carthaginians against Scipio, who enticed him to go over. He had lost his hereditary right, owing to the Carthaginians having favoured a rival of his; for some time, he had roved in the desert: he now wished to try his luck with the Romans, and he showed himself useful to them as a centre, round which a host of Africans gathered. He imparted to Scipio his plan by which he had beguiled the Carthaginians, and Scipio fell upon them from an ambush: the loss was considerable for Carthage, as it comprised a number of her citizens. The Carthaginian general Hanno was taken prisoner, and afterwards exchanged for Masinissa's mother. In the meanwhile, Syphax had had the presumption to act as mediator between the Romans and Carthaginians; which, of course, came to nothing, as everything was then to remain as before, and Hannibal and Scipio were each of them to withdraw from Italy and Africa. But the attempt was of use to Scipio; for while this was going on, he was able to establish himself in Africa.

Scipio besieged Utica with ill success; Hasdrubal and Syphax kept him in check, very likely in open camps. On this, Scipio undertook a sudden night-attack, which shows what wretched discipline there was in their armies. He managed to get in, and to set fire to both the camps, which were of straw-built huts; the enemy, taken by surprise, tried to make their escape, but were pent in like sheep, and slaughtered by the Romans. The two armies were scattered; Syphax left the Carthaginians, and returned to his own country. Masinissa now set himself up as a competitor for his throne, and marched against him: the subjects of Syphax joined him in great masses, and Lælius accomplished the undertaking. Syphax was taken prisoner. Masinissa followed up his advantage, and made himself master of Cirta, the chief town, afterwards called Constantineh, a name which it still bears. There the wife of Syphax was found, and Masinissa immediately married her, without asking the consent of the Romans. But Scipio was positive in his demand, that Sophonis, as a Carthaginian woman and an enemy of the Romans, should be given up; Masinissa, not wishing to let her suffer such a fate, sent her poison, and she killed herself. Part of the kingdom of Syphax was given to his son; he himself was sent as a prisoner to Italy, and led in the triumph of Scipio: he died an old man at Alba in the country of the Marsians. His statues must have been common: there are still several pedestals which have his name and a summary of his history.

The Carthaginians became convinced that their force was not sufficient; they had indeed succeeded in an attempt against the Roman ships, but this was also the only time during the three years of the war in Africa. They sent word to Hannibal and Mago that both of them were to come, which was good news for Italy; yet as it was uncertain, whether the transport of the armies was possible, the Carthaginians also made Scipio proposals of peace, to which he listened the more readily, as he had now for three years been proconsul in Africa, and had always to expect his dismissal, in which case the consul of the following year, Ti. Claudius Nero, would have carried away the glory of having ended the war. Moreover, the issue of the contest with Hannibal was still very doubtful; and therefore the conditions of Scipio, hard as they were, were yet tolerable in comparison with what happened afterwards. The independence of the Carthaginians was acknowledged; they were to be masters of the whole tract of country within the Punic canal, (what its extent was, is uncertain;) to give up Italy, Spain, Sicily, and Sardinia, and likewise all their ships but thirty, probably triremes, and to deliver up the prisoners of war: how much was asked by way of payment for the expenses of the war, is uncertain. Livy says that the annalists stated the numbers very differently: the exact numbers which we meet with in the later Greek writers (fifteen hundred talents in Appian), are taken from these statements, between which Livy does not venture to decide. The latter mentions also a great quantity of corn. On these conditions, the rulers of Carthage were resolved to make peace; but quite different was the feeling of the restless, unruly populace, who fiercely raved against the peace, without, however, being willing to shed a drop of their own blood. These were in despair. After having gloriously fought for so long, were they, it was said, to declare themselves vanquished, while Hannibal was still alive? for the great mass of the people certainly looked upon him as an idol. In the meanwhile, the government carried its point, and a truce was concluded, and ambassadors sent to Rome. There the peace was accepted on condition that Hannibal should leave Italy. But the Carthaginians now heard that Hannibal was really going to evacuate Italy, and they thought that they might try a different tack. The peace was all but sworn to, when a large Roman fleet, which had arrived with provisions, but had not yet landed them, was driven from its moorings by a storm. Carthage had for a long time been in want of food, and the people murmured at this supply being allowed to go to the enemy, when the gods themselves were against them, and they could take it if they liked; so they embarked in a riotous manner, and cut out the Roman ships, which, relying on the truce, had cast anchor there. Scipio on this sent envoys to remonstrate, and to demand satisfaction. This, however, was not to be had, such was the general fermentation, and the Roman emissaries got away with great difficulty; it was only under the protection of a guard, that they managed to return to their ship, which—contrary, it is true, to the wish of the government—was chased by a Carthaginian vessel, and had to save itself, by running ashore. This story reminds one of the murder of the French ambassadors at Rastadt. All hope of peace was now utterly gone, and the Carthaginian ambassadors were commanded to withdraw from Rome.

Mago had landed from Spain at Genua, had taken it, and was trying to change Liguria into a Carthaginian province; just as the Romans had spread in Spain from one single place. Yet he made but little progress in the Apennines and in the Alps, as he had to deal with a host of unmanageable petty tribes. Although indeed he got reinforcements and money, his means at first were inconsiderable; yet he always obliged the Romans to employ some forces against him. Once he defeated them in the country of the Insubrians: so that, if he had not now been recalled, he would certainly have given them a great deal of trouble. He embarked, but died of the wounds which he had received in that engagement.

Hannibal had likewise had positive orders to embark, and one cannot understand why the Romans did not do their utmost to destroy his fleet: he reached Africa without an accident. Against Carthage itself, the Romans were not able to undertake anything: it was too strong a town. Nor had Scipio as yet taken any other city that was fortified, though he was master of many open places. Hannibal landed near Adrumetum; he had taken with him all those whom he could find in Bruttium able to bear arms, and he had embodied among his troops all the Roman and Italian deserters, whose only chance of life depended on the war with Rome. His army consisted of about forty thousand men. Yet when he beheld the state of things at Carthage, he made an attempt to negotiate; for he saw how unlikely it was that the war would be successfully carried on, and he knew well that, if a battle were lost, the city would obtain a peace from which it might never recover. Scipio likewise was very anxious for peace; for he was always afraid that they would not prolong his *imperium*. The conditions which Hannibal offered, were too low, as he demanded for the Carthaginians the sovereignty over Africa, leaving indeed to the Romans the countries which they had conquered, but refusing everything else; Scipio still wished to keep to the former conditions, with a trifling compensation for the wrong which had been done. All was spoilt at last by the folly of the Carthaginian people, who, now that Hannibal was come, thought that Scipio's army would be destroyed like that of Regulus; and thus the famous battle of Zama was brought on (550). Hannibal, according to the testimony of Polybius, here also displayed the qualities of a great general. He drew up his army in three lines. The foremost was formed of a medley of foreign troops enlisted from among the most opposite races; behind these were placed the Carthaginian citizens, who only took up arms in times of the utmost need, but were forced by these very circumstances to be brave; behind these again, as a reserve, were the Italians whom he had brought over, and they were a considerable body: in front of the whole were eighty elephants, and on the wings were the cavalry. This is the only battle in which Hannibal made use of elephants. The Romans were set in their usual array of *hastati*, *principes*, and *triarii*, save only that Scipio left large spaces between each of these three divisions, whereas otherwise they were so placed behind each other, that the maniples of the one always covered the intervals between two maniples of the others. In these wide spaces, as well as in front of the lines, he put the light troops, that when the elephants approached, they might hurl their missiles at them, and then, should they enter these open lanes, assail them with javelins. On the wings, he set the Numidian and Roman horse. The result of the battle shows that this cavalry was now superior, in quality at least, to that of the Carthaginians; for the latter was soon put to flight. The object with regard to the elephants was partly attained, as most of them ran right through these lanes, although there were some, who turned themselves sideways upon the men who were armed with javelins. Now began the shock between the *hastati* and the Carthaginian mercenaries, who, after a gallant fight, were forced to throw themselves upon the Carthaginian phalanx behind them, but were driven back again by these upon the Romans; so that they were trampled down between the two. The *hastati*, however, had to give way before the Carthaginians; Scipio then made them fall back, and the *principes* and the *triarii* move sideways towards the wings, so as to attack the Carthaginians in the flank: this had the fullest success. The Italians alone fought with desperate courage; but the Carthaginian cavalry had been all destroyed, and the Romans burst upon the Carthaginian rear, on which the rout became such, that nearly the whole of the army was cut to pieces. Hannibal himself escaped with a small handful of men to Adrumetum.

Nothing else was now thought of in Carthage, but peace. It was the great Hannibal who principally negociated it, and accepted the conditions, which of course were much harder than the former ones; the eagerness, however, of Scipio to hurry on the peace, was the saving of Carthage. Her independence was acknowledged; the towns and provinces which had belonged to the Carthaginians in Africa before the war, they were indeed still to keep as subjects; but in this there was trickery, as they were to prove, what they had possessed. Instead of thirty triremes being left to them, as at first, only ten were now allowed them; they had to deliver over their elephants, and were no more to tame any; they were to pay ten thousand Euboïc talents (15,000,000 dollars) within fifty years; to give a hundred and fifty hostages to be chosen by the Romans themselves, (which was very hard, as hostages were so badly treated among the ancients;) and to yield up all the Roman prisoners and deserters, and likewise the unfortunate Italians who had come over with Hannibal. Whether these were all put to death as rebels, or sold for slaves, is not told us by Livy, who indeed says not a word about the whole of this article: Appian has given the account of it, and therefore so did Polybius likewise. They were moreover to acknowledge Masinissa as king of the Numidians within the boundaries prescribed by the Romans; to conclude a passive alliance offensive and defensive, with the Romans, on whom, however, it was not to be binding; and to feed and keep the Roman soldiers for six months longer. In Africa, they might wage war only with the consent of the Romans; out of Africa, not at all; and they were not to enlist mercenaries anywhere in Europe.

Some fools in Carthage wanted to speak against these conditions; but Hannibal seized hold of one Gisgo, and dragged him down from the platform on which he was haranguing. An outcry was raised about the violation of the liberty of the citizen; Hannibal, however, justified himself, saying that ever since his ninth year, he had been for six and thirty years away from his country, and therefore was not so accurately acquainted with the law; that, moreover, he deemed the peace to be necessary. All men of sense had become aware that the peace was now unavoidable, and that matters would have taken a different turn, if Hannibal had been supported at the right time.

Scipio now evacuated Africa; all the Carthaginian ships of war were brought to sea, and there set fire to. Thus ended, after sixteen years, the second Punic war and the rivalry of Carthage. Rome had made an immense booty.[30]

THE MACEDONIAN WAR[31]

Immediately after the battle of Cannæ, Philip III. of Macedon had sent ambassadors to Hannibal, and had concluded a treaty, which fell, by chance, into the hands of the Romans. Even without this accident, it could not have been kept secret, not at least for any length of time. By this treaty, of which we certainly read in Polybius a genuine text, and of which the form is not at all Greek, but quite foreign, undoubtedly Carthaginian, the two states had not after all bound themselves to much. Hannibal secured to Philip in case of victory, that the Romans were to give up their possessions beyond the Adriatic, Corcyra, Apollonia, Epidamnus, the colony of Pharus, the Atintanians (an Epirote people), Dimalus, and the Parthinian Illyrians; and in return for this, Philip was to let the Carthaginians have the supremacy over Italy. Had Philip then been what he became in his riper years, this alliance would have proved dangerous to the Romans. But they, with that perseverance and heroic courage which distinguished them in the whole war, sent out a fleet under the prætor M. Valerius Lævinus, to protect Illyria, and to raise a party against him in Greece. Hostilities began in the year 537, or 538 (Lævinus not being a consul, the commencement is not quite certain), and the war lasted until the peace of P. Sempronius 548. This war was carried on very sluggishly on the side of the Romans, and Philip, who had to limit his exertions only to the few points on the mainland of Illyria, could have made himself master of these, had he not managed his affairs quite as feebly. His conduct then gives us quite a different idea of his powers from that which we are led to form afterwards. Had he given to Hannibal but ten thousand Macedonians as auxiliaries, Rome would have been in a sad plight; but he was too vain to do so.

Philip was at that time very young, hardly in his twenty-first or second year. His father Demetrius II. had left him at his death yet a child, and had given him for guardian an uncle, or elder cousin, Antigonus Epitropus (likewise called Doson). This Antigonus showed a conscientiousness which, considering the time in which he lived, really awakens our wonder; he seems to have taken as much care of the education of his ward, as of his rights: of this we see the traces in Philip, especially in the first years of his reign, in which he is said to have been very amiable. But there was something bad-hearted in him, which soon shook off that influence: like an eastern youth, he then wallowed in lust. Yet he was endowed with remarkable talents; he was highly gifted as a general, and he had courage and skill, to employ and to increase the resources of his empire. In the war against the Romans under Flamininus, he displayed much ability; and when in the peace he had lost part of his kingdom, he cleverly took advantage of circumstances to be set up again by Rome herself. Thus he managed to leave behind to his son a power, such as he himself had never possessed before.

The empire of Macedon, during the latter days of Antigonus Gonatas, had fallen into decay: the Ætolians had risen, the Achæans had made themselves free. Under Demetrius, it was going down hill still faster. From this condition, it only recovered in the last years of the guardianship of Antigonus, and that by the treason of old Aratus, who sacrificed the whole glory of a well-spent life; for he chose, rather to yield up Corinth and the liberty of Greece, and to make the Achæans sink into utter insignificance, than to let Cleomenes have that authority in the state, which was due to him, and without which the Lacedæmonians could not have joined the Achæan league. Philip, in the beginning of his reign, had, in conjunction with the Achæans, undertaken a war against the Ætolians, by which the latter were considerably humbled, important fortresses in Thessaly having been taken from them and their estimation in Greece lowered. They were obliged to agree to a disadvantageous peace, yet they still kept their independence. When Philip leagued himself with Hannibal, and began the war with the Romans, Greece was at peace. Thessaly, with the exception of that part which was Ætolian, Phocis, Locris, Eubœa with Chalcis, Corinth, Heræa, and Aliphera were well affected to Macedon, and had Macedonian garrisons. The Achæans were nominally free and united, but in reality dependent on their allies the Macedonians; so were likewise the Bœotians and Acarnanians. The Ætolians, who were hostile, were free, and had a territory of considerable extent. In Lacedæmon, at that time one revolution followed upon another: it was subjected to a nominal king, probably a son of Eudamidas; but soon afterwards Machanidas seized upon the government. The Syrian kings ruled over Western Asia, with the exception of Caria and Samos, which, as well as the Hellespont, Chersonesus, and the towns on the southern coast of Thrace, belonged to Egypt. Chios, Lesbos, and Byzantium formed together a confederacy of free cities. Rhodes was free, the mistress of the sea, and powerful; she was a friend of the Romans, without being actually allied with them. Egypt and Syria were at war with each other. The former retained Cœlesyria when the peace was made; but she lost the northern fortresses of Phœnicia to Syria. The Athenians were on friendly terms with the Romans; in their enfeebled state they kept aloof from all political activity. There was peace everywhere; the eyes of Greece were already very much turned towards Rome.

One would have thought that under these circumstances Philip might have undertaken something of importance against Rome; yet he did not exert himself. In the beginning of the contest, there were only little skirmishes going on, and he had some success; he overcame the Atintanians, and also the Ardyæans in the north of Illyricum, who were under the protection of Rome. About the fourth year of the war, the Romans made an alliance with the Ætolians, and from that time, unhappily for Greece, they became enterprising in those parts. They sent over indeed but one legion, in fact, only marines; but they also had a fleet in those seas, which was of some consequence, as the Macedonians had scarcely any at all. Through the Ætolians, the Romans also became connected with Attalus, who having begun with the small realm of Pergamus, had conquered Lydia, and created a rich principality. The Roman fleets of Lævinus, and after him of Sulpicius, were a real curse for ill-fated Greece. The treaty with the Ætolians stipulated, that of all the places beyond Corcyra which they should conquer together, the soil should belong to the Ætolians, the inhabitants with their goods and chattels to the Romans. Such a stipulation is indeed not unheard of; yet it shows what the Ætolians really were. After the Lamian war, they deserve praise; but all that happened afterwards, shows them to have been morally barbarians: their language may indeed have been partly Greek. This treaty had the saddest consequences. The Roman fleet made its appearance off the Greek coast; Ægina, Dyme, Oreus, were taken, and the whole population swept away by the Romans. These two last places the Ætolians were not able to keep; but Ægina with its harbour they sold to Attalus for thirty talents,—that noble Greek island to a prince of Pergamus! These atrocities drew upon the Ætolians and Romans the abhorrence of the whole of Greece. Philip, who thereby became popular, penetrated with the Greeks, for the first time, into Ætolia, and requited them in their own country for their devastations. The Ætolians, abandoned by the Romans, concluded a very disadvantageous peace. Philip made considerable conquests. Two or three years afterwards, (Livy's chronology here is very little to be relied on,) about 548, the Romans also by means of Tib. Sempronius concluded a peace with Philip, beneath the conditions of which some great disadvantage again is veiled. Not only the country of the Atintanians, which had become subject to them,—a district not unimportant of itself, but of very great consequence on account of the pass of Argyrocastro, through which Philip had now a free passage between the Roman territory and the then republic of Epirus,—was by it expressly ceded to Philip, but also the country of the Ardyæans. The Romans, of course, had this mental reservation, that the time would not be long before they would break this peace, and gain back what they had lost. This is one of the few instances in which the Romans renounced part of their possessions. One ought to have remembered this, when such violent reproaches were made against Jovian, who, to save his army, ceded a tract of country to the Persians: there was an outcry at the time, as if such a thing had never happened before in the history of Rome. Aurelian had yielded Dacia to the Goths; Hadrian had given up the conquests of Trajan in the east; not to mention the peace with the Volscians in the earliest times.

Philip, after having concluded peace with the Romans, allied himself with Antiochus the Great against the infant Ptolemy Epiphanes, the child of the unworthy Ptolemy Philopator. The Egyptian kings since Philadelphus and Euergetes, were in possession of extensive districts and strongholds on the coasts of Syria and Asia Minor, as far as the coast of Thrace: Lycia at least was subject to their supremacy. As under Ptolemy Philopator the empire had already fallen into utter decay, and his infant successor was growing up under the charge of an unworthy guardian, Antiochus and Philip took advantage of the moment. Egypt had since the rise of the Alexandrine empire been on friendly terms with Rhodes, and the Rhodians had a strong interest in being friends with Alexandria, as they had much more to fear from Macedon than from Egypt; they therefore defended Epiphanes. Yet their power was no match for that of Macedon and Syria; especially as the wretched Egyptian government hardly did anything, but on the contrary let the allies, among whom, besides Rhodes, there were also Byzantium, Chios, and Attalus of Pergamus, bear the whole brunt of the war. The two kings were therefore most successful. Philip conquered for himself the whole of the Thracian coast; Perinthus, Ephesus, and Lycia, fell to the lot of Syria, although the allies of the Egyptians had shortly before had some success in a sea-fight near Chios.

Philip had now reached the pinnacle of his greatness. Even from Crete, where Macedon had never before exercised any influence, he was applied to for his mediation.

The immediate cause, or at least the pretext for the second Macedonian war, was afforded to the Romans by the distress of Athens. That city was utterly impoverished and decayed; but it kept up a sort of independence, and as early as about twenty-five years after the first Illyrian war, it had made an alliance with the Romans, and had granted them isopolity. [32] Perhaps the Romans received the gift with a smile; yet such bright rays of her old departed glory still lingered upon Athens, that on her side at least, there was nothing ridiculous in the proffer. Pausanias tells us, that among the cenotaphs for those who had been slain, there were also some for the men belonging to three triremes, who had fallen in battle abroad as allies of the Romans; but he does not give the date. It is not likely that this was a figment of the Athenians; the time may have been that of the second Illyrian war, as they were keen enough to see that they might gain the Romans by sending them a few ships. During the first Macedonian war, they very wisely kept neutral; but in the last years of the war of Hannibal they got involved in hostilities with Philip. The murder of two young Acarnanians who had intruded when the Eleusinian mysteries were celebrated, led their countrymen to call upon Philip for help. He had long wished to get possession of Athens, and he now savagely devastated the whole of Attica to the very walls of the city: all the temples in the Athenian territory were pulled down, and even the tombs were demolished. The Athenians betook themselves to the Rhodians, to Attalus, and in general to all the allies of that suddenly decayed Alexandrine empire, which had once been so highly blooming under Euergetes; yet their hopes were chiefly bent upon the Romans. In Rome there was much consultation what to do. The senate and the leading men, who already had unbounded views of extending the Roman power, would not have hesitated for a moment to declare war, and the more so, as they were likewise eager to make up for what they had lost by the unfortunate issue of the former one: but the people, who were most wretchedly off, and longed for rest, threw out the first motion for a war.

It is a most erroneous thing, for one to believe that a constitution remains the same, so long as its outward forms still last. When alterations have taken place in the distribution of property, in public opinion, and in the way in which people live, the constitution, even without any outward change, may become quite different from what it was, and the self-same form may at one time be democratical, and at another aristocratical. This internal revolution is hardly ever traced by modern writers of history, and yet it is one of those very things which in history ought to be particularly searched into. That strange and wonderful preponderance of the oligarchy of wealth existed already at that time in Rome, and the many—who generally speaking have neither judgment nor a will of their own—now decree the very things which they did not wish. Here indeed we have one of the first and most remarkable symptoms of this: the people, contrary to their own wishes, vote for the war with Philip. It was the great misfortune of Rome, that after the war of Hannibal, there was no great man who had the genius to restore the constitution in accordance with its spirit. For great states always decline and fall, because, after great exertions, everything is left to the blind spirit of the age, and no healing of what is diseased is attempted.

The Romans now, with great zeal, sent ambassadors to Philip to demand indemnification for the Athenians, and cessation of all hostilities against the allies of Rome, to the number of whom Ptolemy also belonged. Philip clearly saw that this was but a pretext to raise a quarrel, and he had bitterly to repent of not having taken better advantage of the war with Hannibal. In the year 552, the war was decreed, and the command was given to the consul P. Sulpicius Galba, who had already made a campaign before in those parts, though not of the most glorious kind, as he devastated Dyme, Oreus, and Ægina. It must have been resolved upon late in the season, and as the consul besides fell ill, nothing more could be undertaken that year: Galba's expedition therefore entirely belongs to the year which followed his consulship, a fact which is overlooked by Livy. Villius, the next consul, was only present at the seat of war for a very short period, towards the end of his time of office.

In Greece, the Ætolians just then were very much weakened, but independent, and hostile to Macedon. They possessed Ætolia, part of Acarnania, the country of the Ænianians, that of the Ozolian Locrians, most of Phthiotis, the land of the Dolopians, part of southern Thessaly, and Thermopylæ; and they had isopolity with Lacedæmon, and with a number of distant places in Elis and Messene: yet for the last thirty years they had been going down hill. In the Peloponnesus, the Achæans held Achaia, Sicyon, Phlius, and Argolis, and Arcadia; but in reality they were entirely dependent on the Macedonians, and were protected by them against Ætolia and Lacedæmon. The Lacedæmonians were confined within very narrow limits in their old country, and they had lost their ancient constitution; they had no ephors, perhaps not even a senate, but they were ruled by a tyrant, Nabis, one of the worst of monsters. The Messenians stood apart from the Ætolians and Achæans, and were become sworn foes to the latter; the Eleans were independent, and leagued with the Ætolians; the Bœotians remained independent in appearance only, under the supremacy of Macedon; Corinth, Eubœa, Phocis, Locris, were nominally allies of the Macedonians, but in fact were subject to their rule. Thessaly was held to be a state which had become blended with Macedon. In Epirus, the house of the Æacidæ was extirpated, and the remainder of the people hemmed in by the Ætolians, formed a republic, sometimes under Ætolian, and at other times under Macedonian influence. On the Greek mainland, Athens survived as a mere name, without a connexion belonging to her, an object of Philip's hate. The Acarnanians were, properly speaking, none of the subjects of the Macedonians, but were only united with them by their common enmity against the Ætolians. The Cyclades had formerly belonged to Egypt, and they were now in an unsettled state. Crete was independent, but torn by factions, owing to which Philip had been called upon to mediate. Chios and Mitylene were free; Rhodes was great and powerful; Byzantium also was free, and allied with Chios and Mitylene: they had taken as little part as possible in all the quarrels; but now they were drawn into them, particularly Chios, and in a league with Attalus. As to their intellectual life, the Greeks were utterly fallen. There were indeed still some schools at Athens; but poesy was dead, and even the art of speech, that last blossom of the Greek spirit, had vanished away, and had sought a new home among the Asiatic peoples which had been hellenized, but without imbibing any of the excellencies of the Greek nation. Most places were mere shadows of what they had been; there were but few indeed which had not been destroyed more than once: of the number of those spared was Corinth, which therefore was the most flourishing of all Greek towns. The Achæans, ever since Aratus, out of spite to the Lacedæmonians, had given over his country into the hands of the Macedonians, were mere clients to their new patrons. Owing to this connexion, which had lasted nearly twenty years, they had many a time received the deepest cause for provocation; but they were on bad terms with their neighbours, and if their patriots had any wish, it was to have their dependence upon Macedon changed into a freer form of clientship; none, however, dreamed of independence. But then many were filled with bitter indignation at the cruelty with which several towns had been laid waste by the Romans. The Ætolians felt inclined to undertake the war; but they did not come to any decision, a misunderstanding having arisen between them and the Romans, whom they reproached with having given them unfounded hopes, whilst, on the other hand, the Romans complained of not having been supported by them in the Illyrian war.

In the first campaign of Sulpicius (553), the Romans could do nothing: they took the bull by the horns, and attacked Macedon from Illyria. Philip kept on the defensive. That part of Illyria, as far as Scutari, is a country of rather low hills, very much like Franconia; in many places it is flat. On the eastern frontier, near Macedon, a ridge of high mountains runs down, which takes in western Macedon, and from Scodrus, or Scardus, reaches southwards to Pindus and Parnassus. This range of mountains, lofty and broad, cold, barren, and naturally poor, is now hardly inhabited any longer; even the valleys are inhospitable. Here are the highlands of Macedon, the true home of the earliest Macedonians, who had formerly held under their own liege-lords, being dependent upon Philip, but at that time were entirely united with Macedon. The Romans found every thing here against them: nearly the whole of the population, consisting as it did of Macedonians, was hostile with the exception of the Epirote Orestians, and provisions were scarce everywhere. Sulpicius therefore retreated, and passed the winter in the fertile country of lower Illyria, near Apollonia and Epidamnus. However carefully historians may disguise the fact, certain it is that his undertaking was a complete failure.

T. Quinctius Flamininus, immediately after his being made consul, in the year 554, led reinforcements across the Adriatic, and changed the whole plan. This time also, the Macedonians had fortified their frontiers, and they kept on the defensive. The principal camp of the king was near what is now Argyrocastro, the old Antigonea, founded by Pyrrhus, where the Aous—so we must read instead of Apsus, in Plutarch's life of Flamininus—has worn its way between two high ridges of limestone: both these mountain ranges are wild and impassable; they stretch out on one side as far as the Acroceraunian heights, on the other towards Pindus. The place cannot be mistaken from its very nature (*fauces Antigoneæ*); even to this day, the true road from Illyria into the interior of Epirus passes through it, part of which, on the brink of the river, is cut in the mountains. The Romans had renewed their alliance with the Ætolians, who took up arms and threatened the frontier of Thessaly, but undertook nothing of consequence. Philip was much bent on hindering the Ætolians, now that they were the allies of the Romans, from attacking the Thessalian frontiers in right earnest, and uniting with them; and this he effected by taking up his position near Antigonea. Before this defile, Villius also who, when Flamininus arrived, was still in Greece, had during his proconsulship stood his ground against Philip; yet it was hopeless to attack him in front, and several attempts had miscarried. Perhaps the Romans expected that the Ætolians would compel the Macedonian army to change their position, as otherwise it would be incomprehensible why they should have encamped in that place.

Flamininus, who now entered upon the consulship, was a distinguished man, and had moreover been chosen by the people before he was thirty years old, owing to their confidence in his personal qualities. It is indeed a proof of the utter falsehood of the notion that the Romans had only in later times sought to make themselves acquainted with Greek literature, when we find it distinctly stated of men like Flamininus that they were imbued with Greek learning. His conduct towards Greece is not indeed to be approved of in every respect; but he was provoked, when his noble attempt to win her applause, was darkened by the ingratitude of a nation which was already partly degenerated. Had the Greeks been able to suit themselves to the actual state of things, they might have been spared many a sad experience. Flamininus became convinced that it was necessary to try and drive the Macedonians from their vantage ground, and he attained his end by means of that faithlessness then so general in Greece. He tampered with a chieftain belonging to the Epirote republic of the name of Charops; and the latter, being gained over by money and promises, undertook to lead a small Roman division of four thousand men through unknown roads to the rear of the Macedonian army. The Romans did not indeed trust their guides, and they carried them bound along with them; but no treachery was committed, and on the third day they reached the heights above the Macedonians. That day had been appointed for the attack. At sunrise, Flamininus began the battle in front, and thus engaged the attention of the Macedonians; he had already lost a great many men, when the detachment which had gone round the Macedonians, gave the signal with fire from the heights. He now renewed the attack with redoubled vigour: the other Romans fell upon the Macedonians from the rear, and these were panic-struck and fled; so that the Romans by one blow became masters of Epirus, where all the towns opened their gates to them. Philip escaped across mount Pindus into Thessaly. Flamininus did not follow, as he wished first to take advantage of these circumstances, entirely to drive the Macedonians out of Greece. But an expedition to Thessaly had no great results. He united with the Ætolians in Ambracia, and took up his winter-quarters in Phocis, where he besieged the strong town of Elatea.

During the campaign, the combined fleet of Attalus, the Rhodians, and the Romans, was in the Greek seas; they made several undertakings, which, however, led to nothing but the ravaging of unhappy Greece. Thus Chalcis, once so flourishing, was destroyed and pillaged. The Achæans had before been obliged to give up Megara and Corinth to Philip, who had likewise kept Orchomenus without asking their leave; at a later period only, that is to say at the beginning of the second war, he gave it back to them. Had he now after his defeat, likewise restored to them Corinth, they would hardly have forsaken him; for they had an implacable hatred against the Ætolians, and also against the Romans on account of the savage devastations of the former war. But now that Philip had not been able to stand his ground, and all the country as far as Thermopylæ was in the hands of the Romans, the Macedonian party, although certainly still considerable, could not come forward, and the proposal was discussed of concluding an alliance with the Romans. Roman ambassadors appeared at Sicyon; the Achæan strategus Aristænus, a shrewd statesman, took advantage of the disposition which was felt by many to yield to sense and reason, and to dwell on the injuries suffered from Philip; and he got the alliance with him dissolved, though not without difficulty, and another one concluded with the Romans. The restoration of the places of which Philip had stripped them, was promised; Nabis and the Ætolians were not to exercise any hostility against them. It was no longer possible, as Demosthenes once had done, to lead the nation by inspired eloquence and high feeling, but shrewdness had its effect. The Achæans were not warlike, although Philopœmen had done everything he could to make them so. The war with Macedon was very irksome to them; for, although there was only a small Macedonian garrison stationed at Corinth, yet it was able by its allies to do much harm to the neighbouring places in the Peloponnesus. The governor of Corinth, Philocles, even took Argos.

In the meanwhile, Flamininus called upon the Bœotians to enter into the league with Rome; yet they showed themselves wavering, as after a hundred and forty years of the Macedonian yoke, it seemed impossible that that power should have been suddenly broken. It was only by what was almost a stratagem, that Flamininus managed to bring them to that alliance (555). The proconsul (Flamininus' consular year had expired, but his *imperium* had been prolonged) appeared before Thebes, and demanded to be let in, that he might negotiate; now he had brought soldiers with him, who came forward whilst he was before the town, and so he marched in without asking leave. The decree which the Bœotians still made, was now but a mere form: there was, however, also a Macedonian garrison in the place.

One hundred and twenty-five years had passed away since the death of Alexander; the proud waves had gone down, and the Greeks no longer deemed themselves to be the people which alone had been called to rule the world. They no longer thought Macedonians upstarts, but they beheld in them their protectors against the Gauls, Scordiscans, Thracians, and other Northern peoples; they looked up to the Macedonian court; Macedonian money also did its work; in short, they acknowledged their leadership. Nor did they indeed any more reckon them to be barbarians. At Pella, Greek was no doubt as much spoken as Macedonian; at court, and among all the educated classes, it was the language in vogue; so that the difference between Hellenes and Macedonians had by this time been effaced.

Before the new campaign had begun, but when the Achæans had already declared against him, Philip sought to negotiate. He would not, however, yield to the demand of the Romans that he should evacuate the whole of Greece; and so determined again to try his luck in war, as he had become much more spirited in the course of his reign. These negotiations failed, and the hostile armies marched against each other in the year 555. Thessaly was the natural scene of the campaign of this year, in which Philip had put forth all his strength. If what Livy tells us of his levy be true, and he was indeed able to raise but so small an army, then must the Gauls have dreadfully visited his country. But the statement does not seem to be correct; for if Macedon had any thing of a population, it must easily have furnished a hundred thousand men. The Romans took the field, reinforced by the Ætolians; no other allies are spoken of, and the Ætolians themselves are said not to have been more than a few thousand foot and four or five hundred horse, unless this be another mistake; altogether, we are told, the army of Flamininus consisted of twenty-six thousand men and a small body of horse. The struggle began rather early in the year. The harvest in Thessaly is gathered in about the middle of June, and by that time the battle of Cynoscephalæ must have taken place; for the corn was ripe, but not yet cut, so that the soldiers, when foraging, had only to reap it. The Romans and Macedonians, who were each advancing, fell in with each other at a spot where they were separated only by a range of low hills. This was on the borders of the Thessalian plain, at which the Phthiotic hills gently slope away into Thessaly proper. Here the two armies were marching in the same direction, without knowing it, each believing the other to be far behind: the object on both sides, was to take up their quarters wherever they might find provisions, and they wished to avail themselves of the ripe corn. Both were on their way to Scotussa. It had rained the day before, and in the morning there arose a thick fog; so that they scarcely saw the hills along which they were marching to the right and left, and the Romans chanced to hit upon one which the Macedonians were about to ascend. Philip had no wish whatever to fight; the Roman general also would rather have chosen another battle-field, as the country thereabouts was still too open: the force of circumstances, however, compelled them to engage. The Romans were already on the height when the Macedonians came up; but their number was small, and at first they were driven back, until they got reinforced. This took place on the left of the Macedonian army, and thus both generals became aware of the nearness of the enemy, and quickly sent troops to the help of their own men. With the support of the Ætolians, the Romans gained the upperhand on the hill; but this led the foe to make a grand attack upon them, and they were pushed down again by the whole of the Macedonian left wing. The Macedonians now thought themselves sure of victory, and Philip was obliged to risk a battle, lest he should damp the spirit of his soldiers. He therefore had only to choose the best line for their advance; and, what was bad for the Macedonian phalanx, he had to take up his position on the hill, where the moveable array of the Romans was much more efficient. The description of this battle in Polybius' fragments is masterly. The whole of the left wing had pressed forward, and had driven the Romans down the hill on the other side; but when the right wing had with great exertion ascended thither, the Roman left wing was already there before it, and thus was this part of the Macedonian army soon defeated. The Ætolian cavalry, to whom this success was owing, went in pursuit of the fugitives. On the left wing of the Romans, which had to encounter the phalanx, the struggle was undecided; at first, they had even the worst of it: the phalanx, which was once sixteen deep, and now fourteen, charged heavily with its immense masses and its terrible *sarissæ*, the rear ranks pushing those in front with almost irresistible force against the enemy. But the Romans wheeled half round to the right, and drove the Macedonians on the other side up the heights from which they had come down; and in this position, in which the phalanx was not able to move, the battle was won. There is no denying that the Romans owed their victory mainly to the Ætolian cavalry: the rout of the phalanx was the work of these alone. Philip had a narrow escape. The Macedonians lifted up their lances in token of submission; but the Romans, who did not understand this signal, fell upon them, and thus most of them were killed, and the rest taken prisoners. After this overthrow, in which the loss of the Macedonians, according to the lowest estimates, those which Polybius gives, was eight thousand killed, and five thousand prisoners, Philip fled to Larissa, and from thence to Tempe. He had led the whole of his forces into the field, so that he had no reserve left: this was his fatal mistake. He therefore began to negotiate, and after two vain attempts, a truce was agreed upon: he was to send ambassadors to Rome, and in the meanwhile to furnish supplies to the Roman army, and to pay a contribution.

The Romans were inclined to peace, as there had begun to be much ill-blood between them and the Ætolians. These had plundered the Macedonian camp after the battle of Cynoscephalæ, and in consequence dissension had arisen. The Romans were in much greater numbers in that fight than the Ætolians; but the cavalry of the Ætolians had indeed decided the victory, and moreover, in the beginning these had stood the brunt of the battle on the heights, by which the Romans were enabled to make an orderly retreat. As there was no blinking these arguments, the Ætolians, even if they had not been a vain people, might very well have taken to themselves the honour of the victory; and this indeed they did in a way which gave great offence to the sensitive Flamininus, who therefore, immediately after the day was won, tried to cut them out of all its advantages. Throughout the whole of Greece, the Ætolians were sung of as conquerors, and the Romans with their consul looked upon only as auxiliaries: there came out at that time a fine epigram still extant of Alcæus of Messene on the victory of Cynoscephalæ, full of scorn against Philip, in which it is said in plain words that the Ætolians, and with them the Latins under T. Quinctius, had beaten the Macedonians, and that thirty thousand Macedonians had been slain. This insolence the Greeks had dearly to pay for, as Flamininus was provoked by it; yet it would have done them still greater mischief, had any other than he been general. It is difficult to form an idea of the blind infatuation of the Ætolians,—a people, whose territory was not larger than the canton of Berne, and who yet could have been mad enough to think themselves the equals of the Romans: one of their generals, who had a quarrel with Flamininus, told him, that arms would decide it on the banks of the Tiber. The only clue for this is in the character of the southern nations, who, though unable to do anything, fancy that they can do everything. Even so it was with the Spaniards in their relations with the English: they are always talking of the immortal day of Salamanca, on which they beat the French, whereas they did not lose more than one man in that battle. And thus did the Ætolians, without any substantial cause, become at variance with the Romans. It is true that Flamininus was too irritable: he ought to have treated this with contempt, as his mission to give freedom to Greece was such a fine one. Nor were the Romans by any means just to the Ætolians: by the original conditions, these had a right to claim the restoration of all the places which had been taken from them by Philip; but the Romans decided against them, and they either kept the places themselves, or embodied them with other states, or else they left them independent. This would not have happened, unless there had been indeed some provocation; but it made the Ætolians quite furious.

It was, of course, the policy of the Romans, to restore Greece in such a manner, that the separate nations should balance each other. The peace was concluded in 556, and a most mortifying one for Philip it was. By its terms he was limited to the kingdom of Macedon, which, however, was larger than the old one of that name, as it reached as far as the Nestus, taking in part of Thrace, and many Illyrian and Dardanian tribes, and he had to give up all his places in Greece and on the Thracian coast, and all his conquests in Asia Minor and Caria: these last ought to have been restored to Ptolemy; yet, for appearance's sake, they got their freedom. Moreover, he had to bind himself to keep no more than five thousand men as a standing army, and only five galleys, and his royal ship; to pay a thousand talents in ten years; and also to give hostages, among whom was his own son Demetrius.

Of this peace the Romans made a generous use. It would be hardly fair to search keenly into their reasons for it; yet it was perhaps that they might leave no vantage ground to Antiochus. Flamininus himself seems to have had very pure motives. The whole of Thessaly, the countries south of Thermopylæ, and the three fortresses, Acrocorinth, Chalcis, and Demetrias, were in the occupation of the Romans, and it was now a question what was to be done with them. Men were not wanting, who never would have sacrificed the positive advantage of the moment for the sake of a fair fame, and who strongly urged that these three places, with some others besides, should still be retained, so as to ensure the dependence of Greece; but Flamininus declared himself against this, and so effectually, that Corinth, the citadel of which had as yet been provisionally held by the Romans, was now already restored to the Achæans. This was the more nobly done, as not only the Ætolians, but also the Achæans, with Philopœmen at their head, claimed to be equal with the Romans; so that it certainly cost Flamininus a struggle with himself to follow his generous impulse. It was lucky for the Greeks, that, in spirit and education, he was a Greek, to which the epigrams on his votive gifts also bear witness.

On the day of the Isthmian games, the decision of the senate was to be made known, from which people expected different things according to their different dispositions. An immense throng was gathered together at Corinth; and there, in the theatre, Flamininus had the decree of the senate proclaimed, by which freedom was granted to all the Greeks. This beautiful moment of enthusiasm gave Greece fifty years of happiness. In the history of the world, fifty years are a long period,—not long enough indeed for a man to go down to his grave without having lived to see evil times; yet to many the sad experience of early youth was requited by a cheerful old age.

The Ætolians did not rejoice with the rest, neither did Nabis of Lacedæmon. The alliance with the latter was a disgrace to Rome. He had made it a condition that he should keep Argos, which he had got Philip to sell to him, and Flamininus was afterwards glad indeed to lay hold of an opportunity of setting aside the treaty, and of waging war against him. Livy is here very explicit, as he copies from Polybius, to whom these events had a peculiar interest. In this war, the tyrant showed himself to be not without ability; but he would have been crushed and Sparta taken, had not Flamininus, guided no doubt by his instructions, followed the baneful policy of not wishing to rid Greece of this source of apprehension, in order that the Achæans might be obliged to make great efforts, and thus want the help of Rome. A large part of Laconia, the district which is now called Maina, was wrested from the grasp of the tyrant, and formed into an independent state, inhabited by the former periœcians; the Achæans got Argos; and Nabis had to pay a war-contribution of a hundred talents down, and of four hundred more within eight years, and also to give his son as a hostage. This did not last long. When Flamininus was absent, the Achæans took advantage of a riot in which Nabis was slain, to unite Sparta with the rest of the Peloponnesus; which was very disagreeable to the Romans, but at that time could not be helped.

The two fortresses, Chalcis and Demetrius, the Romans bound themselves to evacuate, as soon as their affairs with Antiochus stood on a firm footing. Thessaly was made much larger than it had hitherto been;

joined with Phthiotis, it formed the Thessalian republic: on the other hand, Perrhæbia and some other districts were detached from it. Orestis, which had fallen away from Macedon, was proclaimed free, and probably united with Thessaly, as I conclude from the list of the Thessalian generals. Magnesia became independent. Eubœa, Locris, Acarnania, Bœotia, Phocis, Athens, Elis, Messene, and Lacedæmon became separate states; the rest of the Peloponnesus and Megara were Achæan. Whilst, however, the Romans called themselves the liberators of Greece, they, in spite of principles which they had publicly professed, yielded up Ægina to Eumenes, the son of Attalus. Athens, down to the times of Sylla, was treated by Rome with peculiar favour: never were the Muses so beneficial to any people. The Romans gave them Scyros, Delos, Imbros, Paros.

THE INSUBRIANS AND BOIANS VANQUISHED. WAR WITH ANTIOCHUS. WAR WITH THE GALATIANS

We have now reached much beyond the times of the development of the constitution at home, and the rest of the history has not for us the same interest which it had for the ancients. Even the wars are losing that grand character which arose from the display of native energy. What sort of a subject for description, for instance, is the battle of Magnesia, in which a well-ordered Roman army came off victorious over a horde of eastern barbarians, which did not even deserve the name of army? Some wars, like the Cimbric, form an exception. Livy from henceforth becomes more and more diffuse; for he had other interests in his history, and more than two-thirds of his work are taken up by the two centuries which now follow. We are going to adopt just the opposite plan, and are able to be more and more concise.

The Insubrians had risen against the Romans. During the second Punic war, they had been quiet; except in the first years, they took no part in it, as the scene of operations was in general too far distant from them, and they kept up but little communication with Hannibal. But now they were in arms, and the Romans met with peculiar difficulty, owing to Hamilcar, an enterprising Carthaginian who had remained behind from Mago's army, and had organised the Ligurian and Gallic forces. The Insubrians were very different from the Boians: the former made their submission after one or two campaigns; but the war with the latter lasted to the tenth year. They defended themselves with distinguished bravery, and they destroyed the fortresses of Placentia and Cremona; for they knew that the Romans were carrying on against them a war of extermination, and they therefore fought with all the energy of despair. Historians do not state as explicitly as a fragment of Cato does, that they were utterly rooted out. The fate of this people is remarkable. After their emigration from Gaul, they had either turned themselves to Italy, or had gone to the Danube: in Gaul, their seats are now hardly known; in the country near the Danube, they were probably exterminated in the Cimbric war, and hence the *desertum Boiorum* (*Böheim*, Bohemia), which was afterwards occupied by the Marcomanni: in Italy they are said to have had a hundred and twelve cantons. That in Italy they were extirpated, and that there could therefore have been no question about them, was not at all understood by the jurists who have written on the *lex de Gallia Cisalpina*. But all the Celts south of the Po were destroyed, and the whole of their land taken up by Roman colonies: Bologna, Modena, Parma, and also Lucca, were founded at that time, and received a considerable territory. Yet even in the days of Polybius, that country was nearly without inhabitants, and it was repeopled only by slow degrees. The *Lex Julia* united the Cispadana as to political rights with Italy.

At the close of the war with Philip, the Ætolians were filled with the most envenomed resentment. This bitterness of feeling was by no means softened down in the course of time; for the Ætolians made too great pretensions, and the Romans were unfair towards them. Yet even without that, they would have moved heaven and earth to drive the Romans out of Greece. They therefore turned their eyes towards Antiochus.

Antiochus is one of those princes, who unjustly bear in history the surname of the Great. The Seleucidæ were poorer in great men than any of the dynasties which succeeded Alexander; even Seleucus himself hardly deserved to be so called: the Asiatic degeneracy shows itself in them much earlier than among the Ptolemies. Antiochus got that surname because his reign was happy: compared with the princes of his house who had the same name, Antiochus Soter, and the utterly infamous Theos, his grandfather and great-grandfather, he may have been the better man. He certainly restored his empire, which had come to him almost in a state of dissolution from his brother Seleucus; but he did this without any grand achievement of his own, as he only put forth against his cowardly enemies the comparatively great might of his dominion. He had no real difficulties in his way, and those, which he had to face, he did not overcome like a great man. He might have called himself εὐτυχής; for before his war with the Romans he had a more extensive monarchy than the kings of Syria had ever possessed. He ruled from the Hellespont to the borders of India, over Phrygia, Cilicia, Syria, Palæstine, Cœle-Syria, Mesopotamia, Kurdistan, Media, Persia as far as Sidgistan and Cabool; he had made treaties with Indian princes, and his riches were immense: but with all this, there was nowhere the vigour of a warlike state, but Asiatic effeminacy throughout. His strength had not been put to the proof. The descendants of the Macedonians and Greeks in the colonies of Alexander and Seleucus, had become quite unwarlike; just as the *Pullani* (the offspring of the crusaders) in the Holy Land, a set of people with all the vices of the east without its virtues. Yet, as he possessed the whole extent of the Persian empire, Antiochus was looked upon in Asia as the μέγας βασιλεύς, and in Europe, as the terrible adversary of the Romans: the Ætolians therefore built great hopes on him.

It was natural that Hannibal should turn himself towards this prince, and try to stir him up to a war against Rome; although as things then were, he did not wish to begin it at once, especially as he had the prospect of still remaining for a long time in the prime of life. The Romans had, since the war with Philip, entered into negotiations with Antiochus, which, however, led to nothing: it was a step, such as they had often taken before, as they would risk an enterprise, and not mind if it miscarried. When leagued with Philip, Antiochus had gained the Egyptian possessions in Asia Minor, and he dreamt of nothing less than of extending his empire to Europe. Philip, in consequence of his peace with the Romans, had been obliged to abandon the towns which he had conquered from the Egyptians; these were exposed to the inroads of the savage Thracian tribes, and they called upon Antiochus for help. This prince also meddled in the feuds in the Chersonesus, and restored Lysimachia which had been destroyed by the Thracians. But the Romans forbade him to set his foot in Europe; they declared that they would never let him overstep the natural boundaries of his empire, in which they very wisely kept to this undefined expression: he was also to acknowledge the independence of the Greek towns in Asia,—this was a piece of immense presumption, put forth by those who wanted a war. Antiochus refused; and thus the negotiations were carried on for four years, during which he fortified Lysimachia and the Chersonesus as the outworks of Asia. He also fitted out a fleet, for which he possessed the most ample resources, having taken the Phœnician coast from the Ægyptians, and being likewise master of Cilicia and Pamphylia. In Greece the Ætolians were on his side; but the Rhodians were decidedly against him, as they were allies of the Egyptians, and though not actually leagued with the Romans, yet on terms of such good understanding with them, that it came nearly to the same thing.

Antiochus had not always his abode at Antioch; he had at that time chosen the beautiful city of Ephesus for his capital: thither Hannibal came, and was received with the greatest distinction. The latter, who had passed the first years after the conclusion of the second Punic war in his native city, had by no means given himself up to despair: he soon showed himself, after the peace, to be as great as during the war. He had been made Suffete, a term which we also find in the Book of Judges, meaning the head of the state in peace; and though this was a dignity which had not any longer much weight, as the ruling power in Carthage was already seriously paralysed by the democratical element, while in office, he by his ability had given it its former influence. He reformed abuses of every kind,[33] and turned his attention particularly to the finances, in which he had found out an immense deficit, as the great men had helped themselves to all the good things: in short, he brought with him new life and new hopes into his native city. But the more he laid abuses bare, the faster grew the party of the traitors, who at that time were to be met with in Carthage as well as in all the states,—a set of men who sought their own individual power, whilst sacrificing their country to the Romans. The latter, who, to use Livy's fine expression, had made peace with Carthage, but not with Hannibal, looked upon him with great mistrust; which was very natural, as his only thought was to raise his country. Rome had long ceased to be a conscientious state; her unsullied moral purity, which in her earlier days was far from being a mere dream, was quite gone, and just when she had the power, and therefore the opportunity of acting uprightly, she broke all the laws of honour and virtue. The Romans had already more than once complained of Hannibal; and now they regularly charged him with the design of preparing war, and demanded that he should be given up to them. This embassy, however, was not set on foot without the strongest opposition from the great Scipio, who denounced such conduct as unworthy, as shameful indeed. But before the Carthaginians had come to a resolution which would perhaps have been wrung from them, Hannibal fled to Antiochus, the king of Syria.

Hannibal was startled, when he saw the state of the Syrian troops. He found a host, of which the great mass were barbarians, which though apparently trained in some measure to the Macedonian way of fighting, was unsound to the core, and quite as cowardly as under the Persian rule: it was only from single divisions of such an army that he could expect anything. But his plan was worthy of him. He advised Antiochus to bestow his greatest exertions on the fleet, and by means of it to carry the war into Italy; the picked troops and those which he himself still hoped to train, might then be embarked on it and landed in southern Italy, which was so exasperated against Rome on account of the revenge which she had taken. Greece he should not touch; for that would irritate Philip, to whom he should rather leave it, and seek to aggrandize himself in Egypt. But it was natural that men of small minds should reject this plan; and it was resolved to transfer the war to Greece, where the Ætolians were their allies, and to try and gain over Philip. The latter plan was the more hazardous, and in fact quite impracticable, owing to the folly which the advisers of Antiochus displayed in all that they did: they wished to work upon Philip, not by fair means only, but also by fear. Thus at the very moment, when everything turned upon Philip's goodwill being won, a pretender, who gave himself out to be a descendant of Alexander the Great, and who had been with the Acarnanians in Epirus, was received at Ephesus as the rightful sovereign of

Macedon: they even fostered the fond hope of bringing about a revolution there. This was childish folly. As matters now stood, Hannibal gave his advice against war; and this was accounted to him as treachery, and the wretched king with his wretched councillors so thoroughly misunderstood this great man as to think him capable of playing into the hands of Rome. In this belief they were confirmed by a stratagem of the Romans by which bad men only could have been taken in. Scipio was sent over to Asia for a last negotiation with Antiochus. He and Hannibal were personally acquainted, and two such great men passed lightly over the circumstance of their having faced each other as enemies. They were not mere tools of the state; but they were as two great moral powers arrayed against each other, which after a mighty struggle had made peace, and not as ordinary men. In such cases, there is kindled in truly great souls a mutual love. They met familiarly, and Hannibal was thus led to offer hospitality to Scipio, which the latter said that he would have accepted, had not Hannibal been dependent on an enemy of Rome. Scipio was perhaps less frank in this conversation than Hannibal, and he may have taken advantage of him: this may have contributed to make Hannibal suspected.

When it became known, that the Romans began to arm, the Ætolians demanded that Antiochus should come over with his forces to Greece. Hannibal saw that Antiochus was running to his destruction, if he undertook the war with his present means; and he told him, that he must gain over Philip, and if possible, the Egyptians. Yet there were great difficulties in the way of these alliances. If Philip united with the Ætolians, the Achæans were thrown into the arms of the Romans. Philip also was angry, because Antiochus had not supported him in his war; and moreover, should everything turn out most favourably, the object of Antiochus was no other than to conquer Greece: if it therefore became possible to weaken Rome, the Macedonians thereby merely got another dangerous neighbour. Thus the negotiations did not advance matters; and if Antiochus had been wise, he would not have listened to the blind rage of the Ætolians, and he would have been aware of their insignificance: but he thought them to be a great nation.

The preparations were made with so little method, that Antiochus had no more than ten thousand men ready to embark. The Ætolians, who expected an innumerable army, had likewise described their own power as much larger than it really was; so that he was highly astonished to find that they had scarcely four thousand men. He landed at Demetrias, which, as we shall see, was already evacuated by the Romans, and now occupied by the Ætolians. He now reduced Phthiotis, and passed over to Eubœa, and made himself master of the strong town of Chalcis. It was fated that the

Romans should be justified in their unwillingness to intrust their fortresses to the Greeks, who did not know how to behave. From thence he went on to Bœotia, where he was joyfully welcomed, to Phocis, and into Thessaly. This last country had been converted by the Romans into a republic; yet it had never known how to govern itself, and owing to its having been so long dependent on Macedon, it had become quite unable to take care of its own affairs: the Magnesians and Phthiotes had been detached, and formed into an independent state. He met with a good reception on both sides of mount Œta, and here he made fresh acquisitions. This was the critical moment: had Philip energetically declared himself, the Romans would have been driven back as far as Illyricum. But Philip was diverted from it by the Romans. He saw that the war had been begun with so little judgment that there was not much to be expected from it: moreover, he had not himself acquired strength enough, and he knew well, that if the issue were unfavourable, he should fare the worst; and if he were to wait awhile, he might hope that the Romans would crush his enemies the Ætolians, whilst his position would be none the worse, and then he might quietly abide his time when the Greeks would begin to be hostile to the Romans. He therefore only took possession of the town of Demetrias, one of the three chief strongholds of Greece, which gave him the command of Thessaly. There must have been a secret treaty about it with the Romans; for it henceforth remained Macedonian until the fall of that empire, without its evacuation having been called for. The district of Magnesia was also incorporated with Macedon.

In the war of Nabis already, a bitterness of feeling between the Romans and Achæans had begun to show itself: the latter were mistrustful, because the Romans had not yet withdrawn their garrisons from the Acrocorinth, Chalcis, and Demetrias. But as Antiochus was approaching, of whose power quite an exaggerated opinion was entertained, the Romans were wise enough now to remove those garrisons. The other Greek states likewise fell off one by one from Rome, and there was everywhere a Roman and a Macedonian party. Flamininus now sullied his fair fame by allowing the faction devoted to himself and to the Romans in Bœotia to murder the leader of the Macedonian faction, and by screening the guilty from justice. The Achæans were still his friends, but very negative ones: they did not wish to join themselves with the Ætolians.

Antiochus and the Ætolians had now on both sides their eyes opened with regard to the expectations which they had entertained of each other. Hannibal, who from the very first had been a prophet of evil, was now called in. This is the usual fate of great men. So long as one is doing well, and one can still follow their advice, they are not listened to; but if one has got into trouble by acting against it, then are they charged with obstinacy, if they declare that nothing any more is to be done. Hannibal could only propose that they should renew the attempts to gain over Philip. But the latter had already concluded his alliance with Rome, hoping thereby to regain Thessaly; at the same time, to him the thought was delightful of revenging himself on the Ætolians by means of a union with the Romans. Antiochus now ventured no more on any greater undertaking; but by the advice of his courtiers, he sought to employ the winter in making preparations in Asia. This, however, was only done to a small extent, and in the meanwhile he wasted his time in feasts at Chalcis. By the beginning of spring, a new consular army under M'. Acilius Glabrio, which was reinforced by the Macedonians, appeared in Thessaly, where it was opposed by no more than ten thousand Asiatics and a few Ætolians; and it encamped near Heraclea, whilst Antiochus occupied Thermopylæ, just the reverse of what happened in the days of the Persians: for this time it was the Asiatics, though indeed these were half-Macedonians, who in their turn defended the pass. The Achæans had now again decidedly joined the Romans, and they did them good service. That the pass at Thermopylæ could be turned, unless Œta, over which there lay a path, were occupied as well, was then generally known already, as experience had twice shown it. The order to take two mountains which covered the defile, was given to old Cato, and to his friend L. Valerius Flaccus. The latter was unsuccessful; but the former got possession of the heights, and dashed into the enemy's camp along with the flying Ætolians, whilst M'. Acilius beat the Syrians in front. The army of Antiochus broke, and was scattered; he himself escaped to Chalcis, where a short time before he had been revelling in Asiatic luxury and childish festivities. That town he abandoned, leaving behind a weak garrison which made no stand against the Romans, who, however, did not pursue him; and he went to Asia. His fleet also, at the sight of a Roman one which had now arrived, sheered off to Asia Minor. Antiochus looked upon the war as ended; yet he gathered together a new army, and again gave himself up to his pleasures. There is no doubt but that he would have agreed to any peace, however indifferent it might have been.

M'. Acilius Glabrio now turned the war against the Ætolians. Heraclea and Lamia, on the Thessalian side of Thermopylæ, belonged to Ætolia Epictetus: the former of these was besieged by the consul, Lamia by Philip. The siege of Heraclea, where the main force of the Ætolians lay, was carried on with the utmost spirit, according to all the rules of military art. The town was taken by storm, and the garrison surrendered at discretion. The Ætolians now lost courage. Yet they were still saved by the eagerness of the Romans to pass over into the rich country of Asia, and to have done with this toilsome mountain war against a race which had nothing; and also by the anxiety of these that Philip should not gain his ends. When Lamia was about to fall, although without doubt possession of it had been promised to Philip, the consul sent him word, that he had made a convention for Lamia, and that therefore the king was to give up the siege. Hereupon Philip took no further share in the war, beyond reducing the Athamanians and the Dolopians.

The Ætolians would have been extirpated, had not the Romans themselves wished to have them preserved. The latter besieged Naupactus. Had they urged on this siege with true vigour and earnestness the town must have yielded; but they went to work sluggishly and with much forbearance, which enabled the Ætolians to save the place. The war ended with the siege of Ambracia, which at that time was Ætolian, and in the defence of which the little people of the Ætolians, though abandoned by all the Greeks, and without any great man to head them, displayed the highest gallantry. The siege is one of the most scientific in the whole of ancient history: the description of it is delightful, owing to the cleverness of invention, and the stedfastness of the besieged: it does one good to see physical weakness holding its own by means of skill. This defence does honour to the Ætolians, whose wars are otherwise not very glorious: it is of a somewhat later date (564). At length, peace was mediated by the Athenians. The Ætolians had to pay a few hundred talents as a war-contribution; to acknowledge the supremacy of Rome, and to bind themselves to follow the Romans in their wars; to evacuate Ambracia, and to give it up to them, as well as Cephallenia, which was taken and laid waste by the conquerors: a like fate had already befallen the Acarnanians. The peace was a hard one, yet under the circumstances fair enough. Thus the Romans gained possession of the country along the coast, and of the landing places in Greece.

Antiochus now confined himself to holding out with his fleet against the Rhodians and the ships of Eumenes, amongst which there were only a very few Roman ones. An unimportant battle was fought, in which these had the best of it; but after the fleets had separated, the Rhodians were shamefully deceived, surprised, and defeated by the Syrians. The Roman admiral, M. Æmilius Regillus, now came up with a new fleet of not more than eighty ships: the Romans were so little made for the sea-service, that they kept no fleet whatever, when they did not actually want one. Hence likewise, at least one half of their crews were then Rhodians; for these were the best seamen of the age, being yet in their prime, as in the best days of Greece. The fleet of Antiochus had been furnished almost entirely by the Phœnician towns, which, however, important as they were during the Persian rule, must now have very much gone down; and it was commanded by Hannibal. Yet though led by Hannibal, it was not able to effect a junction with another division, when a battle was fought near Myonnesus. The victory was altogether on the side of the Romans and their allies: the fleet of Antiochus was all but destroyed; the ships which were left, fled away into two harbours in Caria. This success had been achieved by the Rhodians; it was won, however, by means of fire, the Rhodians having engines on board their ships which hurled fire upon the enemy, most likely a kind of what was afterwards called Greek fire: it was not thrown with rockets, and from the way in which historians speak of it, this at least is certain, that the masses of it were quite extraordinary, and that it could not be quenched. This naval victory decided the war. Antiochus, by the advice of Hannibal, had meant to occupy the Chersonesus, which is joined to Thrace only by a narrow tongue of land about half a mile in length; on this lay Lysimachia, a well fortified town, from whence strong walls stretched out to the Melas Colpos and the Propontis, so that on the landside it could only be taken by a siege: one could land indeed at several places, but the Syrian fleet might have prevented it, and ought to have done so. He would then have been unassailable in Asia, so long as he chose to keep on the defensive. Yet such was the blindness of this king, that he sent Hannibal, as a hateful reminder of rejected counsels to Pamphylia, and banished him from his presence. It is possible that Antiochus by occupying the Chersonesus might have protected Asia, although he could not have kept it in the long run; but what was senseless, was his giving it up without making even so much as an attempt to defend it: the rich magazines there, which had been laid up for a long campaign, were abandoned to the Romans, and the garrisons withdrawn from the towns. He beguiled himself, or his subjects, with the thought that he should be able to make a stand behind the Hellespont; yet this coast also he forsook at the approach of the Romans, and fell back into Lydia. In the same way, the troops of Philip, which, even before Alexander's days, had set foot on those shores, were not hindered by the Persians from crossing.[34]

In the year 562, L. Scipio and C. Lælius were consuls. They both of them wished for the command of the expedition to Asia, and the senate gave it to Scipio, who would not, however, have gotten it, had not his great brother offered to serve as a legate under him. For the latter could not be appointed consul, as the law by which ten years were to elapse between two consulships of the same individual, was now very strictly adhered to. P. Scipio had in the meantime been censor, and his influence was still almost unbounded, as was plainly shown on this occasion, when L. Scipio, a most insignificant being, was chosen merely for the sake of his brother; just as the great Fabius Maximus in former times had procured the consulship for his son, under whom he then acted as legate. The Roman fleet had scarcely appeared off the coast of Asia, the Scipios being still in Macedonia, when ambassadors arrived from Antiochus, to ask for the conditions of peace. He offered to give up the Chersonesus; to acknowledge the freedom of the Asiatic towns, Smyrna and Abydos, which had been taken by the Romans; and to bear half of the expenses of the war. These conditions, coming from one who owned himself vanquished, the Romans did not accept: Scipio declared that they would have been good enough before Antiochus had evacuated the Chersonesus, but that now the bridle was put upon Asia. They marched through Macedon and Thrace over very difficult roads, aided, however, by Philip, whom they rewarded by giving up to him the possession of the towns on the Thracian coast. When the Romans had now crossed the Hellespont, P. Scipio fell sick, a thing which often happened to him, and as he was not able to follow the army, he was obliged to stay behind at Elæa, an Æolian town. This put a stop to all the operations, and Antiochus took advantage of the delay to set on foot fresh negotiations, which, however, led to nothing. Scipio proposed very fair terms; but they offended the pride of Antiochus. A son of the great Scipio had in some way or other been taken prisoner in Asia, and was treated with the greatest distinction. The ambassadors first offered to set him free; then Antiochus sent him back without ransom, hoping that it would now be easier for him to obtain peace. Scipio wished that a decisive battle might be put off until his recovery; Antiochus, on the other hand, was in a hurry to have it fought. The armies encountered on the borders of Lydia, near Magnesia, at the foot of mount Sipylus, in a country of moderately high hills, which is one of the finest in the world, being, like all the lands along the coast of Asia Minor, quite a contrast to the inland regions which are barren and devastated by volcanic convulsions. The army of Antiochus consisted of eighty thousand men, its chief strength being the Macedonian phalanx, which in all likelihood was made up of men of all countries: there were likewise some Macedonians among these, the descendants of the troops of Alexander, who, however, were already mingled in blood with the Asiatic population. Besides these, he had peltasts armed in the Greek manner, and a host of Asiatics, concerning whose arms and equipments Livy and Appian tell us nothing. The Romans had only a consular army, as the other was still fighting against the Ætolians: besides two legions and the proportionate number of allies, there were a few thousand Achæans, and a small number of auxiliaries from Eumenes (who only ruled over Pergamus and some Ionian and Mysian towns), the whole being much less than thirty thousand men. They had been advancing against each other for three days; on the fourth, the battle came on. The large army of Antiochus outflanked the Romans: their left wing rested on a river, which, however, had no depth, and thus they were outflanked on the opposite bank. The Syrian army consisted of the phalanx, of a medley of troops attached to it, of cavalry, elephants, and war-chariots. The Romans also had elephants, but African ones, which they did not use because they were far weaker, and much more timid than those of India. The battle was decided at the very first onset, the victory being contested for a moment, only by the mass of the Macedonian phalanx, and on one single point: on another, Antiochus drove the Roman troops back as far as their own camp, whereupon, however, he was repulsed. A good general might with the aid of the phalanx have given the Romans a great deal of trouble, as was still done at Cynoscephalæ; but all was lost by the king's wretched tactics. The phalanx at first was formed into a number of smaller bodies with intervals; and instead of their keeping that order, and acting together in masses, these gathered from fear into one huge cluster, which could have been of use only in a plain, and in extreme danger: but here, on uneven ground, there arose an immense confusion, in which the light troops of the Romans so harassed them with their javelins and slings, that they all broke and fled. Just as vain had been the attempt, in the beginning of the battle, to use the scythed chariots against the Romans, whose skirmishers put them to flight, as the horses were soon made to shy: this is an Asiatic invention, but it is also to be found among the Celts, especially in Britain. The overthrow was so complete, that it was impossible to bring together again the small remnants of the army. The king fled through Phrygia, and sent Xeuxis as his ambassador to Scipio to beg for peace, stooping at the same time to the meanest offers. Scipio was glad to come to terms. It is possible that L. Scipio received also some presents, which was the charge afterwards brought against him; yet there is no need for supposing this, as a Roman consul could not have wished for anything better than to make peace before the coming of his successor. The conditions were, as follows:—Antiochus was at once to pay down five hundred talents (675,000 dollars) for the truce;[35] the definitive peace was to be settled in Rome, and as soon as it was concluded, he was again to pay two thousand five hundred: this latter condition, very likely by accident, is never mentioned again. Then he was to pay twelve thousand talents (16,200,000 dollars) in yearly instalments of one thousand each, and to give twenty hostages, among whom was his own son. He was to place at the disposition of the Romans the whole of the country on this side of the Taurus which belonged to him, that is to say, Asia Minor with the exception of the two Cilicias north of the Taurus, the Halys was to be the boundary. Thus Antiochus was to yield up all that he possessed in Phrygia. It was afterwards a moot point, whether Pamphylia was also included therein: Livy and the fragments of Polybius throw no light upon it, and, on the whole, the geography of these countries is very obscure; as far, however, as I can understand Appian, Pamphylia did not remain under the rule of Antiochus, nor was it bestowed upon Eumenes, but it existed as an independent state between both. Moreover the king was not to meddle with the affairs of Europe without leave from Rome, nor to wage war with nations which were allies of the Romans, unless he were attacked; he was to give up his ships of war, even the triremes, all but ten; to keep no elephants; to enlist no mercenaries from countries which were subject to the Romans; to pay a specified sum to Eumenes; and also to deliver up Hannibal, and some others whom he had received at his court: (these last were added only for the sake of appearances, to give a good colouring to the demand for the surrender of Hannibal). But these made their escape. This happened in the year 562, the definitive peace being concluded somewhat later. A rashly undertaken war could have led by one battle to such a peace; but that a prince capable of making it should have been called the Great, is quite inconceivable: and yet he had still an immense empire, as large as Germany, France, and Spain put together.

In the following year, Cn. Manlius, the successor of L. Scipio, took the command, quite impatient to do something. This, and the hope of booty, led him in compliance with the wishes of the Asiatics to undertake a campaign against the Galatians or Gallo-Grecians in Phrygia. About the time of Pyrrhus, the Gauls overran Macedonia, and had forced their way as far as Delphi: then—whether moved, as the Greeks relate, by awful natural phenomena, or allured by the accounts which they had heard of the beautiful countries in Asia—they marched off out of Greece eastward to Thrace: there many of them remained, and established their rule in it; others, twenty thousand in number, crossed in two divisions, the one over the Hellespont, the other over the Bosporus, being favoured by the feuds of the Asiatic princes. Here they gained settlements in Ancyræan Phrygia, on the northern coast; just as in later times the Normans did in Neustria; and henceforth they lived in thirty free towns, in a land which is meant by nature to be the seat of the greatest wealth and happiness, but which now under the rule of barbarians has become a wilderness. There were three tribes of them, the Trocmi, Tolistoboii, and Tectosages, the two first of which seem to have been formed in the course of their migrations; for we do not meet with them elsewhere, as we certainly do with the third. They united themselves with the Bithynians, among whom two small kingdoms arose. The latter were Thracians, and they dwelt between Nicomedia and Heraclea: during the Persian domination, they were under their native princes; but after the breaking up of the Persian and the Macedonian empires, which had always been least consolidated in Asia Minor, they widened their sway, and became proportionally important. Nicomedes, who was then king, took the Gauls, among whom there were still but ten thousand armed men, into his pay; he defeated his rival, and founded the Bithynian state, which now became hellenized. From that time, the Gauls sold their aid to whosoever wanted it, and made the whole of western Asia tributary to themselves. This part of history is still very confused; but it may be disentangled, as we have many materials for it. They were defeated by Antiochus Soter, on which they withdrew into the mountains, and when circumstances had changed, they burst forth again: every one paid them tribute to escape their ravages. When the war broke out between Ptolemy Euergetes and Seleucus Callinicus, and afterwards between the former and Antiochus Hierax, they sold themselves, being thoroughly faithless, now to one now to the other, and they became the scourge of the whole of Asia, until to the astonishment of everybody, Attalus of Pergamus, refusing to pay them tribute any longer, attacked, and defeated them; which is only to be accounted for by the fact, that sloth had made them utterly effeminate and unwarlike; just like the Goths whom Belisarius encountered in Italy. From this blow they never quite recovered; yet they still retained considerable influence, as Asia was always divided, and although Antiochus was living in their neighbourhood, he was too busy notwithstanding to be able to protect that part of Phrygia which bordered on the country where they dwelt. They therefore went on raising tribute far and wide; and now, after the downfall of Antiochus, the Asiatic peoples were afraid that they should not be able to defend themselves: this gave Cn. Manlius an opportunity of taking the field as the defender of these against the Galatians. Those barbarians had answered his summons to yield, with a *stolida ferocia*. He marched through Phrygia, and attacked them in their mountains, without, however, exterminating them; they remained there, and retained the Celtic language for a remarkably long period, even down to the times of Augustus. By degrees they also hellenized themselves, and such we find them to have been in the days of St. Paul.[36] The war was most desirable for the inhabitants of Asia Minor; but thoroughly unjust on the side of the Romans. Cn. Manlius undertook it contrary to the expressed will of the *decem legati* who followed him. It was ended in two campaigns, and brought the Romans no other fruits but the booty and the sum of money which may perhaps have been paid; for the countries between western Asia and the land of the Galatians, were not the subjects, but the allies of Rome. The Gauls suffered such severe defeats, that thenceforth they lived quietly, and in subjection to the Romans.

The Romans now divided their conquests. Eumenes, who until then had had quite a small dominion, very much like that of a petty German prince, now became a great king. Mysia, Lydia, Phrygia on the Hellespont and Great Phrygia (the two were afterwards made one under the name of the kingdom of Asia, and the inhabitants were called Asians), Ionia with the exception of Smyrna, Phocæa, Erythræ, and some other Greek towns, which retained their freedom, became his. It was a great, and an enviable empire, but for all that a feeble one, owing to Asiatic effeminacy. The Rhodians got Caria and Lycia, with the exception of Telmissus which, heaven knows why, fell to the share of Eumenes. This was for a little republic an immense windfall, as these were fine rich countries, from which they might draw millions of our money: the taxes among the ancients were very heavy, and mostly on land, being a third of the whole produce. Revenues like these made the Rhodians very rich, and they spent them partly in armaments, and partly on the embellishment of their city, which, even without this, was already so beautiful. The Rhodians are a thoroughly respectable people; the Romans themselves acknowledged that they had none of the *levitas Græcorum* about them, but were quite their equals as to *severitas disciplinæ*.

IMPEACHMENT OF L. SCIPIO. END OF P. SCIPIO AFRICANUS AND OF HANNIBAL. DOMESTIC AFFAIRS. M. PORCIUS CATO

The contradictions which, according to Livy, were everywhere rife with regard to P. Scipio's end, are a remarkable instance of the way in which even impossible statements were got up; and we see from thence, that even at a time in which contemporary history was already written, when the work of Fabius was ended, and that of Acilius began, these accounts were very little substantiated. We do not know for certain the year in which Scipio died. What is quoted in Livy from the speech of Tib. Gracchus, must be deemed to be worth more than the stories of the annalists. There is no doubt that L. Scipio was once called upon in the senate by the Petillii to answer to the charge of having received sums of money from Antiochus, and of not having accounted to the republic for those which had been gained during the course of the war. This kind of impeachment is one of the earliest which we meet with among the Romans. The consuls might indeed freely dispose of the *manubia*; they might distribute them among the soldiers, or deposit them in the *ærarium*; but they were always to be ready to give account, as the Romans in money matters were very particular with regard to this point. L. Scipio sent for his books, and produced them in the senate; but his brother snatched them out of his hands and destroyed them, saying that it was a shame, when he and his brother had made the state so rich, to ask an account for such a trifle as a million of drachmæ. Thus 225,000 dollars were already then a trifle! Hereupon an impeachment was brought against P. Scipio; he spoke a few proud words, and then it was—which can hardly be otherwise than authentic—that he cried out, "This is the day that I conquered Hannibal at Zama, on which ye are always wont to offer sacrifice: let those who are well disposed, follow me." The tribunes alone are said to have staid behind. This accusation may perhaps be made to agree with the fact that Gracchus himself had wanted to have L. Scipio arrested, and that on this, when the prætor Terentius Culleo was about to try the case, P. Scipio had in all haste come up from Etruria, and rescued his brother from the beadles. And therefore as P. Africanus *plus quam civiles animos gerebat*, he too was impeached. He either did not wait for this prosecution, and retired to Liternum, a Latin colony, or *colonia maritima*, between Cumæ and Minturnæ, or he had lived there already before. Thus much is certain, that the last years of his life he did not pass in Rome. That he lived at Liternum in exile, and not for his own pleasure, becomes probable from the circumstance, that before his death, some one else was *princeps senatus*. Such an exile was easy to bring about; for, if he settled at Liternum as a citizen, he had thereby renounced the right of Roman citizenship.

L. Scipio, with his quæstor and legate, was found guilty of having embezzled the sum with which he had been charged. He was not addicted; but his property was seized by the state, and it is said not to have been sufficient to cover the demand. To conclude from thence that he was innocent, would be quite absurd; for he might have been a spendthrift in the meanwhile.

After the first Punic war, the number of the tribes had been raised to five and thirty, as a great part of the Sabines had acquired the full right of citizenship, and had formed two new tribes, the Quirina and Velina. This was nearly sixty years after the last increase, and thus, there were considerable signs already of a state of political stagnation. At the same time, perhaps as early as before the first Punic war, many towns were made præfectures with Cærite rights. During the second Punic war, there were four prætors; and while it yet lasted, their number was increased to six. Like Sicily, Spain now became a province; or rather, it was divided into two provinces, *Citerior* and *Ulterior*, to which two prætors were sent. Southern Italy had likewise taken the form of a province, owing to the war with Hannibal, and it continued as such for some time after: the prætor there was most likely in Tarentum or Bruttium. But Gaul was not yet reduced *in provinciæ formam*, and there was, of course, no prætor there. The greatest change, which reached deepest, and had the most lasting consequences, had been caused by the falling away of many peoples to Hannibal: they were punished, and the places which had belonged to them lost all the privileges of Italian allies; some were treated as conquered, their lands being either confiscated, or merely left to them on sufferance; others, who had submitted, had but met with forbearance. This was the fate of a great many places in Samnium and Apulia, which were severed from their communities. Those which had remained faithful, kept indeed their ancient constitution. As the Lucanians, in the war with Hannibal, had their own prætor whom they elected themselves, they may have still enjoyed this privilege; but all their subject towns which had revolted, were detached from them. The Bruttians, who had persisted the longest in their revolt, were altogether deprived of their constitution: they were mere *dediticii*, no more allies at all; they had some of them to become serfs, and the whole of their land was confiscated. It is uncertain, whether they had been formerly on the same footing with the Samnites and Lucanians: as being of Greek descent, they were most likely treated as foreigners, yet they had still held an honourable position, which was now gone. Tarentum lost all its rights, and lingered on forsaken within its own walls, until little by little it fell to nothing. This change among the allies, made it more difficult for those who remained to fulfil their engagements to Rome than before; and owing to the rebellion likewise, a bitter and long-lived hatred had grown up between Rome and many of the Italian peoples. And what had much exhausted the allies, was the drain upon their citizens, many of whom had taken advantage of the isopolity, to settle in Rome or in the colonies. Some of the Latin colonies, moreover, had neglected their duty, twelve out of thirty having furnished no contingent during the expedition of Hasdrubal; and now, when circumstances allowed of it, their rights were abridged. The traces of the war with Hannibal had never been done away: the Samnites, Apulians, and Lucanians had already been hardly dealt with before; Etruria alone found herself in a state of high prosperity. Many colonies were planted in the south of Italy, not so much for security's sake, as thus to provide for the poorer Romans. The veterans of Scipio's army were rewarded by a special grant of land in Apulia and Lucania, which is the first example known to us of a provision made for veterans on a large scale; if we had the second decade of Livy, we might perhaps discover some earlier instances, but indeed they can only have been single cases. The condition of Italy must have been one of extreme distress: the price of every thing was unnaturally high, and, owing to the heavy war-taxes, the middle classes must have been utterly impoverished. In the latter periods of the war, we meet with a public debt, which was repaid in three instalments; but the Macedonian war had so drained the exchequer, that the third instalment was made in public lands. The Roman people itself was affected in its very life's blood. The war had cost an immense host of men; and if notwithstanding the census now gives a like number, we have only a proof that in the meanwhile a crowd of foreigners, especially freedmen, had been received as citizens, and that thus the body of the Roman commonalty had become quite a different thing from what it had been before: those who had stood the war, were for the most part grown wretchedly poor. All this misery is not to be detected in Livy's narrative; but we know from other sources, that in Rome almost continual famine and epidemics were raging; many families had their estates in the Falernian country and in Campania, which districts were entirely laid waste; others which had possessed landed property in the revolted provinces, had lost their all; so that this struggle quite destroyed the wealth of the nation. The Greek towns, Croton and others, were never able to recover. Another consequence was, that the soldiers remained for years under arms; that the legions, which had been composed of men enlisted for a campaign, were converted into a standing army. This continued to be the case after the war; and the soldiers became accustomed to look upon themselves as a permanent order, which they had never been before, as the legions were disbanded every year, and newly raised the next. This condition of the preservation of republican freedom was now changed by the war with Hannibal, and thus were the seeds here sown of the later troubles. Owing to the great confiscations, immense landed estates had been gained, the possession of which was divided between the great men among the patricians and plebeians, as there was no one now to control them, and the Licinian law had become a dead letter.

At that time, not a soul actually thought of danger; yet the beginning of dissolution most decidedly existed already. It is said that, owing to the victories in Asia, luxury and its concomitant vices had spread; but this was an accidental symptom, the real cause lay deeper. After such long, savage, and destructive wars, in which so many deeds of outrage and ferocity had been wrought; in which the poor had become poorer and poorer, and the middle classes had gone down more and more, whilst the rich were crammed with wealth; many things must have changed for the worse. The same soldiers who formerly had earned glory under Scipio, and then as hungry plunderers went to Asia, enriched themselves immensely, and returned with ill-gotten treasures: they had no real wants, and did not know how to use their suddenly acquired riches. Even in the character of the great men, as in every thing else, we everywhere meet with a great alteration: the dismal spectacle of an utter degeneracy is already preparing itself. The generals appear like robbers; they carry on wars merely for the sake of pillage and booty, and the exceptions among them are few, and far between. The men of high rank are overbearing towards the allies: in former times a Roman magistrate, when travelling through Italy, would put up at the house of his own guest-friend, but it was now customary for such travellers to be everywhere received with pomp. The games were got up in a style and on a scale which required an immense fortune; in 580, there were at one funeral no less than a hundred and fifty gladiators: in the forum, banquets were given to the people. It was already the fashion to seek for choice specimens of art and luxury; the officers and the nobles filled their houses with furniture, tapestry, and plate of every description. A brutal expenditure of wealth got in vogue, a judicious and liberal use of riches being one of the most difficult things in the world. Thus, when several years ago, the inhabitants of Dittmarsch all at once made a great deal of money, it immediately gave rise to a sluttish wastefulness, until, before long, they were reduced again. The cooks, who hitherto had been the most despised of slaves at Rome, now became the most highly valued: in earlier times, the consul lived like the peasant; only the pontiffs, whose bills of fare we may still read in Macrobius,[37] were held to keep as good a table as the most dignified of canons. With the Athenians it was quite different. The Greek is naturally very temperate, and the Italian can be so too; but when the latter has an opportunity of feasting, he makes a beast of himself. Moreover, although the constitution was most democratical in appearance, yet we already see the overweening pride of the nobles on the increase: the rich were almost above punishment. L. Quinctius Flamininus, the brother of Titus, to amuse his catamite, caused a man who was either a convict, or a Gallic hostage, to be beheaded; for which Cato expelled him from the senate. And though fifty years afterwards, Polybius conscientiously places the Romans above the Greeks, peculation and extortions from the allies were notwithstanding very common, as we may see from an excellent fragment of Cato *de sumtu suo*, the gem of the collection of Fronto: it shows that towards the end of the sixth century, it was the general belief that the servants of the state seized upon every opportunity of feathering their own nests. All distinctions between the different orders had entirely ceased; the only thing looked to, was whether a man were noble or not, the patricians, as an order, having quite lost their importance. The last of their privileges, that one consul should always belong to one of the two orders, was done away with at the time of the war with Perseus, as the patrician houses were nearly extinct: for the ædiles only, this was still the rule, but in the case of the prætorship it was altogether abolished. It was, however, extremely difficult for a plebeian to rise, who was not of high rank: for only a few *novi homines*, like Cato, could make their way, and the whole of the nobility seem to have been in a league to check such intrusion.

On the other hand, the city was very much embellished. Stately buildings were erected, and instead of the courts of justice being held any longer with no other covering but heaven, as was done by our (German) forefathers, *basilicæ* were built. This name was derived from the στοὰ βασιλική under which the βασιλεύς at Athens used to sit: it was a triple portico in which the judges assembled in the open air, though not under the open sky. Cato was the first who built a *basilica* (Porcia) in the forum; by and by several others followed. They were afterwards enclosed with walls; and when the Christian religion was introduced into Rome, this form was deemed to be the one best suited to the Christian worship, as the different *stoæ* might be assigned as separate places, the men and the matrons being in the aisles on each side, and the clergy in the middle; at the tribunal, was the high altar, and the throne of the bishop. Hence the name of *basilica* was applied to all Christian churches, even when they were no longer in this form. The material of the buildings was still the old, simple one; the style, the ancient Doric or Tuscan: marble was not yet to be seen.

M. Porcius Cato is the most remarkable man of that age, he is quite a man of the old times: (the surname Priscus, however, merely indicates his Latin origin from Tusculum.) The account of him in Plutarch is excellent, as his life may be understood without any knowledge of the constitution, or deep insight into politics: nothing else was needed but a keen perception of individual character, which was Plutarch's strong point. Perhaps Rome never again gave birth to so original a genius as his. Whilst all around him had their science and erudition from Greece, Cato had it from himself; he learned Greek only late in life; his language, his style, his knowledge, were altogether Roman. A more versatile mind than his, the world has never known: he was a great statesman,—his censorship was a distinguished one,—an excellent agriculturist, an active man in every business of life, gifted with remarkable eloquence, which was pure nature, and not at all formed after artificial rules; and he was also a very eminent scholar, indefatigable in research, an excellent prose-writer in his own way, although harsh and uncouth. Livy, who otherwise is fond of him, applies to him in jest the phrase, *qui vivo eo* ALLATRARE *ejus (Scipionis) magnitudinem solitus erat.* His peculiarities were those of a man of low birth, who, being endowed with immense energy, had worked his way by dint of it through countless difficulties: all his life long, he kept up a feud with the nobles and the rich; he abhorred their manners from the bottom of his heart,—there was no affectation in it. The only one like him in feeling, was his colleague in the censorship and the tribunate, L. Valerius Flaccus. Cato was a fanatical Roman: he bore a hatred against every thing that was polished and elegant, his nationality therefore led him to dwell fondly on the past; he looked upon the men of his day as quite degenerate; his ideal dated a hundred years back, and with him the height of happiness was in simplicity, thriftiness, and stern morality. His constitution was of iron strength: in his eighty-sixth year, he still carried on a troublesome lawsuit; and even as late as in his ninetieth, he impeached Servius Sulpicius Galba. He stood up without flinching for Rome's supremacy; but at the same time he had an extraordinary sense of justice: though he did not like the Greeks, he yet defended the Rhodians, as he likewise did the Lusitanians against the perjury and the extortions of Galba. On the whole, he is very like the great German characters of the sixteenth century, in whom what is called coarseness by no means deserves that name.

Whilst Cato was almost the only really great man, virtue was then on the wane, and genius becoming more and more rare. The moneyed interest also in those days was already of great importance. Since the acquisition of Sicily, there had been a wide field opened for employment of capital; people went into the provinces to make their fortunes. In Rome, as by canon law, it was forbidden to take interest; yet the prohibition was unavailing, as ways and means were sought out of evading it. As in the middle ages business was done through the Jews, so in Rome it was carried on by means of foreigners and freedmen; and it was still more easily managed in the provinces, where there were none of these checks. And when the property (*publicum*) of the Roman state had grown immensely great, it became the custom to lease it out in single lots, such as the mines of Spain, the tithes of Sicily or Illyricum, or the tunny-fisheries on the Sardinian coast; so that those who farmed them made enormous profits, and many suddenly found themselves rich, as people now do by stock-jobbing. If a war-contribution were laid on a state, there was immediately a *publicanus* at hand, who advanced the money at twelve per cent. at the very lowest, but often at twenty-four, and even at thirty-six per cent.: the governors of the provinces then helped him to get paid. Thus a reckless circulation of money began, of which there had never been a trace before. The first signs of the class of the *publicani* are to be met with in Livy as early as in the war with Hannibal, and there are rather more in the decade which follows; these men did not, however, gain their extraordinary influence until nearly a hundred years afterwards, when in the nature and extent of their wealth they form a counterpart to the fortunes of the eighteenth century.

P. Scipio and Hannibal, according to the common account, died in the year 569, the latter by his own hand, as the Romans had basely called upon Prusias, the king of Bithynia, to yield him up. It happened that the extensive and wealthy state of Eumenes, who was in a sort of thraldom to the Romans, was so unwarlike, that the small kingdom of Bithynia was formidable to him; and the latter had spread, and had wrested from him a great part of Phrygia on the Hellespont. In this war, Hannibal directed the undertakings of Prusias, and forthwith Roman ambassadors demanded his surrender. The king was loth to arrest him; but he ordered his house to be surrounded by soldiers, that he might secure him until he had made up his mind whether he should give him up. When Hannibal saw that every way of escape was shut out from him, he swallowed poison and died. This demand of the Romans is one of the infamies of that age. But even in their brightest times, they would not have been more generous to an enemy like Hannibal, as is shown by the case of C. Pontius in the Samnite war. Hannibal had been unaccountably overlooked by the Romans for some years. T. Quinctius Flamininus lent himself to the office of getting him to be delivered up.

LITERATURE OF THE ROMANS AT THIS PERIOD. ATELLANÆ, PRÆTEXTATÆ; LIVIUS ANDRONICUS; NÆVIUS; ENNIUS; PLAUTUS. ROMAN HISTORIANS IN GREEK

We are by no means to fancy that the Romans, before they were acquainted with the Greeks, knew as little of Greek literature, as, for instance, our forefathers did at the time of the revival of learning, or that indeed they had had no literature whatever. The class of scholars and writers was then unknown; but the Romans, and all the Italian nations in general, were very well versed in Greek poetry. This is shown by their pictures and monuments of every kind, by the many representations of Greek fables on the vases of the Etruscans and other peoples, and by the idiomatic names of Grecian heroes which were current in Italy; for instance, Ulixes,[38] instead of Odysseus; Catamitus, instead of Ganymedes; Alumentus, instead of Laomedon, and so forth; which are proofs that they really were in the mouths of the people. The religion of the Romans was not mythological, but a regular theology; their deities were νοούμενα, the myths referring but to the gods of lesser rank: they were therefore wanting in that which gives so much life to the Greek poetry. This of course applies rather to the Sabine element in the Roman population; the Pelasgian one was evidently more akin to the Grecian. By the other element, as well as by the Sibylline books and by the oracle of Apollo, they were familiarized with the mythology, and, therefore, likewise with the poetry of the Greeks: that mythology, there can be no doubt, was perfectly intelligible to the Romans. In Rome, after the end of the first Punic war, Greek poetry became still more known through the medium of the Latin language: it is true, however, that it awakened less interest there than in other Italian towns. The theatre at Tusculum, which, if we may judge from the bases found in the orchestra, dates at latest from the war with Hannibal, presupposes the performance of native or Greek pieces.

The Atellan plays, which are mentioned even before the end of the fourth century, are to us a distinct sign of a national literature. The statement that they were extemporised, is surely correct. Thus, before the great change of manners in Italy, there was often some improvisation interwoven with the pantomimes. As in the Atellanæ they possessed a sort of comedy, so in the *prætextatæ*, they had not only a native, but also a most ancient national tragedy. I believe that there is no mistake in connecting with the *prætextatæ*, the solemn processions at funerals, in which the masks of deceased men, who had curule ancestors (*jus imaginum*), were represented in the dress of their rank by men of similar size; yet even without any reference to this, we may ascribe to them a very great antiquity. The first poet whom we know to have treated them according to the rules of art, was Attius: earlier *prætextatæ* than his are not mentioned; yet this is no proof that they did not exist a long time before.

The translation of Greek poetry into the Latin tongue was a step of immense consequence. That Livius Andronicus had been taken prisoner at Tarentum, may be a mistake, as he is perhaps confounded with M. Livius Macatus; Livius Andronicus could at that time have been but a mere child. The accounts of him are very uncertain; in the earlier ages, little heed was bestowed upon the lives of the first poets, and their sayings and doings were only gathered afterwards: thus it still happened with Plautus and Terence. As far as we can judge from his fragments, he seems not even to have attained to the Greek form at all. The Odyssey, which, from its reference to the native country of the Romans, went indeed nearer home to their hearts, and had greater attraction for them than the Iliad,[39] he seems not to have translated at full length, but to have made an abridgment of it, which was also in the homely Italian measure. The great poem of Nævius was likewise in the saturnian rhythm. Besides the Odyssey, there are only tragedies mentioned of Livius, which, however, like the Atellanæ, were not acted in the theatre, but on a stage in the circus.

Nævius blended the history of the most recent times with Greek mythology; in his great historical poem, for instance, he brought in the myth of the giants. Besides this, he wrote tragedies as well as comedies, as we may see from the titles. That he was a good poet, we may indeed believe on Cicero's word, who, on the whole, found the old writers very little to his taste.

When Nævius was an old man, Plautus, who was undoubtedly one of the greatest poetical geniuses of ancient times, was growing up by his side. This poet takes Greek plays and treats them with a finished irony, not making a mere version from the original, but displaying in his characters the peculiarities of Roman life, which is that of the lower orders, freedmen, strangers, and naturalized citizens. The scene is at Athens, or Epidamnus, or elsewhere; but he has also Greek characters (for instance, the parasite is thoroughly Greek), and then one is again reminded that one is in the midst of Romans. The cleverness with which he managed this, and with which, on the slippery path where he might so easily have stumbled, he always hits the right point, is quite miraculous. We see how wonderfully rich and refined his language was, a proof that even before his time it had been very much cultivated, otherwise it would not have been changed so quickly. For we have a *senatus consultum* of the fifth century,[40] and the epitaph of Scipio Barbatus, with which we may compare his style, and we find a remarkable difference.

Livius was a foreign client; Nævius a moneyed man, a maniceps; being too bold for a foreigner, he was prosecuted because he had given offence to one of the Metelli.[41] Of Plautus, we do not even know whether he was a Roman citizen: he must have been poor; but the story of his having worked at a mill does not rest upon any trustworthy authority. The first who really was a Roman citizen, being somewhat younger than Nævius, but standing in quite a different position from his, was Ennius, a *gentleman*,[42] and certainly a member of the tribes: he lived with Scipio, Fulvius Nobilior, and the first men, and was treated with the highest distinction. It is he who gained for poetry and literature the respect and esteem of the Romans. Among his fragments, there are some very fair pieces; his poetry, however, was not directed to higher objects: in comedy he seems to have been weak, nor does he appear to have held it in particular regard; in epic poetry, on the other hand, he has decided merit. Some of his things were written in a purely Roman form,—this was probably the case with the *Sabinæ*,[43] and also with the *Saturæ*,—yet he followed out quite a different idea. Plautus' metres are by no means thoroughly Greek, though they very often coincide with the latter: the scansion by long and short syllables is Greek, but the Romans were not so strict in their measures, not having the quick ear of the Greeks. A trochaic or iambic movement was of native use among the Romans, and was not measured in the same way as among the Greeks: so it is with anapæsts among the modern Greeks, and with all the metres among some of the Slavonic nations. The *senarius* may be Greek, and as little peculiar to the Romans as to us (Germans). Even as Plautus introduced the latter, so did Ennius the hexameter, which was quite foreign; and this brought about just such revolution in metres as with us. His hexameters were still clumsy and full of faults, and without any *cæsura*, or with a false one, though not so bad as in Klopstock. Much as I like the old *numeri*, the verses of Ennius have something in them which is unpleasing to me. Besides the metres which are properly lyric, he has tried all the *rhythmi*; and indeed he has done it with much greater trueness than the older dramatists. The *senarius* has already more of measured syllables, which gave it a firmer hold; but there is between the verses of Ennius and those of Virgil, as wide a gulf as between the first attempts of Klopstock and that height of perfection in metrical art, to which Count Platen has reached. A peculiarity of the old versification which as yet is far from being clearly made out, was the slurring of the short syllables (*ecthlipsis*): *ego* was pronounced as one syllable, like the Italian *io*; *accipito*, as a dactyl.

Ennius was not an original genius; yet he surely does not deserve the contempt with which Horace speaks of him. He had had a Greek education in Calabria; Greek was his second mother tongue, while the Roman was for him only an acquired language: he therefore wished to help the Romans to a translated Greek literature. If we compare it with what the Greek literature then was, that of the Romans was very brilliant. The Alexandrine period was now already past. Callimachus was dead, when Livius Andronicus began; Antagoras[44] and Aratus were dead; Eratosthenes was a mere versifier. On the other hand, the Romans had a great deal of freshness, and there would have been still more, had not Ennius caused the foreign influence to get so much the upperhand.

Somewhat younger than Ennius was Pacuvius, his sister's son, justly called the Deep. He scorned the pieces of Euripides, which Ennius had chosen, and only took those of Æschylus and Sophocles, thus putting himself altogether in opposition to the taste of the Greeks of that age.

Q. Fabius Pictor and L. Cincius Alimentus then wrote the history of their own nation in Greek. Dionysius, who finds fault with Fabius as an historian, has never made any objection against his language; on the contrary, the fact that Dionysius wrote his own history only down to the beginning of the first Punic war, when Fabius was getting to be more diffuse, proves that the latter was very readable. Of the same standing was Acilius. The great Scipio wrote in the form of a letter to Philip the history of his own wars,[45] and so did his son-in-law Scipio Nasica that of the war with Perseus. Greek grammarians, statuaries, and painters were brought in already by Æmilius Paullus for the education of his children.

WAR WITH THE LIGURIANS; WITH THE CELTIBERIANS. THE THIRD MACEDONIAN WAR. PEACE WITH THE RHODIANS. FURTHER WARS IN SPAIN. STATE OF AFFAIRS AT HOME

During these changes, when on all points a sudden and thorough revolution had taken place in the manners of the people, the Romans were not backward in widening their sway: whilst the state was falling to pieces, they did not know what to do, unless they were making conquests. The evil had become so deep-rooted, that it could hardly have been got rid of; but as it was, nothing was done to heal it, and the degeneracy quickly increased.

The war against the Ligurians is not only insignificant, when measured by the standard of other wars, but it is also obscure, owing to our very defective knowledge of the geography of the country. It has some resemblance to undertakings against the Caucasian tribes of which we now (1829) read; and although the Apennines are not such a high mountain-range as the Caucasus, they yet likewise give great advantages to the inhabitants. As is always the case when a powerful state has once determined upon subjugating a people, the Ligurians also were crushed. Their tribes in fact had their abodes as far as the Rhone; but the Romans, who were chiefly anxious to secure the Tuscan frontier, reduced only the Genoese territory. These wars did not reach beyond the borders of Provence; the hostilities against the Salyans in the neighbourhood of Marseilles belong to a later period.[46] These tribes fought for their freedom with such determination, that the Romans had no other course but to drive them out of their fastnesses,—booty there was none to be got there,—and the consuls Cornelius and Bæbius[47] led away fifty thousand Ligurians from their homes into Samnium where Frontinus,[48] as late as in the second century met with their descendants under the names of the Cornelian and Bæbian Ligurians. The war was ended before that of Perseus. For the especial purpose of commanding Gaul, the highway of Flaminius, which went as far as Ariminum, was now lengthened as the *via*

Æmilia to Placentia; and the whole country south of the Po was filled with colonies, so that the Celtic population disappeared.

All this time, the Romans were likewise establishing their rule in Spain, where they regularly kept troops. This beginning of standing armies had a decided influence, not only upon warfare, but also on all the relations of civil life. In former days, the real burthens of war had fallen upon all ranks alike: every one who was able to bear arms, had served for a time, and he became a citizen again, when the legion was disbanded at the end of the contest; which had this advantage, that the soldier was not separated from the citizen. But now the men remained for a long term of years in Spain, married Spanish women, and became estranged from Italy: many of them never returned. The Roman sway spread itself over Catalonia, Valencia, and Andalusia, as far as the Sierra Morena; for when they waged war with the Celtiberians, the latter had traversed the country of the neighbouring tribes. These wars were therefore not so much for acquisition as for consolidation. Their rule over the nations seems to have become somewhat slippery; but Cato, during his consulate in 557, gained them back by his uprightness. Roman generals who behaved in this way, always won the confidence of the Spaniards; and these would submit, until the injustice of the Romans again drove them to shake off the yoke: the people always appears in a very noble light. Cato, however, was also cunning, this being a feature in his character, as well as in that of the Romans as a nation. He strengthened the power of Rome by circulars which he sent to seventy or eighty Spanish towns, all of which were strongly fortified, and in case of rebellion hard to take, so that they were apt to combine with their neighbours. In these letters, which were all of them to be opened on one and the same day, as containing a secret of very high importance, was the command to pull down their walls forthwith under the threat of a siege and of bondage. The order was generally obeyed; and before they became aware that it was a stratagem, the work of demolition had already made considerable progress.

In the year 575, Ti. Sempronius Gracchus, a son of him who in the war with Hannibal had won a brilliant victory over Hanno and had nobly fallen, and also the father of the two ill-fated brothers, became consul, and went to Spain. (It was he who had deeply deplored that P. Scipio tried to set himself above the law, but who did not wish him to be punished like any other citizen; and Scipio had afterwards chosen him for his son-in-law.) At that time, the feeling of hostility had already been more widely kindled. The Celtiberians, who had spread from the sources of the Ebro to the threefold border of the Mancha, Andalusia, and Valencia, and chiefly dwelt in New Castile and Western Aragon, in the provinces of Soria and Cuença, had never been subject to the Carthaginians, but had furnished them with mercenaries, as they also did the Romans: they now got involved in war with the Romans, who endeavoured to reduce them. They were the bravest people in Spain. With them Gracchus concluded a peace, the conditions of which are unknown to us; but they were so fair, that these tribes, who in reality had no wish whatever for war, ever afterwards looked upon it as the greatest good which could befall them, if they were only allowed to have them. The whole family of the Gracchi is distinguished for an extraordinary mildness and kindness, which otherwise are quite foreign to the Roman character. Had his successors kept the peace, the Celtiberians would have become as true and as useful allies to the Romans as the Marsians and Pelignians. Other generals, however, extended the Roman rule in the west of Spain: the Vaccæans north of the Tagus and the Lusitanians must have been brought under subjection between 570 and 580; yet this was not for long, owing to the extortions of the generals.

In the meantime, a new thunderstorm gathered in the east. Philip's reign had lasted a long while; but he made an excellent use of his time to strengthen his kingdom. His expectations from the war against Antiochus had not been fulfilled; but he had considerably enlarged his dominions: he was again in possession of Demetrias and of part of Magnesia, so that he hemmed in Thessaly; the Dolopians had remained under his sway (although they were detached from his country); he also had Athamania; and he had gotten again the Greek towns on the Thracian coast, Ænos, Maronea, Abdera, and others, which had formerly been Egyptian. The Romans had let him go on quietly for a while; but now they began craftily to undermine his rule. They gave their encouragement when Amynander drove the Macedonian garrisons from Athamania; they received embassies which they themselves had set on foot, from Thessaly and the towns on the Thracian coast, bearing complaints of Philip's encroachments. They must have held the conviction, that he had no other object, but thus to strengthen himself until he should be able to regain his former might; but Philip, in all his preparations, was too cautious to run foul upon the treaty. Particularly hostile to Philip was Eumenes, who longed to have the towns on the Thracian coast, that he might extend his territory to the frontiers of Macedon. Philip heard that many ambassadors were gathering in Rome, and he sent his son Demetrius thither, who had formerly been with the Romans as a hostage, and in that way had made a good many connexions there. These transactions—as was always managed by the Romans at that time with ruthless dexterity—led to nothing; the decision was to be given in Macedonia by Roman commissioners. During that time, there was now a great anxiety not to do anything that might have seemed unfriendly to the Romans. These commissioners were received by Philip with great bitterness: some things he yielded which he could not help; in others, he made evasions, and sought to gain time; misfortune had taught him wisdom. He had carried on the first war with the Romans, in which he might have done them much harm, sluggishly, and without having his heart in it; he had also engaged quite unprepared in that which had been directed against himself, so that after one defeat, every thing was lost for him; but from 555, during the eighteen years which elapsed to his death, he was always preparing himself. On both sides, they vied with each other in faithlessness. Philip set on the Thracians to surprise the Roman army which was coming from Asia, and to rob it of its *impedimenta*: the Romans tried to strip him of his possessions. He therefore strove to make himself as unassailable as possible; and as he was not allowed to have a fleet, and therefore was exposed to constant attacks by sea, he formed the plan of abandoning the sea-port towns, which were by no means strong, and of drawing the inhabitants into the interior: he also directed his whole attention to getting money. For this purpose, he settled in Thrace, where he worked the mines with redoubled activity, and the arsenals were filled with arms: on the other hand, he caused Thracians to emigrate to the wasted Macedonian countries. At the same time, he negotiated with other nations; yet he did not turn his eyes towards the powerless East, but to the Getæ and Bastarnians. The latter then dwelt in Dacia, the present Moldavia and Wallachia: the great move of the Sarmatian peoples on the Dnieper, had made those tribes inclined to leave their abodes. Philip therefore tried to get them to fall upon Italy, a scheme which was carried out seventy years afterwards by the Cimbrians. These transactions had already gone very far, nor would they have been abortive but for the death of the king; and in fact this would have been the only means of assailing Rome. The Romans were universally hated, and they deserved it. The people among whom in former days justice had been the corner-stone of religion, had not even a spark left of their ancient virtue: they tried to stir up infamous intrigues in the free states, and in the families of princes; they everywhere took the bad under their protection, and cheered them on to venture everything on the strength of it. Thus, in the royal house of Macedon, there arose a quarrel between the two sons of Philip, the elder of whom was Perseus, and the younger, Demetrius; the former being the son of a concubine, the latter begotten in lawful wedlock. Demetrius became suspected by the king of being a partisan of the Romans; and the hatred between the two brothers broke out with so much the greater fierceness—Perseus being maddened against the Romans—the more Demetrius took their part. After years of horrid accusations and treacherous wiles, Perseus at last carried the day, and had Demetrius poisoned by his father. Whether Demetrius really engaged in guilty plots, or whether there was nothing more than a passing impulse, cannot be made out now; if we judge from the morality of those times, his complete innocence is not likely: that the charges against the father and Perseus in Livy, according to which Perseus tells false-hearted slanders against his brother to the king, are highly exaggerated, however beautifully they read, may be asserted with the greatest probability. Thus it is no doubt one of those unjust insinuations which we meet with but too often, when the *mors opportuna* of Philip is spoken of. How frequently, when such a *mors opportuna* happened, was it represented as having been intentionally brought about! Philip had reached the age when he might very well have died a natural death; he was sixty years old when he died (573): he is said to have deeply rued the foul deed which he had committed against Demetrius, and to have died of a broken heart. And it still remains a question, whether, and how far, he could have had the thought of passing over his son, who was no fool, and bequeathing the kingdom to his cousin, a son of Antigonus Doson. In short, the country was left to his son Perseus in a state of power and greatness, which no one could have dreamed of at the beginning of his reign, and still less at the time of the disadvantageous peace with Rome.

It is difficult to form a correct opinion of Perseus, who was an inconsistent character. A marked feature in his disposition was avarice: he could not tear himself away from his treasures, even when there was the strongest necessity for it, and he grudged them when they might have gotten him the most formidable troops; and this is particularly the case when he promises subsidies to foreign peoples. Moreover, he showed himself wavering in war, which indeed was partly the result of circumstances, but was also deep-rooted in his nature. He was no general; for he had no presence of mind in an emergency: as long as circumstances were not appalling, he was very clever in hitting upon and doing the right thing; with regard to his courage the ancients themselves differed in their judgment. In his first years, it was his endeavour to win the hearts of the Greeks, in which he was signally successful: he gained over the Achæans, Bœotians, Acarnanians, Epirotes, and Thessalians, one after another, and besides these, even the Rhodians and other islanders. Here he did not indeed show his avarice: he remitted taxes, recalled convicted persons from banishment, and opened Macedon as a refuge for unfortunate and exiled Greeks. Thus he got adherents among all the Greeks, and we meet everywhere with a Roman and a Macedonian party. Among the Achæans there even arose three factions, a Roman, a Macedonian, and a third one of the patriots, which was hated by the other two. Thus Perseus came to Greece, and was welcomed with enthusiasm, as the Roman rule grew more oppressive every day. The Greeks looked upon him as the man who would restore the old Macedonian sway, and drive the Romans back again across the Adriatic. With Carthage also he entered into negociations: but things had already come to that pass that there was not much to be expected any more even from a general coalition; for although Rome's moral power was blighted, yet she had acquired the influence of a wealthy state, being able to hire and to arm troops in distant lands.

The Rhodians stood quite free: having entered into no league with the Romans, they might, if they chose, ally themselves with Perseus. The latter married a Syrian princess, daughter of Antiochus Epiphanes, a crazy tyrant, but who displayed no common energy: (he is very correctly described in the book of the Maccabees, and in the fragments of Polybius.) Perseus' sister was married to Prusias. He also went on with the negociations with the Bastarnians, and even entered into new ones with the Illyrians. But Eumenes became suspicious of these connexions of Perseus with Rhodes, Antiochus, and Prusias; for he saw fast enough, that he could not but fall a victim, if Perseus should be successful against the Romans: Perseus held out as a bait to the other powers the kingdom of Pergamus, which would be the natural prey for them to share. Eumenes therefore complained to the Romans; and these listened to him, and took up all sorts of other grievances against Perseus and the Rhodians, which had been set forth against the former by the Thracian petty princes, and against the latter by the Carians and Lycians, who had rather be independent than have to pay heavy taxes to the Rhodians. To these ambassadors they gave the most encouraging answers, without, however, committing themselves by any thing positive. In this way, they irritated the Rhodians, but did not break with them: their policy at that time was truly Macchiavellian. The peace-party, although indeed very weak in Rhodes, had yet sufficiently the upperhand to prevent their fellow citizens from declaring against the Romans. Eumenes himself came to Rome and got a splendid reception, the Romans wishing even by this very means to display their hostile dispositions. Perseus, however, kept quiet: he was acknowledged by the Romans, having been termed the friend and ally of the Roman people, and his ambassadors were received and rewarded.

On his return from Rome, Eumenes was attacked by assassins in Delphi. This plot may have been laid by Perseus; it was very like him, although he positively disavowed it: perhaps also it was a farce of Eumenes himself, intended to give the Romans a handle for war; yet it would, after all, have been too bad. The demand of the Romans, that Perseus should deliver up persons who stood highest in his estimation, because they were accused of having been the instigators of that attack, met with a flat refusal, and thence arose the war, which lasted until the fourth year, from 581-584. This war took a different turn from what the Romans had expected. They had hoped to be able to bring it to an end, like the second Macedonian one and that against Antiochus, in one campaign; besides which, they wished to crush Macedon, and to reconstruct the whole state of things in the eastern countries. But Perseus began the struggle with extraordinary resources: Macedon, for the first time, had enjoyed a twenty-five years' peace, and it was thriving; so that besides his auxiliaries and four thousand horse, he had an army of forty thousand foot. The last books of Livy are mutilated, and thus we are without any clear view of part of the operations. The duration of the war, considering the disproportion between the two powers, is very great; but indeed the Roman generals carried it on at first in the worst way that could be, and strategical talent seems to have very much fallen off just then among the Romans. P. Licinius Crassus appeared in Thessaly, where Perseus advanced to meet him, and gained a pretty considerable advantage over his cavalry: the Romans had many killed and taken prisoners. The king, in waging the war, did it with the wish to obtain a favourable peace; and he believed that by showing himself resolute, he would get it on better terms. Yet this was contrary to the settled maxim of the Romans; in fact, it was exactly a case in which they felt that they must humble him. Perseus immediately began to negociate; but it was answered, that he was to make his submission, and to await the decision of the senate. This led to the battle in Thessaly, the result of which was favourable to the king. This victory threw such lustre on the arms of Perseus, that the whole of Greece was ready to go over to him. Yet the Romans had a vast advantage in their fleet, which was a dreadful scourge to the Greek sea-port towns; and though indeed it was now opposed by a Macedonian squadron, which did more than any one expected, they had still the best of it. Only some few party-leaders in Greece, such as Charops in Epirus (who had been brought up in Rome, and made it his boast that he was able to speak Latin), Lyciscus in Ætolia, and Callicrates in Achaia, were for the Romans: the public opinion was altogether against them. Whilst men like Polybius, who certainly hated the Romans as bitterly as his father Lycortas did,—but this was a different hatred from that of the common herd,—and like Philopœmen, now saw plainly that Perseus would not be able to stand his ground against the Romans, and only supported him with pious wishes and prayers, the many dreamt that he could not fail to be victorious. They egregiously exaggerated trifling successes, such as the battle in Thessaly, and were guilty of the worst outrages and insolence against the Romans; just as was done in Germany, when the French were at the height of their power. Such men also as Polybius had a very strong feeling against the Romans: it was not till afterwards, when he was living among them, that he became aware of the good that was in them. The state of affairs at that time is clearly shown by the fragments of his history. The Romans now also, on their side, everywhere looked upon the Greeks as enemies; and this gave rise to the most cruel deeds, for which the prætor Lucretius was particularly notorious. A number of Greek towns on the sea-coast were taken and utterly destroyed, under the command of this Lucretius and of Hostilius, and the inhabitants were led away as slaves: in Bœotia, Haliartus and Coronea were burned to ashes. If Perseus had taken advantage of these circumstances, and had pressed the consul hard, the whole country on the other side of the Adriatic would have risen in revolt: but he was irresolute and narrow-minded; he had made out for himself a petty plan, within the range of which alone he could do any thing, and of those great enterprises, which would have been needed to overthrow the Roman empire, he was utterly incapable. Thus he listened to the delusive offers of the Roman consul to make a lasting peace; and in the meanwhile Crassus got himself out of his wretched plight, and the negociations were, of course, broken off. In the same way, when Marcius Philippus subsequently opposed Perseus again with insufficient means, he was allowed to offer the king a truce, which, it was given out, was to lead to a peace, whereas the Romans merely availed themselves of it to send the consul the reinforcements which he wanted. In the second and third years of the war, Perseus was very successful; he even drove back the Romans out of Macedon into Illyria, and also gained time to protect his empire against the attacks of the savage Dardanians.

In the third year of the war, Perseus had withdrawn from Thessaly; but he kept Magnesia, his army held Tempe, and thus he lay safely in winter-quarters in Pieria. Here Q. Marcius Philippus undertook a bold piece of daring. He stood at the entrance of Tempe, and as he was not able to force the pass, he endeavoured with an immense effort to cross the huge heights of Olympus, so as to turn the army of the Macedonians, who did not dream of the enemy having thus gone round them. Yet this enterprise of the Romans ought only to be blamed; for their army got into a position, in which, if Perseus had only had common presence of mind and attacked them, they might have been cut off to a man. Perseus abandoned Dium, having set fire to part of the town; evacuated Pieria, that narrow strip of beautiful land along the coast, extending from Olympus to the Thermaic gulf; and retired to Pydna. The Roman general himself, finding his own situation to be a very dangerous one, retreated, and the Macedonians, in their turn, advanced again. This undertaking, however, ended in the Macedonians evacuating Tempe.

The state of opinion with regard to the issue of the war shifted more and more, though the Romans were slowly creeping on. It was thought that a formidable coalition would be made; and that fortune would turn against the Romans, as Rome had reached the crowning height of her power, and now must needs sink down, as all the Greek states had done. The Rhodians believed that they might now set up an independent system, as they hoped, if the wars ended unfavourably for Rome, to consolidate their own rule over Caria and Lycia: they too allowed themselves to be beguiled by their wishes. The connexion of Perseus with Prusias and Antiochus became more active; Antiochus, however, entered with less spirit into these affairs, as he wished first of all to take advantage of the crisis to gain Egypt. Since he therefore no longer threatened Asia Minor, even old Eumenes changed his policy, and likewise espoused the interests of Perseus; so that not only was he backward in supporting the Romans, but he even entered into secret negociations with Perseus: these, however, could not be kept altogether concealed, and for this the Romans afterwards bore him a bitter grudge. The Bastarnians also were stirring again; and there was likewise a closer alliance with Genthius, king of Illyricum, of whose kingdom and descent we have no distinct accounts, though this we know for certain, that Scutari (Scodra) was his residence; (his country seems to have very nearly comprised what is now Upper Albania.) He was not a great prince, yet, if he took a determined part, a dangerous neighbour to the Romans. But the Illyrians and Bastarnians reckoned upon getting subsidies from Perseus: his not granting them to the Bastarnians was downright madness; he ought at any price to have induced them to invade Italy. The three hundred talents which he had agreed upon for Genthius, he kept back, after having drawn him in to commit an outrage against the Roman ambassadors at his court; for he thought that he had thus bound him fast to himself by a tie which could not be broken. This was a pitiful trick!

In 584, the Romans chose L. Æmilius Paullus, the son of the general who was killed at Cannæ, to be consul for the second time; and as they saw that considerable efforts were needed to finish the war, they furnished him with every possible means for it. The Rhodians, most unfortunately for themselves, had wished to act as mediators: the war interfered with their trade, and they by no means wanted the Romans to conquer, as they owed their own independence to the balance of the different states. They came forward, using violent language, and engaged to get Perseus to make peace; but the Romans, though hard pressed by the war, did not desire peace, and the speech of the Rhodians even offended them. At home, and among their neighbours, the Rhodians felt strong, and there by their weight they could turn the scales, which indeed they had done in the war of Antiochus by means of their fleet; but they forgot the immense disproportion between the power of the Romans and their own. Perseus opened the campaign without any further increase of force, except that Genthius declared himself for him. The king had taken up his winter-quarters in Macedonia, and when the Romans broke up theirs, he retreated behind the Cambunian hills and Olympus, the lofty ridge of mountains which separates Thessaly from the Macedonian coast, a country which is one of the most beautiful on earth. Yet this time also the Romans succeeded in going round the mountains. Between the Peneus and Pieria, there is the high and broad range of Olympus, the peaks of which are almost all covered with everlasting snow. The chief pass was through Tempe, which was fortified; besides this, there were several ways across Olympus, and these also were most of them so well secured, that Æmilius did not expect any good from an attack. But he discovered a road, just over one of the most towering summits of the mountains, which, inasmuch as it seemed to be inaccessible, was less strongly guarded. Thither he sent the son-in-law of Scipio Africanus, young Scipio Nasica, with eight thousand men, so as to go round the camp. This enterprise could not have succeeded, had Perseus been a great general; the aggressor, however, has always an advantage. The impassable mountain was got over; the Macedonian army saw the Roman detachment in its rear; the vanguard was defeated by Scipio Nasica, and Perseus was obliged to change his position. He now took up another at the back of Pydna, behind a deep torrent: for in this narrow strip of coast, in which a number of deep mountain streams run down alongside of each other from Olympus to the sea, lines were thrown up behind every one of these, so that a stand might be made at every point successively, in case the enemy should force the pass at Tempe. But now that the Romans had crossed the mountains on the extreme left wing of the Macedonians, these entrenchments were useless; and the Macedonians had then to retreat behind the last of them near Pydna. Thus the Romans were in Pieria, the country of Orpheus, which was a great advance. Yet the Macedonian power was still unshaken. Near Pydna, the final battle was fought, in which the Macedonian monarchy ingloriously fell; it was decided in one hour, and with it the fate of Macedon: the infantry was cut to pieces, the cavalry saved itself without much loss, but with disgrace. The loss of the Romans was trifling: according to some, it was only ninety-one, according to others, one hundred men; and moreover the former of these estimates is that of a man, who was no friend of the Romans, namely Posidonius,—not the celebrated one, but a writer who lived at the time of this war, and who wished to justify Perseus.[49] The king had no hope of a rising; for he had drained the resources of the country to the utmost, and the great fault of the Macedonians was want of faithfulness to their princes in the day of need: he fled, and, escorted by some Cretans, tried to escape with what treasures he had left, as if there had been a place where they were safe from the Romans. Part of these he therefore offered to give up to his followers; yet when he had taken breath at Amphipolis, with the madness of avarice, he repented of his promise, and cheated them of their due. He ought to have gone to Thrace where he had allies, and from thence to some Greek town on the Black sea, as these would not have delivered him up; but he was utterly blinded, and betook himself to Samothrace, where there was an inviolable temple, which he may have looked upon as so much safer an asylum, as indeed the worship of the *penates* at Lavinium, and that of the Samothracian gods, were akin. He would doubtless have been safe in that island as a private person; but it could not possibly have been expected, that the Romans would let him alone there in his present capacity. His chief motive was certainly the thought, that he might then also have saved his money; yet he soon found out that he could not trust those who were about him, and he even went so far as to have one of them put to death, on which the others treacherously left him. He now wished to embark for Crete, or, according to others, to go to Cotys in Thrace; but the master of the ship, whom he had paid beforehand, deceived him, and all that he could do was to take away his own life, as the Roman prætor had already made his appearance, either to seize or to starve him. From a cowardly love of life, he was led to surrender himself to the Roman admiral Cn. Octavius; and he was kept as a prisoner for the triumph of Æmilius Paullus, as was also the case with Genthius.[50]

Æmilius now executed the commission of regulating affairs according to the instructions which he had from Rome, and this he did in a way which is shocking to our ideas. The Epirotes were involved in the fate of Perseus: although they were not faithful to the treaties which bound them to Rome, yet the dreadful revenge which the Romans took upon them, can never be justified. The Roman soldiers were quartered upon the Molossians, and the senate determined to reward them with the plundering of the Epirote towns: it was undoubtedly meant to requite them for the calamities which formerly had been brought upon the Romans by Pyrrhus. Æmilius was charged with the business of exterminating the Epirote nation. In seventy places, the Roman army was stationed, and the Epirotes were ordered to gather together and deliver up all their gold and valuables, having already been obliged before that to yield up their arms. When in this manner everything was collected which in a general plunder might have been spoilt and wasted, all the troops on the self-same day turned their arms against the inhabitants. One hundred and fifty thousand Epirotes are said to have been either slain or led away as slaves, and seventy places to have been destroyed. This is horrible; it shows the rank degeneracy of the Roman people, as there is no longer in it any balance of its different elements, but only the dead weight of one promiscuous mass. Slavery strips man of half of his virtue, but absolute liberty to do what one lists creates double vice: as rulers of the world, the Romans thought themselves privileged to do any thing and everything. After such a deed as this, we cannot agree with Plutarch in ranking Æmilius among great and virtuous men. Throughout the whole of Greece, and particularly in Bœotia, things were just as bad: the sword was put into the hands of the partisans of the Romans, and their rage was ruthless. In Ætolia, as in all Greek countries, there were two factions, the one devoted, and the other hostile to the Romans; the Roman party ruled without any one to control it, and the lengths to which it went in its outrages, beggar all belief. Besides other atrocities, it broke into the senate house, and butchered all the senators who were accused of being friendly to the Macedonians. Roman troops were sent thither under the command of A. Bæbius. This frightful state of things extended likewise to the Achæans: there the party of Perseus had not been very strong, but so much the stronger was that which had striven to uphold that dignity, which had been injured by the Romans. These had kept none of the treaties with them, and they had received separate embassies from some of the towns, which they had even encouraged; as in the case of Lacedæmon and Messene, which brought complaints against the Achæans, whilst, according to the treaty, none were to be listened to but those which came from the whole of the Achæan league. It was seen how much the Romans were endeavouring to disturb the peace of the people; they even required that the exiles should be reinstated. There was among the Achæans a traitor, Callicrates, who had entirely sold himself to the Romans, and who was so detested and execrated, that people were loth to go near him, or even to touch his garment: the more he became an object of contempt, the deeper he sank in his infamy. After the victory over Perseus, ten Roman commissioners appeared in Greece, two of whom, C. Claudius and Cn. Domitius, went to the Achæans. They asserted that among the papers of Perseus clear proofs had been discovered of the treachery of many eminent Achæans, and they now demanded that the Achæans should pronounce sentence of death upon all whom the Romans had found guilty. This the senate at once refused to do, declaring most properly, that the names must be given, the evidence produced, and the parties regularly tried; those who were brought in guilty should then be punished without mercy. But the envoys would have nothing to say to this, they wanted to give in the list after the executions only; and when they were urged to mention names, they said, that all those who had been *strategi* were guilty. Then Xeno, who had formerly been *strategus*, got up, and declared that he was so conscious of his innocence, that he would take his trial before a tribunal in Achaia, and, if this were not sufficient, he would even defend himself at Rome. The Roman commissioners eagerly caught at this, and they had a list drawn up by Callicrates of those who were to be sent to Italy and judged there. There were more than a thousand of these; some of them made their escape, for which they were denounced as convicted offenders, and the punishment of death was inflicted upon them when they were taken. The rest were not brought before a court of justice at all, but were distributed as hostages in the municipal towns: it was only after the lapse of seventeen years, that the three hundred who were still alive, were let go.

On this occasion, Polybius also came to Rome: his lot was soon bettered; for he got intimate with several families of high rank, and Æmilius Paullus himself made him the companion of his sons, that he might guide them into Greek learning.

Macedon was nominally declared free; but half the taxes were laid upon it, which had been formerly paid to the kings,—an example, how the Romans still exacted tribute from those countries which they did not convert into Roman provinces. The country was divided into four states. This splitting into cantons of the strangest shape; the taking away of all *connubium* and *commercium* between them; and the geographical division of these districts, by which tribes belonging to the same stock were torn asunder, and others which were quite distinct were united, are masterpieces of Macchiavellian policy: those which suited each other were disjoined, and those which clashed were jumbled together, in order that no moral strength and unity might ever grow up in the whole. The consequence of this was, that the power of the Macedonians was completely broken. And yet the Romans were behaving all the time as if they were giving them a republican constitution: to every one of these quarters they granted a *synedrium*, and on pretext of removing those who were dangerous to this new equality, they drove all the men of rank and distinction out of the country. The advantage of this arrangement showed itself afterwards in the rebellion of the pseudo-Philip.

The triumph of Æmilius Paullus is the most brilliant of any which had been seen until then, owing to the quantity of costly things displayed in it. The life of Paullus by Plutarch is very well worth reading, and the account also of the triumph is very instructive: twelve millions of dollars in hard money were carried in the procession. Yet the people did not find itself the better for all these riches; its condition, on the contrary, became worse and worse: the bane of downright poverty was showing itself; the rabble and beggars were increasing fast. We likewise now see, and even somewhat earlier already, traces of a debased moral state: at times, a series of the most monstrous crimes makes its appearance. Even before the war with Perseus, frightful atrocities are met with, which have the most incredible ramifications. In the beginning of the seventh century, two Roman matrons of the highest rank, the wives of men who had been consuls, were accused of having poisoned their husbands, and were put to death by their cousins. Whilst the moral condition grew worse every day, the wealth of the republic became greater. During the war with Perseus, taxes had still been paid, which was done no longer, except, no doubt, in the Social War, when everything was turned into money. This is indeed mentioned nowhere. Historians talk as if the Macedonian booty, which Æmilius Paullus brought with him, had been inexhaustible; but the fact is rather, that the permanent revenues from Macedonia, Illyricum, and elsewhere, made it now quite superfluous to lay on direct taxes. The indirect duties only, as the customs for instance, were still paid: they were part of them rather high, at least in after times, and they had this peculiarity, that they were raised in a number of harbours as an excise, whilst in the interior of the country everything circulated quite freely.

The Rhodians, who had aroused the wrath of the Romans by their pride, were still left: to these the Romans now turned their attention, and declared war against them. They on the other hand, being well aware that resistance was impossible, stooped to the lowest humiliations to appease the Romans. Those who had actually corresponded with Perseus, made the negotiations more easy for the republic by laying hands on their own lives, on which their dead bodies were given up. Others fled, but could nowhere find a refuge, and were likewise forced to kill themselves. Polyaratus and Dinon, unfortunately, were really guilty; they were banished, and they fell into the power of the Romans. Dealing one blow after another, the Romans now took from the Rhodians all that they had formerly granted them; nay, even places of which they had long before been masters: Stratonicea had belonged to them for seventy years. With great difficulty, by the skill of the Rhodian ambassador, and through the intercession of Cato who interested himself for the Rhodians, the war was prevented. The Romans got Caria and Lycia, hardly leaving to them their nearest possessions on the coast; and the Rhodians, who for so long a time had lived in friendship with Rome, had to think themselves lucky in obtaining an alliance, in which they had to acknowledge the supremacy of Rome, and to support it in war. They, however, still kept their independent government; and they showed their sound judgment in confining themselves to their small but noble island, making themselves everywhere respected by their commerce.

Now follows a period, from the end of the Macedonian to the beginning of the third Punic war, which is quite barren of events. Polybius had concluded the first edition of his history with the destruction of the Macedonian empire, and the reconciliation of the Rhodians. When, after the fall of Carthage and of Corinth, he once more took his work in hand, he wrote the wars by which this was achieved, separately; but he prefixed to them an introduction connecting this account with his first history, which also contained in a short summary all that happened in the times between. They are therefore two different works, a fact which has been frequently overlooked.[51] We follow his example, giving only what is absolutely indispensable.

Towards the end of the sixth century, the Romans began to attack the Gauls in the Alps; and soon after the war with Perseus, they took the Massaliote colonies of Antibes and Nizza from the Ligurians. It now was their object to bring the coast as far as Spain under their own rule (601). About the same time, they also tried on the other side of the Adriatic to subdue the Dalmatians, from Zara to about as far as Ragusa. They compelled them to acknowledge their supremacy, though not for long. In Corsica likewise, they made some progress.

The two kings, Prusias and Eumenes, were each of them compromised, yet in a different way; the former, owing to his connexion by marriage with Perseus, the latter by his breach of faith. Prusias disgusted his contemporaries by his abject baseness. In Roman attire, with his head shaved, and wearing the cap of a slave made free, he came humbly to Rome, prostrated himself in the senate, and declared himself a freedman of the Romans. He attained his end so far, that the Romans did not curtail his territory: he had to give his son Nicomedes as an hostage, by whom he was afterwards to be overthrown. Eumenes was forbidden to come to Rome, when his brother Attalus implored for him the mercy of the Romans.

At the same time, Antiochus Epiphanes waged war against the two infant princes of Egypt, Ptolemy Philometor and Euergetes II. (Physcon), and their sister Cleopatra: Cœlesyria was lost; they still possessed only Egypt, Cyprus, and Cyrene. All these likewise, Antiochus made successful attempts to conquer; he had advanced as far as Memphis, and, as the Egyptian towns were nearly all of them open places, he was all but sure of victory: Alexandria alone could have withstood him. But the Romans did not wish to let him grow powerful; they sent the celebrated embassy of M. Popillius, who with his staff drew a circle round the king, within which he forced him to decide upon evacuating Egypt. The Romans now mediated between the two princes, giving to Physcon, the younger of the two, Cyrene, and afterwards Cyprus also, on which he made up, and then again quarrelled with his brother, who had all the rest. The details do not belong to Roman history.

In the meanwhile, the Parthians had begun to spread. They had taken the country east of the desert, and ancient Hyrcania which bordered on the Caspian sea; nor did the Syrian kings keep Media, Susiana, and Persia long (until 620). The great Parthian empire was then founded, and in the year 630, the Parthians had already taken Babylon.

In Spain, the wars still lasted. Most of the undertakings there were directed against the Celtiberians, whom the Romans tried to bring under subjection. The terms granted by Gracchus were not kept with them, and thus insurrections and wars sprang up, the history of which is a dismal one. The Romans had laid upon the Celtiberians the condition not to build any new towns; at the end of the sixth century therefore, the war broke out anew, because they had considerably enlarged the circuit of the walls of Segida, that they might gather together thither. With this the Romans interfered, and thence the first Celtiberian war arose. The Romans at first made some progress; but on many occasions they were also soundly beaten. The small tribes in the mountains of eastern Castile, and western Aragon, were on the whole an heroic race; there were four peoples altogether, of which the Arevaci were the most important: in former days they might indeed have been dangerous also to their neighbours; but now, all their efforts were only put forth for the maintenance of their independence. Yet the Romans had so much the superiority in force, that the wars generally turned out in their favour, although they did not bring on any final decision. A Roman general, M. Claudius Marcellus,—the grandson of the great Marcellus of the second Punic war, and well worthy of him, who also was thrice consul, a thing which is without example in those times,—in some measure brought back to the Spaniards the days of Gracchus: he was quite a man of the old virtue and humanity, and he honoured and respected these people who were struggling for their freedom, and tried to mediate for them. But the senate would have it, that the honour of the republic did not allow of a peace being made with them as with equals: they must surrender at discretion; then only could one deal mildly with them. Marcellus, who well knew that a successor might treat these poor creatures much more harshly, won their confidence in a way which is so often seen in ancient Spanish history. He concluded a very fair peace, making them send hostages to him whom he gave back: they were merely bound to furnish the Romans with horsemen for their wars in Spain, and perhaps also in Africa. Other generals followed quite a different course, as, for instance, L. Lucullus, who, after Marcellus, commanded in Spain: he had flattered himself with the hope of conquering the Celtiberians, and as he was now hindered from doing this by the peace of Marcellus, he picked up a war against the Vaccæans who dwelt in the neighbourhood of Salamanca. He carried it on with varying success. Had the Spanish nations trusted each other, and had they chosen to go forth as one man to fight the Romans, they might have stood their ground against them, and have pent them to the sea-coast. But they were utterly wanting in unity. So long, for instance, as the Lusitanians were not attacked, they were glad to be able to till their fields, nor did they mind if the Romans waged war against another people. Hence it was, that the Romans gradually made their way. With the Lusitanians also, a war had arisen about the same time as that with the Vaccæans: these did not inhabit the whole of Portugal, as they had only a little land to the north of the Tagus, but the southern part, all but Algarve; and they were in a league with the Vettones in Spanish Estremadura. The Lusitanians were a race of robbers, and were just as troublesome to the ancient Spaniards themselves as to the Romans; but they had not yet the great leader, who soon afterwards arose among them. They plundered the subjects of Rome in Andalusia, and thereby drew down upon themselves the vengeance of the Romans. How horribly the Romans were wont to act in those times, is shown by the fate of Cauca. The men of that town had been bidden by Lucullus, as a condition of his pardon, to yield up their arms; and when they relied upon his word, all were put to the sword. This breach of faith made the resistance of the Spaniards so desperate. The Lusitanians, who were excellent light troops, were, owing to their forays, very dangerous to the Romans; nothing, however, can justify the conduct of the latter towards them. Sulpicius Galba, a distinguished rhetorician and lawyer, who belonged to one of the first patrician houses, and was a pillar of the aristocracy, by such behaviour sullied his own fair fame, and that of his forefathers. He vanquished the Lusitanians, and they sought for mercy, gave hostages, and surrendered their horses: they were not, however, the whole of the nation, but only part of it, and as they were inclined for peace, he declared to them, that he was quite aware that distress had driven them into war, and that therefore he would assign them abodes in more fruitful lands. They agreed to this, on which he made them gather together in three bodies into three different places; then, under a lying pretext, he got them to deliver up their weapons, which were to be returned to them in their new dwellings; and now, whilst they were divided and unarmed, he had them massacred, perhaps from sheer ferocity, or indeed because he did not trust them. Among those who escaped was Viriathus, who, by a war of several years in which they had nothing but shame, made the Romans smart for their faithlessness. This, however, belongs to a later period. Unhappily, the crime of Galba had not at Rome the consequences for him which it deserved. Honest old Cato brought an impeachment against him, and he was tried for his life, and would have been condemned, had he not raised the pity of the people by leading forth his own infant children and those of a cousin.

Of organic changes in the constitution, none can be mentioned as having taken place at this period: it remains quite the same in its outward form as it had been since the first Punic war. Some laws are given, and some little attempts made to remedy existing evils, but without any effect. Thus the *lex Voconia* was passed, which forbids the leaving of property to females either by will or by legacy, except in the case of an only daughter and child: this clause respecting the only daughter (ἐπίκληρος) had its reason in the relations of the clans, such a daughter being bound, just as in Attica, to marry within her own *gens*, so that the fortune did not go out of it. Yet the law proves that the spirit of family had already died away: Cicero, in his Republic, is wrong in judging of it according to the standard of his own times. The Romans had already gone so far downhill, that no single law, like the *lex Voconia*, could any longer have staved off the impending crash. It was then, as forty years ago in England, a time in which a thorough-going, deep-searching legislation might still have checked the wayward course of the state. But such timely and thorough reforms are very rare indeed in history. Fate leads states onward towards their downfall; and thus I prophesy of the English state, that within fifty years it will be radically changed.[52] In Rome also, single laws were now brought in, which were carried against the wishes of individuals; yet one always made shift to find some quibble by which it might be evaded. The *lex Ælia et Fufia* is another remarkable law: when, and how it was passed, is very obscure; it is generally considered as one law, but according to Cicero, it is probable that there were two: they must have been of great importance. As far as we know of its contents, it enacted that the proceedings of the tribunes might be interrupted by auguries which had been observed. This shows in what estimation, even at that time, the old forms still were. To us, who, of course, look upon the whole system of auguries as a tissue of lies, this has only the appearance of an extension of priestcraft, and we wonder how this could have been done in an enlightened age. Yet it was meant as a mere form. The power of the tribunes had risen to a fearful height, and now that the augurs received authority to set forth what might break up an assembly of the people called together by the tribunes, no one thought in this of signs given by the powers above: it was only a means for the *optimates*, to check the unbounded encroachments of the tribunes. By the *Lex Hortensia* the tribunes might have laws passed without the consent of the senate; but now the augurs, who were chosen, half of them from the patricians, and the other half from the plebeians, but from the most eminent families, might oppose these enactments, and restrain that unbridled power. The form indeed is unworthy and offensive, as the augurs evidently were obliged to tell a lie; yet the meaning of the law, to create a counter-tribunate in matters of legislation, was a good one. The law is to be met with in Cicero only; Clodius repealed it.

Among the events which show how greatly the state of things at Rome had changed, is the circumstance that in the year 600, either a tribune, or the whole college, ordered the consuls to be led to prison for having been guilty of unfairness at the enlistment, particularly L. Licinius Lucullus.[53] Such a decree of the tribunes is so much against the spirit of the ancient constitution, that this is of itself enough to show the completeness of the change. This change is a proof that personal conscientiousness could no more be relied upon. In early times, the consuls designated every one singly who was to serve in war, and this had continued to be the custom ever since: at first, nearly all were taken; afterwards, those who were most able-bodied, and who were already well trained in war, were picked out. As the legions were now stationed longer and longer in distant provinces, the burthen of military service grew more and more oppressive, and many tried to screen themselves from it by making interest; for the tribunes would, without giving any reason, get off those whom they favoured. Moreover, the enlistments, owing to the wide extent of the empire, must have been fraught with still greater difficulties, as the men had to appear in person. The system of selection was now done away with, and the general conscription so managed, that the lot decided the obligation to serve, and the grounds for exemption were to be considered afterwards. This was not a change for the worse, but it was still a change. The tribunes, however, on this demanded that each of them should have the right of liberating ten, and when the consuls would not allow this, they arrested them.[54] Still more significant is the fact, that even before the end of the sixth century, it became necessary to make laws against canvassing which were directly aimed at venality; for the form of the organization by centuries was now changed, and attempts at bribery had become possible. Whether the *Lex Cornelia* against *ambitus* is that of Cornelius Cethegus, or of Sulla, cannot be ascertained, although it has been held to be the former beyond a doubt; certain it is, however, that as early as in the year 570 a law was passed against *ambitus,* a circumstance which has become somewhat better known from the Milan scholia on Cicero.[55]

THE THIRD PUNIC WAR

The third Punic war had been long threatened, owing to the relations between Carthage and Masinissa. The peace lasted more than fifty years, during which the Carthaginians had never given any handle for complaint, nor do we know of any mentioned on the side of Rome. It may be said that this must have been a time of some prosperity for Carthage, as at the end of it we find the city wealthy and well-peopled. This we may also easily understand: the wars in the east were highly profitable to Carthage, since as a neutral state it had free intercourse everywhere; as, for instance, during the war between Syria and Egypt, when the trade of these two countries was altogether stopped. The energy of the Carthaginians could not turn itself to foreign affairs, and therefore it was engaged at home in accumulating wealth. Whilst, however, Carthage by the peace of Scipio was placed in fact in a kind of pupillage, its national character and constitution seem to have quite fallen away: the rottenness of the government, and the anarchical preponderance of the rabble, was, to use Polybius' remarkable words, an old evil, older even than at Rome. We see that a power like that of the consuls at Rome had by this time long ceased to exist in Carthage, and that the authority of the senate was also very much reduced. A people of eastern origin, with republican self-government, but without institutions like those which among the Greeks and Romans checked democratical degeneracy, could not but sink into utter lawlessness.

The real thorn in their side from abroad, was the neighbourhood of Masinissa. He may have had instructions from Rome; yet, even if it were not so, he knew well, that however much he worried the Carthaginians, even though he were hatefully in the wrong, the Romans would never declare against him. The Carthaginians showed immense forbearance, and resigned themselves to their hard lot. In such cases, one should indeed yield to necessity, yet always cling to the feeling of being unfortunate; for as soon as that is lost, cowardice and baseness spring up: we can hardly help believing that the Carthaginians had fallen into this condition, and given themselves up.

Very soon after the end of the second Punic war, quarrels already began. Masinissa put forth impudent claims to the oldest Phœnician settlements, to the rich coast of Bysacene which the Carthaginians had possessed from the very first. Polybius says that those districts had belonged to Carthage as early as in the days of the Roman kings. This was so barefaced, that the Romans had not the hardihood to declare for him openly. Scipio Africanus went over as Roman commissioner and umpire. The facts were so glaring, that he could not possibly decide for Masinissa; yet he did not scruple with unjustifiable policy to refuse to give sentence, and thus Carthage and Masinissa remained at enmity with each other, and the Carthaginians must have felt convinced, that any active resistance would involve them in a war with the Romans: they were therefore obliged to confine themselves to the defensive. Their position was a most unhappy one; just like that of the states with which Napoleon had made peace in order to bring on their ruin, in which cases he set everything like truth at defiance. Unluckily for Carthage, Masinissa reigned upwards of fifty years after the peace of Scipio, and during the whole of his life played his game with Rome so cleverly, that her sad condition grew worse and worse. Already before the war with Perseus, soon after the death of Philip, they complained bitterly of Masinissa, who wrested from them one district after another. The Romans for the sake of appearances sent over arbitrators, who, however, allowed the affair to drag on and never decided anything. And the plot thickened so much, that at last it came to a war between Carthage and Masinissa, the date of which cannot be stated with chronological precision,—very likely, not quite so close upon the breaking out of the third Punic war.[56] The territory of Carthage at that time was about as much as modern Tunis, and the western part of Tripoli; Masinissa, by his continual conquests, was the lord of one of the mightiest kingdoms which the world then knew, and was much stronger than the Carthaginians. The Carthaginians had gathered together a considerable army under Hasdrubal, one of their generals; but their former disasters had not made them more warlike: they did not what Macchiavell had wished for his own native city, not having yet come to the conviction that they ought ever to rely on their own bravery, and likewise to lighten the lot of their own subjects: had it not been for this, the war might, after all, have taken quite a different turn. They had amended none of the faults of their military system, and they still carried on the war by means of mercenaries. Hasdrubal went out to meet Masinissa with an army of fifty thousand men; but he was quite an incapable general, and though the battle was not decisively lost, he looked upon himself as beaten, and retreated without securing his connexion with Carthage: he was, therefore, cut off, and now began to make offers of peace, which, however, Masinissa haughtily rejected. The latter would not consent to let go the army thus hemmed in, which hunger and distress had driven to extremity, until the Carthaginians gave hostages as pledges for the peace being kept, undertook to pay five thousand talents within fifty years, and recognised his encroachments upon them. When the defenceless and disarmed soldiers were now marching off, Gulussa, Masinissa's youngest son, fell upon them, and cut most of them to pieces. Masinissa had the hostages, and so he still demanded that the peace should be kept, and even complained to the Romans of the Carthaginians not being disposed to abide by it. The Romans had already for some time turned their attention again to Carthage, very likely on account of the flourishing state of its trade, and because they had been told that stores of timber for building ships were heaped up in the arsenals: for though indeed this had been by no means forbidden in the treaties, the Carthaginians were thus able at a moment's warning to build a fleet. Rome now called for the surrender or the destruction of this timber; and while the debates on the subject were going on, old Cato incessantly urged in the senate, that Carthage should be destroyed. The government of the world had given the senate an importance which made up for the loss of power at home from the growth of the democratic principle, and the senators felt more and more like kings. Now the senate, with regard to Carthage, was divided between two opinions,—the one of blind dogged hatred, that Carthage should be destroyed, at the bottom of which was the consciousness that Rome was the object of universal hatred; the other, that of P. Cornelius Scipio Nasica, which held on the other hand that Carthage was a godsend, as nothing else could keep Rome well balanced. Nasica seems to have been fully aware of the actual condition of the state, and so were many others; but with regard to the remedy, opinions were divided. Some thought that there was no help for it, and that therefore one ought to go ahead, and make the most of a short life. Cato was one of these. Others, like Nasica, believed that the evil might at least be checked by superficial means, as a thorough reform could not perhaps be carried out. A small party, which afterwards came forward with Tib. Gracchus at its head, tried to root out the disease by desperate remedies. Whether this justice to Carthage in Nasica sprang indeed from a love of righteousness, is more than we can tell; yet it may be that the son of him who was called "the Best" wished to behave uprightly: certain it is that he was powerless, and the destruction of Carthage was decreed. When Masinissa had beaten the Carthaginians, and it was fancied that the end might be easily gained, the Romans began to reproach the Carthaginians for that war with Masinissa, as if it had been a breach of the treaty, when in fact it had only been a measure of self-defence. The Carthaginians in their alarm sent embassy after embassy, begging of the Romans to tell them what they were to do to preserve the peace. But they were put off with crooked answers, and assured that it was not meant to undertake anything against them, only they ought to do their best to give satisfaction to Rome. Resistance seemed so hopeless, that the utmost humiliation was a necessity for Carthage: there was peace in all the rest of the world, and Rome was fully at leisure.

In the year 603, two consular armies under L. Marcius Censorinus and M'. Manilius, amounting, it is said, to eighty thousand men, were sent in a large fleet to Sicily, and put on shore near Lilybæum. Thither also the last Carthaginian ambassadors were directed to repair, as the consuls were furnished with instructions. The Carthaginians saw that the Romans were bent upon their ruin, and that nothing was left to them, but to defend themselves to the last gasp; and yet the ambassadors still appeared before the consuls. These gave as their answer, that they could not then explain themselves; but that it was not the wish of the Romans to bereave them of their freedom, and that if they yielded to the commands which they would receive, they should retain their liberties: still, it was added, as they had too often already broken the peace, and as great preparations of theirs had been observed, and too many factions were at work among them, Rome was to have a guarantee; they should give three hundred children of the first families as hostages. These, to the despair of their parents, were sent to Sicily. Carthage had not a friend in the wide world: her very oldest allies became faithless; even Utica, which hitherto had always stood by her, now hopeless of her fate had thrown itself into the arms of the Romans, by whom it was received, although this was against the treaties. When the hostages were given, the Romans still sailed over to Africa, and landed, partly near Utica, and partly at the old camp of Scipio (*castra Cornelia*); here they took up a regular military position, and the consuls now summoned the magistrates of Carthage to receive their commands. They raised complaints that the Carthaginians had built ships beyond the number allowed by the treaty; that they had filled their arsenals with offensive weapons, which they meant to use against Rome only; and it was therefore required of them that they should surrender all their ships of war, and all the catapults, and that moreover they should deliver up all their arms and stores. Rome, it was also declared, would fully protect them, and the peace with Masinissa would be sanctioned. Hard as they felt this to be, the Carthaginians yielded to it; and the whole of the arms were brought on a thousand waggons, and under the eyes of the Roman commissioners, to the Roman camp. The Romans, on first landing, had demanded a supply of corn for their army, and received the grain from the magazines of the city, which was thus very nearly reduced to a state of famine. With this the Carthaginians thought to have done enough; but now the ambassadors received the last audience. They were led through the ranks of the whole army to the tribunal of the consuls, who now told them, that all that had been done betokened the good will of the Carthaginian government, yet that the latter was not even master of the town; that so long as this strong city was standing, Rome was not safe; and that Carthage therefore must be demolished, and its inhabitants were to build for themselves an open town in the inland country, two (German) miles away from the sea. When the ambassadors remonstrated, the consuls said that they had promised safety to the men, and not to the walls; that the people should not be harmed, and they might just as well live ten (Roman) miles from the sea as those who dwelt in Rome. The outbursts of rage and despair at this infamous deceit were of no avail; the last awful prayer was, that the consuls would, before the ambassadors returned, cause the Roman fleet to make its appearance before Carthage, to strike it with dismay. This was no treason in them; it was prompted by despair. Those among them who had advised their countrymen to yield, saw full well that, if they went home, they should fall victims to the rage of the people; and they therefore remained under the protection of the Romans. Those who came back, refused to answer the people, who had gone out to meet them, and they weeping brought the answer into the senate. It was resolved to die upon the ruins of the city; the gates were immediately shut, and all the Romans and Italians in the town were seized and tortured to death. This the consuls had not expected. They were indeed well informed men,—Manilius was even a highly distinguished jurist,—but they were unfit for war; it may be that the fate of the town appeared to themselves so dreadful, that their heart sickened, and they went to work without spirit. Had they at once advanced to the city, they would have taken it, and the misery been less; but they loitered in the camp, waiting till the Carthaginians should surrender. Things, however, took quite a different turn. The citizens made up their minds not to yield themselves up; they laid hold of everything that might serve as a weapon, and worked day and night with unexampled energy; the women gave their hair for the ropes of the catapults, the slaves were set free, the walls were manned, and the war declared. When the consuls saw that they had made a bad business of it, they wished to storm the town. But across that neck of land on which Carthage lay, it was fortified by a threefold wall, three miles long, forty-five feet (thirty πήχεις) high, and twenty-five feet thick, in which in former times there had been arsenals; and on the side towards the sea, there was one somewhat lower. Both of these the Romans tried to storm, but were beaten back. The country in the neighbourhood of the city was left to Hasdrubal, the general who had fought against Masinissa, and whom they had been obliged to sacrifice. This Hasdrubal, with an army of twenty thousand men, formed of outcasts and refugees, and acting independently, had ravaged the country, and at the same time had waged a war of pillage against Masinissa. He and all the rest who had been banished were reinstated, and Carthage appointed him as her general without the city.

This war is so dismal, that I can hardly bear to think of it, and still less to tell of it at any length. There is nothing more heartrending than this struggle of despair, which indeed could not end otherwise than in the destruction of the whole people, and that most miserably, but which yet must be gone through. At first, one is glad to see the discomfiture of the Romans, the whole might of the unskilful consuls being baffled by the despair of the besieged. The Carthaginians defended themselves bravely within the city: their commander is unknown; without, there were Hasdrubal and Himilco Phameas as partisans. The way in which the latter carried on the war, so as by means of diversions to give the town a free opening to provision itself, strongly reminds one of the achievements of Francesco Ferrucci at the siege of Florence by Charles V., in the years 1529 and 1530; who was at last taken prisoner and hanged by the Spaniards, whose behaviour there was like that of the French in Tyrol. But although Phameas distinguished himself very much as a military man, yet his end shows how great was the corruption of those times. After having done things which were so brilliant, that he ought to have felt called upon indeed to remain true, he entered into negotiations with the Roman consul; and he told his men that the fate of Carthage was decided, that every one must now take care of himself, and that he could pledge himself for the safety of all those who should join him. A few thousand men went over. The Roman senate did not blush to give this traitor splendid garments, money, landed estates, and other things of the same kind. This was a heavy blow for Carthage; and yet at this very time it seemed as if its fate was about to take a more propitious turn.

Masinissa again showed himself to be a base perfidious oriental. His faithfulness to Rome had hitherto been quite natural, as to this connexion he owed his greatness; but now he had rather see Carthage saved than destroyed, although still weakened. He could not shut his eyes to the fact that if Carthage was once a Roman province, he should no longer be able to fleece it; and that moreover, as the Romans held the maxim *bella ex bellis serendi*, they would soon find a handle for quarrels: for if Carthage was no more, they would then have no reason whatever for sparing him. And thus mistrust betrayed itself between him and the Romans: he sent no troops, but merely asked what they wanted? Offended at this, they told him that they would let him know it in time, and thereupon he answered that he would wait for it. Yet they afterwards called upon him for his help, and it was granted them. He even began to treat with Carthage, wishing that it would unconditionally throw itself into his arms. This is a thing which often happens in eastern history: the same bashaw, for instance, who had stirred up the Sultan against Ali Pacha, would at last, when he was weakened, have been glad to see him saved. After the death of Masinissa, his son Gulussa was very suspicious of the Romans. Had the Carthaginians thrown themselves into the arms of Masinissa or his son, these would have declared for them, and it is very possible that the Roman rule in Africa would then have been broken.

The attacks on Carthage were left off, the siege was raised, and the two consuls confined themselves to waging war against Hasdrubal and Himilco. But Hasdrubal defeated the consul Manilius, who was obliged to fall back with his army to Utica: on this occasion P. Scipio first distinguished himself. In the following year (604), the consuls L. Calpurnius Piso and L. Mancinus came over, and carried on the war in a very bungling manner. Hasdrubal posted himself at Nepheris, a fortified place a few days' marches from the city, and every attempt to drive him out was unsuccessful; and what is really astonishing, the sea was open to the Carthaginians, although they had no fleet, and they continued to get supplies from thence. The bad progress of the war, in which the Romans took only single towns, was the amazement of the whole world, and it strengthened the belief that the Nemesis for Rome's ambition would at length appear. At the same time happened the rising in Macedonia under the pseudo-Philip; the Spaniards also roused themselves to new hopes, and the Carthaginians tried to stir up commotions every where. This general agitation, which reached far into Asia, gave Carthage the courage to hold out, and not to enter into a league with the Numidians.

The Romans were so much the more ashamed, as such base conduct as theirs had been towards Carthage could not but rise up in judgment against them; and therefore their dissatisfaction with the generals was very great. In the year 605, P. Scipio was chosen consul. He is in the classical ages never called Æmilianus, although the analogy of this appellation is quite correct; but he is spoken of as *P. Scipio, Paulli filius*. Thus it is always in Cicero, there being no manuscript which has Æmilianus: in the *fasti*, this surname is always of modern interpolation.[57]

Scipio is one of those characters, which have a great name in history, but of which we may ask, do they deserve their fame? I do not gainsay his great qualities: he is a distinguished general, a very eminent man in his day, and he has done many praise-worthy and righteous deeds. But he made a display of this worthiness; even quite ordinary acts of his were to be cried up as great achievements: one really blushes for the age in which such things could have been given out as being above common. From what we are told by his teacher and friend Polybius himself, who loved him dearly, we may see that he also thought that there was much in him which was mere ostentation. He had received from Polybius a most varied education, and had been particularly instructed by him in the art of war. Besides this military ability, he was remarkable as a political character: he was one of those who were for upholding the existing state of things; he found himself comfortable in it; for him what was established was all right, and he did not trouble himself with asking whether it might not have been wrong in its origin. Perhaps he looked upon the condition of the republic as so hopeless, that he believed, that any change must have shaken it: such views are held by many otherwise true-hearted and honest men. In no respect is he to be compared to the elder Scipio, who was a man of real genius, and felt himself to be far above all his contemporaries, so that with great love for his countrymen, he had hatred against any one who wanted to put himself on a par with him. The latter was artless, even to rashness; whereas, on the contrary, his adopted grandson was a made up man, in whom genius was wanting. The education of the younger Scipio was much more finished than that of the elder one; for he had all the knowledge of a well instructed Greek, and he lived with the most distinguished men, such as Polybius and Panætius. He allowed himself to be employed by his nation for two terrible destructions, which were quite against his feelings; yet he did not all he could to prevent them: the elder Scipio would not have destroyed Carthage. Besides which, his behaviour towards his brother-in-law Tib. Gracchus is altogether blameable: for with all his influence and might he backed the thoroughly bad party; whence also he was so much hated by the people, as was seen at his death. The introduction to the *Somnium Scipionis* is not to be considered as historical by any means: the very fact that he had first come to Africa as a military tribune under Manilius and Censorinus, is incorrect; it is one of Cicero's historical blunders. Cicero has treated him with particular favour. Thus it often happens that we identify ourselves with some personage in history or in literature; we learn to feel like him, and to feel as his case were ours, and we then ascribe to him quite a different character from that which is really his. Scipio's position was not altogether unlike that of Cicero.

Whilst still very young, Scipio stood for the ædileship, instead of which he was chosen to be consul, although the *lex Villia annalis* was then rigorously observed. The provisions of this law we cannot state for certain: they were not the same as in aftertimes; the statutes which were in force in Cicero's days, dated from the age of Sylla. Nevertheless Scipio was elected consul by the unanimous voice of public opinion.

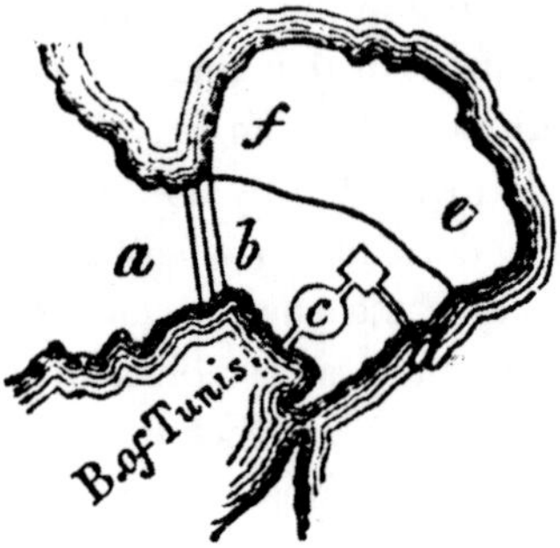

a. triple wall.

b. Byrsa.

c. harbour.

d. newly dug canal.

e. Megara (Magalia).

f. Roman Carthage.

Carthage was built on a peninsula, of which, however, it did not take up the whole, as indeed has been supposed, but only the southern half: this mistake arose from its having been said that the city was twenty-three (Roman) miles in circumference. It seems to have been entirely surrounded by a sort of breastwork. This is now known from the excavations of Colonel Humbert, who was several years in the service of the Dey of Tunis; but the results of his researches have not yet found their way into books.[58] (His papers fell into the hands of a downright adventurer, Count Camillo Borgia, who copied his drawings, and passed them off as his own.) The old town of Carthage was so thoroughly destroyed, that no traces of it are found above ground;—the place on which it stood was laid under a curse, and therefore the later Roman Carthage was founded by the side of it;—yet there is still to be seen a quay built of great blocks of hewn stone, from which I had a piece broken off as a relic, which is, however, still lying at Leghorn. Where it faced the isthmus, the city, as has been remarked before, was fenced by a triple wall; next to this was the Bozra; on the south was the port, which was detached, as at Cadiz. The harbour (Cothon), which was dug out, had several basins with a narrow entrance, like the docks in London: from the offing one sailed into the harbour for merchant vessels, and from thence by a canal to the arsenal, which was situated on an island, and strongly fortified; round the basins, there were storehouses with the equipments for every ship. This port was of later origin; probably there was a third district also. In the course of time, there had likewise grown up a large suburb, Megara or Magalia, the situation of which cannot be exactly defined: it was quite covered with gardens, but was also surrounded by a wall. As the coast was very steep, it was difficult to land there. It is the present El Marsa. The Roman Carthage, founded again by C. Gracchus and Cæsar, was in this neighbourhood, as may be clearly made out from the antiquities, which are brought to light there. The only Carthaginian relics to be found in it, are tombs; which is easily accounted for, as it lay outside of the city.

Appian is the only source, which gives us the details of this war. Fortunately he has copied from Polybius; for otherwise he is below criticism. Yet even then, his account, like that of Zonaras, is very obscure and unconnected. We merely gather from thence that Scipio landed on the outer part of the peninsula, where he took up his position, and made himself master of the suburb; so that Carthage was confined to the old town and the harbours. About a year before his consulship already, a Roman officer had discovered the possibility of landing at Megara, and of taking possession of it; and by this means Carthage was brought to great distress, as a large part of the provisions used to come in that way. Nothing could be done against the walls on the landside; Scipio, therefore, directed his attack against the side from the bay with redoubled energy. In the meanwhile, the Carthaginians summoned Hasdrubal to the city, and he entrenched himself on the isthmus before it; but when the suburb was taken, he threw himself panic-struck into the town, and the Romans occupied his fortified camp; so that the Carthaginians were entirely hemmed in. Another Carthaginian general, Bithyas, had remained in the interior of the country; and he behaved admirably, always supplying the city with provisions, which he conveyed to it through the very midst of the unwieldy Roman ships. To cut off from Carthage this support, Scipio now chose as a last expedient, the gulf being shallow, to choke up the mouth of the harbour by running a dam across; and this was so much the easier, as the swell, when coming from the Syrtes, carries with it a good deal of mud. The harbour has ceased to exist; yet one may still very distinctly make out its site and shape from the silt which has been washed in. From the dam, Scipio tried to batter the wall of the harbour with his engines: the desperate struggles of the Carthaginians to hinder this, beggar all description. The greatest feat which they accomplished, was the building of a whole fleet of fifty triremes in the arsenal, and then,—as the latter was connected by a canal with the outer harbour, the entrance of which Scipio was endeavouring to block up,—digging from thence an outlet on the other side to the sea, by which they brought out their ships to attack the Roman fleet in the gulf. Polybius (in Appian) justly remarks, that, if at that moment they had fearlessly fallen upon the Roman fleet, they would undoubtedly have destroyed it, as the Romans had utterly neglected their naval concerns. Unhappily, they slackened after their more than human effort, and, lingering for some days, irretrievably lost time, and with it all the fruits of their labour: the Romans got their ships ready as well as they could, and thus the Carthaginians were driven back, particularly by the Græco-Asiatic ships of Sida, which fought quite in a way of their own. Four of these small vessels would cast anchor, on which they swung round as on a pivot, and thus defended themselves against the Carthaginians, an example which was followed by the others. The Carthaginians retreated. The next day, they wished to renew the attack: but they got foul of each other in the narrow entrance, the canal, which they had dug, being unfortunately not wide enough, and the Romans bore down upon them, and drove them against the wall of the harbour; so that this gigantic undertaking was again baffled. The Carthaginians now saw nothing but ruin before their eyes. Scipio first took the harbour for merchantmen, and from thence he advanced through the canal against the arsenal. Thus the city was conquered bit for bit, and the Romans made their way as far as the arsenal; as this could not have been held, the Carthaginians, perhaps too hastily, at once set fire to it, and then to the storehouses for the ships. The Romans were in possession of both harbours, and the fight was for the old city, Bozra (Byrsa), which had no walls on that side, but only leant upon the threefold wall on the isthmus: from the harbour, three large streets led up to the Byrsa, and in these the rich and the old families seem to have lived:—one may still trace in the description the gradual development of the city. The houses there were most of them seven or eight stories high, with flat roofs. (We must look upon Carthage as having been with regard to art and beauty like the fine towns of Greece, but with much more of Roman grandeur and massiveness: the building of stately streets is ascribed to them by the Romans as a thing peculiarly their own; the Greeks knew nothing of it.) There was now the same struggle as at Saragossa. House after house was defended and taken; the enemy broke through the party-walls, they fought from room to room, and when they had forced their way up the stairs, and driven the unfortunate inmates from the last stories, they tried to throw bridges from the roofs across the streets. The superior strength of the Romans assured them the victory, besides which, a most fearful famine was raging in the city where people were already feeding on dead bodies: and yet the besieged would not hear of surrender, though indeed such a thing could hardly have been mooted, as Hasdrubal had treated the Roman prisoners with the most horrible barbarity. When, after much bloodshed, part of the city was already taken, the Romans stopped short, and set fire to the buildings; on which the Carthaginians, fleeing before the flames, pulled up the houses, and thus raised up a huge mound of rubbish against the wall and the citadel: the harrowing description of this fire is evidently from Polybius, the unfortunate eye-witness of the horrors which now took place. The soldiers deliberately buried the wounded alive under the ruins! Thus the old town was reached, and now every one tried only to save himself; the priests went as suppliants with signs of truce, and begged for mercy: Scipio then caused it to be announced that the lives of those who would come out should be spared. On this, the people which still survived, fifty thousand in number, came forth; the Roman deserters only, with Hasdrubal and his family, retreated to the highest part of the citadel, a most hallowed place which was called Ἀσκληπιεῖον. Hasdrubal was base enough to sue for his life; but his wife slew her children, and cursing him, even from the pinnacle of the temple, threw herself into the flames, an example which was followed by the deserters. Thus Scipio became master of a heap of smouldering ruins drenched with blood. Much must, however, have been preserved, as he took from the temples many Sicilian trophies, which he sent back to that island. Neither Tarentum nor Capua had been destroyed by the senate; but Scipio had to raze Carthage to the ground at their command. He now completed the work already begun, and drove a plough-share across the site as a sign of its everlasting desolation: the army, when it went away, left only that utter wilderness in the midst of which Marius seated himself sixty years afterwards. The prisoners were treated with more or less humanity: most of them were sold for slaves, some also were slain; a few of those of higher rank met with a better fate, and were distributed among the Italian towns. Bithyas was one of these; their race and their name perished from the earth. The Romans, whose forefathers had put to death the great C. Pontius, spared the life of Hasdrubal: he was kept for the triumph.

Carthage had stood for seven hundred years. Part of its territory was given to the Numidian kings, the three sons of Masinissa; the rest became a Roman province, under the rule of a proconsul or prætor.

THE PSEUDO-PHILIP. THE ACHÆAN WAR. DESTRUCTION OF CORINTH

When Carthage was overpowered, the Macedonian war was already ended, and Corinth near its downfall. The Macedonian war of Andriscus is a striking example of the way in which the whole of a people may be taken in. The false Demetrius, as he was called, was in the opinion of those who knew history well, by no means an impostor: but he had been brought up in Poland, had gone over to the Roman catholic religion, and had adopted European manners; whence the mistrust which he met with in Russia. There is a very strong likelihood that one of the Sebastians in Portugal, was the true king: (Lessing, in the "*Literatur briefe,*" has also written a masterly article on this subject, though it was one which was out of his beat.) But Andriscus was really an impostor, most likely a Thracian gladiator; heaven knows how he could have dreamed of the venturesome idea of giving himself out as the son of Perseus: perhaps he bore some likeness to him. Such personifications are not unseldom attempted in the East; in Europe, some instances of the kind are met with in the middle ages. The war had already broken out when Scipio became consul, perhaps even a year before: (the destruction of Carthage was in the time of his proconsulship.)

Perseus and his sons were, after the triumph of Æmilius Paullus, sent as prisoners to Alba on the lake Fucinus, where they were treated in a way which clearly showed that their extinction was determined on. The king did not outlive this cruel usage more than two years; he had so childishly clung to life, that he would not listen to the hints of Æmilius Paullus, to take it himself: they probably killed him by constantly disturbing his sleep. His eldest son died in the same manner; the youngest lived in the most abject degradation. Being clever, he learnt the Latin language, and earned his daily bread as clerk to the municipal council of Alba: beyond this, we have no further trace of him.

During the Carthaginian war, Andriscus now set forth that he was a son of Perseus, and he found a party in Macedonia; being, however, unable to stand his ground, he went to Demetrius in Syria, and was by him given up to the Romans. Such an act is just what one would have expected from

Demetrius, who had every reason to do his best to regain his footing with the Romans, now that he had only just escaped being punished by them. He had fled indeed from Rome after the death of his brother Antiochus Epiphanes, to secure the throne; and the Romans had sent commissioners to Syria, on hearing that the Syrians, contrary to the existing treaties, were keeping elephants, and had moreover built a greater number of ships than they were allowed. One of these commissioners was slain in a riot at Laodicea, and Demetrius, with great difficulty, turned aside the vengeance of the Romans, by yielding up the murderers and killing the elephants. Under these circumstances, it was but natural that Andriscus was given up. At Rome, this man was, as an adventurer, held in such contempt, that he was not properly guarded; and he again made his escape. He came to Thrace, where the Romans were already feared and hated; all sorts of people flocked to him there, and he made an inroad into Macedon. A war in that country was very inconvenient to the Romans, who were engaged in their enterprise against Carthage, and had no troops in the north of Greece. To the amazement of every body, Andriscus routed the Macedonians on the eastern bank of the Strymon; he then crossed the river, and beat them once more, whereupon they all joined him. His success was quite wonderful; he put on the diadem under the name of Philip. Things must at that time have been in a very dismal state in Macedon. The Romans had brought in the wretched republican constitution, and the most eminent men had been led away to Italy; so that the people, who from the earliest times had been accustomed to kingly rule, eagerly caught at this hope of bettering its lot. In Thessaly also, he found partizans. Nasica, who happened to be there, got together the contingents of the Greeks, and with their aid repulsed Philip when he invaded it: at that time, therefore, the Greeks were still faithful. Andriscus was a tyrannical fellow at bottom: Polybius calls him στυγνὸς ἀνήϱ. Yet he knew how to make himself respected: his armaments were on an extraordinary scale, and he ventured to wage war even against the Roman prætor, P. Juventius Thalna; after having beaten him, he marched once more into Thessaly. Matters looked serious enough: Q. Metellus, the prætor, was obliged to go with a large army to Greece, where he landed on the coast, which could not have been easily defended; in the meanwhile, the Achæans already showed themselves very mutinous, and the war, if it lasted, could not but lead to a rising. Metellus drove the king from Thessaly, who, like Perseus, fell back upon Pydna, followed by the Romans. The Macedonians, who were superior in numbers, divided their forces for a foray; and Metellus took advantage of this, and attacked and utterly routed them. The conquest of Macedonia in this insurrection was not, however, so easy as the former one had been; for many places held out, expecting a worse fate. On this occasion Pella must have been destroyed: Dio Chrysostom, in the first century after the birth of Christ, speaks of it as a ruined city; it now lies buried under mounds of earth, and is only to be traced by the row of hills which marked its site. Undoubtedly the most interesting antiquities might be found there, especially works of art; but unfortunately, the present condition of European affairs gives little hope of any thorough researches being made there so very soon. Andriscus was taken prisoner in Thrace, and put to death: Macedon became a regular province, and from henceforth a governor seems to have been constantly sent thither; its few remaining privileges were taken away.

Had the Achæans known what they wanted, the revolt of the pseudo-Philip would have been the moment for them to act: but they allowed themselves to be beguiled into folly and absurdity. Although we cannot disguise from ourselves, that the causes which hastened on the fall of Achaia, were disgraceful to the Achæans, yet it is a fact that its ruin made the condition of the survivors not better but worse; and this awakens our sympathy for them. And moreover, this degenerate people still had among them many excellent men. The Romans had for a long time been bent on the destruction of Achaia, and by means of traitors, such as Callicrates and Andronidas, they ruled there with unlimited sway; hence causes for grievances arose, and when these fellows had once gained a settled position, they too were no longer as ready to do the dirty work as before. The catastrophe was wholly brought on by one unhappy violent act of the otherwise excellent Philopœmen, a man who was justly called the last of the Greeks. He entertained from his very childhood a deadly hatred against Sparta, since Cleomenes had destroyed his native town of Megalopolis; and to bring down Sparta, was what he ever had most at heart. He took advantage of Rome's being entangled in the war of Antiochus, to compel Sparta to join the Achæan league, and to adopt its customs and forms; for among the Achæans, unlike the other confederacies of the same kind in the ancient world, such a fusion existed. Achaia then comprised the whole of the Peloponnesus: that strange federal system was full as mischievous as that of our unfortunate German confederacy, in which the least of the petty princes has just as good a vote as he on whom the safety of the country hinges;—or as the state of things in America before the constitution of Washington, when Delaware with seventy thousand inhabitants, had an equal vote with Virginia, the population of which amounted to half a million; or as in the republics of the Netherlands, where Zeeland, which paid three per cent. of the taxes, had by its votes as much weight as Holland which paid fifty-eight per cent. This absurdity was the ruin of the Achæan league. Elis was a large town and country, while Lacedæmon, even after the sea-coast had been already severed from it, was yet greater than all Achaia;

nevertheless, each of the twelve little Achæan townships, many of which were not larger than some of our German villages,[59] had just as many votes as Lacedæmon. But the second article was the most galling of all. Even as Sicyon had adopted the Achæan νόμιμα, which was all very well, so was Sparta likewise to do away with the laws of Lycurgus, to which it had clung with so much pride, and to put up with those of the Achæans: this was done some years before the war with Perseus. Spartiates, in the true sense of the word, there were none at that time, but only Lacedæmonians; the former had died away, and since the days of Cleomenes, the population of the town, which consisted of descendants of the Periœcians and Neodamodes, under the name of Lacedæmonians, stepped into the full rights of citizens. But as these Lacedæmonians had adopted the laws and the ἀγωγή of Lycurgus, and prided themselves in them, it was a great piece of cruelty in Philopœmen to force them to drop them again: for this was a change which was felt throughout the whole business of every day life. Moreover, there is not much to be said in praise of the Achæan forms, and however little good there may have been in the Spartan system, if it did nothing else, it made good soldiers. For these reasons, the Lacedæmonians strove to rid themselves of this hateful alliance, and there were long negotiations in consequence: yet it was still binding on them in the beginning of the seventh century, when even a Lacedæmonian, Menalcidas, was the general of the Achæan league.

About this time, some unlucky quarrels having arisen between the Oropians and Athenians, the former bribed Menalcidas with ten talents to help them. The assistance, however, came too late; notwithstanding which he exacted the money from them, and though he had previously promised part of it to Callicrates, he kept the whole for himself. From the charge which the latter brought against him, sprang all the woes which befell Achaia. Menalcidas did his utmost to sever Lacedæmon from the league, and he succeeded. At the time of the negotiations which took place about it at Rome, both Menalcidas and the Achæan ambassador deceived the people who had sent them: each of them carried home a false decision. It was just then the most unfortunate period of the third Punic war. Lacedæmon now severed itself, and a war broke out between the Achæans and Lacedæmonians, in which the latter had the worst of it: for Menalcidas was a wretched general, and they were so hard pressed that they had to consent to an agreement by which the Achæans got every thing that they wanted. Menalcidas laid hands upon his own life, and the Lacedæmonians again joined the Achæan league.

When the Romans, in the year 605, now saw that they were about to overthrow Carthage, they also took a different tone towards Achaia. The

Achæans had acted in direct disobedience to them, and had thus drawn down their vengeance upon themselves, although they had remained faithful during the revolt of the pseudo-Philip, and had given them their aid. But the very prosperity of Achaia may have led the Romans to break it up. Its extent in those times cannot be stated with exactness: it very likely took in the whole of Peloponnesus and Megara, and although Attica, Phocis, and Locris did not belong to it, several places yet farther off, by having isopolity, were in the league; for instance, Heraclea, by mount Oeta, Pleuron, in Ætolia. The Roman commissioners, C. Aurelius Orestes and his colleagues, appeared at Corinth, and announced it to be the will of the Roman senate, that Lacedæmon should be declared independent; and that all the places, which, at the time of the alliance with Philip, had not belonged to Achaia, but had been under Philip's sway, should be separated from it: these were Corinth, Orchomenus in Arcadia, Heraclea, Pleuron. (Whether Elis and Messene belonged to the same category, is more than we know, as Appian's notices are so scanty: the *excerpta* of Constantinus Porphyrogenitus will very likely still bring to light a great deal more of this period.) This was about the half of the Peloponnesus, and the most distinguished of their towns. The Achæan council, then assembled in Corinth, would not listen to the end of this message; they ordered the doors to be thrown open, and the people to be called together to hear the insolence of the Romans. The rage of the people was beyond all bounds: the Romans returned to their lodgings, without having gotten an answer; the citizens spread themselves about the town and fell upon the Lacedæmonians; everywhere the houses were searched to see whether any Lacedæmonian had hidden himself within, and not even that of the Roman ambassadors was spared. The first of these, Aurelius Orestes, was bent upon revenge; but the Roman senate was not yet inclined to inflict immediate punishment. We find it often stated that Corinth had been destroyed *ob pulsatos legatos*; this is not to be understood literally of personal violence, *pulsare* being the technical expression for every violation of the law of nations. Even a derogatory *appellatio* of the ambassador, by which his dignity was insulted, was termed *pulsatio*.

The Roman senate did not trust its allies, and again sent commissioners; so that the Achæans might have easily saved themselves by submission. The demand of the Romans was a most glaring injustice; but unhappily there is henceforward in all the dealings of the Roman people with foreign nations, nothing but insolence and unrighteousness. And yet, now that the moral interest of the Roman history is quite at an end, a new one begins: the history of Rome becomes neither more nor less than the general history of those ages, and the events in the latter which find no place in the former, are so insignificant that they cannot be made into an independent history. Now though the Achæans could hardly have succeeded in getting the Romans to desist from their demands, they ought at all events to have submitted to their will: it was madness to kick against it. But it was with them as with the ill-fated Jews, in that last struggle with the Romans of which we read the history in Josephus; those who had the language of freedom on their lips, were the fiercest tyrants of the nation. He who votes for yielding to necessity, is often held to be a vile traitor; the man, on the contrary, who is for risking everything, is looked up to as a lover of his country. The prophet Jeremy already had good reason to complain of the false prophets who beguiled the people to mad undertakings. Just so it was with the Achæans. Those among them who talked the most loudly of freedom, were by no means its best friends; the true patriots indeed were those who gave their advice for peace. The Romans were now still waiting for more favourable circumstances, as they were not in a condition to take the field, on account of the Macedonian and Punic wars: embassies therefore went backwards and forwards on both sides. Achaia had formerly been under the lead of Callicrates, one of its citizens, who had sold himself to the Romans; and it was now under the influence of a couple of madmen, Critolaus and Diæus, his most violent foes, who were for resistance, even to the last gasp. Critolaus amused the Roman ambassadors. As the Achæans only met twice a-year, he now sent to call one of these meetings, and promised to introduce the Roman ambassadors; but he secretly warned all the members not to come, and then declared that, according to the laws, a new assembly could not be held for six months.

The Achæans now armed themselves. Yet one can hardly conceive how so small and insignificant a people could have the madness even to dream of being able to stand against the Romans. During the fifty years which had elapsed since they had been under their protection, they had been quite inactive: they had only carried on petty and trifling wars, and as they had ceased to have a standing army, they had nothing but militia, which was still to be properly trained. They had spent their time, while they were well off, in sensual indulgence, and had neglected everything which they ought to have done for their armament; so that they were not prepared for the chance of a danger which might try their utmost strength, as may be seen from the newly discovered fragments of Polybius. A wanton luxury and moral degeneracy, the contemplation of which awakens most dismal thoughts, was now rife among them. They came, as we have said, to the resolution of waging war; and they were joined by the Bœotians and Chalcidians, the latter of whom may have feared for their newly recovered freedom. These transactions are, however, very obscure. The Ætolians did not take part with them, perhaps from revenge and a malignant joy at seeing the downfall of their rivals. Critolaus led a small army to Thessaly, in all likelihood with the hope that the false Philip would still be able to hold out, and that the Romans would thus be placed between two fires: for it was thought that the Macedonians would go on with the war, and that the Thessalians perhaps would rise in a body. But in Macedon all was over. Heraclea, which before had sided with the Achæans, was in fact separated from them by the Romans: an Achæan detachment, which had already penetrated through Thermopylæ, and was besieging Heraclea, quickly fled at the approach of Metellus and the Romans to the main army, and joined Critolaus, who had not yet reached Thermopylæ. Experience indeed had shown that this pass could be turned; yet the very place ought surely to have called upon the Greeks to die a glorious death: but they did the very worst thing that they could have done; for they made off in all haste for the Isthmus, and when near Scarphea,[60] Metellus came up with their rear-guard, being seized by a sudden panic, they were scattered like chaff before the wind. Critolaus disappeared: the most likely supposition is that he sank with his horse in the marshes on the sea-shore, though it is possible that they who told this, may also have meant by this mysterious account to designate him as the evil genius of Greece. The Romans now entered Bœotia, and fell in at Chæronea with the Arcadian contingent of one thousand men, which, at the tidings of the battle, was trying to retreat. The misery of Greece is described by Polybius, and we then see how unjust it was to this great man to have looked upon him as having no feeling for the fate of his native country. Metellus advanced towards the Isthmus. The whole population of Thebes had left it, and had fled for refuge to Cithæron and Helicon; Metellus took the town, and treated it with much forbearance: he wished to end the war, and to deal mildly with the Greeks. But that he could not do; for which the Greeks themselves, as well as their stars, are to be blamed. In almost all the towns it was the same as in Thebes; no one thought of making a stand. At the same time, a Roman fleet went to Peloponnesus, and, landing on the coast of Elis, barbarously ravaged the country, the Achæans not being able anywhere to protect their shores: the contingent belonging to those parts did not now go to the Isthmus; it tried to defend its own towns, but in vain. Diæus, who, on the death of Critolaus, had seized upon the office of *strategus*, and had posted himself near Megara, at the approach of Metellus, retreated to the Isthmus. Now indeed the Achæans might have made peace; for Metellus was a great soul, and had the safety of Greece at heart. He offered to negotiate; but Diæus, whose faction had the upperhand at Corinth, thought that he was able to maintain the Isthmus: reckless as he was, he scouted every proffer like a madman. How lucky it would have been if, like Papius Brutulus, he had thought of opening, by his own death, to his country, the prospect of tranquillity! It would then have been an easy thing for the Achæans to have gotten a peace, in which the existence of the single states would have been maintained.

Before Metellus reached the Isthmus, Mummius hastened to take the command of the army. Mummius was not of so mild a disposition as Metellus; he sought laurels for himself, and booty for the Romans. He tried to come up before Metellus could have concluded a peace: for the latter, although a plebeian like Mummius, was of a family which had long been in possession of the curule dignities, and being a *nobilis*, he could easily have carried the peace in the senate; Mummius was a *novus homo*, and not one of the aristocracy. Diæus had enlisted all the slaves who were able to bear arms, and yet he had only got together an army of fourteen thousand men, though there had been more than half a century of peace: this, more than anything, shows in what a wretched moral and political condition the country was; for wealthy the Achæans undoubtedly were. These had their heads turned by an advantage which they won in a cavalry fight, and they provoked the Romans to a battle, which was soon so utterly lost as to leave no hope of safety. They ought to have defended the impregnable Acrocorinthus; but the whole population of Corinth fled into the Arcadian mountains, and the town and the citadel were abandoned, not a soul having remained behind. On the third day after the battle, Mummius, who would not believe it possible that they had given up every thought of defence, ordered the gates to be broken open, and convinced himself that the city was deserted. The pillage of Corinth; Mummius' barbarian honesty; and the burning of the most wealthy commercial town then in Europe, are well known facts. The booty was immense: all the Corinthians were sold for slaves, and the most noble works of art were carried away. In the same manner, Thebes and Chalcis were destroyed: with regard to other towns, we have no distinct information. Thebes, in Pausanias' times, was only a small village within the Cadmea. The inhabitants of the whole of the Peloponnesus would have been sold into slavery, had not Polybius, through his friend Scipio, managed to get some merciful decrees from the senate.

Greece was changed into a Roman province, a few places only, like Sparta and Athens, remaining *liberæ civitates*: the real province was Achaia, the prætor of which had the other Greek districts under his rule as dependencies. Phocis and Bœotia were to pay tribute, a thing which they had never done even in the days of the Macedonian sway. Moreover, they got a uniform constitution, which Polybius had a hand in bringing about, and which is said to have contributed greatly towards the reviving of the country. But the national strength was paralysed by the law, that no one should possess landed property in a state to which he did not politically belong; all the συστήματα of the peoples were done away with; all *concilia*, and most likely, all *connubia* and *commercia* were forbidden: the territory of Corinth was added to the *ager publicus*. Polybius now returned to the land of his fathers, to obtain for his unhappy countrymen as fair conditions as he could. But his lot was that of a physician who performs on his wife or his child the most painful and dangerous cure: it is his love which animates him in his task; and yet it is that very love which, in such an operation, rends his heart with thrice the agony that it does that of others. This courage is more than heroism: to bear up under such a trial, where once he had lived happily; not to despair amid the general dismay, and even then only to get the tyrants to keep within bounds; and after all to attain at last to a certain end, truly bespeaks a great soul. The author of a petulant essay on Polybius which was published a few years ago, has only exposed himself by his incapability of understanding the sterling greatness of the man. It was through Polybius that the statue of Philopœmen was restored; and all the concessions which were at all favourable to Greece, were owing to nothing but his endeavours alone.

WARS IN SPAIN. VIRIATHUS. DESTRUCTION OF NUMANTIA

In Spain, fortune was so far from smiling on the Romans, that it seemed as if fate wished to remind them of a Nemesis, as the slave did the warrior in his triumph. The Spanish wars may be divided into periods. The first goes down to the end of the second Punic war; the second, to the treaty of Gracchus by which the Romans ruled over Catalonia, Valencia, Andalusia, as well as western Aragon and eastern Castile, and also acquired a kind of supremacy over the Celtiberians. The violation of this peace by the fortification of Segida, called forth a fresh struggle which we may name as the first Celtiberian war: M. Claudius Marcellus had then the command; it lasted three or four years.

Out of the war against the Lusitanians, in which Galba by his faithlessness had branded the Roman name with dishonour, that of Viriathus sprang. This man, who was a Lusitanian, had been a common shepherd and also a robber, as is very often the case with herdsmen in southern Europe, even as it is to this very day in Italy; and having been among those Lusitanians towards whom Galba had behaved with such infamous treachery, he had vowed implacable revenge against the Romans. He placed himself at the head of a small band; for in Spain it is characteristic of the nation to have a continual guerilla warfare, for which the Spaniards have a turn, owing to the nature of their country, and also from their disposition, law and order not having the least power over them, while personal qualities are everything. Viriathus enjoyed unbounded confidence as the hero of the nation. He seldom engaged with the Romans in a pitched battle; but to lie in ambush, to cut off supplies, to go round the enemy, to scatter quickly after a defeat, were the ways in which he would wage war. By his great skill he wore out the Roman generals, more than one of whom lost his life against him. The history of his achievements, imperfectly as we know it, is exceedingly interesting. For eight years[61] (605-612), he maintained himself against the Romans; they would march against him with a superior force, and yet he always got out of their reach, and then would suddenly show himself in their rear, or hem them in on impassable roads, and rob them of their baggage, and cut them to pieces in detail. By these means, he gained the whole of the country for himself; only the inhabitants of the coast of Andalusia, who had ever been the least warlike, remained subject to the Romans, being quickly latinized. Among these, therefore, Viriathus made his appearance as a foe; but the ground which was particularly friendly to him, lay from Portugal, all through Estremadura, as far as Aragon: here he moved remarkably quickly with his light horse and foot. Seldom did he meet with loss against the Romans. The Celtiberians also he managed to win over to his side: they did not indeed carry on their warfare according to his plan, but still, as is always the case with Spaniards, they sought the same end in a way of their own. The Romans saw themselves reduced to the necessity of concluding with him a formal peace, in which they acknowledge him as *socius* and *amicus populi Romani æquissimo jure*, and by which he and his people became completely sovereign,—a peace the like of which the Romans had hardly ever made before. On his side it was honestly meant; whereas the Romans, on the contrary, did not deem themselves bound to keep a treaty which was so utterly at variance with their maxims. The Roman proconsul Cæpio wished for a triumph and booty, like all the Roman generals of that time; and so he rekindled the war, having with an utter want of faith been authorized by the senate to do harm to Viriathus, wherever it was in his power. Thus the war broke out anew, though negotiations were seemingly going on. Traitors were found who offered to murder Viriathus: they accomplished the deed in his tent, and, before any body was aware of his death, escaped to the Romans, from whom they received the price of blood. All that the Lusitanians could now do, was to bury him with an enthusiasm which has become famous in history (612): the friends of this great man fought with each other over his grave, until they fell. Treachery like this is often met with among the Iberians:—the Celtiberians, however, are to be excepted. The character of the Spaniards has in many points remained entirely the same; and though we must lay not a few such cases to the charge of that fearful party spirit of theirs, which still displays itself as strong as ever, of them most particularly the saying holds good, that friendship dies, but that hatred is immortal. Another characteristic has continued to distinguish them even to this day: they are hardly fit for any thing in the lines, and they have shown themselves great in battles only at times, and under great generals,—under Hamilcar and Hannibal, in ancient history; in the middle ages and afterwards, under Gonsalvo de Cordova who formed the Spanish infantry, down to the duke of Alva, under whom it still was excellent: from thence it began to decline.[62]

The Lusitanians now went on with the war under several other generals; but none of the successors of Viriathus was as great as he was,—there was not the same confidence in their personal qualities. D. Junius Brutus

Callaicus concluded a peace with them, and they accepted the offer of settling as a sort of Roman colony in Valencia, where they founded the town of that name: the climate there is most softening, so that they soon lost their warlike character. It is remarkable with what ease the same Brutus made conquests in the north-west of Spain, and the north-east of Portugal; and also in modern times, these peoples have shown little perseverance, except against the Moorish rule. He is the first Roman who advanced beyond the Minho into the country of the Callæcians; but his campaign did not leave any lasting consequences, although it made a deep impression in those parts.

These conquests, which shed such lustre upon Rome, took place at the very time when the wars with the Celtiberians were carrying on so unsuccessfully. This people was divided in several small tribes, of which the Belli, Titthi, and Arevaci were the chief. Of their constitution we have no satisfactory idea. Southern Spain seems to have been ruled by kings; the Celtiberians were republican, and perhaps had highly popular institutions: besides which, as in Greece, the most important towns had a free and independent existence of their own, Termantia or Termestia, and Numantia being in the first rank among those of the Arevaci. The Celtiberian wars began in 609, and ended in 619 or 620: when we bear in mind what the races were which held out in them, their great length is well nigh inconceivable. At first, most of the Celtiberians were under arms; little by little, one place after the other fell off. Numantia lay in a very strong position, amid ravines and torrents, near the spot where Soria now stands: whether it is true that it had no walls, or whether this be only said in imitation of the accounts of Sparta, can no longer be made out. They were able to send but eight thousand men into the field, a number which was greatly lessened in the course of the war: at the time of the blockade, there were not more than four thousand left. Twice the Romans make a peace with them, and twice did they break it again: at last, Scipio was once more charged with the commission of torturing to death a noble people.

The year 611 was that of the consulship of Q. Pompeius, who, to distinguish him from another of the same name, is called *Auli filius*: he was appointed to the command in Spain. He is the ancestor of Cn. Pompeius Magnus, who stood at the head of the aristocracy of his day, and he himself figured as one of the leaders of that class, although the son of a very humble musician. As he leagued himself with the *nobiles*, he was welcome to them, and was received into their ranks; so that even before he was consul, he had already a powerful party. How he raised himself, is uncertain: according to some, he did it by dishonourable means; yet he was a man of talent. His very opposite was Tib. Sempronius Gracchus, who was of a plebeian house, but of most ancient nobility: the latter was at the head of the popular party. Q. Pompeius led his army against the Numantines, and was unsuccessful: they took his camp, and brought him to very great straits. Being in this plight, he offered peace: the Numantines, but only for form's sake, were to give hostages, whom he was to return to them; they were also to pay a certain sum, and to promise to serve in the field. This they also did. But this most reasonable peace did not please at Rome, nor was Pompeius fool enough to believe that it would; his successor, by order of the senate, disregarded it altogether. The Numantines sent ambassadors to Rome, and appealed to the treaties, in which they were borne out by the Roman staff-officers: but the senate annulled the peace, Pompeius himself doing his utmost to bring this about, that he might not be called to account for the way in which he had conducted the war. Hostilities were renewed on a greater scale; and a few years afterwards the command fell to C. Hostilius Mancinus, a man who had the ill luck to gain a great celebrity and a sort of moral notoriety which indeed is of a very doubtful nature. The frightened Spaniards had abandoned Numantia to its fate, and Mancinus had reached as far as the *suburbana*, the gardens and cemeteries of the town: there he was driven back in an engagement; the Numantines pursued, and the Romans, retreating in blind haste, got into a place from which there was no way out, so that they had to make up their minds either to sue for peace or perish. At first, the Numantines would have nothing to say to the conditions offered by Mancinus, favourable as they were; it was only Tib. Gracchus, then serving as a quæstor, who could save the army. The Numantines had not forgotten the equitable peace which his father had made, but the remembrance of his upright conduct towards all the Celtiberians was so dear to them, that they accepted the son as a mediator, being convinced that he meant honestly. So great was the respect in which he was held by them, that he betook himself in the midst of them to Numantia, to get back his account-books, which, as well as the camp, had fallen into their hands; and these were also returned to him uninjured. The army, which, without reckoning the allies, numbered twenty thousand men, was allowed to march off without disgrace, and independence and friendship were stipulated for Numantia. Mancinus afterwards played at Rome the same part which Sp. Postumius had done after the Caudine peace: he recommended the senate to yield up himself and the officers, to atone for the unauthorized peace. The people agreed to this, so far as he was concerned; but it threw out the clause as to the officers, out of regard for Tib. Gracchus. Mancinus was delivered up: the noble-minded Numantines would not have him, that the curse of a broken oath might fall upon those who were guilty.

The war lasted yet a few years longer without any result; so that the Romans were driven, in spite of the laws, (as Appian says,) to elect Scipio Africanus consul. Ten years had already passed away since his first consulship, and the *leges annales* could not have prescribed an age which he had not reached already; perhaps there was a law that no one should be consul twice. Scipio went forth with many recruits, allies, and volunteers from all parts, with Numidians and men from the far East, against that small people, to root it out from the earth. All the proffers of the Numantines were rejected. Scipio found a great degeneracy in the Roman troops; and it cost him a vast deal of trouble to restore discipline, as the loose morals and the luxury which were rife among individuals, were likewise spreading in the army: he purified it, and then marched with sixty thousand men against Numantia. This city was surrounded on three sides by the Douro, and it lay therefore on an isthmus, which was strongly fortified. Around the town, the circumference not being more than three Roman miles, (one German,) Scipio now drew a line of pallisades with a rampart, and behind it a second one,—just as Platææ was shut in by the Spartans,—and here he distributed his army. On these lines, he placed engines for hurling missiles, with which the Romans tried to keep off their desperate foes, as they wanted to destroy them by hunger. For a while, some of them escaped on the Douro, by which the besieged also got supplies; but he cut them off even from this, by sinking above the town huge beams armed with saws into the river, so that the rafts with flour could no longer float down that way. How long this dreadful blockade lasted, is more than we can tell. Once, however, some Numantines climbed over the walls, and came to a distant town where some hundred youths enthusiastically took up arms; and thus a general rising against the Romans was on the eve of bursting forth. When Scipio found this out, he forthwith marched thither, and had the hands of those who were guilty cut off. Such an atrocity stamps the man. The Numantines, when they had fed, first on the dead bodies of the enemy, and then on those of their own countrymen, and gone through all those horrors which Missolunghi had to suffer, wished at length to capitulate. Scipio demanded that their arms should be given up, and that they should surrender at discretion: they asked for three days, which they spent in freeing their wives and children by death from slavery; so that a few of them only came out, who were like skeletons. Of these, Scipio picked out fifty for his triumph, who seem to have been beheaded afterwards: the rest were sold; but they are said to have broken out with such rage, some of them killing themselves, and others murdering their masters, that after a short time not a Numantine was left alive. The place where the town had stood, from henceforth became a waste.

THE SERVILE WAR IN SICILY. ACQUISITION OF THE KINGDOM OF PERGAMUS. ARISTONICUS. DOMESTIC AFFAIRS

The punishment for so foul a deed was not slow in overtaking the Romans. Even before the fall of Numantia, a servile war broke out in Sicily; though indeed this does not so much belong to Roman, as to Grecian history. It was brought on by the depopulation of the island owing to the many wars in which famine and pestilence were raging, as in Germany during the Thirty Years' war. Twenty-four years had not yet passed since the first Punic war, when the second completed the misery of Sicily: it was in a state of desolation, like that of Ireland after the peace of Limerick, in the times of William III. Much of the land was made *ager publicus*, and thus fell into the hands of speculators; in this way there arose large estates in Sicily, which were chiefly used for grazing. Thus (according to the *Codex Theodosianus*) nearly the whole of Lucania, Bruttium, and Calabria, in the days of Honorius and Arcadius, was pasture land, of which the owners, who were partly Romans, partly Siciliotes, kept large studs of horses and herds of cattle. Herdsmen in Italy are a degenerate race of men: they are, almost all of them, as far as I know, (in the States of the Church and in the kingdom of Naples,—in Tuscany there are few of them,) the associates of robbers: the herdsman is as bad and as robber-like, as the peasant, on the other hand, is respectable. On these large estates, there was an immense number of slaves,—often as many as thousands together on one alone. The traffic in slaves, owing to the wars and the continual piracy of those times, had reached a fearful height; so that at the slave-market in Delos, ten thousand are said to have been sold in one day, and they were to be had for a mere trifle. They were treated with the greatest cruelty, and had to work in the fields in chains; of course, there were among them many respectable men from all parts, Carthaginians, Achæans, Macedonians, Celtiberians, and others, who deserved quite a different fate, and could not but thirst for the blood of their tyrants. Thus the Servile war broke out in Sicily, and it is not to be wondered at that there was then another of these risings in

Greece: the cause was everywhere the same. In Greece, tillage had formerly been mostly the business of the freedmen, and it was only of late that it had fallen into the hands of the slaves. The war had now reached its fourth year; several Roman armies had been utterly routed, and it required a consular one under P. Rupilius to reduce the island (620): for the slaves were masters of the strongest places, Enna and Tauromenium, and they had for their leader Eunus (Εὔνους), a Syrian, who, like Jean François at St. Domingo in the year 1791, put on the diadem in due form. The struggle was carried on with the same relentless cruelty which slaves have met with everywhere, as in the West Indies and in North America. Sicily was laid utterly waste by it, and thirty years afterwards, the same circumstances led to the same results. The details are awfully interesting; yet, as we have said before, they are not in their place here.

In the meanwhile, Attalus Philometor of Pergamus, the son of Eumenes, died, and with him the race of Philetærus became extinct. The first kings of Pergamus whom the Romans had raised to greatness, were on the whole clever men and mild princes; and under their rule the country flourished: this state of things was a desirable one, although, if looked upon in a moral point of view, much might be said against it. But the last Attalus was a tyrant and a wicked wretch, such as is only to be met with in the East, where a certain perversity reaches its highest pitch, and takes delight in what is most unnatural and revolting: in a word, he was an incarnate fiend, like Sultan Ibrahim. The only art in which he employed himself, was that of cultivating deadly plants and of preparing poison: it was sport to him, to get those who were his nearest kindred out of the world. He bequeathed the whole of his kingdom to the Romans; and indeed he could not well have done otherwise, as every one of his dispositions had still to be approved of by the Romans, who would hardly have acknowledged the rule of any one else. They took it as a property which of right belonged to them, very much as a master might take the goods of one of his freedmen who had not been fully emancipated, and had died without leaving a will. Thus Rome had a new province, which, however, was to be won by the sword, as Aristonicus, a bastard son of Eumenes, laid claim to the throne. According to the notions of the East, this defect of birth was not a bar to the succession, so that, but for the will of Attalus, he would have been the lawful heir. He had very little trouble in getting hold of the diadem soon after the death of his brother; for the people had a horror of the Roman rule, and they had learned to know the tyranny and rapacity of the Roman prætors and proconsuls who made their appearance every year: many towns declared for him; others, like Ephesus, which had lately gained their freedom by the help of Rome, took up arms against him. How he came to believe that he could hold out, is quite inconceivable. He had no aid whatever: in his neighbourhood were Pontus, Cappadocia, and Bithynia, all three of which were only small kingdoms, and the two last quite unwarlike; the Syrian kings were likewise tottering to their fall, and their whole attention was turned to the East, where the Parthian empire was spreading farther and farther, and Babylon was already conquered. There was not a soul in the world who could help Andronicus; and yet he would engage in the mad undertaking of raising war against the Romans. But the struggle lasted longer than one would have thought: not only did the womanish inhabitants of Lydia and Ionia, countries which are an earthly paradise, carry it on with great resolution, but the pretender had likewise many Thracians in his pay. The Romans, on the other hand, were badly commanded: their leaders thought of nothing but enriching themselves; they were very glad when wealthy towns rebelled, as they could then plunder them. Rome had not only a consular army, but also troops from Bithynia and Pontus; a Roman general, P. Licinius Crassus, was even defeated and taken prisoner. This man has some name in history; and yet, his rapacity was so abominable, that the Asiatics ill-treated his dead body because of it: so cheap was it at that time to be deemed a man of honour. He died, however, a noble death, himself asking to be killed. At length, M. Perperna overcame Aristonicus, and took him prisoner; but M. Aquillius snatched the triumph from him. This is of later date than the tribuneship of Tib. Gracchus (619); that is to say, in 622.[63]

The province of Asia was now regularly formed, but within narrower limits. Rome was generous to the native princes: Nicomedes had his territory enlarged, and Great Phrygia was given to Mithridates of Pontus. But in the latter case, this was not done before the tribuneship of C. Gracchus, who, however, seems to have spoken against it, Mithridates having perhaps gotten this quite unnecessary cession of land by bribing the Roman commissioners.

The changes in the constitution of Rome in those days, are most of them unimportant, as the distinction between patrician and plebeian was now at an end. In 622, for the first time, two plebeians are censors; in 580 already, both the consuls were from the same order. Here we find this entry in the Capitoline Fasti, *ambo primi de plebe*: Livy makes no remark whatever about it, circumstances having become so ripe for the change, that no one even thought any longer of putting any obstacle in the way of a plebeian. Dionysius says, that in his time not more than fifty patrician families were still left, which is to be understood of actual families, and not of *gentes*, of which there may have been only about fifteen. As *gentes*, they are no longer held in any account: these had lost their importance together with the curies. In a *gens*, moreover, all the families were not ennobled: of the Claudia, there was only one; of the Valeria, the Messalæ; the Cornelia consisted of Scipiones, Lentuli, Cethegi, Sullæ (these last being added but of late); in the Æmilia, were the Lepidi, and perhaps also the Scauri. But of the plebeian *familiæ nobiles* there was a very great number, and they were still ever increasing. Of the senate, by far the larger part belonged to them; ever since the end of the war with Hannibal, most of the prætors were likewise plebeians, scarcely one out of six being a patrician: nor does it seem as if any stress had been laid on it; it was merely the effect of time. In the troubles of the Gracchi, we find the families quite indiscriminately in both parties. Appius Claudius, sprung from a family which in former times had headed the patricians against the plebeians, was the father-in-law of Tib. Gracchus, and sided with him, and carried through all the laws put forth by him; whilst, on the other hand, those, who were the most enraged against the Gracchi, and the most interested in withstanding them, were, with the exception of Scipio Nasica, all of them plebeians. The feuds had long been settled, and they had passed to the *novi homines* and *nobiles*, the latter of whom were in the last century very incorrectly called patricians, especially by foreigners (the French). This change has been known ever since the revival of learning. The censorship remained forty years longer than the consulship in the possession of the patricians; for as the elections for this were only every five years, there were still men enough to fill it.

About the same time, the holding the ædileship by turns must have been done away with; and certainly this office must of late have been a heavy burthen upon the patricians, as it entailed considerable expense.

The tribuneship of the people had quite changed character; the tribune holding arbitrary sway just like any tyrant. A tribune (C. Atinius Labeo), a few years after Gracchus, wanted to have the censor Metellus thrown from the Tarpeian rock for having excluded him from the senate; and it was only with difficulty that his family succeeded in getting another tribune to intercede for him. Such instances are not unseldom met with, as the tribunes themselves no longer knew what their office meant. It was very likely the same Atinius, who brought in the law that the tribunes were *eo ipso* senators, and could only be excluded by the same rules as other senators.

TIBERIUS SEMPRONIUS GRACCHUS.

There was a time when the name of the Gracchi was cried down, when they were looked upon as the leaders of a tyrannical onslaught upon the property of others; and there was another time, when they had a renown which would have certainly been most hateful to themselves. Both of these opinions are now entirely exploded; and, although the complicated system of the *ager publicus* is not yet understood everywhere, still I do not believe that any one in Germany—unless indeed it be in some corner of Austria—holds the old views with regard to the Gracchi. The French still cling a little to their false prejudices; but in America my account of the matter is already the one generally received, as a reviewer of my history in a North American periodical has especially pointed out.

Tiberius Gracchus was the son of Tiberius Gracchus the elder who had made the peace with the Celtiberians, and of Cornelia, the daughter of the first Scipio Africanus, who was given in marriage to her husband, not, as Livy says, by her father, but, after his death, by her family: both of these were, even in the midst of the thorough corruption of that age, acknowledged to have been people of the highest virtue, in whom the olden times were living again. Of their many children, few only remained alive—in fact, out of twelve not more than three, namely the two brothers, Tiberius and Caius, and the daughter, who was married to the younger Scipio (*Paulli fil.*). The sons were brought up under the eye of the mother by distinguished Greeks, and by a Campanian, C. Blossius, who was a perfect Grecian, writing Greek, and even composing poetry in Greek: he was, as we now know, the author of Rhintonian comedies,[64] a proof of the flourishing state of Greek literature at that time in Italy, of which Cicero also informs us. He was the teacher and friend of Tiberius of whom he was somewhat the elder, and a follower of Stoic philosophy, a system which in those days was congenial to the aspirations of all generous minds, and was particularly welcome to a nation like the Romans. When Tiberius, owing to the great favour which he had with the people, had been raised step by step to honours, and he had gained glory already at Carthage, where with C. Fannius he was the first to mount the wall, he became a quæstor and made the peace with Numantia. Its not being ratified greatly exasperated him. Unfortunately, we have for this period only desultory works from second or third hand, such as those of Appian and Plutarch: the latter of these wrote the lives of the Gracchi with much feeling, but without any knowledge of the true state of affairs, the moral part in him, being, however, really beautiful; moreover, like Appian, he is led astray by the gossip of any writer. Thus Plutarch allows himself to be beguiled into the belief that the vanity of Tiberius had been hurt by the repudiation of the peace; but of a soul such as that of Tiberius, we may safely say that its motives for anger were different. He had concluded the peace as an honest man, and to see it trampled upon in defiance of all good faith, embittered him against the men who then were in power. How a character like Gracchus in such times as those must have felt bound to take in hand these dangerous πολιτεύματα, may best be shown from the Servile war in Sicily, where the real canker which lay at the root of the whole state of society is laid bare.

The *ager publicus*[65] was the land taken in war, of which the ownership belonged to the commonwealth, but the possession was given up to Roman citizens, or to foreigners, on the payment of certain outgoings, such as the tithes on the produce of the arable land and of the live stock; a *scriptura* on the pasture land according to the number of the cattle; and other things of the kind. By the Licinian law[66] it had been enacted that no one should possess more than five hundred *jugera* of the *ager publicus*, but that he might transfer the occupancy as if it were his property: yet the possessor was, after all, only a precarious occupant, *a tenant at will*,[67] whom the real owner might turn out, whenever he liked. If he possessed more than was allowed by law, he was liable to punishment, and what was above the quantity was to be confiscated: the state, however, might, of course, at any time take back the whole.

The way in which the Licinian law was kept, was just what might be expected under such circumstances: one or two incidents give us light enough to see this. P. Postumius Megillus, for instance, was fined for having employed the soldiers of the legion in converting a large forest into arable land; Licinius Stolo himself was accused of having tried by emancipating his son to evade his own law, as under his name he held more than its clauses would have allowed him. The amount of land was everywhere exceeded; and the very fact of these estates being no freeholds, as they had the authority of the prætor for their only title, so that, where they were situated, there existed no jurisdiction, gave to those who wished to enrich themselves a great means of driving out the small farmers, which was now done more and more. Whilst in Germany, as well as in France and in England, the small estates are worth much more taken singly, than when combined in large masses; in the South, particularly in Italy, the larger properties are more profitable, and thus the small estates go on decaying, and all the land keeps falling into the hands of a few owners. Until the war with Pyrrhus, an immense deal of land had been won, and so likewise after the war with Hannibal: part of it was taken up for colonies, and another share was left to the Latin allies, whose claims were thereby satisfied, though even in this case also, the right of ownership seems to have been reserved to the Roman commonwealth. Only in Samnium and Apulia, and I believe also in Lucania,[68] had an extraordinary distribution been made to the veterans of Scipio's army; but besides this, no general assignment had been made to the plebeians *viritim*, as in olden times.

It is in the nature of things, that the husbandman is able to pay a far higher rent for a piece of land, than we could, who do not till it ourselves, provided, however, that no capital is needed for it. We have to pay the labourer, whereas the other gets the double gain of the labourer and of the farmer. I know the farming in Italy well, having taken much trouble to become acquainted with all kinds of land-owners and farmers there, particularly with the larger ones, who understand husbandry very well. The latter manage their farms in an excellent style, and yet they are a curse to the country: on the other hand, I quite love the poor peasants. Among others, I knew of a small farmer at Tivoli, who did his very utmost to get himself out of the clutches of the usurers, and to free his bit of ground; on which occasion I fully learnt how great the value of labour is in Italy, and what an advantage it is there for a man to farm his own land. But as the money is in very few hands, only indeed in those of the men of rank, the small proprietor, if any ill luck befalls him, is unable to keep his freehold, and therefore this class of men dwindles faster and faster every year. The poor man, for instance, lived near the rich one; the former in hard times had taxes to pay, but, having had losses owing to murrain among the cattle and other visitations, he could not raise the money: thus he borrowed from his wealthy neighbour, and as he had no other pledge to offer but his farm, he had to pay a heavy rate of interest. Nor was this the whole of his troubles: his son, perhaps, served in a legion, in which case, if the father was taken ill and had to keep labourers, he could not pay the interest; and now, if his neighbour called upon him for the principal and interest, he must needs give up to him the possession of his land at a low price. He who is once in the fangs of the large proprietors, will never get out again. And so Tib. Gracchus found the many small allotments on which the soldiers had settled, either burthened with debt after the long series of disasters during the late campaigns (in which the war-taxes moreover were most heavily felt), or already fallen into the hands of the rich. Such a change of property goes on increasing like an avalanche. In Tivoli, the number of land-owners is now perhaps not a fifth of what it was forty years back, and not one-fiftieth of what it was four hundred years ago; as I have learned from an old survey of the fifteenth century. I made inquiries to know what became of many of the olive-yards there, which (in former times) belonged to certain families in the town, and one by one have been got hold of by the rich. Sonnino[69] has four thousand inhabitants, and some five or six men own the whole of the land: all the rest are beggars and robbers.

By the Licinian law it was enacted, that on every five hundred *jugera*, a certain number of free labourers (*cottagers*)[70] should be employed, that slaves might not work on them. But the rule had not been kept: thousands of slaves came in, as was also the case in Portugal from the sixteenth century to Pombal's days, when negro slaves were so very cheap within the kingdom, owing to which indeed so many mulattoes are found there. The condition of Italy was now this: on the one hand, the number of Roman citizens had increased, partly—which was desirable—from the allies, but chiefly in a worse way from the freedmen, the common run of whom bore the brand of slavery; and on the other hand, the numbers of the hereditary land-holders and land-owners were dwindling fast. It is very likely that the first thought of amending this state of things, came into the mind of Tib. Gracchus on his return from Spain through Etruria, where he saw large tracts of country with nothing but slaves, who worked at the ground in chains, while the free-born men were begging and starving. The population of Rome had become more and more a true rabble, and in the country the poor increased at a fearful rate, an evil which alas! is now a growing one in Europe. The Romans did not blind themselves to the condition in which they were; they mourned over it, and acknowledged that, if the Licinian law had been observed and the poor had been allowed to occupy the land, there never would have been that wretchedness. Every body wished, like the king[71] in Goethe's play, that "all were otherwise;" but no one had the courage to do anything. There is no doubt that just after the war with Hannibal, it would not have been hard to stop the mischief, and that was one of those momentous periods which sometimes follow after great convulsions, and must be taken advantage of, or else they are irrecoverably lost: one ought then to have created a magistracy to watch over the way in which the Licinian law was kept, and to distribute part of the conquered *ager publicus*, and to see that the occupation was fairly managed. Since that time, seventy years had passed, and every one must have looked blank at the very mention of a reform. C. Lælius is said to have thought of it, but to have given up the plan as impracticable; so that he got the surname of *Sapiens*. This was either a nickname, or else *sapiens* here means prudent; for prudent it is not to stir up a wasp's nest. There were now but few great families indeed which did not possess far more than the lawful quantity, and which did not keep more than a hundred head of cattle, and five hundred sheep and goats, upon their estates: all these were sure to be offended, if the Licinian law were carried out in all its rigour. As our governments have now the right, when a lease is out, of warning off a tenant on the crown-land, although his forefathers held it perhaps for many years before him; thus also the Roman government had never given up its right to the *ager publicus*, although it had not exercised it for a long time. The law was quite clear; yet as it had not been enforced for ages, it might be said on the other side, that it was only common equity not to root out an old abuse at once, and thus wound many interests. The rich might plead, that "when C. Flaminius made his agrarian law to apply to the new conquests only, he thereby tacitly acknowledged what had hitherto been held by right of possession; moreover when the loan was contracted in the war with Hannibal the *ager publicus* was pledged to us, and has thus become our property." A hundred years had already passed since then; some of the estates had also been laid waste during the war; in the full trust that every one would remain in possession of what belonged to him, they had planted them anew,[72] they had raised buildings on them, they had drained fens: and now they were to sacrifice all this, and to be turned out of what was their own.

Of purer intentions than Tiberius Gracchus, no man could ever have been: even they have owned it, who a long time after, blinded by party spirit, have railed against this undertaking; nay, Cicero himself, whose generous heart always gets the better of him whenever he views a subject with unprejudiced eyes, calls him *sanctissimus homo*. The statesmen of old were not such as our fancy would generally lead us to paint them; but they had the self-same ends in view as those of our times: Tiberius Gracchus saw clearly, that, if things were to go on in this way, utter ruin must follow, and Rome would fall into despotism. Had he now wished to enforce the Licinian rogations to the very letter, this would indeed have been just in law, but in reality most unfair. He therefore laid down the rule, that every one should be allowed to have, and that as freehold property, five hundred *jugera* for himself, and two hundred and fifty for every son who was still *in patria potestate*, though as it seems, not for more than two of these (for so must the passage in the Epitome of Livy be interpreted according to the correct reading);[73] and moreover, that buildings erected on that part of the land which was to be given up, should be valued, and an indemnity paid to those who had owned them. Thus, instead of infringing upon vested rights, he, on the contrary, converted a mere tenure at will into a regular freehold which no man could touch. One case, however, Gracchus had not considered: many had bought the *ager publicus* of the former occupant for ready money, or had taken it at its value as their share of an inheritance; these could not be expected to lose their capital. When this had happened, the overplus ought to have been bought in at a fair price by the state, and then there would have been nothing to say against the law: the great wealth of the state would have certainly sufficed for this, as there could not, after all, have been so many cases of people having more than a thousand *jugera*. Five hundred *jugera* are a very good-sized estate, as much as seventy *rubbii* are now, which is still looked upon as not a bad property in Italy. I should not in that country wish for a larger one: one may get from it in a fruitful district, if well managed, a net income of five thousand crowns, merely by letting it out in farms. That the money which was hoarded up in the treasury, could not have been better spent than for such a purpose, is as clear as day. In this way it might have become possible to remove from the city the *sentina rei publicæ*, the disgrace of the Roman people, which weighed like a heavy burthen upon it, and which always sold its votes in the *comitia*. To this class allotments ought to have been given, but with the condition that they should never be alienated, as otherwise they would have fallen again into the hands of the rich. It is ever to be lamented that Gracchus did not do this: however great the cost might have been, the state ought to have borne it. In all likelihood he would have escaped the fate which befell him, though indeed the hatred against him would always have been bitter.

Gracchus is said also to have thought of widening the extent of the Roman franchise; yet this is only dimly hinted at, as, generally speaking, the accounts which we have of the whole of his undertaking are so very scanty. He saw clearly that the middle class of the Roman people had almost entirely disappeared, and that its restoration was one of the principal wants of the time; and therefore he wished to open the citizenship to the allies. This regeneration is quite in the spirit of the old laws: its aim was to infuse fresh blood into the higher orders, and to enlarge their numbers; just as in former times the Licinian laws gave new life to the republic which was dwindling to an oligarchy, and began the second brilliant epoch of Rome. There were in Italy thirty Latin colonies, and in these there were many citizens of great respectability, who might vote among the tribes in the Roman assemblies, and who felt second only to the Romans, if not quite their equals. These Latins actually now held the same rank which the plebeians did two hundred and fifty years before: there was even much more refinement in those towns than in Rome. Tiberius Gracchus wished therefore to admit these to the full rights of Roman citizens, and he likewise undoubtedly meant to grant the *suffragium* to any *municipia sine suffragio* which at that time may have still existed.

On the side of Gracchus were many of the most eminent men, who certainly were owners of large estates as well as the Scipios, but who gave up their private advantage for the common good. There was even his father-in-law Appius Claudius, who in other respects was just as proud as any of his forefathers, but who in this behaved as Appius Claudius Cæcus had done in his most glorious moments; moreover, there was the great P. Mucius Scævola who was then consul; there was also the father-in-law of his brother, P. Licinius Crassus, and others. The rage which broke out against Tib. Gracchus in the senate, is difficult to describe; it went beyond all the bounds of decency. Men of rank, when they are the champions of oligarchy, as soon as ever their interests are touched, not only display the same greedy covetousness as the worst bred, but likewise a fury which one could hardly have believed. Hitherto no one had lost sight of what was due to Gracchus and his family: he enjoyed the same respect among the Romans, as among barbarians; every one acknowledged his virtue, and even those who looked upon all virtue as folly, were forced to own that he was afflicted with that folly. But now the heroes of triumphs, and the first men of the state, railed against him as a mutinous fellow who was actuated by the most detestable motives. P. Cornelius Nasica, he who was grandson of him who in the war with Hannibal had been declared to be the most virtuous of men; and son of Scipio Nasica, who was likewise said to have been an example to the whole nation, and who had tried hard to bring back the good ways of the olden time; a man who himself also was deemed to be the very soul of honour, and perhaps deserved to be so in many respects—became hand and glove with the infamous Q. Pompeius. From this it does not follow that he was a knave; it may be that, hardened in his oligarchical notions, he really saw Ti. Gracchus as he fancied him to be. The senate did not possess the same means which the patricians once had against the plebeians: it had not the old negative of the curies, the Hortensian law having conceded to the tribes the most unbounded power of legislation, so that the senate could not step in with a senatus consultum. By the strangest anomaly, the tribunes could now only check each other, since there was no veto where it would have been most needed: the only means of defeating a law was the intercession of a tribune.

There are hereditary family principles in Rome, as there were also family characters; and these are more than mere political maxims.[74] Throughout the family of the Gracchi, as has been already mentioned, we find a certain mildness, and an unaffected kindliness towards those who were in need of help. This is shown in the three generations which are remarkable in history, by Tib. Gracchus in the Second Punic War, by Tib. Gracchus the censor, and by the two unfortunate brothers Tiberius and Caius; it is a disposition moreover which in Rome was not often met with, and which had now disappeared entirely. The same thing is to be seen in every free state, and it is one of those spells by which a commonwealth is upheld. Those who are born in certain families, are, as it were, predestined to such and such political principles: thus in England it is known at once to which party a Russel is sure to belong, just as every one receives from his church the doctrines which he is to follow.[75]

If the notion that the tribunes belonged to a different class from the ruling one, is quite erroneous at the very outset, it is utterly groundless now. At this time, we may positively say that as a rule the tribunes—though they did not all become consuls themselves, as every year there were ten tribunes elected, and not more than two consuls—belonged to the consular families, and that it was only very rarely that a plebeian was made consul who had not once been tribune. This is a point, which we must not lose sight of. It now happened not unseldom that a man like Gracchus was among the tribunes. M. Octavius, who was tribune with him, belonged to a good family, although not one of the very first rank. Him the opposite party gained over, to put in his veto. There is nothing to say against his character: he had formerly been a friend of Tiberius Gracchus, but party spirit had now got the better of him. He himself had much to lose, and Gracchus offered to make it up to him out of his own property; but this, of course, he could not accept. In vain did Gracchus try to convince him of his error, and adjure him to recal his intercession: it was all to no purpose, as Octavius had bound himself by his word of honour, and could not act otherwise than in the trammels of his faction, which is the worst thing that a man can do in a struggle of parties. The question now was, whether Gracchus should give up a law which might save the nation and check the spread of vice, merely because a man who was his friend had sold his soul to the evil faction; or whether he should do a thing which was indeed contrary to the letter, but quite in the spirit of the constitution. He made up his mind to the latter course, which was to move in the assembly of the people, that Octavius should be put out of his tribuneship. This was an irregularity; but, properly speaking, the independence of the tribunes was an abuse: consuls had been deposed more than once, and an office from which its holder cannot be removed, is an absurdity in a republic. The tribunes were merely commissioned to bring motions before the people, and whoever has given a commission can also take it away again. But what Gracchus did, was wrong in point of form. That he might swerve from the law as little as he could, he proposed to Octavius, first to put himself to the vote; and when Octavius refused, he went on with his motion. Seventeen tribes had already voted against Octavius, when Gracchus once more besought him to give up his opposition, or else to resign. But he would do neither, and was deposed. As he wished to make a scene, he would not leave the rostra, until Gracchus had him dragged down by force, thus awakening that feeling of disgust among the beholders, which the senate and the men in power were eager to call forth.

The opponents of Tib. Gracchus had now the advantage of seeing him wrong in form. The agrarian law was carried, and a standing triumvirate was appointed to watch over the way in which it was kept. Tib. Gracchus, his brother, and his father-in-law, were named as triumvirs. From the *Somnium Scipionis*, we see that the *socii* and *Latini* attached themselves to P. Scipio, and we have even a great many statements which show that they, like the senate, were against the agrarian law: the reason for this we may make out by laying things together, there being several ways of accounting for it, one of which must undoubtedly be the true one. The Roman laws, unless it were expressly stipulated, did not apply to the allies, as we know from the usury laws, which are a case in point. Now it may be that the law of Licinius had said nothing about the *socii* and *Latini*; so that if these had a *possessio*, they were not tied down to the maximum of five hundred *jugera*. Those who were rich, may have bought up in remote districts the *latifundia* of former Roman possessors, and they would now have been disturbed by the Sempronian law. Certain it is, that the *socii* and *Latini* had always been granted a certain portion of the *ager publicus*: thus for instance the Campanians had a very large one, which they could only have acquired as allies; the Marsians had a share in the Apulian pastures. That Gracchus had meddled with these holdings, is not very likely, though it cannot be positively denied. It is more probable, on the other hand, that many places had been allowed, till further orders, to have the use of their *ager* on condition of their paying tribute for it, though the right of ownership, which these had lost in war, had not been restored to them by the Roman people: if this indulgence were now taken away, it was hard upon them. They also got compensations, as we know for certain in the case of Carthage. Those who held on such tenures, had now the same interest as the wealthy Romans. However this may have been, the allies felt themselves aggrieved.—The plea then of defending the rights of the subjects, was the mask behind which the covetousness of those who were in power was hidden: they put on the guise of being the champions of these without thinking at all of themselves, an hypocrisy, which has taken in even a clear-headed man like Cicero, who is remarkably wavering with regard to these and other like transactions: his heart is with the Gracchi, but led by *a priori* reasoning, he decides against them; and thus he feels quite at a loss, and is afraid to speak out. The circumstances under which he wrote the books *de Re publica* and *de Legibus*, are his excuse. The opposition of the

Latins was a great stumblingblock in the way of Gracchus; the *optimates* were only able to counterbalance the popular party by thus leaguing themselves with the allies. But when the oligarchy had gained the victory by the help of the *socii*, they afterwards basely sacrificed them, very nearly as the Irish Roman Catholics were sacrificed at the Union.

About this time, already in the beginning of the year, Attalus died. The establishment of the province of Asia now forms an episode in the tribunate of Gracchus, in which he again showed himself to have been a statesman of deep thought, and earned great honour. Among the goods which the king left, was a large treasure, as is always the case with eastern princes, who, much as they spend, hoard as much again; and this was sent to Rome. Now it is often thrown out as a reproach against Gracchus, that he divided it among the Roman people; but there was nothing wrong in what he did. In Rome, as in the small Swiss cantons, every citizen had a share in the sovereignty; besides which, the public *ærarium* was becoming richer every day, as the tributes already yielded so immense a surplus, that the citizens had no longer to pay any direct taxes. As the great mass of the people had now sunk into the lowest depths of wretchedness, this division was quite justifiable; and the more so, as land was to be assigned to them, and they wanted money to stock it. The triumvirs for the distribution of the land were now first to make out, which estates belonged to the republic, and which to private persons: for many had been sold, and many in the midst of the allotted districts had been left to their former owners; so that the keeping of the registers was exceedingly difficult. The Romans had these registers, just as we have our surveys for the assessment of taxes; but they were very carelessly done, as the seat of government was at Rome alone, and there was hardly anything like sub-delegation.

The time for choosing new tribunes was now at hand. The tribunes entered upon their functions on the ninth of December; but for a longer time than we can tell, the elections had been held at the end of June, or in the beginning of July, that the tribunate might never be vacant. As the tribunes took part in the discussions of the senate, and in these Gracchus was treated with a vulgar and most reckless fury, he could easily foresee, that when once out of office, he would be at the mercy of his foes: as *triumvir agrorum dividundorum*, he was not *sacrosanctus*. He therefore tried, in accordance with the laws, to have his tribuneship renewed. This was done very often in the first ages; but it may have fallen into disuse, and thus the party against him have had the plea of prescription on the score of which they might withstand him. When the *prærogativa* had nominated him, and another tribe had followed on the same side, the opposition declared this vote to be null and void, and demanded that the tribunes should not receive any suffrages for him. Q. Rubrius, a tribune who presided over the election, having become quite at a loss what to do, Mummius, another tribune who had been chosen instead of Octavius, said that Rubrius ought to yield his place to him: on this, as the other tribunes demanded that the matter should be decided by lot, a quarrel arose, and the day passed away without anything being settled. Gracchus already saw that his death was aimed at, and he went about with his child among the people, begging them to stand by him, and to save his life. In the earliest times, the *plebes* assembled on the forum; but in the war with Hannibal already, it always votes on the *area* before the temple in the Capitol; I have not yet been able to find out when it was that this change began. It also seems that the votes were now given by word of mouth, and not, as formerly, on tablets, a custom which afterwards the *Lex Cassia* only restored, so that it is by no means to be looked upon as an innovation, as is generally thought. Professor Wunder has very correctly perceived this. Let no one believe that it is possible to honour Cicero more highly than I do; yet I cannot help saying, that he is to be blamed for all the erroneous notions which are rife on this subject, as well as on so many others. Gracchus now was on the area of the Capitol, and was speaking most movingly to the people, who seemed as if they would uphold him. At any other time of the year, when the country folks were in great numbers in the city, he would undoubtedly have found the strongest protection; but these were away on account of the harvest, and the townspeople were not only lukewarm, but many of them were directly under the influence of the *optimates*. Here also we see how the constitution, owing to circumstances, had become quite different from what it had been formerly under the self-same forms. In the earlier ages, when the territory did not yet reach over many leagues, the citizens might assemble and the *tribus rusticæ* be represented, if not fully, at least in considerable numbers: but now that the Roman peasantry lived so far away, especially, for instance, after the assignments of Flaminius in the Romagna, they were no more able to come to town and vote; and the form of the law, which was suitable to the former size of the city, was now thoroughly preposterous and mischievous. On the following day, the elections were to go on, and people now met together with a gloomy foreboding that blood would be shed. Gracchus came only lightly armed. The senate was assembled in the temple of *Fides*. The votes were about to be given, when a tumult arose. The senate being near, at the news that there was an uproar among the people, Scipio Nasica called upon the consul Mucius Scævola to take strong measures. The latter appears in a doubtful light: according to most of the accounts, he seems to have been favourable to Gracchus; according to others, just the reverse; but if we suppose him to have been a weak-minded man who stood in fear of his faction, this contradiction may be accounted for. Nasica, seeing that a bold stroke would decide the matter, called upon all the senators to follow him; and they all, to a man, while leaving the temple, declared Gracchus a traitor. The people fell back before men of such high rank, and the senators seized hold of everything that might serve as a weapon. There seem to have been scaffoldings erected all round (even now-a-days in Italy, wherever there is anything to be seen, benches are placed); part of these were broken in pieces. The report had been spread, that Gracchus had appeared with a diadem, and that he wanted to have himself proclaimed king: the senators, with the exception of some blockheads who would believe anything, well knew the whole to be a lie; but the people, who could not tell their own mind, and had no leader, many of them dispersed. The senators laid hold of the broken pieces of timber, and made an onset against the few unarmed men that were still gathering round Tiberius Gracchus, who, on their side, did not dare so much as to lift up a hand against the senators. Tiberius fled down the *centum gradus* to the Velabrum; and there his foot slipped, one of his pursuers—according to some, one of the common people; according to others, a senator, or a colleague of Gracchus (there were persons who afterwards disputed for the honour)—having pulled him by the toga: this man struck him on the head with a bit of wood, and when he fell down stunned, the murder was completed. Many of his followers shared the same fate, and their dead bodies were thrown into the Tiber: the carcase of the great man himself, having been washed ashore, was left to rot in the fields. He was not even yet thirty years old when he died. A great number were also arrested as accomplices. But the real persecution only began in the following year, under the consul P. Popillius Lænas, the descendant of one of the leaders of the *plebes* at the time of the Licinian law: he has left a terrible memory behind him. He caused thousands to be imprisoned, and some of them to be put to death without any trial, like a real Duke of Alva; one he condemned to be thrust into a chest filled with snakes, an atrocity which Plutarch expressedly speaks of in his life of Tiberius Gracchus. It is sad that even Cicero looks upon this Popillius Lænas as a man of honour. One anecdote I cannot help telling here. It was either at that time, or very likely some years before, that Diophanes of Mitylene and C. Blossius of Cumæ, the most intimate friends of Tib. Gracchus, were summoned before the inquisitorial tribunal, to give account of their connexion with Gracchus. The latter answered, that his connexion was well known; that Tib. Gracchus had been his most intimate friend. They then asked him, whether he had done everything that Gracchus had told him to do. He answered that he had.—"Whether he would have done anything that Gracchus might subsequently have required of him?"—"Yes," was his answer again.—"Whether then he would at his bidding have set fire to the Capitol?" He said, that Gracchus could never have commanded such a thing.—"But what if he had commanded it notwithstanding?"—"Well then," said he, "I would have done it." This horrid speech was held to be a proof of his utter wickedness; but it is not so much a disgrace to him who looked upon his friend as his better self, as to the man who wrung it out of him by his captious questions. Blossius got off; but he afterwards took away his own life, that he might not fall into the hands of these bloodthirsty wretches.

It is remarkable, that the ruling party did not again abolish the new office of triumvirs, M. Fulvius Flaccus, the friend of Tiberius, being chosen in his room; but the efficiency of these was hampered, and they were able to do nothing, as those who were called upon to show their titles to their estates, did not come forward, or else made no declaration. But when the first burst of their rage was over, they saw that they were playing a dangerous game; and they left the laws of Gracchus untouched, and, for appearance's sake, appointed the consul Tuditanus to pass judgment on the disputed points: instead of doing this, he took the field, and thus the matter was put off. Whether anything was done at all, cannot be made out. When Ap. Claudius also died, he was succeeded by C. Papirius Carbo, an unworthy disciple of Gracchus, who did the same things as his master had done before him, but from bad motives. It is the curse of revolutions, that the onward march of events hurries along with it even good men who have once plunged into them; the power of freeing oneself from the influence of what is passing around us, belongs only to that iron will which neither heeds nor shrinks from anything. A distinguished man, who had gone through all the horrors of the revolution, but had kept his hands unsullied, once said to me, "It is a terrible remembrance to have lived to see a revolution, and to have had a share in it; one goes to the attack along with the noble-minded, and one remains before the breach with the knaves." This one should have before one's eyes as a warning; but perhaps we may not have to dread a revolution for centuries to come. The period in Roman history which we have now reached, is one in which the explanation of forms is no longer sufficient; we must take men psychologically, and make a study of the personal characters of those who tore from each other's grasp the spoils of the state when its life had fled from it. Carbo was a man of much talent; but he was possessed by evil spirits: he might perhaps, in peaceful times, have belonged to the number of fine souls; but in that age, he sank down into the lowest depths of guilt and meanness. His character was such, that the charge of his having murdered Scipio, is not at all impossible in itself: yet, as in the south it is so very common for it, to be reported that a man has been poisoned, if his death has exhibited any symptoms like it (as, for instance, in putrid fevers), we ought not to place unqualified belief in that suspicion.

Scipio was laying siege to Numantia, when he heard the news of his brother-in-law's death; and he expressed his approval of it. After his return to Rome, Carbo called upon him to declare whether he looked upon the death of Gracchus as just; but he shuffled out of this, saying, that it was just, if Gracchus had meant to make himself king. This was mere senseless slander, and thus men's minds were generally embittered against Scipio. The oligarchs themselves were divided: not every one who had clamoured for Gracchus' blood, was therefore Scipio's friend; but they all wanted him, and it flattered his vanity to consider himself also as the protector of the Latins and of the allies. Tiberius' death had by no means brought the dispute to a decision; far from it, it was carried on with unabated violence. Scipio intended to speak in the assembly of the people against the enforcing of the Sempronian law, which was never repealed; as we may see from the original tables of the *Lex Thoria* (640-50), and the few fragments of a later agrarian law. The evening before the day on which he was to address the people, he had betaken himself to rest at an early hour, to think over his speech; but in the morning he was found dead in his bed. This sudden death now raised the suspicion of his having been murdered; yet, strange to say, no inquiry was made, although it would have been the interest of the ruling party to have had one. The result might, however, perhaps have turned against this very party;[76] for instance, against Q. Pompeius, or Metellus: people even went so far as to charge Scipio's wife, Sempronia, a sister of the Gracchi, with having got him out of the world by poison. Yet poisoned he could not have been, by all accounts; for as his corpse was borne upon an open bier, the symptoms of it would have shown themselves. If he died a violent death, he must have been strangled.

From the death of Tiberius, to the first tribunate of Caius Gracchus, several remarkable measures were debated: the question of the new division of land was no more to be got rid of. Unluckily, we do not know the particulars: it is a pity that the books of Livy, from the 50th down to the 60th, have been lost. We have a decree of the tribune M. Junius Pennus, that the allies should be left in possession of their land, but should not be raised to the right of citizenship; which was quite in the spirit of the oligarchy. In many towns of the Marsians, Samnites, and others, there were a great many rich and uncorrupted families, which, had they been engrafted upon the worn out Roman stock, would very soon have thrown the Roman aristocracy into the shade. For this reason, they were not to become citizens, but to keep their land; and by this means it was hoped to quiet them. But when they saw themselves thus taken in in every way, they began to plot together: the details, however, of this conspiracy are shrouded in darkness. In the lifetime of Tib. Gracchus already, there had been a talk of giving the right of citizenship to the Latins, especially to Tibur and Præneste, and perhaps also to the towns of the Hernicans, but above all, to the colonies. These consisted of Romans, Latins, and Hernicans of all kinds, who lived under the Latin law, and had the best claims to the right of citizenship; but Gracchus must either have put off his plans with regard to them, or have quite given them up. Now they insisted upon having it, as it had been chiefly their support which had upheld the senate. It is inconceivable how Fregellæ, the most flourishing of them, could at that time have been so mad as to take up arms; the other Latins would have nothing to do with it, and the colonies were scattered throughout the whole country. The Italians proper, as they stood one step lower down, were perhaps not always glad when the Latins got such privileges; they rejoiced at their trouble, and gave them no help. The prætor L. Opimius besieged, conquered, and destroyed Fregellæ: not a trace is left of the town, and a dreadful revenge was taken on the people.

CAIUS SEMPRONIUS GRACCHUS

It is beyond a doubt, that C. Gracchus surpassed his brother in talent: he was altogether a different man. The parallel drawn by Plutarch between Agis and Cleomenes and the two brothers, is a very happy one. Of the speeches of Tiberius, nothing has been left to us; from those of Caius, many passages are quoted. He was the first refined, polished, and elegant writer of the Roman nation: Scipio and Lælius are still strikingly rough and harsh, as Tib. Gracchus also certainly must have been, more so perhaps, even than Cato; (we see this from a fragment, hitherto unknown,[77] of a speech of Lælius, in an unpublished commentary of Cicero which Maï has discovered.) In what still remains of him, we find Cicero's saying borne out, that he had been the first to come forth in an old literature with a new language; even as among the French, Corneille forms the link between the antique and the classic. In all likelihood, the language of C. Gracchus was far older than that of Cicero, or even Sisenna; but it nevertheless had the stamp of the modern age, and none of the stiffness and mustiness of the earlier times. He was perhaps also more of a statesman than his brother; at least he showed himself more to have been such, the reason of which may have been, that while the career of Tiberius was ended in seven months, he was engaged in public life much longer: his activity began even before his tribuneship; and the two years that he was tribune, and yet a half a year besides, it was in full play. His high accomplishments, and the development of his character, he owed chiefly to his excellent mother: the kindly disposition of the Gracchi is seen also in their affectionate behaviour to their mother, the like of which was very seldom to be found elsewhere among the Romans. On the whole, we know very little indeed of the domestic relations of the Romans; yet we may reckon as examples Horace's loving mention of his father, and that of Agricola by Tacitus.

Caius was driven on by fate into the path in which he met with his ruin. Heart-broken by the death of his brother, he seemed as if he wished to keep away from the higher offices of the state: he rose indeed to be a triumvir,—there he could not help himself,—but even then he would only act where it was possible for him to do so without shaking the existing state of things. But there was an inward call, which would not let him follow his own inclinations, although he foresaw his doom. At a very early age he had the eyes of the people bent upon him; he had served for twelve years, had been quæstor in Sardinia, and thus already had awakened jealousy: for a young man who displayed the most perfect disinterestedness, was a reproach and an object of hatred to every one. When the soldiers were in want of warm clothing, and the miserly senate would not grant any money, he did not rest until he had scraped together in the province, and from other sources, the means of buying warm cloaks; he also got a cargo of corn from Micipsa, the king of Numidia. All these things gave rise to such rancour and ill-feeling, that it was intended to keep him in Sardinia, where, even at that time, the air was so unwholesome, that it was hoped that he would fall a victim to it. By law he was only obliged to be there for one year; but he had been three years in the island, and therefore he now went without leave to Rome, where he publicly justified himself, showing how he had been thwarted in everything. This made such an impression, that not only did the tribunes take him under their protection, but he was himself chosen to be tribune of the people for the following year, and that under more favourable auspices than his brother had been: for among the enlargements of the tribunician power, which the senate had yielded, owing to their evil conscience, since the death of Tib. Gracchus, there had also been a *plebiscitum* passed, by which a tribune who wished to carry through his laws, might be elected twice. In the year 629, C. Gracchus entered upon his tribuneship. He was upright and pure, like Tiberius, but passionate; he was superior to his brother in energy, and he knew more clearly what he was about. With regard to the possession of land, in the outset he had indeed only to enact Tiberius' laws: but he aimed also far beyond these at other reforms: since, as a tribune, he had a power just as lawful as that of the senate itself, and therefore did not act the part of a revolutionist. But had he also a chance of success? That was the question. In his own mind, he was satisfied that his cause could make its way. It is a pity that we do not get a sight of the whole of his plan; the most important points are the very ones which have been the most corrupted: his legislation consisted of a number of detached laws which affected the most different branches of the state. What we know of it, is quite enough to show how little he was of a demagogue. There are seemingly the greatest contradictions in it; but they vanish when we look at them from the right point of view: for we thus see that he did not wish to lend himself to any party. Far from it, he made use of the factions to carry out wholesome reforms, holding out to one side such and such advantage, and to the other something else, while he himself stood quite apart. His first step, as tribune of the people, was, of course, to avenge the death of his brother and his friends. Nasica had gone off with a commission to Asia, and did not return.

His first law was that no one who had been deprived of his office by the people, should be invested with any other: this bill, which was evidently aimed against Octavius, he withdrew at the intercession of his mother. The second enacted that those men should be punished with death, who, without any previous trial, had laid hands upon Roman citizens, and slain them. This was chiefly directed against Lænas, who, when it passed, went into voluntary exile. Of the speech, in which Gracchus made these motions, we have a fine fragment still left, which Gellius pedantically criticises. These were the offerings with which he made atonement to the dead.

The carrying out of the agrarian law had been decreed, and it went on, though rather sluggishly. The measure which has been most found fault with, is his having first brought in the practice of distributing corn to the common people living at Rome: in the way in which he did it, the *modius* of corn was to be given out at three-quarters of an *as*, one-fourth of what it would cost elsewhere. This surely was not by any means a bribe, but a charity to the poor who wanted it. Rome had those great revenues which were paid in grain, and the treasury was so rich that it was not necessary to convert the corn into money. At the time of the Social war, there were about seventy-four millions sterling in the treasury, and these certainly could not be better bestowed than for the good of the poor: besides which, even from of old, corn had been distributed in the temple of Ceres; so that this was not even an innovation. The idea of a certain dignity being inherent in every one who belongs to a free people, lies at the bottom of everything that is done in a republic. A commonwealth has the duty of providing for its members, even for the most humble: this is a principle which England in some measure follows in her poor's rates, whereas there is nothing of the kind in a despotic country, to belong to which gives no privilege. Now it so happened that part of the true Roman citizens, who also had their share with the rest in the sovereignty, were as poor as those paupers among us, who are maintained by the alms of the public: their numbers must have been immense; some of them were not in the tribes at all; others, as, for instance, the descendants of freedmen, were in the *tribus urbanæ*. The Gracchi wished to make peasants of as many of them as possible; but this could not be done with all, nor perhaps had the greater part of that *plebes* even so much as a claim to it, as the division of the land was to be according to tribes. C. Gracchus did not want the corn to be given them entirely for nothing; but at such a rate that they might easily earn their livelihood by their work. From this time, I believe the difference of the *plebes urbana* and the thirty-five tribes to be dated, the free Roman citizens of lower rank being the main elements of that *plebes*.

Another of Gracchus' measures was for the relief of the soldier. Every soldier had formerly to find his arms, and part of his pay was kept back to defray the expense of repairing them. But the treasury was so very full, that the sacrifice was not felt, if those who had to serve, had at least their arms given them. This point C. Gracchus carried. He also established between the quay, the Aventine, and the Monte Testaccio, a corn-magazine (*horrea populi Romani*): this afterwards expanded into immense buildings, the traces of which were very distinctly seen even so late as in the sixteenth century. Moreover, he made highways, and gave a new impulse to paving: it was perhaps under his management that the great Roman roads were brought to that perfection which we still admire in them; for he had them paved with basalt, which until then had been done on a small piece of the Appian road only. By this means he gave employment to the poor man, who was thus enabled to get his living.

All these arrangements were administrative ones; he now went on to make others which affected the constitution itself. The senate was at that time without control with regard to one of the most important branches of civil government: Polybius already remarks, that the great power of the senate in so democratical a republic was owing to two causes. In the first place, it had quite an unbounded power over the finances; so that many were dependent on it for their incomes. All the revenues of the state from customs, mines, tithes, and other sources, were let to companies of wealthy Romans; and these again in their business employed the lower classes down to the very lowest, who, therefore, were all of them under the influence of the senate, which had the supreme direction: thus indeed, though every one engaged in this way did not get his maintenance from a government employment, as with us; the result was practically the same among the Romans, that the state itself provided for a great part of its subjects. Hence swarms of these citizens spread themselves as *negotiatores* over the provinces, and sucked their life's blood. This was one of the circumstances which enabled the small body of the senate to stand its ground so steadily. The other means which it had, was, that all these people were obliged to have their patrons in the senate itself, and that the judges in nearly all the more important causes were senators; at least in all those which did not directly concern Quiritary property. It is one of the erroneous notions to be found everywhere, that in ancient Rome a sort of jury had existed, which was instituted only after the laws of Gracchus. During the earlier times, no trial was required in any case of *delictum manifestum*; the identity of the person being proved, the prætor immediately enforced the law, and that was all. In other cases, as in criminal causes and those civil suits which were not brought before the *centum viri*, the decision of one *arbiter* was needed, before the prætor could pass a sentence which might be acted upon. The complaint was laid before the prætor, who after thirty days named a judge. The latter gave judgment according to certain fixed rules, from which there was no further appeal; for the appeal which there had once been to the people had been done away with, whilst for anything that was not *judicium publicum*, none perhaps had ever been allowed. Since the seventh century, several pleas for which formerly special *quæsitores* had been appointed, from whom they came before the popular tribunals, were now judged according to the common course of law; especially the *actiones repetundarum*, the complaints of the unfortunate provincials against their governors: for these, however, several judges were granted. But this single judge, or, as the case might be, these several judges, were always senators; and this was indeed a strong tie, by which the senate strengthened its authority. But these courts were detestable: the most scandalous judgments were given; and the senator who by lot had become *judex*, allowed himself to be bribed in the most barefaced manner, no one making any secret of it: nor indeed was any body ashamed of doing thus; those who were not to be bought formed but a small exception, and that perhaps merely from calculation. The right of bringing an action made the provinces yet worse off than if they had been utterly debarred from it; for the governor had to plunder so much the more, that he might be able to bribe his judges. This reminds me of the saying of the Neapolitan minister, the prince of Canosa, an eccentric but witty man: he said, that no where out of the kingdom of Naples could one get so many false witnesses for a carlino (about fourpence) each; and that, if one wanted a quantity of them, they were to be had cheaper still. Thus the senators in Rome merely asked, "How many thousands will you give me, that I may acquit you?" One crow does not pick out the eyes of the other. This was revolting, and it was clear that it would bring the state to ruin: a change was necessary, and that of Gracchus was certainly the best as things were, though, on the other hand, it might also have ill consequences. He cast his eyes upon that body of men which now in some measure filled the place of a middle class, although sometimes possessing immense riches: it was composed of those who had more than a hundred thousand *denarii* (400,000 sesterces), there being no longer any other standard but that of wealth. From what is called the people, Gracchus expected nothing whatever; he knew that part of it was a rabble which either did not care for anything, or else was open to the worst bribery; the knights, on the other hand, had no interest to screen the misdeeds of those who were in power. As in the senate there were three hundred members, Gracchus transferred the jurisdiction to a like number of knights in their stead. That the three hundred knights were alone to be the judges, and that, as the case might require, each of these was one by one to be chosen by lot from among them, is placed beyond a doubt by the researches of Manutius. At first, this did not altogether work badly, as these new judges had none of the family and other connexions of the leading senators at Rome; but, on the other hand, they were no fair judges for the provincials. The Roman companies which farmed the revenue, consisted chiefly of knights, and they had been guilty of most unrighteous dealings in the provinces. Hitherto these had been ground down by the magistrates who had been sent to rule over them; and now that a remedy had been found for the evil, if the latter chose to make a bargain with the knights, they could buy them over by letting them go beyond their contracts, and take, for instance, one-fifth, instead of the tenth which was their due. In return for this, the knights would guarantee them impunity, should they be prosecuted for extortion. This was a monstrous abuse, occasioned by accidental circumstances; but for Rome and Italy the change was an improvement: and so it was on the whole for all those places to which the farming companies did not extend.

This fell upon the senators like a thunderbolt. And when an independent body of judges had now been formed, Gracchus went still farther: he substituted their jurisdiction for those popular tribunals which were not worth anything, and which henceforth are only met with as an exception. This was setting bounds to democracy, where democracy was no longer in its right place.

In order to put better blood into the veins of the thirty-five tribes, he wished to extend the full right of citizenship to the Latins, among whom there were some forty colonial towns besides the old Latin cities: they had existed for three hundred years, and had for two centuries been entirely amalgamated by language and manners with the Romans; and in all likelihood he meant to form them into new tribes. The Italian allies, on the other hand, from Lucania to the March of Ancona, nay all the Italian districts as far as to the Alps, he wished to raise to that position which the Latins then held; that is to say, to give them a vote in the assembly of the people, and prepare them to become full citizens after thirty or forty years. It may even be that something was really done to carry this out. This law again was most wise and judicious, and those who were for a reasonable aristocracy must have rejoiced at it. In the Latin towns, there were many good families of local celebrity, which were now to be ranked among the Roman citizens. In Augustus' times, the most distinguished families came from the allied towns: the Asinii were Marrucinians; thus also, the Munatii and others; according to Cicero, literature was more cultivated among them than at Rome. Thus, an aristocracy of wealth and refinement was to be brought in; a wiser and more praise-worthy scheme than that of C. Gracchus, there could not possibly have been.

Many of his laws are either not known to us at all, or only from occasional notices. Though he wished to make the plebeians good husbandmen, if he could, and therefore assigned land to them, he did not make them a present of it. The state, the interests of which Gracchus did not lose sight of, had hitherto always had the tithes from the occupants; and this burthen he allowed to continue, as we learn from a passage in Plutarch which can have no other meaning. To him it seemed evident, that Rome could only hold her own by returning to her first principles: he therefore gave the Italians hopes of the right of citizenship, and also moved for a reform of the manner of voting; so that the republic would no longer have comprised one city, but the whole of Italy.

The distribution of the provinces had until now given rise to the greatest intrigues in the senate. Sometimes the tribunes even interfered. When the new consuls and prætors had come in, and the reference was made *de provinciis*, every one would apply for himself, and try to get what seemed to him most favourable to his purpose of enriching himself; and the senate decided from personal considerations. At that time already, the elections took place long before the end of the year. C. Gracchus now made the wise rule, that the senate should settle before the elections, to what provinces a consul or a prætor was to be sent, and then assign them afterwards to the persons who were to have them: this was wont to be done by lot, and thus anything like favouritism was put an end to. This rid the republic of a great many evils. He, no doubt, was also the one who brought in the rule of having the *comitia* held so early, that the year might not come to an end without the curule chair being filled. This is one of the real and lasting improvements of Gracchus, and it was still in force seventy years after his death.

These laws of his, Gracchus made in 629 and 630, having been tribune for two years running. His tribunate was less stormy than that of his brother, as he had much greater power, and was less thwarted. He got himself, and his friend M. Fulvius Flaccus, and very likely Q. Rubrius also, to be appointed triumvirs for the establishing of colonies; for his activity was unwearied, and it was felt in all the branches of the state to which his influence as tribune could reach. Among others, he had founded a colony by the side of old Carthage, and against this settlement a hypocritical outcry was raised, as if it might one day become dangerous to Rome; a most senseless notion, which some folks even held in good earnest. The jealousy and spite against him had now risen to the highest pitch, and the present opportunity was seized to harass him. The senate, with fiendish cunning, egged on another tribune, M. Livius Drusus, to outbid him in liberality to the people, and that in the name of the senate, so as to undermine his popularity. The great mass did not care, who it was that offered a boon to them; they thought, "Gracchus wants to buy and cheat us, Livius bids more: let us take what we can get, and not let ourselves be cheated." Such, the Italians are even to this day. I myself have seen a striking example of this in the citizen of a small town, who had some coins which I valued for him. He fancied that I wanted to overreach him; and immediately after, he asked me, for a piece which I wished to buy, three times as much as I had told him, whereas before that, I might have had all of them for the third part of what they were worth. When one gives the modern Romans any advice from real kindness, and with perfect disinterestness, they will at once suspect you of having some secret end in view; for indeed they will not trust anybody. Thus it was also in those times. Livius did away with the tithes with which the lands were still burthened; and instead of the two colonies which Gracchus had proposed, he founded twelve, each of which was to consist of three thousand citizens. This the rich could easily grant, the only losers by it being the old inhabitants, unhappy men who hitherto had dwelt by sufferance on the soil where their ancestors had been conquered; for the estates of the rich were only in those places where the old towns had been destroyed. With regard to these colonies of Livius, we may ask, have they really been founded? There seems to be no doubt of it, as those of Gracchus were certainly established; indeed they were in all likelihood those *duodecim coloniæ* in Cicero's oration *pro Cæcina*, about which there has been so much controversy. These cannot have had any reference to what happened in the war with Hannibal, when the number of those which had remained faithful was eighteen; so that eighteen and not twelve must have had the *commercium* given them as a boon. The MSS. have XII.: it has been proposed to write XIIX. instead; but this kind of notation is not met with in any of the old manuscripts. If, as I take it for granted, they were not twelve new colonies, but twelve Latin towns which, as they had a great deal of unoccupied ground, were increased by three thousand citizens, it is quite easy to understand why they had better rights than the other colonies.

Gracchus saw that the thoughtless people turned away from him to the senate, and to the tools of the senate who deceived them. There are many men, frank and kindly souls, who heartily love the Beautiful, and are delighted at seeing distinguished men play their part, and look upon them as the ornaments of their age; others think of nothing but themselves: driven on by envy and jealousy, and grieved at hearing any name praised be it ever so slightly, even when it does not harm them in the least, they are glad if they can discover any weaknesses in great men. All this tribe now raised an outcry against Gracchus, laughing at him as a *doctrinaire*, a man of crotchets and theories. He had now for so long a time enjoyed great consideration, and he stood forth in too full a blaze of light not to become an eyesore to many people; just as the Athenian citizen gave his vote against Aristides, because he was called the Just. Thus it came to pass, that when he again offered himself as a candidate for the tribuneship, he was rejected; nor is there any reason to believe that his colleagues had been guilty of foul play. Among the independent educated middle classes only, Gracchus seems to have had many partisans; but these had not much political weight, and his friends of high rank were hot-headed people. In the year 631, his enemy L. Opimius, the destroyer of Fregellæ, whom, the year before, he had kept out of the consulship, was chosen consul. For when he was in the heyday of his popularity, he once asked the people to promise him a favour; this they granted, and while it was thought that he would demand great things, he begged the consulship for C. Fannius. The latter was a *homo novus,* at least for the consulship, and it would have been hard for him to get it without the help of Gracchus: he, however, soon left him, and went over to his foes. Opimius also was a plebeian; but, like Popillius Lænas, he sided with the aristocracy against Gracchus. The oligarchical party was bent upon getting up a quarrel. Gracchus, now that he was no longer *sacrosanctus,* did not feel sure of his life, and was therefore always surrounded by many of his friends. The measures of the senate became more and more hostile: the colonies granted to him were to be broken up by a decree of that body, and there was a deliberation on the subject; one of the tribunes moreover, who had been nominated by the oligarchs, spoke to the people then assembled before the Capitol, against Gracchus, and when the latter came forward to defend himself, he was charged in a tumultuous manner with having interrupted the tribune. The consul, who just then was offering a sacrifice on the Capitol, sent one of his lictors, as if to fetch something for the sacrifice, but in reality for another purpose; and the man while forcing his way across the friends of Gracchus, cried out, "Ye evil-minded fellows! make room for the good citizens!" One of them was rash enough to strike him; a tumult arose, and the lictor was murdered. His dead body was displayed in the forum, and a scene was got up, as if he had been a martyr to the good cause. For the first time,[78] the senate now passed the decree, *viderent Consules, ne quid detrimenti res publica caperet.* Opimius was invested with dictatorial power; for the custom of making dictators had fallen into disuse, as it could no longer be managed in the old forms, the curies having ceased to exist. Gracchus now took leave of his wife and children; after which, he and Fulvius went to the Aventine, the ancient refuge for persecuted innocence. He had had no foreboding of the misfortune which had come upon him: his whole party was all in confusion, and he could not make up his mind to let things go on to extremity. His friend and colleague, the consular M. Fulvius Flaccus, who was more resolute, armed some of the common people, and slaves; in short, any one whom he could get. The mob itself—

from henceforth we meet with nothing better—for which Gracchus had no sympathies, left him to his fate, taking him for a knave or a fool, and being quite content, so long as they kept the benefits which he had gained for them. Thus it cost the consuls no trouble to attack the Aventine, though they had only a small force, the city being either paralyzed or indifferent. The knights, whom Gracchus had nearly remodelled as an order, were likewise idle lookers on, owing to that fear which is inherent in rich men whose wealth is not in landed property, but merely in money. This class shows itself lukewarm in every commotion, and lets itself be trampled on in every possible way, as we see, for instance, in the history of Florence.

Gracchus sent to the senate to effect a compromise; but unconditional surrender was demanded. The Aventine being feebly defended, the *clivus Publicius*, by which one ascended from the Circus, was taken by storm; and now Fulvius sent his son, a fine, handsome youth, to the senate, to ask for a truce. He was sent back the first time; and when he came again, Opimius had him arrested, thrown into a dungeon, and afterwards put to death. When the Aventine was taken, Fulvius, who had hidden himself, was found and slain; Gracchus leaped from the temple of Diana down the sharp steep of the Aventine, and sprained his ankle; not being able to find a horse, he, leaning on his friends, could hardly reach the *Pons sublicius*. The two friends, Pomponius and Lætorius, who were knights, and formed an honourable exception to the majority of the higher classes, fought like Horatius Cocles on the bridge, to keep the pursuers at bay, and allowed themselves to be cut down. In the meanwhile, Gracchus fled across the Tiber into a sacred grove (*lucus Furiarum*), which, however, did not shelter him. Opimius had promised for his head its weight in gold. According to the most likely account, a faithful slave did him the friendly service of killing him. An Anagnian, Septimuleius, got the head, and filled it with molten lead. Upwards of three thousand men were denounced as partisans of Gracchus, and nearly all of them were put to death by Opimius; a few only may have made their escape. This war of extermination was waged against all who were in any way distinguished: it was a downright butchery, like that of the year 1799 at Naples. For two years the bloodshed lasted, and these murderers called themselves *boni homines, boni cives*. There were many renegades, and there is no doubt but that C. Carbo was very early one of them. He became consul, and then defended Opimius against the charges brought against him by the tribune Q. Decius. Carbo, after he had saved Opimius, became the darling of the oligarchs; but now there arose against him P. Licinius Crassus, a near kinsman of his, perhaps a brother of the wife of C. Gracchus, and the very one of whom Cicero so often speaks, especially in the masterly dialogue *de Oratore*, and in his "Brutus." Crassus was a man of uncommon mind and powers; but like all the orators of that age (with the exception of C. Gracchus), wanting in cultivation. He too began on the side of the people, and then he went over to the senate, and became one of the foremost champions of the oligarchy; yet he is a very respectable oligarch, and quite free from the reproach which clings to so many others. He now spoke against Carbo, and attacked him in such a manner, that he took away his own life by means of poison (a solution of vitriol, *atramentum sutorium*). [79] This was a satisfaction to men's feelings, and it gave a hope of the possibility that things would still change for the better. But for all that, they remained as they were: the knights were intimidated; the courts of justice were no better, nor were any fruits whatever of their independence yet to be seen. The utter worthlessness of those who were in power is strikingly shown in the war of Jugurtha, which Sallust, with his fine tact, has therefore made the subject of his historical work. But we must first speak of the conquests of the empire.

FOREIGN CONQUESTS DOWN TO THE WAR WITH JUGURTHA

In Spain, few events of any importance happened between the time of Tib. Gracchus and the war with Jugurtha. The Balearic isles were subdued by one of the four sons of Metellus Macedonicus, all of whom were consuls. The Metelli were plebeians, but one of the most powerful families which formed the aristocracy; and they were truly great characters: Metellus Numidicus also, notwithstanding the reproaches which have been brought against him, is one of the most spotless of men. Another son of Metellus conquered the Dalmatians, who from henceforth remained subject to the Romans; so that one might now go by land to Greece round the Adriatic.

Soon after the death of Tib. Gracchus, the Romans made their first expedition into Transalpine Gaul. They were masters of nearly the whole of Spain, and of Italy almost as far as the Alps (Aosta did not yet belong to them); but in Gaul itself, between the Alps and the Pyrenees, they had not yet even tried to gain a firm footing: all that they did, was to secure for the Massilians, their old allies, in the beginning of the seventh century, a strip of country along the coast against the Ligurians. The first occasion for their establishing themselves there, was a war of the Salluvians or Salyans against the Ligurians: the Salluvians, who dwelt from Aix to Marseilles, were conquered by them. This tribe had been supported by the Allobroges, one of the greatest peoples of Gaul, who had their abodes in Dauphiné and Savoy, as far as Lyons; and when these had likewise been defeated, the Romans turned their arms against the Arvernians, a race governed by rich and powerful kings, which as far back as the second Punic War, held the supremacy in Gaul. These last were utterly routed on the banks of the Rhone near Vienne, in the days of C. Gracchus. Bituitus, of whose wealth various accounts have been preserved, was at that time their king: he tried to make his peace with the Romans, and the generals, Q. Fabius Maximus (who was afterwards surnamed Allobrogicus), and Cn. Domitius, sent him to Rome to beg the mercy of the senate. Without having come *in deditionem*, he went thither, trusting to the good faith of those who were in power; but they arrested him, and kept him a prisoner to the day of his death at Alba on the lake Fucinus, where Syphax and Perseus had died. The Roman province now reached as far as Dauphiné. The Allobroges in that country, though they acknowledged the *majestas populi Romani*, did not become subjects; but Provence and Lower Languedoc, were real provinces, although there was not always a prætor there. The time when the Roman provincial institutions were introduced, cannot be exactly made out, owing to the loss of the books of Livy. Aquæ Sextiæ was the first Roman colony beyond the Alps.

In 638 the Cimbri make their first appearance. After the reduction of Dalmatia, the Romans had attacked Carniola, which is said to have roused the anger of the Scordiscans. It is, however, more likely that the immigration of the Sarmatians from the east stirred up the Scordiscans, who now fell upon Macedon and Greece. This was one of the greatest calamities of the unfortunate sixth and seventh centuries of the city, which were some of the most awful for the world itself; just as the sixteenth and seventeenth of our era in modern history: it destroyed most of the beautiful works of ancient art. In Italy, that havoc went on until the times of Augustus, which were the first beginning of a kind of material prosperity. The consul C. Porcius Cato was routed in Thrace by the Scordiscans, and Macedon, Thessaly, and part of Greece, were overrun by the barbarians.

THE WAR AGAINST JUGURTHA. Q. CÆCILIUS METELLUS NUMIDICUS. C. MARIUS

Sallust's description of the war against Jugurtha, is one of the best specimens which we have in either language of the ancient literature, and I would even rate it above that of Catiline's conspiracy. They are monographies, almost the only ones which the Romans had, except perhaps the history of the war with Hannibal by Cœlius Antipater, of which, however, we know nothing: the memoirs of Fannius were something quite different. Sallust takes indeed the utmost care to avoid anything that has an annalistic look; he leaves out every mention of dates, to give his work the greatest possible finish. It is a book which, the more one reads it, the more worthy of admiration it seems: it is a real study for every one who wants to know what excellent historical writing is. To him I refer you.

When Masinissa died, he had put his kingdom in order, and made Scipio executor of his will. He left his dominions to his three sons, Gulussa, Micipsa, and Mastanabal, whom we are by no means to look upon as having been somewhat like the chieftains of the tribes which now dwell in those countries; for Livy says of Mastanabal, that he had been *litteris Græcis apprime eruditus*. He knew Greek so well, that he wrote it; a fact which shows us how wrongly we deem the Numidians and all such races to have been mere barbarians. Even among the rude Thracians, there can be no doubt that at that time Greek learning was not unknown; we meet with it afterwards even among the Parthians. The civilization of the Greeks had spread very widely, more especially since the fall of the nation. The Numidians, as well as the Libyans, had an alphabet of their own, as one sees from remains which are found in several towns in those parts. Colonel Humbert has discovered over the gate of a city an *inscriptio bilinguis*, Punic and Libyan; in Cyrene, there are inscriptions in three languages, Punic, Greek, and one which is unknown; in the desert of Sahara, among the Tuariks, the travellers Clapperton and Denham have met with an alphabet which is quite distinct from the Arabic. I am convinced that it belongs to the Libyan language, which is spoken in the Canary isles, throughout the whole of the desert and the oases, as far as the Nile and the Barabras in Upper Egypt. Denham[80] is too shallow, to see his way through it; we shall be able to read the Libyan inscriptions when we fully know the alphabet, of which Denham gives one letter. The whole of this matter will one day be cleared up. The Numidian kings likewise had the Carthaginian library given them as a present by the Romans. Gulussa died early, as also did Mastanabal, who left behind him only a son by a concubine, Jugurtha. The Numidian empire, which reached from the borders of Morocco to the Syrtes as far as Leptis and Tripolis, was now in the hands of Micipsa alone. He had two sons, Adherbal and Hiempsal. Jugurtha, who had excellent abilities, at first won the heart of the old king; but when the latter discovered in him talents superior to those of his own sons, he became jealous of him, and sent him to Spain, where Scipio was gathering troops together from all parts for the siege of Numantia: there he hoped that he would perish. But Jugurtha was befriended by fortune; and he gained great favour with Scipio, under whose protection he desired to be placed, lest Micipsa should murder him. Many Romans of rank even encouraged him to revolt, and provided him with money, as he had no prospect of coming to the throne lawfully; for after Micipsa's death, the whole of the kingdom was to be kept together. He now got letters of recommendation to Micipsa, who, taking fright, adopted him, and in his will divided the sovereignty among the three princes, who were to reign together as colleagues. The proud and fierce Hiempsal, who looked upon his cousin as an intruder, would insult him without any provocation: it was then agreed upon to share the inheritance, and in the meanwhile Jugurtha had him murdered. Jugurtha, who was no common man, being shrewd and versatile, but without any notion of truth and honesty, like an Albanian chief, now took up arms and attacked Adherbal also. The latter betook himself to the Romans, and owing to their predilection for him obtained a favourable decision: a commission was sent from Rome to divide the country between himself and Jugurtha. The commissioners, however, were so well plied with gold, that, when the division was made, Jugurtha got the most powerful and warlike part of the country. But he longed for the whole, and thus a war was soon brought on again. Adherbal imploringly besought the help of Rome against this criminal and restless man, and in the senate, at first, his cause was found to be a just one; but the ruling oligarchs, headed by Opimius, and bought over with bribes, declared for Jugurtha, and hindered every decision. In the meantime, Adherbal was beset in Cirta, and driven to the last distress: his representations to the Roman senate were all baffled by the influence of L. Opimius, as the envoys of Jugurtha, who were at Rome with a large sum of money, purchased the votes of every one. But when Cirta had been brought to extremity, some of the friends of Adherbal stole out of the town, and carried to the senate most dismal letters: a new commission was now sent, which was likewise bribed, and returned without having raised the siege. Jugurtha, however, was impelled by Nemesis not to keep his promise to Adherbal, when he yielded himself up and stipulated for his life only; nor to the Roman and Italian *negotiatores*, who alone had upheld that prince, and who now also surrendered. He had them slaughtered to sate his vengeance. This was too bad, and even those who had hitherto spoken most loudly for him, had no longer a word to say. A Roman embassy arrived at Utica, to call Jugurtha to account; but he gave evasive answers and completely took them in.

This embassy was headed by M. Æmilius Scaurus, a man who has a great name in history, but of whom one is at a loss what to think. Horace says,

> *Regulum et Scauros*
>
> *Gratus insigni referam Camena,*
>
> *Fabriciumque.*

As for Horace, it is remarkable that no one could be more ignorant of the history of his own people than he was; thus, for instance, he confounds the two Scipios, and he had so little read Ennius whom he laughs at, as to believe that he had sung of Scipio, the destroyer of Carthage.[81] When he names Scaurus, he says *Scauri*, not knowing that Scaurus the son was a most worthless fellow, the Verres of Sardinia, whom Cicero defended merely out of regard for his family. It is owing to this un-Roman spirit, that he is utterly unable to appreciate the great minds of the earlier literature; he is a man of elegant, superficial learning, and, even in his knowledge of the Greek writers, not to be compared with Virgil. Hence then so many strange things in his Odes, where he misunderstood the Greek. The stock-in-trade which he had for his odes, was taken from a few Greek lyrics. When he says that Homer was wont to slumber, he merely shows his ignorance; he writes to Lollius that he had again read Homer, which may perhaps have been for the first time since he left school. Still he is a noble genius, much more versatile and prolific than Virgil, who, indeed, was far more industrious and painstaking. Horace was lazy, ever bent on refined enjoyments. The contrast between the two poets is very striking; it would be an excellent subject, if worked out.—What speaks well for Scaurus, is the great respect in which he was held by Cicero, who mentions, as one of the finest remembrances of his earlier days, that as a youth of seventeen he was introduced by his father into the presence of the great statesmen of the age, among whom Scaurus then shone as a venerable old man: the youth met with a distinguished reception from them, as they recognised in him the future great man; and he, on his side, had come to them with that longing which is felt by all generous minds, to attach himself to those who are more matured, and to purify himself after their example. Thus he idealized these men, and the impression which he had received, lasted his whole life through; even, when an old man himself, he looked up to the men of his youth, and in this spirit he also remembers Scaurus. Sallust is reproached with malignity; but surely he is not sinning against truth, when, filled with indignation, he is branding a guilty man for ever. Scaurus, as Sallust describes him, was on the verge of that time of life, when the vigour and energy needed for waging war are already weakened, but are still equal to ruling the state; yet when he actually became old, he got out of the perplexing position in which he had been entangled, and he stood forth as one who had belonged to an age of gigantic minds, and having to keep up a high character, he then seems to have lived outwardly blameless and upright. Thus Cicero knew him. The same person may at different times be quite a different being; he may be an excellent citizen, and then again a bad one: I am not speaking here of real virtue before God, but only of political virtue. This was the case, for instance, in England with Shaftesbury and others in the seventeenth century. I knew one of the most eminent men of our own day, who (with the consent indeed of his government) very indelicately availed himself of an advantage, whereas at other times he showed himself to be a true hero. The leading features in the character of Scaurus, are very great pride, very determined party spirit, and first-rate talent. That his behaviour during the war with Jugurtha is not an invention of Sallust's, may be seen from the history itself.

In the commission at Utica, Scaurus was blameless; just as in former times. After Adherbal's downfall, the consul L. Calpurnius Bestia wished to enrich himself by an African war, or at all events to be able to sell a peace; he therefore joined with some lovers of justice in moving that Jugurtha should be brought to punishment, and he also managed to be sent out to Africa with that commission. The war began in good earnest; but negotiations were soon set on foot, Jugurtha having convinced Bestia and Scaurus that this was more for their advantage. He remained indeed in possession of his kingdom; but to save appearances, he surrendered himself *in fidem populi Romani*; so that the senate only had to ratify the peace, the *fœdus* being changed into a *clientela*. He delivered up the deserters, thirty elephants, and much cattle; and he bound himself to pay several instalments of money. Yet the whole thing was but a vile farce. Instead of the deserters being sent to Rome, where they were to be put to death, they were allowed to run away; and the elephants were returned to Jugurtha for money. This treaty, however, raised such an outcry at Rome, that a bold tribune of the name of C. Memmius got the people to have the matter inquired into; and L. Cassius, who at that time was honoured as the justest of men, was commissioned personally to investigate the case in Africa itself. Cassius, beyond all doubt, was a man of very high rank,—a patrician,[82] but not identified with any party: being himself pure in a corrupt time, he condemned without any respect of persons. Cassius' word of honour was of such weight, that Jugurtha on the strength of it deemed himself quite safe in going to Rome, and publicly making his appearance there. Here we find Jugurtha—and this is a marked feature in the whole of his deportment—wavering between his own boldness and the feeling that he was not able to withstand the power of Rome. He was on the point of giving up his accomplices; but a tribune of the people had been bribed to forbid his speaking, just as he was getting up in the assembly of the people. Thus the authority of the tribunes had become powerful for evil, but powerless for good. During his stay in Rome, Jugurtha caused another descendant of Masinissa, Massiva, a young Numidian, who likewise happened to be there at the very time, and to whom the consul Sp. Albinus had held out a hope of the succession, to be murdered: after this he fled from the city, leaving his sureties behind. The consul Albinus and the senate now declared the negotiations for peace to have been null and void; yet the guilty still remained unpunished. The war was renewed in Africa, but in a lukewarm manner. The consul Sp. Albinus, who had the chief command, wished for war; but his arrangements were bad. As he had to return to Rome for the consular elections, he intrusted the command to his brother Aulus, who behaved in such a bungling way that he was surrounded by the enemy. Jugurtha now plied the army with his money, and not only mere foreigners, but even Roman tribunes were bribed; so that when the time came for attacking Albinus, he was utterly overpowered, and his camp was taken. He was forced to make a disgraceful treaty, which, however, was disowned at Rome.

Things could now no longer be hushed up. Metellus got the command with ample forces to carry on the war. Three *quæsitores* were now to be appointed, and thus Scaurus was in danger of being involved in the enquiry: but, according to Sallust's account, he played his cards so well, that, instead of being impeached, he himself became one of the *quæsitores*, and proceeded against the accused only so far as seemed consistent with his own safety. A great number were condemned, and the slow vengeance for the murder of C. Gracchus now reached L. Opimius. It is inconceivable how Cicero is mistaken with regard to the latter: no man's judgment indeed ought to be implicitly followed. Those who fell at that time, were certainly all of them guilty. Unfortunately, we have no exact knowledge of these *quæstiones*; but thus much is certain, that the *optimates*, who wanted to pass themselves off as being the best, received by the exposure of the infamy of some among them, a blow from which they never recovered. The *equites*, as judges, now took a decided part against the senators: it would have been most interesting for us, if we could have had further details about it. Here begins the split which afterwards led to the civil war between the factions of Marius and Sylla. Calpurnius Bestia was likewise condemned; of the fate of others we know very little.

Metellus was the son of Macedonicus, and has the surname of Numidicus. He is one of those characters which people are very apt to see in a wrong light:—a noble-hearted man, he cannot be called without qualification; he was, though a plebeian, fully imbued with the prejudices and jealousies of the nobility. From a child, he had come to the conviction that the government ought to be honestly carried on: he was the patron of men of low degree who were making their way upwards; for he loved merit, so long as it kept within bounds, and did not aspire to the very highest place. This accounts for his behaviour to Marius, to whom at first he showed kindness; for as soon as Marius stood for the consulship, he was so blinded by his rage that he became his enemy. To this very day, one meets among the high English nobility with men like Metellus, who look upon the privileges of their order as the first inviolable rights, and whenever offences committed by any of their own body come to light, will step in with their protection to prevent an exposure. Thus the remarkable character of Metellus becomes quite clear: he was estimable for the integrity of his motives, but utterly incapable of being just. He spurned all the offers of Jugurtha against whom he used his own Punic arts, so that that prince was obliged to disarm entirely as the price of hopes which were never fulfilled; and when Jugurtha wished actually to buy himself off from the ruin which he clearly saw before his eyes, Metellus put forth conditions which would have rendered him quite defenceless. At last, Metellus demanded, that he should appear in person; this Jugurtha refused to do, and the war broke out afresh. Metellus carried it on for two years; and though he was sometimes worsted, he deserves very great praise for the manner in which he overcame the difficulties which he had to encounter: several of his undertakings are some of the most brilliant in history. Jugurtha, on the whole, avoided pitched battles; he risked an engagement only once, and then he was beaten. We now again see that mixture of cowardice and boldness which there was in him, and his inability to meet his fate. He wanted to surrender to Metellus, and had already given up all his arms, all his elephants, and two hundred thousand pounds of silver; but when he was to yield up his own person, he withdrew into the wilds of mount Atlas, having now stripped himself of all his resources. Thus the war was protracted in spite of the efforts of Metellus, and the opinion gained ground in Rome, that he had purposely allowed it to drag on: yet there was no reason for doubting his disinterestedness and incorruptibility.

He was a great general and statesman, and his personal character stood high; but his pretensions were unbearable. They may indeed have been the ruin of the country: that fearful irritability which we afterwards find in Marius, would never have been roused, had not the *optimates* done everything in their power to crush him.

On the subject of Marius' birth, even the ancients were not agreed. Some of them make him out to have been of a very low origin; others (Velleius Paterculus) place him somewhat higher: certain it is that his ancestors were clients of a municipal family in Arpinum, from which, however, it does not follow that they were serfs. The name is Oscan, and it is likely that his family had come from Campania to Arpinum, where it had entered into the clientship of the Herennii. At all events, he was poor, and had served as a private soldier, and before that, even as a day labourer. His extraordinary qualities must have displayed themselves very soon: at an early age, he was known at Rome as an able centurion; and when he applied for the military tribuneship, he was elected with great applause. Otherwise, it was very seldom indeed—particularly in those later times—that any one who had been in the ranks, was ever raised to the higher military commands. Marius rose without the help of any connexions or relations; yet he must have made some money, or he could not have stood for the ædileship, on which occasion he failed. Notwithstanding this repulse, he got the prætorship, which office he discharged very creditably; and though the oligarchs even then gave him trouble by charging him with *ambitus*, he kept his ground against them. In was in those days already most common for candidates to spend money; and yet every one would try and fix this charge upon his opponents, that he might drive them out of the field. He was now with the army of Metellus as a *legatus*: for the higher employments were by no means permanent. For a *homo novus* to become a prætor, was at that time not at all a thing unheard of; but that he should have risen to the consular dignity, was, according to Sallust's description, all but an impossibility. Of the six prætors moreover, four, as a matter of course, could not become consuls: the children of a prætor, however, were not *homines novi*.

Marius distinguished himself in Numidia. He was then indeed an elderly man already, even as I am now (1829), somewhat past fifty. He was moreover superstitious. We here meet for the first time with a superstition which is to be traced to the East; for he had with him a Syrian (or perhaps a Jewish) fortune teller of the name of Martha, by whose prophecies he allowed himself to be guided. As he was offering a sacrifice, he beheld an *omen* by which every thing that was highest in the state was promised him; and this gave him courage to stand for the consulship. Metellus advised him not to do it, tried to keep him back, and thwarted him in an underhand way;

nay, when Marius declared that he would positively become a candidate, he forgot himself so far as to tell him, that he need not forsooth be in such a hurry; and that indeed it would be still time enough for him to be thrown out, when his own son should stand. That son was then twenty years old, and by the *leges annales* no one could be a consul until he was about forty years of age. Marius never forgot this: he felt bitterly offended, and caused the people to be canvassed by his friends in Rome, on which Metellus seemingly yielded, in the hope that he would be too late: for he gave him leave of absence but twelve days before the elections. But Marius by dint of wonderful exertions reached the coast; and the wind being fair, he arrived in Rome, even making his appearance before the day of the election, and was almost unanimously chosen consul.

Whilst C. Gracchus is unjustly called a demagogue, this name may well be given to Marius, who was one in every sense of the word; for he would fawn upon the lowest rabble as others would upon powerful individuals, and delight in appearing to the common people as if he were one of them. He was not suited to those times: for he had a sensitive pride which was continually wounded, and thus he fell into those unhappy ways which have disgraced him. Moreover, it was then looked upon as indispensable for a man of rank to be well versed in the manners, and literature, and language of the Greeks; just as those of the French were deemed essential in Germany, even to the days of my youth. Old Cato learned Greek only late; yet he learned it, and was well read in the literature of his own country. Unlike him, Marius did not cling to the old traditions which began already to vanish away, and he disdained modern refinement, because he knew nothing of it: he spoke Greek, it is true, which at that time was quite necessary in society, but he despised it. His honesty was without a stain: for though his great wealth must have been acquired in war, he was held to be a *vir sanctus*, since he had not robbed the commonwealth as the greater part of his contemporaries had done. From this we may judge of the state of morals then. Fabricius, Curius, and others, who centuries before had likewise been called *sancti*, were also poor. Marius was a first-rate general, the consciousness of which carried him high: he was great in drawing up an army, especially in the day of battle, unrivalled in his mode of conducting a campaign, and just as skilful in encampment. But he had few friends: the leading features of his character were bitterness and hatred, and he was cruel and unamiable. Fate had raised him up to save Rome, the degeneracy of which is to be charged upon those who crushed and irritated so extraordinary, so distinguished a man. Metellus was an ordinary general: had he ever had to face Marius in the field, he would at once have been beaten. Marius, on the contrary, was no common commander; besides the greatest foresight in making his preparations, he was gifted with unbounded energy to execute, and with a quickness of eye which could see everything at a glance. It was his hatred against the so-called *optimates*, which, perhaps without his being aware of it, led him into his many unrighteous acts against them.

The tribunes of the people at Rome now moved that the province of Numidia should, out of turn, be the first assigned; and as this was unanimously agreed to by the people, Marius got the chief command. Metellus again showed his littleness of mind. Not being able to brook the sight of his successor, he stole away, leaving the army to his legate Rutilius, an excellent man, who afterwards became a victim to party spirit, as he went over to the other side: for, as hitherto the oligarchical faction had shown itself malignant, so did the democrats in their turn, now that they had got the upperhand. Marius ended the war with Jugurtha in less than two years, having displayed the greatest ability and boldness. Sallust particularly mentions, how in the siege of Capsa, he put to flight the enemy's cavalry, &c. The Romans did not advance much beyond Cirta; Jugurtha went to Bocchus, king of the Mauritanians, a connexion of his by marriage. This prince at first had taken up arms on his side; but he soon listened to the proposal of the Romans, to make his peace with them by betraying his ally. This was done after a great deal of negotiation, Bocchus having wavered for a long time, and even thought of arresting Sylla, by whom this business was transacted: at length he gave up Jugurtha, who was now led by Marius in his triumph. Part of Numidia was united with the province of Africa; most of it, however, was left as an independent kingdom, the kings of which in all likelihood—in what way, we do not know—belonged to Masinissa's house. Juba, in the time of Cæsar's wars, was descended from the nameless king who then succeeded. Bocchus was acknowledged as an independent sovereign.

WAR WITH THE CIMBRI AND TEUTONES

The war in Africa had come to an end, and it was high time that it should; for the republic had quite a different employment for Marius, in comparison with which the war against Jugurtha was mere child's play. The Cimbri and Teutones were expected on the frontiers of Italy, and they had already routed the armies of Manlius and Cæpio. Contrary to all existing rules, Marius at the unanimous call of the nation was made consul; for the laws both forbade the choice of a man who was absent from the city, and required that ten years should elapse between two consulships of the same person. Marius had his triumph the new year's day on which he entered upon his second consulate.

The Cimbri[83] were not, properly speaking, Gaels; but they were akin to the Cymri, the inhabitants of the greater part of the western coast of England, of Wales, and of Cumberland (which has its name from them, and where even so late as a hundred years ago, traces of the Cymric tongue were met with): the *Basbretons* also belonged to the same race. Whether any Cymri dwelt in Ulster, is problematical: the Picts were likewise of the Cymric stock; and so were the Belgians: for though these were not unmingled with Gaels, the Cymri must have been predominant among them. On their great migration, they went in the fourth or fifth century to the borders of the Ukraine, and ruled as Celto-Scythians as far as the banks of the Dnieper, or even beyond: there they were called Galatians. Owing to circumstances of which we have no exact knowledge, very likely in consequence of the advance of the Sarmatians or Sclavonians, they were driven out of their settlements,—and they fell back upon their countrymen in Moldavia, Wallachia, Hungary, and the neighbouring countries: they first of all expelled the Bastarnians; then the Scordiscans and Tauriscans; and in 639, before the outbreak of the war with Jugurtha, they threw themselves upon the country of the Noricans in Carniola and Carinthia. Here, on the frontier of Italy, were the abodes of the Carnians and other Gallic tribes, which, though not subject to the Romans, were of course in a state of dependence, as is always the case with small nations when they are neighbours of great ones. The Cimbri made their appearance on the banks of the middle Danube and in

Bohemia, and attacked the Boians; but they were repelled. It must have been while they were on the middle Danube, that they fell upon every people which they met with, and leagued themselves with the Teutones. These, as even their name seems to show, were of German stock, quite as certainly as the Cimbri were of Gallic race in the widest sense of the word (thus many Gallic words are found in the Cymric language, and there is a general affinity between them, although Gauls and Cymri did not understand each other). The Teutones may, like the Cimbri, have been chased out of the East by the advance of the Sarmatians: if what we are told from the travels of Pytheas be true, and he fell in with the Teutones on the eastern coast of Prussia, it is likely that they were pushed on from northern Poland by the Sarmatians. In Gaul they clearly appear as the allies of the Cimbrians, and the names of the leaders betoken a Gallic and a German people. When now they rushed forth from Noricum, either together or in separate hosts, the Romans came to the help of the Carnians, and the consul Cn. Papirius Carbo, in all likelihood a son of him who had been driven by Crassus to commit suicide, was defeated and killed near Noreia by the Cimbrians, and his whole army perished with him. But the barbarians did not follow up their victory, nor did they penetrate into Italy; but, what is very strange, they overran the bleak provinces of Austria and Bavaria north of the Alps, which were then inhabited by Celts, and thus went on to Gaul. At the general break up which ensued, they were also joined by the Tigurini, who were Gauls from Helvetia, and by the Ambrones: whence these last came, is more than we can say; most likely, they were Ligurians from the Alps. All of these moved into Gaul, bringing with them a countless number of waggons with women, children, and booty; and now the four peoples, sometimes in one huge host, at other times apart, burst upon the civilized world. It is difficult to say where they defeated either Silanus or Scaurus; for our accounts are scanty beyond belief, as Livy fails us here, and the seventeen books of Dio Cassius which we have not, were also no longer to be found by Zonaras. It might be inferred from one statement, that the Romans advanced as far as the neighbourhood of Rochelle, between Poitou and the Garonne. They had to suffer another defeat under the consul L. Cassius Longinus, near the lake of Geneva, and they purchased their retreat with the loss of half their baggage. Although they wished to protect the Transalpine Gauls, all their efforts were unsuccessful. The devastation of Gaul by these wars was one of the most dreadful calamities ever known: the whole of the country bounded by the Rhone, even from the Rhine to the Pyrenees, was ravaged, which may account for its weakened state in the days of Cæsar; the towns were taken and laid waste, and the inhabitants cruelly treated. Of all the Gallic tribes, the Belgians alone could stand their ground. The worst defeat which the Romans sustained, was on the banks of the Rhone, the year after the consulship of Marius, under the consul Cn. Mallius and the proconsul Cæpio. That eighty thousand Romans and Italians were killed, does not look at all historical;—if that number be correct, many Gallic auxiliaries must have been with them;—but the statement, according to Orosius, seems to rest merely on the authority of Valerius Antias. At all events, both of the Roman armies were completely routed. But most providentially for Rome, when Gaul had everywhere been ransacked, the Cimbri and Teutones, either deterred by the Alps, or perhaps because they also feared the Romans more than they did any other people, turned towards Spain, which country they overran, as the Romans were utterly unable to protect it. Even those places which surrendered to them were horribly treated; and this led the Celtiberians to stand sieges in which they were at last driven to feed on dead bodies, rather than fall into the hands of barbarians. This resolute spirit made the invaders give up all thoughts of conquering Spain, and they retreated back again into Gaul.

The devastation of Gaul took place at the time when Metellus was conducting the war against Jugurtha; the expedition into Spain happened during Marius' second and third consulships. For the reverses which had befallen the Roman arms, had now caused Marius to be made consul for the third time; even his enemies wished him to be chosen, as they saw that no one else could save the state. Every army but that of Numidia had been annihilated; and to train the new soldiers, was the great task which Marius alone was able to achieve, he being himself as thoroughly practised a soldier as he desired every one to be. Marius is beyond all doubt the author of the great change in the Roman tactics, as may be known from Cæsar: this supposition is already to be found in those who have written before us, Colonel Guichard in particular. And moreover this change could only have been the work of a man who always adapted his system to the wants of his age. Down to Marius' days, even during the Numidian wars, we read of *principes, triarii,* and *hastati*; of Marius' time itself we have indeed no history of any note, written in Latin, though we have an exact knowledge of Cæsar's legion, in which there are neither *hastati,* nor *principes,* nor *triarii,* but only *pilani*; the lance is done away with, and the *pilum* and sword alone are used; the men are no more drawn up in maniples, the legion being now formed in a line which was ten deep, with a proportionate reserve; and when there are several lines of battle, these do not affect the disposition, as they likewise were not placed in maniples, *en échelons,* but in parallels, one behind the other. The legion is divided into sixty centuries (not as in the earliest times, into five cohorts, each having thirty centuries of thirty men); and its strength besides is raised from 4,500 to 6,000 men. The light troops are detached, the legion being no longer a brigade, but a very strong regiment, all of the same arm; and the cavalry is not a part of the legion. Another, and very essential difference, is, that Marius—and he was very much blamed for it—in levying the troops did not now follow the old system by which all who had less than 12,500 *asses*, and more than 4,500, were set aside for the reserve; nor yet the later plan by which every one who had even 1,000 sesterces (400 *denarii*), was enlisted in the line, and those who were below that standard could only serve in the fleet; but he took every able-bodied man, although he might not be above beggary. This was indeed very bad according to the notions of the old times, when there were good reasons for employing in the defence of the country none but those who might be deemed to have an interest in upholding the constitution. But in those days, there were no standing armies; whereas, when once these began to be kept, it was less hard for a man who had nothing to remain for years in the provinces, than it was for an only son who possessed property: thus what had formerly been quite right, had ceased to be so, now that circumstances were changed. On the whole, though I am by no means blind to the grievous faults of Marius,—nay, if you will, to his vices,—it certainly shows a want of sense, to speak of him as if it had been better for the republic that he had never been born. That he was worthy of his high renown, is undeniable; and though his cruelties are not to be excused, he was indeed a great man, and one ought to try to understand and account for his failings. Two such different men, as Cicero and Cæsar, had a great fondness for Marius: Cæsar, when a boy, loved with all his soul the husband of his aunt Julia; and Cicero, even in spite of his party, felt proud of being, as an Arpinate, the countryman of Marius.

Marius now employed his second and third consulships in forming a new army. Happily for Rome, the Cimbri were all this while in Spain. Eleven years had now passed since their first appearance; so that we see how quickly the tide of emigration which no bounds could hitherto stay, set in towards the west: had they succeeded in Spain, it is very possible that they would have gone to Africa. Marius had to find soldiers as he best could: what was left of the old army, was shattered and demoralized, all but the troops which had returned from Numidia; he was therefore obliged to train his raw levies for the field, by mingling them with the few veterans who had won many a battle: in his fourth consulship, his army was formed. In the third already, he had been in the south of France near the Rhone, probably on the frontiers of Provence and Dauphiné, between Arles and Avignon; and that part of the country, which was as near the enemy as could be, he had chosen as his exercising ground, that he might force his men to keep with all their might on the alert: those who were not able to stand the work, sank under it; the rest were so much the better soldiers. As the Rhone, like all the rivers of the Mediterranean, has its mouth choked up with silt, he dug in all haste a canal to open a free communication with the sea. During his fourth consulship he advanced towards the spot where the Isere and the Rhone meet, expecting that the Cimbri and Teutones would return from Spain: it was thought that they would cross the Alps, and follow the same road which Hannibal had once chosen. All feelings of hatred in the Gauls, had of course died away. If it be true that Marius was obliged to use intrigues to get this consulship, it is a very bad case, and a proof of the blind infatuation of the oligarchy.

The barbarians had no wish to attack Marius, and so they separated: the Cimbri went round the northern range of the Alps, that they might invade Italy from the other side, where it was more easily entered; the Teutones remained in Gaul. For what reason Marius should have now retreated from Valence to Aquæ Sextiæ, our scanty sources do not tell us: probably it was for the purpose of getting provisions. The Cimbrians passed with jeers by the camp of Marius, and went round Switzerland: for between the Pennine and the Tridentine Alps, there was not yet at that time any practicable road for such hosts of men with their waggons and baggage: the only way was that across the little St. Bernard, which they could not take on account of the Romans; single troops may have gone by the St. Gotthard and the Splügen. The Romans had opposed to them, near Trent in Italian Tyrol, another army under the command of the consul Q. Lutatius Catulus, a man who was the very opposite of Marius, as he was one of those persons of high rank in that day who had had a Greek education: according to Cicero, he was even a fair author, and he left behind him memoirs in Greek, as was then much the fashion among people of refinement at Rome, Latin prose not being yet cultivated by great writers; just as Frederic the Great wrote his memoirs in French. Incalculable is the loss to us of the books of Livy which treat of this period, as we do not know any thing more about it than we do of earlier centuries; in fact, we know less of the gigantic struggles against the Cimbri and Teutones, than we do of the national emigrations and the wars against the barbarians in the beginning of the fifth century. Here we find Orosius on the whole an unadulterated source, and now and then we have to make shift with Florus; all the epitomizers, however, as Orosius, Eutropius, Florus, are full of discrepancies when compared together, though they every one of them drew from Livy. Quite independent of these is the account of Plutarch, which is the most detailed narrative we have of the Cimbric war.

When the Cimbri were gone away, the Teutones and Ambrones followed in the track of Marius: whither the Tigurini went, we cannot tell. To judge from an expression of the epitomizers, the barbarians—a fact which Plutarch does not mention—must have taken the camp of Marius;

but this could not have been the one near the ground where the battle was fought, as from the march towards it, and the whole of Marius' disposition, we may see that he had been stopped when retreating. He had therefore to encamp in a spot where there was no water, and the soldiers were obliged to go out armed and fetch it from a distant well; so that they asked to be led out to fight. Marius wished first to entrench himself, as his foes were quite close, and everything was against him; yet he could not carry out his intention, the distress being so great that the camp-followers in despair went to some water which was in the neighbourhood of the enemy. Here the Ambrones attacked them, on which the soldiers came to their help: the Ligurians first set out, and then cohort after cohort hastened up, without any orders from Marius. Thus an engagement was brought on, in which, strange to say, the Teutones took no share whatever: perhaps they had not yet come up. Even in this conflict, a brilliant victory was gained, most of the Ambrones being destroyed; notwithstanding which, the Romans, who were without entrenchments, now passed an anxious night in which they were busily throwing up works. The next battle was not fought on the following day, as had been expected, but on the day after; most likely because the Teutones and the rest of the Ambrones had only just now arrived. Marius laid all his plans with the talent of a true general, and he sent M. Claudius Marcellus—a man whose family was always distinguished, he being undoubtedly a grandson of that worthy Marcellus so well known in the Iberian war, who had five times been consul—with a division of allies, as it would seem, to attack the enemy's rear. Yet even before this, the fury of the Teutones had spent itself in vain against the steadfastness and dogged resolution of the Romans, and the more so as it was summer: for the men of the South, owing to their more muscular frame, are able to stand both heat and frost better than others: the Italians in Napoleon's Russian campaign, suffered much less than the northern nations did. And therefore, as one might easily believe, the natives of Rome bore the glowing heat of the sun much better than the Teutones. The Romans, who were posted on a hill, awaited the onset of the barbarians; these were beaten back, and when they were endeavouring to rally in the plain, Marcellus fell upon them from behind. Part of them tried to make their escape, and were overpowered and slain by the Gallic tribes. The prince of the Teutones was taken prisoner by the Sequani, and the remnant of his army retreated within their rampart of waggons; but the Romans now broke in, and nearly the whole of the nation was destroyed, some very few only being made slaves.

Half of the danger was now warded off. Soon afterwards, the Cimbri burst upon Italy through Tyrol and the Alps of Trent; and this was not from any fault of Catulus, but it was altogether owing to their overwhelming numbers, and the terror which they spread far and wide. The account in Florus of the manner in which the Cimbri opened the way for themselves, is quite childish; just as if these had been the dullest of savages, and had wanted to stop the tide of the Adige with their hands: this shows what a *homo umbraticus* that writer was. There are indeed some fords in the Adige, and in passing such a river one makes the cavalry cross higher up, and somewhat lower down a close column of infantry, which will break the force of a moderate stream. This the Cimbri may also have tried to do, thinking perhaps that with their huge bodies they would be able to stem the flood; but in the Adige, as it is near Legnano, such a thing is impossible. Afterwards they are said to have thrown trees into the river to dam it up; which is also incredible. They wished rather to have a bridge and to destroy that of the Romans by means of their floats of timbers, and this they succeeded in doing. The Romans being posted at each end of the bridge, on both sides of the stream, one of their two divisions was cut off from the other, and was obliged to surrender to the Cimbri; but these, with unwonted humanity, let it go free. This, however, is true, that in crossing the most impassable parts of the Alps, they glided on their large shields, as on sleighs, down the steepest declivities. At this irruption, Catulus fell back as far as the Po, or yet beyond it: the whole country north of that river was laid waste; the towns of Mantua, Verona, Brescia, which were left to the protection of their walls, defended themselves; but the open places were destroyed. From the winter to the following summer, the Cimbri most unaccountably remained on that side of the Po.

Marius heard in Gaul of the irruption of the barbarians, and he ordered his army to march to Genua in Liguria (as it would seem), and went himself to Rome. Here every one was now full of admiration for him; and the feeling that he was the only man who could save the country, was become so general, that even the oligarchs were for his being made consul for the fifth time. People were so eager to gain his goodwill, that they offered him a triumph; but this he declined until he should have destroyed the Cimbri, and his assurance communicated itself to every one. He accordingly united his army with that of Catulus, who had remained in command as proconsul. They both of them now passed the Po with somewhat more than fifty-two thousand men. It is said that the Cimbri knew nothing of the defeat of the Teutones; which is a downright absurdity, as it is impossible that from autumn to the end of July, they should not have got any news. It was surely for this very reason, that they asked Marius for land and places of abode, as they felt that half of their power had been overthrown: if they also demanded this for their brethren, these must have been the Tigurini. Whether the Cimbri now wished to secure the passes to Gaul, that they might keep the road over the little St. Bernard open for any emergency, and this was why they came to Vercellæ, is uncertain; yet notwithstanding all the variations in the readings, there seems to be no doubt that a battle was fought near Vercelli on the declivity of the Alps: for one cannot see how any body should have thought of placing it in this corner of Lombardy. Writers call the spot *Campi Raudii.* The battle, contrary to the Roman custom, was announced three days beforehand, and on the third day before the calends of the Sextilis (July 29th as the calendar was then), it was fought. So much time had the Cimbri spent in their ravages since the beginning of winter, in this unwholesome aguish country, where the water is so bad: epidemics also had already broken out among them. On the day of the battle, Marius put the army of Catulus in the centre, disposing his own on the two wings: the account of it, which is found in Plutarch only, is so confused, that nothing distinct can be made out of it. It is incredible that the Cimbri should have formed a great square, each side of which was three-quarters of a (German) mile long, the men in the outside ranks having, as we are told, their girdles linked together with chains: such a mass would amount to many millions of men. Marius is said to have so placed his troops that the sun and the wind were in the faces of the barbarians; such a thing may be history, or it may be fiction. Catulus had to stand the brunt of the battle; at least the fight was hottest where he was: and yet it was only a proof of party spirit, when people disputed whether it was to Marius or to Catulus that the victory was due; for it seems beyond all doubt that Marius decided the battle in the wings, and thus had the chief merit of it. The Cimbrians fled within their rampart of waggons, where even the women and children fought, and killed themselves at last: a great many were taken prisoners, as the Alps blocked up their retreat. In short, every thing belonging to the Cimbri which had crossed these mountains, was cut off, all but the tribe of the Aduatici, who had settled hereabouts,[84] on the Lower Rhine, where they must therefore have had fixed abodes at one time.

As a reward for his unexampled achievements, Marius had now his sixth consulship given him. He led the most brilliant triumph which any general had ever had; but even then he already showed how much his head was turned, as he entered the senate in his triumphal garments. There was a belief that some one before him had been six times consul; but this can no longer be ascertained, as the ancients themselves could not tell. Perhaps Valerius Corvus was six times consul; it may, however, have been, that in what is accounted his sixth consulship, one of his family was mistaken for him. Marius was called the third founder of Rome after Romulus and Camillus. But this consulship, although Marius at last became useful to the state, had such dismal consequences, as to make one wish that he had died on the day of his triumph: then his memory would have been glorious and blessed, and he would have thrown even Scipio into the shade.

MARIUS' SIXTH CONSULSHIP. L. APULEIUS SATURNINUS. C. SERVILIUS GLAUCIA

Marius was not the man who could play his part well in quiet, peaceful times; and yet Rome was hastening towards dissolution in a way which compelled him to act. There are very many kinds of courage, as the greatest men have owned; there is a courage with regard to danger, which either looks death in the face with indifference, or forgets it altogether in the excitement of action. This is a fine quality in itself; but it does not follow, that the motive for its display should be as noble: he alone in whom this constancy is allied to a pure mind, and who is conscious of a lofty aim, will enjoy with it the full sense of personal freedom, and be enabled to achieve great things. Many are wanting in this sort of prowess, who yet possess a determined moral courage, owing to which they hold themselves above the opinion of those around them, it being all the same to them whether they be misjudged or not; others, who in the hour of danger show the courage of lions, are exceedingly timid in this respect, and afraid of acting up to a conviction which has been branded by the world's anathema. It was in this latter sense that Marius was weak; for if one was to say that he let himself be used as a tool by the men who exercised such influence during his sixth consulship, this would be making him out to have been a most pitiful wretch; whereas it is the clue to his conduct, that he was at one time afraid of the demagogues, and at another of the senate, a deplorable, although partial, weakness of a great man who had no greatness of character.

Marius had joined himself with a sad knave, to get his sixth consulship. This was L. Apuleius Saturninus, who, undeservedly enough, is often named with the Gracchi, although there cannot be a wider interval than that between them and Saturninus. He was a man like Catiline, one indeed of whom the like is seldom seen; for though one can understand how ambition will lead people blindfold into acts of dangerous daring, yet how a man could have taken in his head to be so mad, is all but incomprehensible. It would seem that his was a revolutionary mind; that he formed no clear notion of what things would come to, being utterly regardless of institutions and government, and only thinking of violence and confusion. He had sprung from one of the richest and most eminent plebeian families; just as in the French revolution, men of the first nobility put themselves at the head of the rabble. I do not recollect whether it is of him, or of Servilius Glaucia, that Cicero says, that no one had been gifted with a more malignant wit:[85] it was by this means that they managed the people. He had started in life as an aristocrat. There were at that time eight quæstorships, which were given partly to consulars, and partly to other persons. They were places with an income attached to them, one of them being the *quæstura Ostiensis*, which had the charge of the granaries at Rome. Saturninus had, as quæstor, availed himself of the privilege of *peculatus* taken by the men of rank; but when the tables were suddenly turned, and the oligarchs were no longer able to screen the sins of their own body, owing to an honest party having been formed from both factions under the lead of the straight-forward C. Memmius, he got liable to the punishment of being deposed, and so he threw himself into the arms of the mob: it was a conspiracy of the dregs of the upper and middle classes. He now became a tribune of the people, and behaved in the most savage manner towards the very first men, for instance, the censors and others. When, on his standing the second time for the tribuneship, another candidate, A. Nonius was set up against him, he so hounded on the rabble against that unfortunate man, that they murdered him; and thus he made himself by force a tribune again. The magistrates had no more any authority; those who had the power, did just what they liked.

His accomplice was C. Servilius Glaucia, like him a man of very high rank, not a freedman, as might be inferred from his name: in a similar manner, a Scipio was nicknamed Serapio, from an actor to whom he bore a likeness. What these two really wanted, is hard to say: if their madness went even to utter recklessness, it might be assumed that they aimed at a tyranny for one of them; but if they believed that Marius would allow such a thing, this were just as great an insanity as that of the drunkard in Shakspeare's Tempest. We must deem many of the men of that time to have been downright madmen. Of Robespierre also, it can never be said what purpose he had;—very likely he had none whatever. Thus also one of these men wanted to rule, no matter how, and for what end. When now Apuleius was tribune, Marius was consul for the sixth time. It was then that the former really began his career as a legislator, trying to win the favour of the people by a set of seditious motions: his aims were quite different from those which in earlier days were called seditious; he was striving to establish a tyranny, a design indeed which only a general, like Sylla or Cæsar, could have succeeded in carrying out. The legislation of Saturninus, however, has come down to us very obscure: thus much we know, that a most sweeping agrarian law was one of its main features, and that he changed the giving out of corn into a regular distribution of alms. It would seem as if the whole of the lands to be divided by his *Lex agraria*, were situated in Transpadane Gaul; for that they should have been in France itself, is not likely. He is said also to have made a *Lex judiciaria*. He now flattered Marius in every possible way. He wanted to found colonies, and the *coloni* were to consist of Romans and Italians: for as the Italian allies in the army of Marius, had also very much distinguished themselves, Apuleius favoured them as much as the Romans, and this was what exasperated many of the poorer Roman citizens against the law. Marius was moreover to have the power of giving in each of these colonies the Roman citizenship to three Italian allies, a thing which indeed went beyond all bounds of civil authority. Yet though at that time this was still something quite monstrous, as it trenched upon some of the rights of the sovereign people, no umbrage was taken afterwards when an *imperator* bestowed the citizenship. These laws were opposed, both on account of their author and their evident tendency, by all right-minded men, even by those who in former days had with all their might withstood the oligarchy; and likewise by the broken-down oligarchs themselves, who now wanted no more than what was reasonable. Hence it was that C. Memmius became the object of the rage of the seditious, though twelve years before, when tribune, he had called upon the people to quell the oligarchy: he had only behaved, as he ever did, like an honest man.

Owing to the Hortensian law, the new *lex agraria* did not require the sanction of the senate. That that body, however, might not afterwards attack it, Saturninus demanded that the senators should swear to it five days after its adoption by the tribes: and when this was debated in the senate, Marius at first declared, that it ought not to be done; that he would not take the oath, and that he hoped that every well-disposed person would follow his example. It was thought that he acted thus from craftiness, to draw in his enemies, particularly Metellus, to refuse the oath likewise: nor is this impossible. But he may also have honestly meant what he said, though afterwards false friends began to work upon him by means of his unhappy dread of the mob. Cicero had the strength of mind not to allow himself to be thus overawed; he says in a speech of his (*pro Rabirio perduell.*) *nihil me clamor iste commovet, sed consolatur, quum indicat esse quosdam cives imperitos, sed non multos*. Neither Plutarch nor Appian have thrown any light upon this subject. At the end of all the laws, there is the following formula, *si quid sacri sanctique est quod non jus sit rogari, ejus hac lege nihil rogatur*; or else, *si quid jus non esset rogarier ejus ea lege nihilum rogatum*.[86] These unlucky advisers now said that, if the law was not passed, blood would flow; but that if it were passed, this clause would give protection against everything in the body of the enactment which was thus made null and void. By such casuistry as this, they got Marius to declare on the fifth day in the senate, that even if they took the oath, they would still have this loophole left them. Thus the oath was taken by Marius, and after him by all the rest, except Q. Metellus Numidicus, who stood out against it with a constancy truly heroic, which does him greater honour than his Numidian victories, and which would lead one to pardon his haughtiness to Marius. In the day of trial, he showed a resolute consistency, and Saturninus, persisting in the course which he had taken, had him dragged out of the senate by his *viator*, and outlawed him (*aqua et igni interdicebat*); on which he went as an exile to Rhodes. The year was passed in horrors. The stain upon Marius' character is his weakness: from henceforth he always stands in an undecided position, trimming between both factions; and thus he saw himself dependent upon the very storms which surrounded him. As good luck would have it, these fellows carried things so far, that they brought about a fusion of parties, and Marius himself, not wanting to have any more to do with them, was ready to declare against them.

The elections for the consulship were now held, and M. Antonius was unanimously chosen. On the following day, it seemed certain that C. Memmius would be elected: he was one of the most energetic and right-minded men of that age, being probably the tribune in Jugurtha's time, or if not the same, at least a very near kinsman of his. Against this candidate, who was all but returned, Glaucia and Saturninus raised a tumult: they did not, however, venture to have him assailed in the open market-place; but when he fled into a booth, he was murdered in it. This was too bad to be borne; and Marius was applied to, who when he received the command from the senate, *ut videret ne quid detrimenti res publica caperet*, resolved to uphold the cause of order against the outrages of miscreants: he now called upon the *equites* and all respectable citizens. In this peril, it was seen how the great might likewise in other times have warded off many things, had they only had the spirit to make a stand. When the rebels found that all were turning against them, they withdrew to the Capitol, and there they were besieged. Marius now showed himself a good general. The *clivus* was taken, and the culprits sheltered themselves within the strong walls of the Capitoline temple, which it was looked upon as a crime to storm. As the water was conveyed thither by the pipes of the *aqua Marcia*, Marius ordered them to be cut off; so that the besieged must have perished from hunger and thirst. That most ancient well, therefore, which had supplied the Romans with water in the days of the Gallic invasion, must already at this time have been in the same state that it is now: it is altogether neglected, and every kind of filth is thrown into it. Glaucia was for setting fire to the temple, and thus dying; but the others, who had hopes of saving their lives, would not do this, and they surrendered at discretion. The most guilty were shut up in the Curia Hostilia, that they might be brought to justice. Yet either there was a change of feeling in the populace, or else the government, not to bring upon themselves the odium of putting so many men of rank to death, got up a sham riot: the roof of the Curia was scaled, and from thence the rebels were slain by the rioters. Marius' conduct now reconciled to him men's minds again; he retraced some of his steps, and even agreed to have Metellus recalled from banishment. Saturninus' laws seem to have been repealed, as those of Livius were afterwards.

Thus ended this insurrection, which indeed is best understood by Velleius Paterculus. Marius for his own part retired into private life, and he had not a thought of making himself a tyrant.

M. LIVIUS DRUSUS

The republic was shaken to its very centre, the great point of contest being the administration of justice. The *equites* had so abused their power as judges, that they had public opinion against them: this was partly owing to their jealousy against the senate, and partly on account of their quarrels with individual senators in the provinces. The system of general farmers of the revenue had become more and more developed; the companies had leases of the mines, customs, tithes, and such like things, and some of them put their money out to usury; and they exacted from the people in the provinces much more than these were bound to give. They had again their sub-farmers; thus for instance, the *publicans* in the gospel were the agents of the *publicani*. The same thing is done to this day. The contract for feeding the galley slaves, was only a short time since given by the Roman government to an actress, who had a very fair price paid to her for it, so much a head being allowed her; but she sublet the contract to others, each making a trifling profit on it, down to the very last of them, and the prisoners were literally all but starved. If a consul or proconsul had ground the people in the provinces, and screened the *publicani*, he was safe at Rome when prosecuted; but if a man who was just and blameless thwarted the revenue farmers in their exactions, they would revenge themselves by charging him with extortion, and get a verdict against him by means of false witnesses. This was the fate of P. Rutilius, and it excited universal indignation. It was impossible to find any check for this, as each one always supported the rest. The ill-blood which there was at that time between the senate and the knights, is to be found among all nations, at a certain stage of their progress, between the land-owners and the monied men; as is now the case throughout Europe. The senate, the *optimates*, held the great bulk of the landed property; the *equites*, on the other hand, possessed the capital with which the great commercial speculations were carried on. Moreover there were in Rome many circumstances under which monied property might be abused to the detriment of the nation, and every one who belonged to the government, was, owing to the ways in which the courts of justice were constituted, at the mercy of the *equites*. With regard to all these matters, Montesquieu, admirable as he generally is, is mistaken; and on the whole, they have not been well explained by modern writers, though they may be brought very clearly before our mind's eye. There was now an open war against the judicial power, stirred up by the tyranny of the latter.

The happy ending of the war with the Cimbri and Teutones, and the putting down of the rebellion of Saturninus, were followed by a season of precarious tranquillity in which no thinking man could indeed have been blind to the real state of Rome, though the common herd might have felt as if all was going on right. Yet the symptoms of its being necessary to bring the great questions of the age to a definitive decision, showed themselves more and more. Things had come to that pass, that no one seems to have thought of a reform which could have given relief, though many changes were made; and it is one of the signs of the times, that those who wanted to rise in the world, had to begin by making themselves popular, after which they went over to the opposite side. Thus it was that Cn. Domitius Ahenobarbus transferred the nomination to the pontificate and the other priestly offices, from the colleges, which used to fill up their own numbers, to the tribes; and this was indeed so managed that the smaller half of the tribes was chosen by lot to be the electors. In the earliest times, the right of choice undoubtedly belonged to the patricians alone; when, however, the patricians and plebeians shared these offices between them, plebeians also were added to the voters; but afterwards, when the curies were no longer assembled, but were become altogether changed, it was quite natural, that the election should be left to the colleges themselves. The clause that the lesser half of the tribes was to elect, seems to have been based on an old form of expression, the patricians, when they were still in existence, having been called (perhaps in the twelve tables) *minor pars populi*; a different meaning was now given to it. This was the last trace which remained of the old constitution.

The two questions which filled the minds of every one, were the courts of justice and the citizenship of the allies. The want of a change in the former, was strongly felt by the best men as well as the worst. People like Mucius Scævola, whose behaviour in the provinces had been quite exemplary—he came to the Asiatics like an angel from heaven, his conduct was really most touching—ran the greatest risk of being condemned though altogether guiltless; the worst men, from quite opposite motives, had the same wish for a reform of the courts, as they would then be acquitted by the senators. The question of the citizenship of the Italians bore the closest analogy with that of the emancipation of the Roman Catholics in Ireland. Every one was well inclined to it: but then things would take an unfavourable turn; a great many interests came in the way, and people again would have nothing to do with it. This is one of the most melancholy conditions in which a free state can be, when there is no knowing how to heal an evil which is manifest to every one.

The allies had, even from the days of the tribuneship of Tib. Gracchus, been taught to ask for the Roman citizenship, which was their "emancipation." Thirty years had now passed since then; they had often had great hopes, which had been blighted over and over again. Whereas in former times, the relations of Rome towards her allies had been more friendly than those of any ruling city, the most bitter hatred now arose. The very people who sometimes had held out hopes to the Italians, inveighed against it, when those allies put forth their claims too insolently. As far as we can judge of all the facts, nothing had been done for them with the exception of one law, by which the tithe from the *ager publicus* was abolished; this, however, we only know from Appian. They now urged their demands more strongly than ever, and the right of Roman citizenship was even becoming more valuable in their eyes; for they were getting more and more like the Romans, they had learned to speak the same language, and yet in war and in peace they were to be subject to the sway of Roman masters. In this fermentation, the rulers at Rome were greatly terrified; but whenever they came to a decision, they only increased the irritation. Thus some Italians had quietly taken to themselves the right of citizenship; one of them, M. Peperna,[87] had even attained to the consulate and the censorship, and now it was found out that he was not lawfully a citizen. In the general breaking up, everything at Rome fell into confusion: the calendar was in the time of Cæsar, owing to arbitrary intercalations, more than eighty days behindhand; and in a like manner, the census had been disturbed by the admission of allies, as they had assumed the character of citizens, and the censors had classed them in the tribes. Now in the *lex Mucia Licinia*, the mad resolution was suddenly come to, of making strict inquiries into this matter, and striking off all those who were not citizens in the fullest sense of the word. This could not but have exasperated an immense number of people: but the infatuation which then prevailed everywhere was inconceivable.

By degrees however, a considerable party in the senate became convinced that a reform must take place; and these were the sons of the very men who had baffled the plans of the Gracchi. They wanted to make an attempt to remedy the evil, the reform most urgently called for being a change in the judicial system. But this was opposed by all the immense influence of the *equites*, which was so great as to make even Polybius say that, in his times, few people only had nothing to do with them. To carry this out, men now thought of giving the full franchise to the Latins and allies; and this ought to have been done at any rate. Under these circumstances, M. Livius Drusus, the son of him who during the tribuneship of Gracchus had gotten an unhappy celebrity, a man of uncommon talent, whose hands were clean, became tribune, and thought upon remedies: all sensible people and the chief persons in the state joined with him to hinder a revolution by means of a reform. Here again much is obscure; for in what belongs to these later ages, we are sometimes much more under the necessity of guessing, than with regard to the earlier times: then the form was a reality, being based upon numbers; now, it had wholly lost its meaning. What is most likely, is that a statement of Appian after all is correct, according to which it was the chief aim of Drusus to bring in a mixed system, and not to give back the administration of justice to the senators alone, which would have caused a revolution. By the *lex Servilia*, the rule had already been laid down, that the judges in the courts should be divided between the knights and the senators; but this did not last long. The senate consisted of three hundred men, and to these, it is said, he meant to add three hundred knights; from both of them combined, the jury was to be chosen by lot: for ever since the days of C. Gracchus, there was really a system like that of trial by jury. The English antiquaries have wanted to find it even at an earlier period; but they were wrong: in civil cases there were still single *arbitri*; but for political offences, and also for felony, there were *quæstiones perpetuæ* which were analogous to the modern jury courts. It is probable that by this measure of reform, one half of the jury must have been made up of senators, and the other of knights. Thus M. Livius offered to these last an advantage which they might have as a compensation, instead of the exclusive exercise of the judicial power. To this another law was tacked, by which *quæstiones* were to be appointed, to inflict punishment on any one who should be convicted of having given wrong judgment for the sake of a bribe, or from favour. What was to be the form of these *quæstiones*, is more than we can tell; in all likelihood they were to be held by the tribes. But there were very many knights, who had no wish whatever to be in the senate: it was much more agreeable to them to stand highest among those who did not belong to that body, and instead of sharing its moral responsibility, to be always able to find fault and to judge. It seems moreover that the law of Drusus did not enact that the three hundred of each class were to be kept distinct for ever; it is more likely that this filling up of the senate was only thought of as a transitory measure, and that eventually the judicial power was to rest again with the senate. The knights now said that this was neither more nor less than a scheme to outwit them; that they would afterwards have a senate of six hundred, into which more knights were admitted than there used to be, but that the courts of justice would be taken out of their hands. Yet the plan of Drusus seems after all to have been the best thing that could have been done at that time; as he also meant to give the citizenship to the Italians, thus renewing the strength of the higher classes by bringing in a fresh aristocracy, and enlarging the Roman state into a nation. He likewise aimed at restoring the middle classes, and carrying through a new agrarian law in favour of the Romans and Italians: but about this we know very little indeed. Yet as the Italians were more closely connected with the Romans, than with the Umbrians and Etruscans from whom they were politically severed; the same split showed itself between these two masses, which there had been in the time of C. Gracchus between the Romans, on the one hand, and the Latins and Italians, on the other. The Latins were in the colonies scattered all over Italy from Valentia in Bruttium to the foot of the Alps, and in the few old Latin towns which had not yet got the right of citizenship, as Tibur and Præneste; by Italians were meant the Sabellian peoples, the Sabines, the Marsians and their confederates, the Picentines, Samnites, and perhaps also the Lucanians, unless the condition of these had been made worse by the war of Hannibal. Very likely the boon was not intended to be given to Apulians and Sallentines, where the Greek element was paramount. All the rest were looked upon as foreigners; and therefore nothing was said in this matter about the Umbrians, Etruscans, Bruttians, and the Greek maritime towns. Yet we may learn from the history of every free state, how the growth of such claims will keep spreading wider and wider. At Geneva, there had long been a struggle between the *citoyens* and *bourgeois*,[88] and the latter of these won for themselves the same rights as the former. Then started up the claims of the *natifs*, who had been born in Geneva of foreign parents, and had sided with the *representants* in their quarrel with the *negatifs*; and in the revolution of 1789 they were granted the full franchise. But then came also the *habitants*, the strangers, and demanded the same rights. Such a succession of claimants is to be found in all republics, whenever there is any stagnation in them. The history of Drusus is the *crux historicorum*, unless one speculates on the state of things in a thoroughly practical spirit. Freinsheim, who lived entirely among his books, and who never thought of looking at what had happened in his own city of Strasburg, was not able to understand those relations; he was quite bewildered by them. Without this kind of knowledge, the tribuneship of Drusus is a riddle: he is said to have been an aristocrat, and still to have been popular.

The knights opposed the two laws with the utmost fury; notwithstanding which they were carried, as the Italians came in crowds to Rome, ready to take up arms, if need be. As this had therefore been brought about by the most unlawful means, the majority of the senate, with an infatuation which is beyond belief, resolved, when the Italians were gone, that the promise to the allies should not be kept; and on Drusus' urging it, he met with a refusal. This gave rise to the most deadly hatred between him and the faithless senate, which accounts for Cicero's words, *tribunatus Drusi pro senatus auctoritate susceptus infringi jam debilitarique videbatur*.[89] He appeared either in the light of a liar, or a dupe. And even as the knights were displeased with Drusus, so likewise, on the other hand, was the stupid party of the oligarchs then uppermost. They said, "Shall we then for ever place on the same footing with ourselves those three hundred knights who are thorns in our side?" Such people are blind to the inevitable necessity of making some concessions: by merely saying "no!" they think that they can keep everything in its old place. Thus there now happened what, from the nature of the human heart must have come to pass: Drusus, who until then had been a zealous partisan of the government, henceforth began an opposition against the senate which was quite at variance with his former ways. The ruling faction in the senate, as well as the *equites*, wished for the death of Drusus; the consul Philippus was his sworn foe. It was this man who first uttered that terrible saying, that there were not more than two thousand families in Rome which possessed unimpaired property. The unhappy Drusus at once saw himself forsaken. He was a man of a violent temper, and yet he had undertaken that most perilous task of negotiating as a mediator with the Italians; (the Latin colonies were quiet; for as they were sure of being the first enfranchised, they let the others urge their claims, and but few of them had entered into the interests of the Italians.) That curious fragment from the Vatican, which the editor did not understand, and entitled Ὅρκος φιλίππου,[90] gives us the oath which the Italians took. It betokens an association of a very peculiar kind; they bound themselves to obey his orders unconditionally, and to enrol in their districts partisans who would stand by him, as was done thirty years ago in Ireland. Drusus was in such a state, that he could hardly be said any longer to have a will of his own; he was in a perfect fever: had he been fairly supported by those who were in power, he might still have found a way out of his difficulties. But he was already goaded into frenzy; and his behaviour towards Philippus, in which he did things that he ought never to have ventured on, strongly shows in what a fever he must have been. When on the eve of a great debate, he was now walking up and down with his friends in the lobby of his house,—in these corridors which had no windows, and were lit up with candelabras, the men of rank would move about among a throng of people who were assembled there, and give audience,—he was stabbed in the side by an assassin. The man who did it was never discovered, and it is even uncertain by whom he was hired. He had scarcely been dead a few hours, when all his laws, with the exception of those which related to the courts of justice, were annulled; and in doing this, the senate arrogated to itself a power hitherto unheard of.

Drusus' death fell out at a most unfortunate moment. The Italians were excited to the highest pitch, and yet there was no one to take their part: public opinion at Rome was against them, as if they were rebels; just as perhaps in England the great body of the people were hostile to the emancipation of the Irish Roman Catholics, or, when the American war broke out, to the North Americans. The party of Drusus, which now showed itself again in the senate, was entirely without a head: Crassus had just died; the two Scævolas, M. Antonius, and the wisest men, knew no longer what to advise, and were intimidated. Instead of allaying the storm, people rashly dared it, the knights charging the senate with treason. The former had at their beck a tribune, Q. Varius,—whose right of citizenship was not even certain, as he was born in Spain of a Spanish mother, though his father was a Roman: this was a brutal man, *vastus homo et fœdus*, as Cicero calls him, whose impudence served him instead of talent. He moved that a court should be established to discover the traitors who had negotiated with the Italians about their emancipation; and the bill was carried against the strongest opposition of the first men in the senate, the knights joining for this purpose with the rabble, who indeed were most furious. They appeared in the forum in arms when the question was put to the vote. There sprang up now a vast number of impeachments; several of the very noblest were convicted of having given traitorous encouragement to the Italians. A very remarkable state of feeling had at this time arisen in Rome: the senate acted the part of democrats; the people, headed by the knights, that of the aristocrats; and whereas the former wished to emancipate the Italians, the latter would not do it.

THE SOCIAL WAR. MITHRIDATES. CIVIL WAR BETWEEN THE PARTIES OF MARIUS AND SYLLA. L. CORNELIUS CINNA

The Social War is one of those periods of Roman history in which the scantiness of our information is particularly annoying. Livy had described the events of those two years in four books; but the only connected narrative which we have, is the scanty one of Appian, and besides this there are some exceedingly brief notices.[91] And yet the Social War is one of the very greatest, not only on account of the passions which were displayed in it on both sides, but also because of the changes in its fortunes, and the excellent generalship which was to be found in both armies.

The first symptoms of a tendency of the allies to separate themselves, are met with even as early as the second Punic war, when the allies in the camp of Scipio mutinied, and chose two consuls from among themselves;[92] the insurrection of Fregellæ followed soon afterwards. The war was not begun by those who had originally planned it, but by the peoples which lived farther off. Which of these was the first to resolve upon it, is more than we know; but it is stated that in the year 662, during the tribuneship of M. Livius Drusus, there was a plot to kill the Roman consuls (Philippus especially) and the senate at the Latin Feast. At that solemnity indeed, the whole of the Roman magistracy (συναρχία), consuls, prætors, and even tribunes of the people, were present; so that there remained behind but a *præfectus urbi Latinarum causa*, who was a young man of rank. Now as the Latins mustered there in strong numbers, it is very probable that it was they who had entertained that design, especially the men of Tibur and Præneste; at the same time, it may have happened that so many Italians came thither, that they on their part, deemed the thing feasible. Drusus heard of this atrocious project, and denounced it: for, even if he had not been a man of honour, he was still a Roman, and he did what he wanted to do, just as much for the advantage of his own country, as from any love which he bore to the allies. After the death of Drusus, the Italians, making no secret of their unmitigated rage, sent round ambassadors, and gave each other hostages for mutual security. The Roman government, on the other hand, appointed commissioners with proconsular power for Picenum, where the commotion was fiercest, to remind the allies of their duty. There being what we would call a diet of the Picentines at Asculum, the proconsul Q. Servilius Cæpio, accompanied by M. or C. Fonteius (I do not exactly remember his *prænomen*[93]), came forward, and ventured to address the people, so as to induce them, either by exhortation or by threats, to desist from their intention. But their minds were so exasperated, that a rash word made them break out; and he and his companion were murdered in the theatre at Asculum. The Italians now wished no longer for the Roman franchise; but they wanted to form a sovereign Italian people, in which all who got out of the grasp of the Romans were to be received. All the Romans who were at Asculum were seized, and most of them slain. In the fragments of Diodorus, among the *excerpta de sententiis*, there is a little story of a harlequin, who was a great favourite with the Romans, and who just then made his appearance in the games at Asculum; the people, believing him to be a Roman, were going to kill him, when he only saved himself by proving that he was a Latin. (In this passage, instead of Σαυνίων, we are to read Σαννίων, the old name for Pulcinella; and this is the first mention of that mask.[94])

The insurrection now broke out everywhere; but the same atrocities do not seem to have been perpetrated among the other peoples as were done by the Picentines at Asculum, who were a cowardly abject race; the Marsians and other nations were quite equal to the Romans in refinement. The Italian peoples who at that time revolted, are mentioned in the Epitome of Livy, and by Orosius: they are the Picentines, Marsians, Marrucinians, Vestinians and Pelignians, the Samnites and Lucanians. Appian speaks also of the Apulians, who indeed were in arms; but it is very likely that they had no share in the Italian state. Those peoples in fact were all of them Sabellians, or Sabine colonies; the others, as well as the Apulians who were Oscans, may have joined them merely as being their dependents. Some of the towns also round the bay of Naples were among those which rebelled; of the Latin colonies, Venusia sided with them. Afterwards, the Umbrians likewise took up arms, and for a short time, the Etruscans as well; but they too did not belong to the republic.

The Italian peoples, according to Appian,[95] who alone has recorded this fact, had established a senate of five hundred persons, and chosen two consuls and twelve prætors, thus altogether adopting the forms of the Roman republic. One consul was Pompædius Silo, the soul of the undertaking, who was a Marsian and the guest-friend of Drusus, with whom he had formerly negotiated; the second was C. Papius Mutilus, a Sabine. And not to speak of this constitution, the nations were very widely distinct from each other:

they had been parted for centuries, each standing by itself; so that when they now made themselves independent of Rome, there could not but have been a great temptation to be independent of each other, their principles and pursuits being different. The Samnites, whom afterwards C. Pontius Telesinus led against Rome, that he might, as he said, destroy the den of the wolf, had from of old entertained an implacable hatred against Rome; and indeed Pontius Telesinus himself, who in this war with Sylla showed such undaunted resolution, and whose thoughts were ever bent on Rome's annihilation, may have sprung from the *Gens Pontia* of that C. Pontius who had so terribly humbled the Romans at Caudium. The Marsians, on the other hand, had never had a fierce and protracted war with the Romans, as the latter had always faithfully fulfilled their honourable conditions with them. These therefore were quite a heterogeneous element of the league. The seat of the government was Corfinium, in the country of the Pelignians, a small but valiant people, and the town now assumed the name of Italica: denarii are not unseldom found, which have the inscription *Italia* and *Viteliu*. The latter, which is the Oscan way of writing, belongs to the Samnites; the former, the Latin one, to the Marsians, who had a language of their own, but Latin letters: from this we see that those nations differed also in their languages. Among the Samnites, the Oscan was indeed the prevailing language; the Marsians and their allies were of far purer race than the Sabines, although in a wider sense of the word they were all of them Sabines. There are also coins still existing with the likeness of C. Papius Mutilus.

At the outbreak of the war, the allies had decidedly the advantage. The only thing which saved the Romans, was that the Latin colonies remained true to them; as there is no doubt but that as soon as ever the struggle began, the Romans granted the full franchise to the Latins by the *lex Julia*, which was so called from the consul L. Julius Cæsar. It is a common, but yet an incorrect way of speaking, to say that the Italians had got the rights of citizenship through the *lex Julia*; for they did not get these all at once by one law, but by several distinct enactments which were successively enlarged. Unhappily we know of none of their details. The *lex Julia* applied to the forty or fifty Latin colonies; and not only to those in Italy, but also to Narbo and Aquæ Sextiæ (the former is mentioned at a later period as *colonia civium Romanorum*), and without doubt to Tibur and Præneste as well, besides those other old Latin towns which had not received all the rights of citizenship in the year 417.[96] To this last class the Hernican towns especially belonged; and perhaps also Venafrum, Atina, and some others, in which at that time there was a *præfectura*. This gave a great increase to the strength of the Romans, who even in the war with Hannibal had thus brought into the field eighty thousand men able to bear arms, all of whom spoke Latin, Roman citizens likewise being mingled with them. It was now seen how foolish it was in the Romans to have let things go so far; for had they turned a deaf ear to the Latins also, Rome would have been lost. This grant of the franchise dates from the beginning of the year.

Although Hiero in his day had still said that the Romans employed none but Italian troops, yet they now carried on the war with soldiers raised from whatever country they could get them, with Gauls, Mauritanians, Numidians, Asiatics: not a place was spared in the levy. Thus by degrees the preponderance of the Italians was balanced by the Latins, and outweighed at last by the foreigners. Moreover, Rome had an immense advantage from her central position, and her colonies which were scattered all over Italy. By her position, she cut off the North from the South; by her colonies, which it was everywhere necessary to beset with troops, the resources of the allies were frittered away.

The history of the war is chiefly to be found in Diodorus and Appian. I have been at much pains about it, and have tried to put the materials in order; yet I have only just barely succeeded in getting anything like a clear notion of it. The scene of the war was in three different districts: there was an army of the south, a central, and a northern army. The southern army of the allies was in Campania as far as the Liris; that of the centre, was from the Liris, all through the country of the Sabines, to the neighbourhood of Picenum; that of the north, in Picenum: here was the utmost boundary of the operations, whilst the Greek towns in the rear of the Italians kept neutral. Nothing whatever is now said of the Bruttians; so much had that unfortunate nation suffered in the war of Hannibal: nor is there any mention of the Messapians, who may already have been entirely hellenized. The Roman colony of Venusia, as we remarked above, took the side of the allies, its population having at length almost become Apulian and Lucanian, so that indeed the Latin language was scarcely any longer the one most in use. In the army of the South, C. Papius Mutilus held the command against the Roman consul L. Julius Cæsar. Mutilus conquered Nola, Muceria, Pompeii, and Stabiæ, and carried the war into Campania. Capua was kept by the Romans; Naples and the Greek cities remained faithful, acting as if the war was no concern of theirs. The struggle was very sharp around Acerræ: at the end of the year, the allies had the best of it.

With the army of the centre, Pompædius, or Poppædius, Silo opposed P. Rutilius Lupus: the former showed himself to have been a great general, and the Roman commander, who was no match for him, lost his life in the battle. But Sylla and Marius were with the army there, which was the main one, as lieutenant-generals; and Rome owed it to these, that limits were put to the success of the enemy. The Latin colony of Æsernia in the midst of

Samnium, was conquered by the Samnites. Here was seen the hatred of the colonies against the Italians; for the people of Æsernia, who seem to have had faith in the lucky star of Rome, held out until they were reduced by hunger: the Samnites in the beginning of the siege had certainly offered them a free retreat. The first who had any brilliant success, was Cn. Pompeius Strabo, the father of him who afterwards was called *Magnus*, a *prætor proconsulari potestate*: he had all the profligacy of his age, notwithstanding which he was a distinguished man. He defeated the Picentines in a battle near Asculum, where there were 75,000 Italians against 65,000 Romans: the Romans gained a decisive victory, and a terrible chastisement was inflicted upon Asculum. The Picentines, on the whole, had to suffer most grievously for their conduct. Cn. Pompeius now advanced from the north: the Italian peoples lost their feeling of confidence in victory, and owing to the want of hearty union among themselves, were no longer able to stand their ground. First of all, the Vestinians separated from the rest; and now the Romans held out allurements to the nations singly, granting them peace and the franchise. What the conditions were we know not, though there must have been more than the *civitas sine suffragio*: the Romans, however, must have taken care not to lay down a distinct rule; for afterwards there is a dispute about the meaning of the grant. Velleius Paterculus, a very ingenious writer who was perfectly master of his subject, whatever objections one may have to the man himself, tells us that nearly three hundred thousand Italians who were able to bear arms, perished in this war; and that the Romans had not yielded the citizenship to the Italians, until they had spent the last drop of blood which they had to shed. We may, therefore, take it for granted, that half of the whole number of men engaged on both sides were killed, and that therefore the struggle was carried on with the greatest fury, as in a civil war: hence Appian also places it in his work as such.

In the second year, the war is still less to be made out than in the first: thus much only is certain, that the northern Sabellian peoples also, the Marsians, Marrucinians, and Pelignians, had now a separate peace, even as early perhaps as the end of the first year. These new citizens were not distributed among the old tribes, but others were formed out of them: this was quite in keeping with the system of the ancients, as otherwise the old citizens would have been outnumbered in the assemblies of the people, and in the elections, by the new ones. It is not known for certain how many fresh tribes were created: according to a passage in Velleius, there were eight of them. Another statement in Appian[97] is evidently written wrong: there we find δεκατεύοντες ἀπέφηναν ἑτέρας (viz. φυλάς), from which δέκα φυλάς, has been gathered, though perhaps it would then have been better to read δέκα ἐξ αὐτῶν. Yet, from Appian's usual way of speaking, it seems to have been δεκαπέντε. My reasons for this, are from a feeling of symmetry: if we add 15 to 35, we have 50; 35 is quite an awkward number, which had grown up by degrees, and at which one would not wish to stop; 15 is to 35 as 3 to 7, and is therefore somewhat less than half of the original number, which was now of necessity to be changed. That Velleius has eight, I account for by the circumstance that the Latins had eight tribes given them, and afterwards the Etruscans and Umbrians got seven.

The number of battles fought in this war, is even beyond belief. Corfinium took again its old name, and the seat of government was transferred to Æsernia; the Samnites now formed the real centre of the war, and they carried it on with the same perseverance as they had done in former times: this was at least the case with the three cantons of the Hirpinians, the Caudines, and the Pentrians. The Romans marched into Apulia, and entirely surrounded the Samnites; so that already by the end of the year 663, the war was well nigh decided. The Samnites indeed still held out; yet there were none in arms besides them, but a part of the Apulians and Lucanians. These peoples went on with the war from despair alone: they either reckoned on the movement in Asia caused by the war of Mithridates, or they had made up their minds to perish.

In this second year of the war, there was also a rising of the Etruscans and the Umbrians: but they soon made their peace with the Romans. Their rebellion took quite a different character from that of the Italians:—a prætor conquers the Etruscans, and they get the franchise at once. The Etruscans had formerly furnished no troops for the Roman army: yet now they were ready to take up arms for an honour to which they had not hitherto attached any value. The Roman of rank had in the Marsian a very dangerous rival for all the offices; whereas, on the other hand, the Etruscan, being as a foreigner quite distinct from the Roman, had far less chance of getting these places. The Marsians were to the Romans very much like what the Germans of the North are to those of the South; and therefore they readily blended with the Romans, whilst the Etruscans were to these, as the French, or the Slavonians are to the Germans. The Samnites, as in olden times, wished for the destruction of Rome.

The Italian war had raised the glory of Sylla to its highest point, and now his aversion and enmity against Marius showed itself conspicuously. In the year 664, Sylla had been elected consul at the age of forty-nine, while Marius was already past seventy: Sylla therefore decidedly belonged to a later generation. This utterly widened the breach which in everything had existed between them. Sylla (*Sulla*) is a most original character, and it is difficult to give a cut and dry opinion about him. He was a great general, and also a favourite of fortune, a circumstance on which he himself laid great stress, and which also drew the attention of the crowd upon him; nor is it a delusion, that some men are favoured by luck, either always, or for a long run. When still a very young man, being much under forty, he had distinguished himself in the war of Jugurtha, serving as quæstor under Marius; and he had had the good fortune to carry on the negotiations with Bocchus, so that he looked upon the ending of it as his own work. He had likewise won renown in the Cimbric, and still more so in the Italian war, in the which he far outshone Marius, as he was the only Roman who played a brilliant part in it. He was of the illustrious *gens* of the Cornelii, and was descended in the sixth generation from that P. Cornelius Rufinus who is honourably mentioned in the war with Pyrrhus; yet the family to which he belonged was undistinguished. The name of *Sulla* has been rightly derived by Gronovius from *Sura* (*Surula*, by contraction *Sulla*); consequently it is an apparent diminutive which has the same meaning as the root itself. *Sura* was a surname of the Lentuli and others. He was in every respect the opposite of Marius. The latter had risen from the ranks, and was a soldier of fortune; Sylla, on the contrary, was a refined man of the world: for his chief delight was in Greek literature; he was quite a master of the Greek language, and a writer of elegant taste. His family being poor, he rose from under as great difficulties as if he had been of humble parentage: the patrician ties were broken, and the Scipios and Lentuli were of no help to him. Marius had all the unhappy feelings of an old man against a younger one who is making his way: this rising sun troubled him, and made him ill at ease; and by treating that extraordinary man with envy and jealousy, he provoked him to an opposition, which—certainly from Marius' own fault at first—gave birth to their mutual dislike. Ever since the time of the war with Jugurtha, Marius had done his best to keep his rival down; and Sylla must also have said to himself, "had I been in Marius' place, I should have done just as he did." Notwithstanding his old age, Marius was insatiable of ruling and commanding, and demanded for himself the conduct of the war against Mithridates, which had been given to Sylla as the consul of that year.

The motive for this war was the very justest on the side of Mithridates, the wrong done by the Romans being too glaring. Mithridates had sprung from a Persian family, which even as early as under the Persian kings had its satrapy in Pontus: the first whom we know of it, in all likelihood was Ariobarzanes, governor of those countries under Ochus. Perhaps it was one of the seven noble families which alone had freedom, being in some sort *sacrosancti*, and invested with the hereditary dignity of governors of those parts. The nation consisted of Syrians and Assyrians; that is to say, the great mass may originally have been Armenian, but as early as in the times of the Assyrian rule over Asia, a colony of Assyrians may have settled here, who called themselves Leuco-Syrians. It was their good fortune, that Alexander did not devastate their country; it was only under his successors, that they got involved in the Macedonian wars: Mithridates the son of the then governor, who arrogated to himself the dignity of a tributary prince, escaped by the friendship of Demetrius Poliorcetes from the jealousy of Antiochus the One-eyed, the father of Demetrius. These countries afterwards established their power on so firm a footing, that even in the fifth century of Rome, their governors already took the title of kings. During the long wars of the successors of Alexander, particularly those of the Syrian kings with Egypt, their strength was completely consolidated; but they were divided by inheritance into two kingdoms, Cappadocia and Pontus proper: they were either under the same dynasty, or at least both of them subject to Persian families. This separation still continued in the beginning of the seventh century (about the year 620), when a Mithridates ruled over Pontus proper and part of Paphlagonia: he gave help to the Romans against Aristonicus, and had before that sent galleys against Carthage; and as a reward they yielded up to him Great Phrygia, which until then had belonged to the kingdom of Pergamus. From a fragment of a speech of C. Gracchus, we find, however, that he had bought this grant from those, who were in power at Rome. Thus then his kingdom was of great extent, and its strength and its revenues were considerable, on quite a different scale from that of our poor Europe. At that time, Lesser Asia was divided into the kingdoms of Pontus and Bithynia, of which the former was the largest; into the Roman province; and into Cappadocia and the southern coast, where Cilicia, Caria, Pamphylia, and a number of small independent states, were then in a chaotic confusion.

Mithridates, justly called the Great, had at the death of his father—the Mithridates mentioned above—been left an infant, and had come to the throne after hard trials. Though he had given no provocation, he had very early been injured by the Romans, who, we know not why, took back from him that highly important possession of Great Phrygia which his father had gained. This treachery awakened in him an implacable feeling of revenge. Besides his many other remarkable qualities, Mithridates had an extraordinary talent for dissimulation; and thus while he seemed to be altogether quiet, but was silently making his preparations, he sought to widen his dominions without doing any mischief to the Romans. He conquered the Cimmerian Bosporus, the Crimea, and the south of the Ukraine as far as the Dnieper; which gave him a great accession of strength. Soon afterwards he found an opportunity of gaining Cappadocia, where there were quarrels about the succession, the reigning king having been declared supposititious: he now placed his own son or brother on that throne. This aroused the jealousy of the Romans, and they set up against him another pretender. Ever since he had become of age, he had done his utmost to collect a fleet and a large army, evidently against Rome; and in the meanwhile he reckoned on the war which was raging in Italy, nor is there any doubt of his being connected with the allies. Yet he had not completed his preparations at the right moment; and this circumstance, as in so many other cases, saved Rome, this time also, from the impending danger. Had he engaged in this undertaking two years earlier, at the beginning of the Social War, things might indeed have taken a different turn; but he made too sure of the success of the Italians, and he believed that they would render his conquests only still more easy.

Rome in the meanwhile recovered herself from the Marsian war, which lingered on but feebly. In the second year of the struggle, she had sent commissioners to Asia to prescribe laws to Mithridates; and this may have overawed him: for, much as they had fallen off, their political weight was still the same, and threatened as they were by the greatest dangers in Italy, they did not yet lose sight of Asia. Moreover Mithridates then abetted the designs of a brother of king Nicomedes of Bithynia, in whose worthless race parricide and fratricide were quite common occurrences. Nicomedes was expelled, and Mithridates became the ally of the new king; yet he allowed himself to be so far daunted by the Romans as to put up with the restoration of Nicomedes in Bithynia, and of Ariobarzanes in Cappadocia, though he did not indeed give up his plan of revenge. The Romans, however, might if they had wished it, have still kept off the war much longer, and the government would perhaps have liked to have done it; but individuals who governed the provinces, and hoped to gain booty, would not hear of peace, but forced Nicomedes into hostilities against Mithridates, that they might have an opportunity of coming to his assistance. Cappadocia was not allied to the Romans, and Nicomedes foreboded ill of the result. Mithridates, of course, revenged himself by invading Bithynia; and there, when he had defeated the king, he again set up against him his brother as a pretender: the Roman senate now thought it high time to interfere. Treating him as if he were the aggressor, they demanded that he should abstain from all hostilities against Bithynia, and acknowledge as king of Cappadocia the man of their own choice. Mithridates bitterly complained of this injustice, saying that the Romans had indeed already taken away Great Phrygia from him. In the meanwhile, the war in Italy was all but decided, as the Samnites only and the men of Nola were still in arms, all the rest having obtained the citizenship; but the Romans were so exhausted, that they could hardly make war. They opposed to him three armies, in which very few could have been Romans, chiefly consisting of Asiatic troops. The result of this undertaking was just what it deserved. After having utterly routed two armies, Mithridates overran the neighbouring countries, conquered Bithynia, placed his son again on the throne of Cappadocia, and took the whole of the Roman province, the inhabitants of which, to a man, welcomed him with enthusiasm as their liberator. The rage against the Romans was here so great, that the people in all the towns in Asia Minor, which were quite hellenized, looking upon the war as finished, slew on one and the same day, as a proof of their fidelity to Mithridates, all the Romans and Italians who were among them. The number of these is said to have been seventy thousand, which is almost beyond belief, as after all none but those who were well off, and men of business, could have resided there: the massacre was carried out with the greatest cruelty. Thus the many usurers and bloodsuckers perished, who after the hard wars of Aristonicus had wrung the highest rates of interest from the people which was in need of money; and who, backed by the cohort and the protection of the Roman præfect, had ventured upon every sort of outrage, and had raised the tolls and taxes in a most arbitrary and overbearing way. Mithridates met with scarcely any opposition on the peninsula; some maritime towns also surrendered to him. And thus, as he was brought up entirely in the Greek manner,—there are no traces of the Magian doctrines to be found in him, except on his coins on which the sun and the moon are to be seen,—the Greeks looked upon him as a fellow countryman in spite of his Persian descent, and he was received with rapture even in Greece itself. Athens unhappily allowed herself to be beguiled by a sophist of the name of Aristion, to open her gates to him, and this fellow set himself up as tyrant. The Peloponnesus and Bœotia went over to Mithridates; the whole of Greece, with the exception of a few places, and likewise the isles of Mitylene and Chios, began to waver. Cyzicus and Rhodes remained true to the Romans: the latter in its wisdom foresaw the issue of the war, and by unshaken fidelity made amends for the faults of which, in the opinion of the Romans, it had been guilty in the war of Perseus. Mithridates occupied all the Roman province but Magnesia, and laid siege to Rhodes. In Rome, these events called forth unbounded rage, and stirred men up to go on with the war in right earnest; but the debate to whom the command in it should be entrusted, gave rise to the first civil war.

By the Sempronian law, the decision lay with the senate, and it appointed Sylla. But Marius, who could not have kept up his great name by distinguishing himself in peace, wanted likewise to have the command in this war. Twelve years had elapsed since his triumph, and he had lost ground in the public opinion: besides which, he had grown old. He might perhaps have been still an able general, although, in the Social War, he distinguished himself but once. The older indeed he grew, the lower he sank in moral worth: he had no more those great qualities which in former days had thrown his faults into the background; but he had still a party, and was the man whom the foes of the aristocracy put forward. Yet all the commotions of that time are not to be accounted for by the feelings of the contending factions, as everything was soon resolved into a mere question of persons.

When Sylla entered upon his consulship, no one seems to have had a foreboding of any danger threatening the republic from a civil war; and before he marched against Mithridates, he wished to put an end to the struggle in Italy. Nola then held out, we know not by what means: this part of the Social War is called *bellum Nolanum*, even as its beginning is called *bellum Marsicum*. This *bellum Nolanum*, however, was chiefly kept up by the Samnites who were still in arms; it was more of an insurrection in which there were no large armies. It was one of Sylla's great qualities, not for any consideration to leave any undertaking unfinished, in which he had once embarked; and the war with Mithridates which was now impending, did not make him withdraw from Nola. While Sylla was still staying there, P. Sulpicius was tribune of the people at Rome: it is he who in Cicero's books *de Oratore*, as a youth, takes a share in the conversation. Whatever may now have led this young man of high family thus unhappily astray,—personal hatred perhaps against Sylla,—it was with him that the calamities of Rome originated. He brought forward a motion that the command in the war against Mithridates should be transferred to Marius; for according to precedent (since the Hortensian law), the people had the right of settling the matter, even though the senate had already assigned the provinces. At the same time, he proposed that instead of forming the new citizens (by whom are meant the Latins, Etruscans and Umbrians) into fresh tribes, as had been intended, they should be distributed among the old ones. The new tribes were in fact to have voted after the others, as the *urbanæ* did after the *rusticæ*, owing to which, as the *prærogativa* had great weight, their rights were much curtailed. The new citizens might indeed have a vote in their turn; but they deemed it a mockery, that a right was granted them by which, nine times out of ten (the Roman tribes being almost always unanimous), they would not be called upon at all: for as soon as there was a clear majority, the votes were no longer taken. That eighteen polled against seventeen, was what very seldom happened. Sulpicius' motion therefore was in one respect an injustice to the old citizens; yet Velleius Paterculus takes too harsh a view of the case: for, as most of those who were in the *tribus rusticæ* lived far from Rome, and did not come to town at all, whilst, on the other hand, the *libertini*, who dwelt in the city itself, had got themselves enrolled among the *tribus rusticæ*, the measure must after all be termed a substantial improvement. A great deal therefore might have been said for and against it.

P. Sulpicius is very badly spoken of by Plutarch and Appian. That his conduct towards Sylla was unjustifiable, needs no further proof, and it is also possible that he did not act from pure motives; yet I cannot believe that he deserved to be so disparaged. The man of whom Cicero,—even though it be only from the recollections of his youth,—quite contrary to his usual feelings towards democrats, speaks with so much reverence, cannot have sunk so low. Sulpicius must, according to Cicero, have been a man of great refinement, and of the most brilliant genius; and though he may have allowed himself to be beguiled into acts of wickedness, Cicero could not indeed have looked upon the matter in such a bad light as the Greeks did. Cicero admires him also for his talents as a speaker: he had still heard him in his youth. Plutarch's hatred of Sulpicius is not to be wondered at, as he followed the memoirs of Sylla who was most justly exasperated against him: yet for this very reason such statements are suspicious.

As the old citizens opposed the motions of Sulpicius,—for there is no longer any question of aristocrats and democrats,—Sulpicius called whole crowds of new citizens into the town to carry his laws by force. But as the bill for giving the command to Marius was tacked to them, Sylla resolved on taking up arms to prevent this. In former days, a man like Fabius Maximus Rullianus would perhaps with a bleeding heart have bowed himself to the will of fate; but those times were gone. That Sylla had recourse to arms, is a thing which, considering the age in which it was done, ought to be judged of with indulgence: he had to fear that Sulpicius and his party would not stop short, but that they would try and have his life. Calling together his soldiers near Nola, he pointed out to them that Marius would form a new army, and disband them, and thus the rich war would slip out of their grasp, and they would be left in disgrace: they resolved one and all to follow him to Rome. He marched with six legions along the Appian road; the senate, which was under the power of Sulpicius, stood aghast at the approach of an army, and sent delegates to enquire what he wanted. Sylla gave an evasive answer, but kept on advancing, and was joined by his colleague, Cn. Octavius.

Marius and Sulpicius had made preparations for a defence: but these were of little avail, as Rome was no fortress, and the eastern suburbs, which in fact were the most splendid quarters of the city, lay open. It was to no purpose that they closed the gates: for the walls afforded no longer any protection, having gone to ruin in some places, while in many others they could easily be climbed over from the suburbs, owing to the houses which were built against them on both sides, now that the town had so greatly increased. Even as late as the war with Hannibal, Rome might have still been defended; but this could now be done no more. Nor did Marius try to make a stand at the gates; he withdrew into the inner part of the city. There was some fighting at the Carinæ; but Sylla outflanked the enemy with his superior numbers, and he marched down the *Via sacra* to the Forum, on which all dispersed. Marius and Sulpicius made their escape.

Sylla used his victory with moderation; so that at that time he appears in a favourable light: yet he unhappily sinned against the forms of the constitution by causing Marius and his son, Sulpicius and nine of their followers, to be outlawed. Sulpicius was seized and put to death, as were also one or two besides; but these were all. Marius escaped with his son to the sea-coast; came in a boat to Tarracina, where he was in danger of being given up; and from thence he went on to Minturnæ on the Liris: there he hid himself in a marsh, and was taken. The magistrate had him thrown into prison, and as a price had been set on his head, sent a *servus publicus* to kill him. The latter, a Cimbric captive, affrighted at the sight of Marius, whom he recognised as his conqueror, ran away from him with a cry of terror at the fickleness of fortune. The decurions then let Marius go away in a boat; and he first went to Ischia, and from thence in a small vessel to Africa. Here he lived during the troubles which followed, among the ruins of Carthage, forgotten and unheeded: there was either no governor just then in Africa, or the proconsul must have belonged to his party. No one thought of seeking a refuge with Mithridates.

Sylla was so little of a tyrant as to leave the election of consuls for the next year free, owing to which men of both parties were chosen, Cn. Octavius (perhaps a son of the tribune M. Octavius), who belonged to that of Sylla, and L. Cornelius Cinna, who was on the side of Marius: which is another proof how utterly the division into patricians and plebeians was now forgotten, the democracy being headed by one of the Cornelii and one of the Valerii (L. Valerius Flaccus), downright demagogues, who trampled under foot every vested right. At the end of the year, Sylla, when he thought that he had put things in order, as the struggle with the Samnites was one that would last long, went over to Greece: there he carried on the war against Archelaus, who commanded the army of Mithridates.

To Q. Pompeius, the colleague of Sylla, the province of Italy was in the meanwhile given for the following year, that he might withstand Cinna, uphold Octavius, and end the Social War. Cn. Pompeius, the father of Cn. Pompeius Magnus, was still at that time with an army in Apulia, on the shores of the Adriatic. Of this Cn. Pompeius, Cicero says, *homo diis nobilitatique perinvisus*: he might also have said, *populo Romano*; for no one was more generally hated. He was a man of deep cunning and of crooked policy, like the men of the fifteenth and sixteenth centuries, especially in

Italy. Neither party knew, whether he was for, or against them; nor was he for any of them, as in reality he was calculating how, at the end of all this confusion, the power might fall into his own hands. To this Cn. Pompeius, Q. Pompeius turned himself, to take the command from him. Cneius pretended to obey the senate, and to give up the *imperium* to him; but he secretly set the soldiers against Quintus, who, when he wanted to make them take the oaths, was murdered, on which Cneius, under a shallow pretence of popularity, was compelled by the troops to resume the command;—a farce, like those played off in Spanish South America by Bolivar, and others of the same stamp. He then wrote to the senate, reporting what a calamity had befallen him, and asked to be confirmed in his command, that he might set on foot an enquiry, and do what he could for the welfare of the republic; a request which indeed they were weak enough to grant him. He was now at the head of this army, and he waited to see what would happen. Sylla being in Greece, the Samnites had time to take breath.

It was not long (665) before the breach between Cinna and Octavius became an open one. In Italy, owing to the transactions concerning the franchise, the Latins, Italians, and Etruscans had different interests. Cinna, who was evidently aiming at absolute power, stood forth as the leader of the Marian party, and offered the Italians, as a bait to win them over, that they should be distributed among the old tribes. The Samnites were still in arms, hoping to conquer Rome or to remain independent; and therefore they would not hear of accepting the citizenship: this, however, separated them from all the rest, who earnestly wished to have it. Cinna's party consisted of the old Latin towns from Tibur to the neighbourhood of Capua, especially Tibur, Præneste, the Hernican towns, and several places between the Liris and the Vulturnus. He now demanded that all these should be distributed among the old tribes; nor can we understand, why Sylla with his political principles should not have been for this measure, as it indeed was the only effectual means of infusing a sort of aristocracy into democracy:—it may have been that those old shadows of tribes were the very things which he was attached to. The new citizens came thronging in crowds to Rome to carry the law, for they hoped to overawe the people by their numbers. Cn. Octavius declared himself against it, and there was a fight in the city, in which many of the new citizens were killed: ten thousand are said to have fallen; but I consider that number as quite uncertain. The senate had now the courage to oppose Cinna; but it was guilty of the irregularity of depriving him by a *senatus consultum* of his consulship, which it had by no means the right of doing by itself: for according to the existing forms, the assent of the people was needed. Things had indeed come to such a pass, that the sovereignty of the people could not have been acknowledged any more; but in point of form, the step was certainly a revolutionary one. The war at Nola was still going on, that town being besieged by a Roman army which could not have been sufficient to overpower that of the Samnites. Thither Cinna went, and bribed the officers and soldiers. These had been taught by Sylla's success what they could do; and they espoused his cause, and encouraged him to resume the consular *insignia*, to break the pride of the oligarchy, and to march to Rome and assert his dignity by force. It is very likely that a truce was concluded with the Samnites. To give a greater lustre to himself and his party, Cinna invited the aged Marius to return from Libya, and recalled the other outlaws. The old general came to Etruria, where he formed Etruscan cohorts, and gave freedom to all the slaves who joined him. Another man whom they called upon, was Q. Sertorius, a follower of Marius' party, which he had joined from disgust to those who were ruling, though he kept himself quite clear of all the tyranny of the demagogues. He is one of the most spotless characters of that age: he was generous, open-hearted, and humane, free from the haughty exclusiveness of a Roman citizen, and gifted with all the qualities of a great general. He was in that position in which, at the outbreak of a revolution, the very best men will often find themselves, as they get involved at the beginning, and afterwards cannot go back, but without knowing what they are about, and against their own wishes, are made to share in the crimes which are sure to be committed at such times; yet he kept his hands unstained during the scenes of horror which he had to witness after the victory. Sertorius hastened to Cinna, who now marched with his army from Campania along the Appian road to Rome, as Sylla had done before. Cinna was joined by Carbo, a man deeply compromised in his guilt, who in the course of these events became notorious; and Marius likewise advanced from Etruria. In their distress, the senate called upon Cn. Pompeius for help; and the latter gave up the war on the shores of the Adriatic, and came to Rome. Octavius was encamped on the Janiculum; Pompeius, before the *Porta Collina*. For some time his conduct was so doubtful, that the senate only expected that he would betray them. Yet at last, a battle—probably an insignificant one—was fought with Cinna; and though the latter had the best of it, the senate had at least a pledge that Cn. Pompeius was serving them. A plague now broke out in both armies, each of which thus lost many thousands of soldiers. Pompeius also died of it: according to other accounts, he was struck within the camp by a flash of lightning. The people were so exasperated against him, that they tore his corpse from the bier, as it was passing through the city, and mutilated it.

Near Albano, at the foot of the Monte Cavo, there was another Roman army opposed by a rebel one. Latium, which formerly had dreadfully suffered in the Volscian and Samnite wars, but had enjoyed peace for more than two centuries, now got its death-blow. Ostia, Aricia, Lanuvium, and Antium, were taken by storm and laid waste by Marius; Tibur and Præneste joined him of their own accord. Rome was now hemmed in by four camps; and though these were indeed too weak to venture upon an assault, a terrible famine arose in the city, and both soldiers and commanders became so dispirited, that the senate determined upon parleying with Cinna, the very man whom it had denounced as a traitor. As he had not laid aside the consular *insignia*, he at once asked, whether he was treated with as consul; and to this the senate had to submit. Marius stood as a private individual by the side of the curule chair, with a sneering laugh, and with looks in which the delegates might have read their sentence of death. When it was stipulated that no blood should be shed, Cinna only gave the very ambiguous answer, that it should not be done with his wish; and on this he demanded that Merula, who had been chosen consul in his stead, should be deposed. To this humiliation also, the senate seems to have yielded. But Octavius, the other consul, would not give way: he betook himself with a small troop to the Janiculum, having the madness to think of defending himself. When Marius and Cinna entered the city, which was about the end of the year, the bloodshed immediately began, chiefly at Marius' instigation. Cn. Octavius was cut down by the soldiers as soon as they had marched in; and L. Cornelius Merula, the *Flamen Dialis*, opened his veins and died near the altar of the temple of Jupiter.

Marius now had himself proclaimed consul for the seventh, and Cinna for the second time, without any election whatever. He had always hoped for this consulship which had been prophesied to him even from a child, when a nest, with seven young eagles in it, fell down into his lap from a tree which is called in Cicero Marius' oak. His acquaintance also with the Syrian fortune teller may have led him to dwell upon the number seven, which was of high import among the Syrians and Jews, as was the number three with the Romans. The victory was followed up with the fellest cruelty: Marius had his body-guard of freed slaves which he sent out to murder people. All who were distinguished in the hostile party, the very flower of the senate, were put to death without any reason assigned, without even a proscription, on a bare order; especially his personal enemies, as the orators Antonius and Crassus. Q. Catulus, Marius' colleague in the Cimbric war, was likewise marked out to die; but he killed himself: Marius' conduct towards him is one of the most deplorable acts of that wretched man. Some very few persons of real worth were with Cinna, among whom was Sertorius, nor is Marius Gratidianus, a cousin of Marius, to be judged of too harshly; but Cinna, Carbo, and their friends were monsters, whereas those who were at the head of the other side, that of the senate, were the most refined, and, according to the standard of that corrupt age, the noblest of men.

The work of murder went on until Q. Sertorius prevailed upon Cinna, to have that band of assassins surrounded and put to the sword. Marius died in the middle of January, it would seem, a maniac, after having been consul for sixteen days. There now followed the rule of a faction, of which we know but little; the shedding of blood, however, was at an end.

Whilst Cinna was drawing near to the city with his army, the senate had given Metellus, who was stationed near Nola, full power to make peace with the Samnites on any terms. But the Samnites tried to drive the hardest possible bargain, not only demanding the franchise for themselves, the Campanians, and Lucanians, but also that the Romans should yield up their prisoners and deserters, without their doing the same on their side: on the contrary, the deserters, who abode with them were likewise to have the citizenship.[98] All this was granted by Metellus, and confirmed by Marius; and thus, when by a later law the Samnites had likewise become citizens, they were henceforth the main props of the party of Marius. The newly formed tribes were now done away with, and the citizens enrolled in the old tribes; whether in all of them, or in some only, is more than we know. In Cicero's times, there is every reason to think that those Italian peoples which belonged to the same stock, were huddled together into one tribe; as, for instance, the Marsians and their neighbours in the *tribus Sergia*, and all the *municipia* round Arpinum in the *Æmilia*. This seems to have been one of Sylla's changes, who drew the Italians out of the tribes, to take away from them their preponderance.

Three years now passed away, during which Sylla carried on the war in Achaia and Asia, whilst in Italy, Cinna, who was at the helm of the state, was preparing to attack him. But the latter became more and more hated on account of his exactions; so that he mistrusted even his own party, and began to demand hostages, which, however, were refused him. L. Valerius Flaccus, his colleague after the death of Marius, had gotten the command against Mithridates, and had gone to Asia by Illyricum, Macedon, and Greece; and he himself was on the eve of marching into Greece against Sylla, having formed a large army near Ariminum, which was to follow. But the soldiers refused to go on this expedition, and a mutiny broke out in which Cinna was killed. After him ruled Cn. Papirius Carbo, who did not have a colleague chosen: he was nominally a consul, but in reality a tyrant.

THE FIRST MITHRIDATIC WAR. SYLLA RETURNS TO ROME. HIS DICTATORSHIP AND DEATH

In the year 665, Sylla had gone to Achaia and Thessaly. At that time, Archelaus and Taxiles, the generals of Mithridates, were masters of the Peloponnesus, and of Greece south of Thermopylæ. Then Sylla won the battle of Chæronea from a countless host of Asiatics,—a battle which he surely could not have classed among those on which he rested his glory; for the Asiatics, who were a hundred thousand men, showed themselves as cowardly as ever were the troops of Indian princes. They were indeed drawn up in phalanx; but it was true of them what somebody has said with regard to those ingeniously prepared dishes in Lent, that fish, even when dressed by the very best of cooks, is after all nothing but fish. Sylla lost but a few men here and there. A different defence was made by Archelaus in the Piræeus. The walls between the city of Athens and its port had been destroyed, perhaps by Demetrius Poliorcetes, and as early as the siege by Antigonus Gonatas the communication seems not to have been free; but the huge walls of Themistocles, as restored by Conon, were still standing. In the Piræeus, where there was a Pontic garrison, Archelaus gallantly held out; in the city, the tyrant withstood the enemy with hired troops. Archelaus did everything in his power to supply Athens with provisions; but to no purpose, as he was baffled by the vigilance of Sylla, who far surpassed him in talent and resources. The distress in the city rose to such a height, that the inhabitants had no strength left; the circumference of the wall amounted to a German mile, and there were not men enough to defend it. The town was stormed, and a frightful slaughter ensued, as if the Athenians had been the deadliest enemies of the Romans. Afterwards the Piræeus also was taken. In Athens itself, few of the buildings were touched, not even the walls being destroyed: in the Piræeus, however, the walls, the noble arsenal, and other buildings, were completely demolished; so that from that time the place was like the decayed towns in the north of Holland, where the grass grows in the streets: Pausanias found only a small hamlet where it had stood. Athens was almost depopulated, and after this the saying of Lucan held good with regard to it, *Rarus et antiquis habitator in urbibus errat*.

Sylla now gained several other advantages, and drove the generals of the king of Pontus quite out of Europe into Asia. Even before him, L. Valerius Flaccus had come thither as proconsul; but he had been murdered by his quæstor or *legatus*, C. Flavius Fimbria, who took upon himself the *imperium* in his stead. Mithridates, thus hemmed in between two armies which were hostile to each other, marched first against Fimbria who had destroyed Ilium. Sylla now concluded a peace which almost startles one's belief. Mithridates abandoned all his conquests, and renounced all claim to Paphlagonia, Cappadocia, Bithynia, and Phrygia, thus confining himself to his hereditary dominions; moreover, he paid down two thousand talents, and yielded over seventy ships of war: in return for this, Sylla did not insist upon his advisers being given up. Sylla now pressed Fimbria so hard, that he took away his own life, and his soldiers went over to his rival, who, however, did not trust them, as they were as *contaminati cœde consulis*, and partizans of Marius: for most of them were certainly Italians, enlisted against Sylla at the time that Marius was in power. These soldiers still remained there, under the name of Valeriani, for many a year, until the days of Pompey and Lucullus; just as the soldiers of Cannæ had to stay so long in Sicily.

After having made this peace, he laid a fine on the Greeks and the Hellenized inhabitants of Asia Minor, the Ionians, Lydians, and Carians, who had murdered the Romans, even to the amount of five years' taxes,—probably the arrears for the whole period of the war,—and a war contribution besides. This crushed them for a long time: but the countries in those parts may so truly be called an earthly paradise, that even under a bad government, be it only not so barbarous as that of the Turks, the land must, after a few generations, again be rich and thriving, and more so perhaps than any in the south of Europe. Thus they also then recovered, and under the emperors, they were most flourishing; but it had taken indeed several generations to set them up again: the first generation after the days of Sylla, was utterly ruined. An officer once told me, how he had seen a succession of countries, each finer than the other: first Rome; then Naples, which is much more blooming still; then the Peloponnesus, which in fertility and luxuriance of vegetation, is infinitely ahead of Naples; then Smyrna, which, beyond comparison, far surpasses all the rest. The contributions, which amounted to thirty millions (of Prussian dollars), were collected with the greatest harshness within a wonderfully short space. The Roman knights, who always followed in the train of the generals, now advanced the money at the rate of twenty-four, thirty-six, even forty-eight per cent., and afterwards enforced the payment of principal and interest with the help of the governors. This was the most frightful tyranny, the sword itself having wasted those countries not near so much as usury did: but Sylla, it is true, could not have carried on his war without money.

Sylla showed himself to be great indeed. His house was pulled down, and his property destroyed; his family had been obliged to fly the country; his friends were either murdered, or driven into banishment, and many of these last came to him, entreating him to return. Mithridates, moreover, would long since have concluded a peace which indeed would have been less advantageous to the Romans; but Sylla wished to bring the war quite to an end, and to get the most favourable terms possible, first taking care of the interests of his country, before he looked to his own. Thus he now returned with a victorious army which was proud of him, and attached to him, being also in possession of great pecuniary resources. He had not more than thirty thousand men, whereas there were opposed to him in the whole of the Italian peninsula as far as Gaul, four hundred and fifty cohorts, that is to say, more than a hundred and eighty thousand men: (for at that time armies were counted by cohorts of four hundred and twenty men, more rarely by legions.) And this was a party besides, which had to fight for its very existence, containing also the Samnites, who could not under any circumstances have concluded a peace with Sylla. This army he attacked in full reliance on his own strength and good fortune, and conducted the war in a manner which was most glorious to his fame.

When Sylla brought back his army to Italy, L. Cornelius Scipio and C. Norbanus Balbus were consuls: here also we again find patricians siding with the democrats. If any one of them had had dictatorial power, and had known how to make use of it; if therefore the military resources had been properly managed, Sylla must have been lost: for against the overwhelming numbers of the opposite party, his success would have been impossible. But the Roman state was at that time so disorganized, and the leaders after Marius' death so incapable; that it was just as it was in France, in the year 1799, when the Directory was so helpless, that without Buonaparte's return it would have been lost. Under such circumstances, rebellions multiply, as the people expect more from any change, than from the continuance of the existing state of things. Sylla reckoned on the incapacity of the chiefs of the opposite faction, and on the hatred which every one had had for their leaders: that now happened which the judicious Cælius Rufus writes to Cicero of the contest of Cæsar and Pompey.[99] Even of the new citizens, very many were filled with disgust and abhorrence against the actual government, and ready to go over to Sylla, if they had only a hope of being maintained in their rights: could the ruling party have relied on the bulk of the new citizens, and on part of the old ones, Sylla would certainly never have been victorious. He therefore, even while his first campaign was still going on, made an alliance with the new citizens in which he confirmed all their rights. Thus, when he landed at Brundusium, he was received with open arms. Preparations for attacking him had been talked of; but those ordered by Carbo, had miscarried owing to the general opposition. Sylla marched quite peacefully through Apulia; near Canusium,[100] if a statement which certainly is very likely, be correct, he had a battle indeed with the consul Norbanus, although it was but an insignificant one. The main force of the enemy, however, he found encamped near Capua, quite close to which city, in the neighbourhood of Mount Tifata, he once more defeated Norbanus; the very troops arrayed against him already went over to him by whole sections. When still in Greece, he had begun to treat, endeavouring to bring about a fair agreement without any exclusive rights for himself; and now he again entered into negotiations with the consul Scipio, and an armistice was concluded, and hostages given. But this truce was broken by Sertorius, because he saw that Sylla was only temporising that he might deceive the consuls and tamper with the soldiers: he therefore occupied Suessa which had declared for Sylla. The soldiers, however, partly from contempt for their general, and partly because they were dazzled by the renown of Sylla, went over to him in such numbers that Scipio was left quite alone. Towards the end of the year, when Sylla was gaining ground in the south of Italy, several of his partisans took up arms: Metellus Pius, in what is now the Romagna; Cn. Pompeius (Pompey),—who afterwards got the surname of Magnus, and was then twenty-three years of age,—in Picenum, where his influence was great, as that district, which had been subjected by his father, stood in a kind of clientship to him; M. Lucullus and several others. Their party and their forces consisted in some degree of old Romans, but mostly of new citizens; Metellus, however, may have had with him a greater number of the older ones from Cisalpine Gaul and the Romagna.

The beginning of the next year was most bloody and decisive. Marius the younger, said to have been a son or nephew of C. Marius (very likely an adopted son), a young man about twenty-seven years of age, was consul with Cn. Papirius Carbo. The latter took the command in northern Etruria and in the neighbourhood of Ariminum, especially against Metellus, Pompey, and Lucullus; Marius was stationed at the frontier of Latium, whither Sylla came from Campania where he had passed the winter. Here the decisive battle near Sacriportus was fought, probably on the road from Segni to Palestrina, hard by the latter place: perhaps there was only a defile. Marius had concentrated thither all the troops which belonged to him, most of which were Samnites, that he might cover Rome; and so long as he held this position, Sylla could not march by the Appian road against the city. All this country, as well as Etruria, was the stronghold of Cinna's party, the

Latin towns there being most zealous in the cause: the rest of the Italians, on the other hand, with the exception of the Samnites and Lucanians, seem to have been lukewarm, even when they did not keep aloof. Thus at Sacriportus, Sylla gained a decisive victory, and, it is said, with very little loss to himself. Marius fled to the strong town of Præneste, which was quite devoted to him, and was also at that time a very large place; the Palestrina of the present day, a town of six thousand inhabitants, is but a part of the ancient *arx*, and lies within the precincts of the temple of *Fortuna*. Here Sylla hemmed in his conquered foes, intrusting the siege to Q. Lucretius Ofella, who blockaded and starved the city in which, besides the Prænestines, there were old Romans, and Samnites.

Sulla himself marched upon Rome. As yet, he displayed great moderation; nay, had it not been for the infatuation of his opponents, he would perhaps have made up his mind to settle affairs without bloodshed: but these were quite drunk with rage; for there was a fanaticism among them, just as there was at the destruction of Jerusalem. Even in the last days of the rule of Cinna's party, the prætor Damasippus had all the partisans of Sylla, whether open or suspected, put to death, particularly the senators: among those who were thus murdered, was the venerable *pontifex maximus*, Q. Mucius Scævola, who, being conscious of his innocence, had not left the city. But as this fury after all did not give them strength to defend the city, the leaders made their escape. Rome opened her gates to Sylla, and he promised moderation; but his moderation had a terrible meaning. He first went to Etruria, where Carbo was: on the side of the Etruscans, the war was truly a national one, as Sylla took away from them the rights of citizenship which had been granted them: the details of this campaign are shrouded in impenetrable darkness. Carbo had posted himself near Clusium, from whence he made two vain attempts to relieve Præneste; he also engaged in other expeditions which were equally unsuccessful, as, for instance, that against Picenum, in which Carinas was concerned. The troops of the Marian party dwindled to nothing under his hands, desertion spreading more and more among them. Of this there were many cases which are quite inconceivable. Even at the very outset, P. Cethegus, one of the twelve who were outlawed with Marius, had surrendered himself to the mercy of Sylla; and Albinovanus, to make his peace with him likewise, now murdered his colleagues and legates at a banquet.

The last effort was made by Pontius Telesinus, whose brother commanded with Marius the Samnites in Præneste. He and the Lucanian M. Lamponius, had tried to relieve Præneste, and had failed; after which, believing Sylla to be out of the way, they marched in all haste to surprise Rome: but Sylla heard of it, and came up just in time to ward off the danger.

Had they been successful, they would have destroyed Rome; but the very fear of this must have roused the Romans to exert themselves to the utmost. There were said to have been forty thousand Samnites and Lucanians; the dread of such allies led many a partisan of Marius to fight under the banners of Sylla. The terrible battle near the Porta Collina now followed, by which the fate of the world was decided; and it was only after fortune had long wavered, and had often been in favour of the Samnites, that Sylla in the evening of the day broke through the ranks of the enemy: so great was their defeat, that Telesinus died by his own hand. After such a blow, Marius also, and the younger Telesinus in Præneste, gave themselves up for lost. They tried to escape from the town by passages under ground which led into the open fields; but the outlets were guarded, and so they both killed each other. Of the son of Marius, we cannot say as we did of the father, "he was a great man:" he was rather a dreadful man; he had the faults of his father, without any of his great qualities but that of perseverance, in which, under such circumstances, there is nothing so very wonderful. Carbo also soon fled from his men to Africa. Unless perhaps in Spain, the party had no longer an army; and in Italy, although single towns still held out, the war was virtually at an end.

Eight thousand Samnites had been taken prisoners in the battle before the Colline gate; and Sylla had them surrounded with troops in the Campus Martius, and cut down to a man. When also, after the death of the younger Marius, Præneste surrendered at discretion, he caused the Roman citizens, the Prænestines, and the Samnites, to be divided into three bodies: to the first he granted their lives; but the Prænestines and Samnites he ordered to be shot down with javelins. The Etruscan towns yielded to him one after another, and met with the same fate as Præneste, besides being razed to the ground. Thus also fared Clusium, Aretium, Populonia, and Volaterræ; the latter after a two years' siege. So perished likewise all the larger towns of Etruria; with the exception perhaps of Fæsulæ, which, however, may also have been rebuilt afterwards.

At Rome, Sylla now held absolute sway, and although until then had been humane, he all at once showed himself at length a bloodthirsty monster. For he gave for the first time the example of a proscription; that is to say, he made out a list of all those whom not only any one might kill with impunity, but on whose head moreover a price was set. There were among his victims few indeed who were to be compared to those whom Marius and Cinna massacred; but in the extent of suffering inflicted, nothing could surpass the revenge of Sylla, who visited even whole peoples with his wrath. That proscription affected the lives of several thousands; two thousand four hundred knights[101] are said to have been in it: that so many had been on the list, seems doubtful. Twenty-three (according to another, but probably incorrect statement, forty-three,) legions had military colonies allotted them. The first colonies of Rome were settlements, in which one of every *gens* was placed to garrison the conquered towns; these men had a third part of the land, and, of course, they kept themselves under arms. The Latin colonies were divided between the Romans and Latins: very likely, every one who belonged to them had served as a soldier; but this was only an accidental circumstance, that colonisation being no special reward for military service. After the second Punic war, we meet with the first instances of the *ager publicus* being assigned to superannuated soldiers; and in Bononia alone there are signs of a still continuing obligation to serve in war, a difference being made there between the lots given to horsemen, centurions, foot-soldiers, &c. Sylla's are the first true military colonies, a system by which the inhabitants of some particular town were stripped of the whole of their land, and some legion or other, which was now discharged, was to form the population there: should the territory of the town not be sufficient, there was added to it from the adjoining districts as much as was required. Thus the soldiers gained a right of having land assigned to them, a right to which in former days plebeianism only could give a title. According to an old and extremely plausible Florentine tradition,—which cannot indeed be traced to any classic author, but which is all but proved by an old reading in the orations of Cicero against Catiline,[102]—we may say that Florence has risen as such a military colony out of the old Fæsulæ; thus it was also with New Aretium and several places of Etruria, with Præneste and other towns, of which, however, few only can be ascertained by satisfactory evidence; in these cases, the inhabitants had almost everywhere been murdered. These legions were the corner-stone of Sylla's power. Something of the same kind was done in places where the old inhabitants were not exterminated: the new comers became κληροῦχοι, whilst the old residents had to pay a land tax for the allotments which they still retained. This was especially the fate of the old Latin colonies. Those which did not fare thus, had by the *lex Julia* become *municipia,* and remained as such; those, on the other hand, which Sylla had proscribed, were now called *coloniæ,* not, however *Latinæ,* but *Romanæ militares,*—Sylla's military colonies. These are the *coloniæ* of which Pliny[103] speaks, and which always have been mistaken. This matter was an obscure one even for the ancients: Asconius Pedianus, a writer of first-rate historical learning, did not in his time understand how Cicero could have called Placentia a colony, when it had become a *municipium.* [104] Nearly the whole of Etruria became a wilderness, and the towns which had not been turned into military colonies, lay in ruins as late as in the days of Augustus. The Samnite nation he had all but rooted out, the whole of the

Hirpinian country being laid waste: all that had been made *ager publicus*, was left by him to his favourites.

A marked feature of Sylla is a sort of fantastic activity. He looked upon himself as born to be the achiever of great things, especially as a reformer: he was aware of the disorganized condition of the nation; but he did not know that when what is old is worn out, the only thing to be done, is to create, in the spirit of the ancient institutions, new ones which are suited to the age. What Sylla wanted to do, could have been of no avail whatever: it was the restoring of what was dead, the return to a state of things which had fallen away because the life had fled from it;—he recalled the old forms of the republic into existence, and believed that they had strength enough to stand. He thought (as in Tieck's World Turned Upside Down) that he could push the world back to the point at which in his opinion it ought to have stopped. Moreover, he deemed himself called upon to rule; and therefore he stuck at nothing, as he held that he was above all these forms, so that they did not affect him in the least.

He reorganised the senate, which was fearfully diminished after the many executions. It might have been expected that he would have tried to restore it from the ranks of the old nobility; yet instead of doing so, he selected the new senators—with a remarkable inconsistency, which shows that notwithstanding all his arbitrary rule, he was swayed by circumstances—not only from the knights, but also from his own low-born centurions, who were ready, it is true, to lay down their lives for him. He had not the elements of an aristocracy at hand: the party, which really had vitality, influence, and refinement of mind and manners, being that of the monied classes, the knights and the Italian *municipia*. These he hated and wanted to crush; and as in such cases, one has usually recourse to the rabble, thus Sylla, true to the example of all oligarchs and counter-revolutionists, filled up with the lowest of the people his senate which was a mere skeleton, and ought most naturally to have been recruited from the rich class of the *equites*; this was just as in the year 1799 at Naples, when the dregs of the populace were armed. Whilst wishing to save the republic by forms, he began by departing from them himself.

As long as his influence lasted, even for four years running, a patrician and a plebeian were regularly made consuls; before that plebeians alone had often been chosen for four or five years in succession: beyond this Sylla durst not go, as all the leaders of his party were plebeians. This was indeed quite a childish arrangement.

The tribuneship he brought back to its original state, as it was before the Publilian law of the year 283; which was as much as going back four hundred years. For he took away from the tribunes the right of bringing bills into the assembly of the people, and revived the old way of making laws: these were now proposed by the consuls, and passed by the senate and the centuries. One might wonder at his not having restored the curies; yet he could not do this, as they were so changed that he would have had in them a democratical assembly. As he neglected every means which ought to have been tried for raising the state again to a healthy condition, he despaired of all gradual improvement, and therefore he rushed headlong into violent measures and all kinds of makeshifts. Much might be said for his changes in the tribuneship, as at that time the office could no longer be made available for good: it had become a nuisance, every one cried out against it; and so the tribunes were henceforth to be only *ad auxilium ferendum*. No tribune of old could have been allowed to have a curule office, as he was a plebeian; and therefore Sylla, wishing in this respect also to retrograde, lessened the influence of the tribunes by enacting that no tribune, after having laid down his magistracy, should fill any office which was a stepping-stone to the senate.

To secure himself still further, he deprived the children of those who had been proscribed, of part of their rights as citizens, that is to say, of eligibility to hold office. This unjust law remained many years in force until Cæsar repealed it.

The administration of justice he gave back to the senators. The knights had employed the power which they had acquired by the exercise of such jurisdiction, entirely against the nobility. The senators should now have taken some care to do away with the old reproaches made against them, by judging righteously; but the courts were never as venal as they were then. Sylla's faction so basely and infamously abused the advantages which they had gained, that they cut their own throats; and had it not been for the military colonies, a heavy vengeance would soon have been wreaked upon them.

Sylla was a very active legislator, nor are every one of his enactments to be found fault with. For though he showed great want of sense in his constitutional measures, in those which were administrative, as in criminal legislation, he did things which prove that he had excellent advisers; in fact, he was the first who placed these matters on even a tolerable footing. And for the management also of criminal trials, his regulations were real improvements. He likewise made a *lex annalis* to settle the order in which the different offices were to be held.

Moreover, it is one of Sylla's changes that there was a considerable increase in the number of the magistracies and priesthoods. In the earliest times, the pontificate consisted of four members, two from each of the oldest tribes, besides the *pontifex maximus*: so it was with the augurs. Afterwards, the number of the pontiffs was, by the addition of four plebeian ones,[105] raised to nine, in which the *Pontifex Maximus* was included, his office being common to both orders; the augurs were also increased, as it was still intended in those days that the two orders should share the priestly dignities alike. It cannot be stated with certainty, when this was no longer done; yet it must have been before the *Lex Domitia*. Sylla himself thought no more of dividing these between the patricians and plebeians; so much did the power of circumstances prevail over the crotchets which he otherwise used to form! He suspended the *lex Domitia*; restored to the priestly colleges the right of co-optation; and raised the number of the pontiffs[106] and augurs to fifteen.

This had no material influence on the state; but certainly the great increase of the prætors and quæstors had. By his reforms of the criminal law, he assigned to the prætors the *quæstiones perpetuæ*; and because the vast extent of the commonwealth had now made many more accountants necessary, he raised the establishment of quæstors to twenty. Thus there was a considerable multiplication of curule and other dignities. The senate he enlarged to six hundred;[107] and now every year, more as a matter of course than by any wish of his, the twenty quæstors came into it, forming the thirtieth part of the whole body. As no one was quæstor more than once, its numbers were almost always full, and thus the censors all but lost their power of choosing the members. Thus the question whether the senate was elective, is placed in quite a different light. The senate is never to be looked upon as a representative body, unless it were in the very earliest times, when it was elected directly by the curies; its being filled up by the quæstors, makes it indeed an elective assembly.

Sylla had a body-guard of freedmen whom he called Cornelians, and these soon became most powerful people. That at that time, anybody in the country towns who had either interest or connexions with these Cornelians, especially with Chrysogonus, Sylla's favourite, might do whatever he listed, and even commit murder; is borne out by the evidence of Cicero's orations *pro Sexto Roscio Amerino* and *pro Cluentio*. The state of things in those days, was horrible and shocking beyond description.

Sylla gave all these laws as dictator, which, after the deaths of Marius and Carbo, he had caused himself to be made for an indefinite period by the interrex L. Valerius Flaccus. It was thought that he would never again lay down the dictatorship; but he held it only two years. He was tired of every thing around him: he would either have had to wage wars abroad, for which perhaps he felt that he was too old, and for which he had no longer any taste; or he must have gone on with reforms at home, though he thought that this had been done already as far as it was practicable. [108] For this reason he resigned the dictatorship, a step which was not by any means so very bold as it would seem; for the condition of the republic, the utter prostration of the enemy, and his military colonies insured his safety. He went to Puteoli, where he was attacked by that most dreadful of all diseases, the phthiriasis: his whole body became full of boils which bred vermin. This in all likelihood is no romance: the chief cases of this disorder are those of tyrants, like Philip II., Herod the king of the Jews, Antiochus Epiphanes, and of land-owners who have ground down their peasants; but the philosopher Pherecydes likewise had it. Though Sylla's strength was wasted away by this sickness, his death was brought on by an accident, and it was most lucky for him that he died before the whole of the machinery which he had created fell to pieces. He thought, that in Puteoli he might even lead history astray, and make posterity believe that all his measures had only been overthrown by the bad management of those who came after him; yet he still ruled the state, even from thence, by means of his trembling creatures who could not do without him. He amused himself at Puteoli with the legislation of the place, wishing to seem as if he were nothing more than a plain citizen, yet for all that his will was to be law: being contradicted one day, he got into such a rage that he broke a blood vessel and died, at the age of sixty. Even if his death had happened ten years later, his last days would have been peaceful: the party against him was crushed, the tribunes were paralysed, and the whole of Italy was occupied by military colonies on whose devotion he could rely. His body was brought to Rome; and the pomp of his burial, which was not inferior to that of Augustus, shows that his rule was not dependent on his person, nor on the circumstances of the moment.

LITERATURE. MANNERS AND MODE OF LIVING

With the consulship of Lepidus and Catulus began the History of Sallust, the loss of which, to judge from the fragments, is one of the most painful of all those which we have to mourn over in Roman literature, not only on account of the matter in it, but above all, because of its value as a work of art. The history of the Social War was written by Sisenna, who was in some measure a forerunner of Sallust: he was also an earlier acquaintance of Cicero's, who does not speak over favourably of the literary merits of his writings. Yet I am inclined to think that here we should not blindly follow the opinion of Cicero: for Sisenna's manner was one which he did not like; it was the *horridum* of the ancients, an imitation of Clitarchus.[109] He wrote quite differently from his predecessors, in reading whose fragments we can hardly believe that any one could ever have written in such a way. At that time, the whole style of literature was changed. It was as in Germany about the period of the Seven Years' War; and just as there were then some stragglers in our republic of letters, thus was it also in Rome. Among these I class Claudius Quadrigrarius, who has still the stiff, uncouth, quaint manner: the want of refinement in the whole of his performances is quite astonishing.

Pacuvius, who was somewhat younger than Ennius, and very much younger than Plautus, ranks very high among the poets; he was exclusively a tragic writer, and undoubtedly a very good one: not a trace, however, is to be met with among the Romans of anything like the Satyric plays. In the beginning of the seventh century, Terence introduced quite a different manner, which, if compared with Ennius and Pacuvius, and Plautus above all, is infinitely more modern: he is already quite free from the πῖνος of antiquity, as there are good grounds for believing that his writings have never been revised.—Somewhat younger was Cæcilius Statius, a Campanian, whose comic skill and playfulness are praised by Cicero, who, however, finds fault with his language: his fragments, especially a larger one in Gellius, give us no great idea of him. A far greater poet was L. Attius (not Accius, nor Actius either), who lived to so great an age so that even Cicero still knew him. His was a truly tragic genius; and he not only composed after the Greek models, especially after Æschylus,—what we have left to us in this style is so beautiful, that it may very well be placed by the side of what the Greek has written,—but he also wrote *prætextatæ*, that is to say, historical pieces in the manner of Shakspeare, which are not tied down to the unities of time or place. He came much nearer to the form of the Greek dramas than his predecessors had done; at least the anapæsts of four feet in his choruses were strictly according to the rules of Greek verse: in his own tragedies also, the *senarii* and anapæsts seem to have been the prevailing measures, and not the long verses of Ennius and Pacuvius; and though indeed the *senarii* are not formed quite so accurately as in Greek metres, they are much more so than in Terence. His anapæsts are already metrical, and not merely rhythmical; whereas, on the contrary, the *prætextatæ* were composed in long rhythmical *octonarii*, part of which were iambic and part trochaic. In him we have a proof how much quicker the ear of the Romans had already become. It was not so with his contemporary Lucilius, from Suessa Aurunca, who indeed made use of a hexameter of dactyls and spondees, but with much greater licence than even Ennius had done, as the hexameters which can only be scanned according to rhythm, are really *sermoni propiora*: of the laws of Greek versification, he either had no knowledge whatever, or he entirely set them at naught. Most of his books were written in hexameters, some of them in trochaics. Wit and raciness his satires must have had in a high degree; we might indeed have been reconciled to his slovenly manner and have enjoyed him, instead of scornfully turning up our noses at him, as Horace did.—About the same time, the lyric poet Lævius may have written, who perhaps reached the highest point of gracefulness and sweetness in the native style.

Prose was still in a quite neglected state; a fragment of C. Lælius, which has lately come to light, shows how uncouth and harsh it then was, even harsher than in the times of Cato: only C. Gracchus wrote prose in measured periods, which nearly approached perfection. The orators of that age either did not write at all, or they wrote in a dreadfully stiff style, much worse than they spoke. The historians before Sisenna had as little claim to the name of writers, as our knightly authors of the sixteenth century, Schärtlin von Burtenbach and others. The Roman historians were yet inferior to them; for the knights were men of action, whilst these were men of the school, and even then not worth much.

The manners and mode of life had but one aim, that of making money: even before the civil wars, people had become exceedingly immoral. The immense riches which had been heaped together by means of plunder and robbery, were squandered in luxury; the old ways having been abandoned in everything, Greek fashions were copied as much as possible. The orator

L. Crassus was the first who sent for marble pillars from Greece, though indeed he had only four set up in his house; before that, the houses were built of brick plastered over, or of peperino: the furniture was equally mean. The condition of Italy was wretched beyond description. Samnium was a wilderness, and Strabo says that even as late as in his day, no towns there were able to thrive. And yet the misery had not reached its greatest height, but things were still to become much worse.

Cicero was in his eight and twentieth year when Sylla died; he had already made several speeches, and awakened great attention. Older than he, and not altogether free from envy, but rather inclined to keep down the younger man, was Q. Hortensius. The latter was in no way to be compared with Cicero, and being fully tainted with the villainy of his age, he was ever ready to sell his convictions for money. Among Cicero's contemporaries, in those awful times, a number of able men of very different kinds sprang up. Such upheavings of party spirit generally have this effect: the *Ligue* indeed quite blighted the study of antiquity in France; but it sharpened the wit and quickened the minds of the people; the Thirty Years' War did nothing but destroy, whilst the Seven Years' War gave a new impulse to Germany, and awakened the Muses. Sallust was a great deal younger than Cicero, being as yet a mere boy; but he was a full-grown man when Cicero was still in the pride of his strength.

COUNTER-REVOLUTION. LEPIDUS. SERTORIUS. POMPEY

Sylla was still living when M. Æmilius Lepidus, as the head of the democracy, rose against Q. Lutatius Catulus, the head of the aristocracy. This movement was one of those convulsions which will always follow such great events, owing to the infatuation of those who do not understand the things which have happened. Lepidus was working *acta Sullæ rescindere;* this counter-revolution aimed at nothing less than drawing the legions out of the military colonies, dismissing the senators of Sylla, and putting into their places the children of the proscribed. (Of those who had been outlawed, hardly one had escaped.) Lepidus' whole undertaking was an impracticable one; nor did either his abilities or his moral worth fit him for such a task. He had himself taken a part in the struggles of Sylla's times; and, as we may gather from the fragments of Sallust's History, he had purchased confiscated estates for a mere trifle, and thus enriched himself. In the French revolution, many people were forced to buy such estates, so as to bind them to the interests of the revolution; just in the same way, Sylla had gained over thousands who would otherwise have been hostile to him, by letting them have estates of the proscribed at a bargain. Lepidus, however, may have been a worthless man, in which case the split would be a matter of course: he set himself up as the avenger of the old Romans who had been ruined. Any party which rules by bloodshed, must necessarily split: many who had shared in the intoxication of the moment, were afterwards ashamed of it, and now banded themselves together in the cause of humanity. Catulus, the colleague of Lepidus, was an honest man, and devoted heart and soul to Sylla. He undoubtedly had approved of his atrocities in some measure; but he himself was a man of honour to whom no foul deed could be imputed; he had kept himself pure from the purchase of ill-gotten property. As he was a person of great experience, he was looked upon as a judicious adviser, and enjoyed on the whole a great deal of consideration; whilst Lepidus, on the contrary, was not respected at all.

Elements of agitation were not wanting. The old inhabitants of the military colonies were driven from their abodes, with the exception of those who, like Ofellus in Horace, kept their estates as tenants of the new *colonus* (of these there were probably a great number). Thousands from the Etruscan and Umbrian municipal towns roamed about as beggars, ready to fight at any time for whatever cause might engage them: many soldiers of Sylla, who had already run through the land which they had gotten, were likewise to be had. The senate, seeing in the enterprise of Lepidus the beginning of fresh misery, made Catulus and Lepidus swear not to take up arms against each other. This answered so long as they were in Rome. In those days,—owing perhaps to a regulation of Sylla's,—it was the custom for the consuls not to leave Rome during their year of office, and it was only after its expiration that they went to their provinces. As soon then as his consulship was over, Lepidus betook himself into Gaul, and the war broke out; he himself in Etruria, and in Cisalpine Gaul M. Brutus, a kinsman of the last Brutus, had gathered together a great number of desperadoes. An attempt of his on Rome was foiled, Catulus having been wise enough to get reinforcements; and thus the whole undertaking burst like a bubble. After a slight engagement, Lepidus himself gave up all hope, and fled to Sardinia where he died. His soldiers at first roved about for some time in Gaul, under his lieutenant M. Perperna; afterwards, they went to Sertorius in Spain. M. Brutus was defeated by Pompey, and put to death.

Infinitely more important was the war of Sertorius, of which we should have been glad to have read a circumstantial account in Sallust. What was the number of books in his *Historiæ*, we can no longer tell exactly: we have many quotations from the first five; but these could by no means have been all. From the fragments of the speeches, we may presume, that they went down from the war of Lepidus, to which without doubt the history of Sisenna reached, to the end of the war of Pompey in Asia. In this work, Sallust may in some degree have adopted the form of annals, which otherwise he could not bear. It was the last of his works, the Catiline having been the first.

Sertorius was a Sabine of by no means high birth, of Nursia, a *præfectura* where Vespasian also was born, and which even long afterwards was proverbial for its old-fashioned sternness (*durities Nursina*). It is a kind of Alpine valley in the midst of the Apennines (*val di Norcia*), and it only lost its freedom owing to the French revolution, before which time it was a small democratic republic, which even had the right of judging cases of life and death without any further appeal to Rome. On the whole, the different parts of the States of the Church were quite on a different footing; thus also Tivoli had such a free municipal constitution.[111] There is no book which can give us any insight into this state of things in Italy; it is quite unknown. The papal legate, or delegate, arbitrarily interfered, just like the proconsuls of old, though he had no formal powers of government. Some states were under the sternest baronial despotism; others had wretched communal constitutions; others again were real republics. In the march of Ancona, the towns had a diet with great privileges, a system, under which the country was very well off; but there were other places indeed in which the magistrates did just what they liked, there being no check upon them. In the States of the Church alone, there were probably a hundred petty commonwealths whose only point of union was the Pope. All this was done away with by the Revolution, and remained so, the system of præfects being introduced instead.

To this very day, the people of the Val di Norcia are looked upon as rough mountaineers, and indeed also as what the Italians call *facinorosi*. When they come to other parts of the country, they are very apt, from their wild habits, to become malefactors and banditti; but in their own home they behave very quietly, as an old Roman Abbé has assured me. In Cicero's day, they bore the character of having kept up the old Sabellian manners in their purest state, like the Marsians, Hernicans, and Vestinians.[112]

Sertorius had risen by his valour alone. In the times of Cinna, he had delivered Rome from the freedmen of Marius; when Sylla came to Italy, he was a *legatus* of the consuls. And now, when in the following year Carbo had managed affairs in Etruria in a hopelessly wretched way, he succeeded in getting a commission out in Spain to maintain that province for his party. Had he chanced to be at the head of Marius' faction, (which was not the case, as he was above all intrigues,) he would have baffled the plans of Sylla. In Spain, not merely from policy, but because he was a man of noble mind, it was his aim to win over the Spaniards; wherever he could remedy their grievances, he did it, not treating them as despised provincials, but trying as much as possible to amalgamate them with the Romans: he thought of holding out in Spain, even when Italy was entirely lost. He had an army in the eastern Pyrenees, on the road which leads from the country between Perpignan and Collioure, with which he made head against the enemy under Livius[113] Salinator: but his men, after having already beaten off Annius whom Sylla had sent against them, were seduced to go over to the other side; on which he was forced to flee with a few followers who were true to him. This piece of treachery was part of Sylla's astonishing luck. Sertorius at first roved over the sea, where the Romans had little power, and the pirates had greatly spread; then he tried for some time to maintain himself in Ivica. From thence he fled to the Lusitanians, who were the sworn foes of the Romans, and who trusted in his honour and uprightness; but as he could not stand his ground against overwhelming numbers, he embarked for Mauritania: there he declared for one of the two pretenders to the crown, and took Tangier, and got a great deal of booty. He was even thinking of withdrawing from public life altogether, and going to the Canary islands, so as to be out of the reach of Roman rule, and to live there in freedom; when there now came again to him an invitation from the Lusitanians, and with it the hope of being able to achieve something. The Roman commanders had, as usual, given vent to their rage in Spain, and had made the pursuit of Sertorius a pretext for plundering; Sylla moreover was dead, and in so distant a province, the belief that the fabric which he had built would fall to pieces, was quite natural. Romans and Spaniards declared for Sertorius; particularly the half-citizens (*hybridæ*), who, being the children of Roman soldiers by Spanish women, had no franchise, but yet considered themselves as Roman citizens, and had Roman names, and also spake both Roman and Spanish: they were the corner-stone of his power, the link which connected him with the Spaniards. Proscribed Romans who had hidden themselves hitherto, now came forward to join him; the Spaniards likewise, especially the Celtiberians, were filled with enthusiasm for him and took up arms.

As soon as he could look upon himself as having the chief command in Spain, he proceeded, according to a well-arranged plan, to change the Spaniards into Romans, so that they were to take their tone from Roman civilisation and Roman life; but he did not wish to sacrifice any of that loftiness which the Spanish character had of its own. He gathered from among the proscribed, and the other Romans who were scattered in the provinces, from among the *hybridæ*, and partly also, no doubt, from among the noble Spaniards, a senate of three hundred members, which is spoken of in history (*Sall.* Fragm.)[114] as *Senatus Hispanicus*; thus making a Rome out of Rome. Then he established at Osca, a town in the north of Spain (the Huesca of the present day), an academy, into which he got together the sons of the most distinguished men, and had them instructed in the Roman language and grammar, according to the ancient meaning of that word. They were also, like the young Romans of rank, adorned with the *bulla* and dressed in the *prætexta*; it is evident that he secured to them the Roman franchise. These boys were at the same time to be to him the hostages for the fidelity of the parents, a thing which was very necessary, owing to the capricious disposition of the Spaniards. There was moreover formed around him a body-guard of men who, according to a custom which was peculiar to the Spaniards, took a vow not to survive him, and therefore in fighting for him, fought also for their own lives: this he readily agreed to, and it was a very numerous band. He also worked on their imagination, addressing himself to their own fancies. We need not assume with Plutarch, that it was trickery and cunning: it is very possible that, living among them, he shared their prejudices, when he treated a white hind as a fairy who disclosed to him the future. I believe that he was open to such impressions, like his master and instructor Marius.

The war lasted eight years from his first appearance in Spain to his death; but in fact there were not more than six years from the time when, after the downfall of his party, he placed himself at the head of the Spaniards. The Romans sent Q. Metellus—called *Pius* on account of his filial love to his father Q. Metellus Numidicus—against him into Bætica. Metellus was at first successful; but Sertorius soon gained more and more the advantage over him, so that the Romans gave the command to Cn. Pompey.

Cn. Pompey, at that time, was still of the equestrian order, that is to say, he had not yet held any office which entitled him to be chosen into the senate; he was about thirty years old. It is very difficult to speak at all decidedly of Pompey, as he is not one of those characters, like Marius, Sylla, Sertorius, or Cæsar, the outlines of which are distinct and marked; it is even hard to say whether he was a great general or not. He was one of those whose high position depends on their having been, if not altogether, at least to a certain degree favoured by fortune; he had not sufficient strength and greatness of soul to display the same bearing throughout a whole life, even in misfortune itself. There can be no mistake as to his having greatly distinguished himself under Sylla in the Social War, as the latter, who certainly was a competent judge on this point, particularly esteemed him. In the war of Sertorius, Pompey undoubtedly showed himself very different from Metellus, although Sertorius was superior to him in generalship; the war against the pirates was uncommonly well planned and speedily executed; the war with Mithridates was not a difficult one to carry on, still he was quick and resolute, and turned every circumstance to good account. Yet from the time of his triumph over Mithridates to the civil war against Cæsar, he appears to have been any thing but great, either as a citizen or a statesman. In the madness of his folly he wants to crush Cæsar, yet he is intimidated by the factions; just in the same way, he quailed before the faction of Clodius, and he was mean towards Cæsar, to whose superiority he was wilfully blind: he behaved like a trimmer and a thorough coward in the affair of Cicero's impeachment, and he never could be trusted as a friend. In his youth, during the war of Sylla, he showed himself cruel; and Cicero entertains no doubt but that in his old age, he would, if victorious, have renewed the proscriptions of Sylla. Nor is he much to be praised for any other great qualities: in eloquence and education he was nothing remarkable, he was even below mediocrity.

His head on his statues and busts, which we have no reason not to believe true likenesses, has something vulgar and coarse about it; in that of Cæsar's, we see the full expression of his vast and quick intellect. Pompey from weakness was at different times a different man, and had very much fallen off in his later years, though he was not more than fifty-six when he died: in his youth he was a much abler man.

In several campaigns, (in two of them especially,) Sertorius succeeded so well, that Metellus had to retreat to Andalusia, and Pompey across the Pyrenees, whilst he himself was able to return quietly into winter-quarters. Had the Spaniards only stood by each other, he would certainly have beaten both of these enemies; but he had just as much to struggle against the traitors among the Spaniards as against the Romans themselves. In two battles, on the Guadalquivir and on the Sucro, he withstood the united forces of the two Roman generals, and in both, one wing of each army was victorious; but as the Spaniards did not remain true to him, he got at last into very serious difficulties, notwithstanding all the readiness of his inventive mind. Many towns fell away from him; but in other quarters he met with all that faithful attachment is able to do: when Calagurris held out against a very sharp siege, he did his utmost to relieve it, in which he was also at length successful. Yet the cowardice and faithlessness of several towns goaded him into an action which is a stain upon his life: he even sold their hostages for slaves. It is true that other generals have often behaved in the same way; but yet he ought not to have done it, as it was at variance with his noble-heartedness, and his power was altogether a moral one: the consequence of it was, that the attachment of the other towns began likewise to waver.

With Sertorius was M. Perperna, a Roman of very high rank, probably a son of the consular M. Peperna: to judge from his name, he was most likely of Etruscan extraction, *-na* being an Etruscan termination which corresponds to the Roman *-ius*.[115] He had gathered together the remnants of the soldiers of Lepidus, and had wished at first to carry on the war by himself; but he was forced by his own troops to lead them over from Sardinia into Spain, and to acknowledge Sertorius as commander-in-chief. This man conspired with some other Romans against Sertorius, who before that had already had several persons executed for plots of this kind; owing to this circumstance, Perperna found many who were ready to join him. Sertorius was murdered at a feast. At his funeral, an incredible number of Spaniards, faithful to their vow, fell by each other's hands. Perperna was from necessity acknowledged as general; but in the first engagement with Pompey, he was utterly routed, taken prisoner, and put to death.[116]

SERVILE WAR. SPARTACUS. M. LICINIUS CRASSUS

Pompey was now made consul: he was the favourite of the people, as it was expected that he would restore the tribuneship. In no other way can I account for this enthusiasm. It might indeed much rather have been felt for Cæsar, whose nature was such that no worthy hearted man could come near him without loving him, even as Cicero in truth was always fond of him: it is a very noble want of the people, that it longs so often to find an object for its enthusiasm. Pompey had not yet been invested with any curule dignity; notwithstanding which, he was consul with Crassus, a man with whom he was at that time on such ill terms, that the Romans trembled lest the two foes should take up arms against each other. But at the urgent entreaties of the senate they made up their quarrel, and both of them behaved like honourable men; for during nineteen years afterwards they never were really enemies again, and they sometimes even appeared to be very good friends.

Crassus had gained his importance as the conqueror of Spartacus. About three[117] years after Sylla's death, Spartacus, a Thracian, had with forty, others say with seventy-four gladiators, broken out of a barrack of gladiators at Capua. There is a house at Pompeii which is very like a barrack, with rooms in which arms were found, and which has therefore been called the soldiers' quarters. The very fact that there should have been a garrison at Pompeii, seemed to me quite incredible; but on closer examination, I recognised the arms as being of the same description as those described by Livy as having been in use among the Samnites, which were afterwards adopted by the Campanians, and then by the gladiators; there is therefore no doubt but that it was a *ludus gladiatorius*, which we must thus suppose to have been a building of this kind, in which the gladiators were shut up at night. The number of the gladiators had gone on increasing; as the rage for them among the Romans had daily become greater, and such games were the surest means by which the men of rank could make themselves popular.

Spartacus, after having broken out, escaped with his followers to mount Vesuvius: he must have been a very great man, and would undoubtedly have proved himself to be one in any other position. The volcano had at that time quite burnt out: there was on it an old tumbled-down crater very difficult of access, in which they hid themselves, and whither immense crowds of slaves, of which there were then great numbers in Italy, ran to join them. Spartacus at first formed a band of robbers; and when troops were sent to surround and take him, he gave them the slip, and defeated the Romans with much loss on their side. By this means, the slaves began to be provided with good arms; hitherto they had made their own weapons themselves, as well as they could. Spartacus now proclaimed the freedom of the slaves. Lower Italy was in those days either altogether lying waste, or it was overrun by slaves, all of whom forthwith hastened to him: the freemen had so much dwindled since the devastations of Sylla, that there was no one at hand to check the insurrection. It is strange that among the slaves Germans also are positively mentioned: of these there cannot now have been many from the Teutones; they must have come thither from the Gauls by *commercium*. The leaders ruled with dictatorial power; Spartacus was a Thracian, Crixus and Oenomaus were Gauls. The war lasted until the third year. Two consular, and three prætorian armies were utterly routed; a great number of towns like Nola, Grumentum, Thurii, very likely also Compsa in the country of the Hirpinians, were taken and sacked with the atrocious cruelty which might have been looked for in a horde of bandits; we know but the smallest part of these horrors. Crassus defeated them in the third year. They had large forges for making arms, and did not shrink from the mighty thought of conquering the greater part of Italy, not to speak of destroying Rome itself. Rome would have been obliged to concentrate her power from all quarters, had not quarrels arisen among the rebels themselves, owing to which they split into three different bodies, each of which was hostile to the others; thus Crassus was enabled to defeat them one by one. Near Petilia in Lucania, he gained the last decisive victory; and he followed it up with the same cruelty which the German princes displayed after the Peasants' War in the sixteenth century. Every where prisoners were seen speared, hung up mangled on the highways, and tortured to death. The devastations of southern Italy have indeed never been so completely repaired, as to restore it to the same condition as that to which it had reached before the Marsian war; yet I fully believe, that even its present wretched state is better, and that its inhabitants are more numerous, than in the most prosperous times under the emperors. The free population was quite rooted out, the towns were laid waste, and the few places which are mentioned of Lucania in the itineraries, were hardly anything else but posting stages; the whole country moreover was turned into large estates which were used for the breeding of cattle, especially of horses. The number of monuments which one finds of the towns of that period, is incredibly small.

SECOND AND THIRD WAR AGAINST MITHRIDATES

At the same time, Rome was carrying on a war in Asia, against Mithridates. It was also in fact the third against him, and it had sprung out of the one with Sertorius: others, however, call it the second.

After Sylla had left Asia, Mithridates fulfilled most of the conditions of the peace; he gave Bithynia to Nicomedes, and Paphlagonia to the prince set up by the Romans; he also had delivered up ships, money and prisoners; in Cappadocia alone, the surrender had not been complete. Yet he had likewise yielded up the greater part of that country to Ariobarzanes, the prince protected by Romans, and he had kept but a small part of it; nor can we blame his motives for doing so. Having faithfully performed every stipulation with the exception of this single point, he now demanded that the Romans should exchange the treaty in form, and that the peace should be ratified in a regular written document by the senate and people, as Sylla had promised him; for as yet he had but Sylla's word. That he had not put forth these claims at once, was very naturally owing to Sylla's wishing first to regain Italy himself. Afterwards, the blame lay not so much with Sylla, who was not false in such matters, as with the senate, which flatly refused to grant such a document.

L. Murena now proceeded to Cappadocia, and thence he made an inroad into Mithridates' territory, and plundered the rich temple of Anaitis in Comana. Although Mithridates did everything in his power to avoid a collision, Murena carried things so far that a war broke out, in which he was worsted. After this, Mithridates still continued to declare with perfect truth, that he was only acting in self-defence; and he begged the Romans to ratify the treaty. Sertorius being still in arms, the Romans held their peace and took his excuses; but the treaties seem never to have been exchanged.

They left him in possession of that part of Cappadocia, and he affianced to Ariobarzanes one of his daughters who at that time was still a child. This is to be considered as the second Mithridatic War.

The last great war against Mithridates, a war which lasted even to the twelfth year, was brought about by Sertorius, who sent two proscribed persons (L. Marius, probably a Campanian new-citizen, and L. Fannius) to Mithridates, and made an alliance with him. It was stipulated that the latter should aid Sertorius with his naval forces, and place at his disposition the Cilician pirates, who were under his influence; Sertorius, on the other hand, was in the event of success to give up the whole of Asia to Mithridates.

FOOTNOTES

[1] Monte Pellegrino.—Germ. Edit.

[2] This number is stated in the Lex. Rhetoricum (Bekker Anecd. I. p. 298). Herodotus (VII. 184.) mentions eighty as the number of the crews of the penteconters. The number given in the text, rests only on one Manuscript of the lectures, but on a very trustworthy one.—Germ. Ed.

[3] One hundred quinqueremes, and twenty quadriremes. R. H. III, note 1053.—Germ. Edit.

[4] The elephants might perhaps have been introduced but a short time before from India, where they were in use from time immemorial: the Carthaginians had not yet employed them against Dionysius and Agathocles.

[5] The *legiones urbanæ* likewise were only phalangites.

[6] This remark that the story of the horrid death of Regulus originated with the poem of Nævius, was not repeated by Niebuhr in the year 1829, which may perhaps justify the surmise, that he had afterwards abandoned this conjecture; yet it is not to be forgotten, that at that period he treated this point on the whole much more concisely.—Germ. Ed.

[7] Thus the Romans always learned from their enemies; they are also said to have told the Carthaginians in the beginning of the struggle, not to compel them to a war by sea, as they had always learned from their enemies, and then surpassed them.

[8] In some MSS. *grandson,* which is in contradiction to the Fasti, but seems more appropriate, as 58 years intervene between the consulship of the two.

[9] By this is to be understood that, previous to the fourth decade, the office itself is not yet mentioned at all in our

Livy, but from thence, and in the fifth, more frequently. See Sigonius ad Liv. XXXIII. 21, 9.—Germ. Edit.

[10] In Suidas there is a touching story. When Antigonus Gonatas took Athens, which made a stout resistance, and was only compelled by famine to surrender, the old poet Philemon was still living in the Piræeus, whither he had removed, though not perhaps till after the downfall of the city. He was hoary with age, but still a hale old man, and his poetical powers had not yet left him. His last comedy was finished, all but one scene. He lay half dreaming on his couch, when he saw nine maidens in the room before him, who were just going away. Being asked who they were, and why they were leaving, they answered that he might well know them. They were the Muses: turning round towards him, they left him. Then he got up, finished his comedy, and died. Greek literature received its death-blow at the time of the loss of the Piræeus: the spirit may indeed be said to have fled from Greece.

[11] According to Justin, XLIII, extr., Trogus Pompeius was a Vocontian, from south-eastern Gaul. Conf. Niebuhr's Lectures on Ancient History, p. 9.—Germ. Edit.

[12] Montepulciano. (Lectures of 1826)—Germ. Edit.

[13] XXI, 38. R. H. II, 589.—Germ. Edit.

[14] Mistake, instead of, "in Lacinium." Polyb. III, 33, 18; 56, 4.—Germ. Edit.

[15] *Forschungen auf dem Gebiet der Geschichte.*

[16] When Bohemond, to check the Turks in the crusades, had corpses roasted, and shown to the ambassadors, this was a necessity. (See Wilken, History of the Crusades I, 87.)—Germ. Edit.

[17] Zonaras IX, 2. (from Dio Cassius). Appian. Pun. 63.—Germ. Edit.

[18] Cicero (de Oratore II, 18), in the anecdote of the rhetorician who expatiated before Hannibal on the excellencies of a general, says that Hannibal did not speak Greek well (*non optime Græce*).

[19] J. A. de Luc, Histoire du passage des Alpes par Annibal. Genève, 1818.

[20] See Leon. Aretino's description of the roads and inhabitants of Tyrol in the fifteenth century, in his journey to Constance, which quite reminds one of the times of the Romans.

[21] So in the MSS. Probably Niebuhr made a slip of the tongue. According to Polybius, Lilybæum is the place.—Germ. Edit.

[22] In the year 1828, this assertion is expressed quite positively, "Sempronius came from Africa to Genoa," in which of course the soldiers taking their oath that they would be at Rimini by an appointed time, is left out.—Germ. Edit.

[23] There seems to be a mistake here; but the MSS. agree in giving "Apennines." What is to be placed instead, seems to me difficult to say for certain; perhaps "Ariminum."—Germ. Edit.

[24] This name also seems incorrect; yet all the MSS. have either this, or another of a similar sound.

[25] The following account is borrowed from the lectures of 1826-7, which I think I ought not to suppress. "Whether Hannibal now marched along the Arno into the upper valley of that river, or whether he turned towards the district of Siena, is not to be decided. I believe that he did the latter, although Livy talks of a devastation of the upper valley of the Arno (very likely a figment of Cœlius Antipater); but in that case, Flaminius could not have executed his hapless march. Hannibal's object must have been, not the laying waste of some Etrurian districts, but to gain the road to Rome; and that he also did. I believe therefore that on getting out of the swamps, he threw himself into the mountains of Chiusi. Flaminius heard of this movement, and tried by forced marches to reach the road to Rome. If my opinion be correct, even the description of Polybius is wrong; for according to his account, as well as that of Livy, Hannibal had passed by Cortona, and thrown himself between the mountains and the lake Trasimenus, and Flaminius had followed him:

here Hannibal stopped, occupied the hills, and placed an ambush for Flaminius. In my opinion, both the generals went round the lake, but from different sides; otherwise it would be impossible that Flaminius had allowed himself to be surprised. If Hannibal had marched by that road, he would have passed within only a few leagues of Arezzo, and then Flaminius must have long known of his march; if, on the contrary, he went through the district of Siena by San Gemignano and Colle, all may be accounted for. We understand then, that Flaminius, who started in pursuit, was not able to catch him; that Hannibal came to the south side of the Trasimenus, whilst Flaminius imagined that he was already much further advanced on the road to Rome, and that he only intended to cut him off. Then it could happen that Hannibal took up his position on the south side of the lake, and placed his light troops around on the hills, between which and the lake the road lay. This could be done unknown to Flaminius, only when he was not aware, that Hannibal had taken this road." Whilst elsewhere there is reason to presume, that wherever the later lectures differ from the earlier ones, Niebuhr had changed his views, and therefore, generally speaking, his last opinions only are given, the present case seems to have been different; and on this ground, the detailed discussion on the march of Hannibal has been inserted in this note.—Germ. Edit.

[26] V, 17. from Q. Claudius (*Quadrigarius, Annalium* l. V.) and Macrob. Saturn. I, 16.—Germ. Edit.

[27] In the same manner there exist three different accounts of the death of Marcellus.

[28] According to Appian, they were 48,000 foot, 8,000 horse, and 15 elephants.

[29] Liv. XXXVIII, 56. Valer. Max. IV, I. 6. According to both passages, he was, however, to be appointed consul and *dictator* for life.—Germ. Edit.

[30] Here follows in the lectures of 1829 a very brief review of the state of things in Italy after the war of Hannibal, which, however, to avoid repetitions, I have made into

one with the more explicit account, which follows after the war of Antiochus.—Germ. Edit.

[31] The second war of Philip against the Romans is generally reckoned as the first Macedonian War; we more correctly so call the one which coincides with the war with Hannibal.

[32] See above, p. 48.

[33] When we read that Hannibal had changed the *ordo judicum*, this means without a doubt not the Suffetes, whom the Greeks always call βασιλεῖς, but the hundred or hundred and four of Aristotle, a power which was quite distinct from that of the constituted authorities of state, and was very like the state-inquisition at Venice.

[34] Diod. XVI. 91. Just. IX. 5.—Germ. Edit.

[35] A dollar (Prussian) = 3 shillings.—Trans.

[36] St. Jerome, as he says, heard the same language in Phrygia which he had heard in Treves. This does not, however, refer to the Galatians; but St. Jerome probably had seen Germans, who at different times, especially Gothic ones under Theodosius, had settled in Phrygia. For it is to be considered as an undoubted fact, that Treves was German, and the Gallic language could have scarcely maintained itself in Asia to such a late period as his.

[37] II, 9.

[38] Ulixes was Siculian: in a temple in the island of Sicily, there was found some connexion with him. (Plut. Marc. c. 20.—Germ. Ed.)

[39] Circe was quite correctly placed in Circeii, which is the most ancient form of the fable.

[40] If this be meant for *S. C. de Bacchanalibus*, the quotation is a mistake, as that decree is not later than Plautus: probably instead of "*senatus consultum*" it ought to be said inscription, or a similar word, as undoubtedly the inscription of the *columna rostrata* is meant.—Germ. Edit.

[41] See on the other hand vol. i., p. 17.—Germ. Edit.

[42] Niebuhr uses the English word.—Transl.

[43] Jul. Victor, p. 224. Or., and in the same place. Ang. Maius.—Germ. Ed.

[44] Fabr. Bibl. Gr. IV. 461.—Germ. Edit.

[45] Polyb. X. 9, 3.

[46] Gall. 12. A. U. C. 631. Appian.—Germ. Ed.

[47] P. Cornelius Cethegus and M. Bæbius Tamphilus, in the year of the city 571.—Germ. Ed.

[48] De Colon. ed. Goës, p. 106.—Germ. Ed.

[49] Plut. Æmil. Paull. 19.

[50] Schneider in his Latin grammar has a whole chapter on the name of *Perseus*. But all the Greek names ending in εύς had in the old Latin the termination *-es*, and were in the genitive case declined after the second declension. *Piraeeus* makes in the genitive *Piraei*, (*Piraeei* being a barbarism which is not to be met with in any MS.). *Perseus* differs from the rest, in afterwards getting into the third declension. Its accusative is *Persen*: *Persum* does not occur, but certainly *Piraeum* does.

[51] This original opinion on the work of Polybius, which Niebuhr repeated several times (see R. H. III. p. 49.) is probably to be understood thus, that he makes the first edition reach to the conclusion of the thirtieth book, (one MS. states in this passage, books I. to XXVIII., in which very likely the first two books are not included,) and considers the rest as added in the second edition.—Germ. Edit.

[52] This remark dates from 1826, and was therefore anterior to the emancipation of the Roman Catholics.—Germ. Ed.

[53] Liv. Epit. 48.

[54] Liv. Epit. 55.

[55] Schol. Bob. in Orat. pro Sulla. (Orelli vol. V. P. 2. p. 361.) In Liv. XL, 19, the reading is very doubtful, see the commentators, whence the supposition, that the law dates from Sulla. Others refer this *Lex Cornelia* to the consul Cn.

Cornelius Dolabella (595), quoting Liv. Epit. 47.—Germ. Edit.

[56] In several very good MSS., there is here the following reading, "but probably later than is generally assumed; it must have been shortly before the last war with Rome." The editor quotes this, since there are no arguments given, for deciding the question; yet the reading inserted in the text, seems to be more correct, as the general belief places the war of Masinissa very close indeed to the outbreak of the third Punic war.—Germ. Edit.

[57] In the received editions of the Capitoline Fasti, the name *Æmilianus* at the year 618 (19) seems genuine, we also meet with *Æmiliano Scipioni*, Cic. Phil. XIII. 4, 9.—Germ. Ed.

[58] There have been published of him, "J. E. Humbert, Notice sur quatre cippes sepulcraux, et deux fragmens decouverts en 1817 sur le sol de l'ancienne Carthage, à la Haye 1821." The papers of Borgia, which seem to be at Naples, are made use of in H. F. J. Estrup *Lineæ topographicæ Carthaginis Tyriæ Hafn.* 1821. 8.—Germ. Ed.

[59] *Literally*, "villages as large as Sinzig."

[60] Thonium in Locris 1829, probably a *lapsus linguæ*.—Germ. Ed.

[61] If in the Epitome of Livy the time of his war is stated as being fourteen years, one is to add the former war, in which he already distinguished himself in a separate command among the Lusitanians.

[62] See above, p. 60.

[63] Zumpt's annals are very recommendable in their way.

[64] I know of no passage where this is stated. May this not perhaps have been a mistake for Blæsus, who has written Rhintonian pieces?—Germ. Edit.

[65] See vol. I., p. 251.

[66] Ibid. p. 398.

[67] These words are in the original.

[68] In Liv. XXXI, 4. Lucania is not mentioned.—Germ. Edit. II.

[69] I have supplied this name merely from conjecture: the MSS. have *Solino*, a place which I do not find.—Germ. Ed.

[70] This English word is in the original.

[71] A mistake, very likely from misreading the academical shorthand of the MSS. It should be, *the queen*, the quotation being from the mock tragedy "Esther" in the *Jahrmarkt Zu Plundersweilern*.—Transl.

[72] Olive plantations especially are only productive after a long time, so that an ejectment renders entirely fruitless a very great amount of labour bestowed upon them.

[73] For Niebuhr reads Liv. Epit. LVIII, *ne quis ex publica agro plus quam M jugera possideret*. R. H. vol. II., p. 150.—Germ. Edit.

[74] See vol. I., p. 401.

[75] This is one of the instances, when Niebuhr was cut short by the close of the hour in the middle of an idea, the thread of which he did not carefully take up at the beginning of the next lecture.—Germ. Edit.

[76] In Plutarch, *Vit. C. Gracch.*, on the contrary, it is stated, ἐνέστησαν οἱ πολλοὶ καὶ κατέλυσαν τὴν κρίσιν ὑπὲρ τοῦ Γαΐου φοβηθέντες, μὴ περιπετὴς τῇ αἰτίᾳ τοῦ φόνου ζητουμένου γένηται, which, when applying to C. Gracchus, is hardly substantiated.—Germ. Ed.

[77] It is now printed in *Auctores classici e Vaticanis Codd. editi, cur. Ang. Majo, Vol.* II. *Rom.* 1828. (*Schol. Bobiensia in Cic. Milon. c. 7. in Orelli V.* 2. p. 283.)

[78] This is perhaps to be modified thus, that this formula here occurs for the first time since the abolition of the dictatorship (in the middle of the sixth century): it is, on the whole, very old, and we meet with it for the first time in the year 290. Liv. III, 4.—Germ. Edit.

[79] *Cantharidas sumpsisse dicitur. Cic. Fam.* IX. 21: it was another Cn. Papirius Carbo, who put an end to himself by means of *atramentum sutorium. Cic. ibid.*—Germ. Edit.

[80] I cannot answer for the correctness of the name; it occurs, indistinctly written, only in one of my MSS. of 1826-7.—Germ. Edit.

[81] See Bentl. ad Hor. Carm. IV, 8, 17; who, however, strikes out that line, from metrical reasons also. Others conjecture that there is a hiatus in that passage.—Germ. Edit.

[82] In vol. I, p. 258, and R. H. II, 195, the Cassii are considered as plebeians: our passage dates from 1826-7; the former one from 1828-9.—Germ. Edit.

[83] Conf. vol. I, p. 367.

[84] Bonn is here spoken of.—Transl.

[85] Cicero does not seem to say this quite so explicitly in Brutus 62, 224. Longe autem post natos homines improbissimus C. Servilius Glaucia, sed peracutus et callidus imprimisque ridiculus—homo simillimus Atheniensis Hyperboli, cujus improbitatem veteres Atticorum comœdiæ notaverunt. Conf. de Orat. II, 61, 249; 65, 263.—Germ. Edit.

[86] Cic. ad Att. III. 23. pro Cæcina 33. Walter's History of the Roman law (*Geschichte des Römischen Rechts*), 2d edit., vol. II., p. 12, notes 45 & 46.—Germ. Ed.

[87] Valer. Maxim. III, 4, 5. Whether M. Peperna, who was consul in the year 622 is the same person as the consul of the year 660, who was censor in 666, is no more to be made out; yet it is possible, as according to Plin. *H. N.* vii, 49, he reached the age of eighty-nine years. But in that case the censorship would be later than the *lex Licinia et Mucia,* and the proposition would be untenable. If they be two different persons, the words "and the censorship" in the text are to be cast out. But the matter is not quite certain, as in Valerius Maximus it is said, *lege Papia,* which altogether clashes with the account as given above.—Germ. Edit.

[88] Vol. I., p. 167.

[89] De Orat. I, 7, 24.

[90] Diod. Exc. Vatic., p. 128., Dind.—Germ. Ed.

[91] In the year 1827, Niebuhr had remarked, "Now we shall probably know soon some further details about it, thanks to the fragments of Diodorus discovered by Maï, if they be really new ones."—Germ. Ed.

[92] See above, p. 130.

[93] The prænomen is not to be made out with certainty. See *Orellii Onomast. Tull. s. v.* p. 256.—Germ. Edit.

[94] In Terence, in the Eunuchus and the Adelphi, the name indeed occurs, but not in the character which it had afterwards.—Germ. Edit.

[95] Mistake instead of Diodorus Siculus (Fragm. l. xxxvii).—Germ. Ed.

[96] Vol. I, p. 450.

[97] Appian 1, 49. In the year 1827, Niebuhr made the emendation δεκατρεῖς, explaining the number VIII from XIII.—Germ. Edit.

[98] Dio Cass. fragm. I. 27. CLXVI. App. I. 68.—Germ. Ed.

[99] This passage, which is of the year 1827, and is given with the same conciseness in all the MSS. which are at my disposition, is only to be interpreted by conjecture. Probably it is *Epist. Cœl. ad Cic.* (Fam. viii.) 14, 3. *In hac discordia video Cn. Pompeium senatum, quique res judicant, secum habiturum: ad Cæsarem omnes,* QUI CUM TIMORE AUT MALA SPE VIVANT, *accessuros: exercitum conferendum non esse omnino.*—Germ. Ed.

[100] Appian I. 84.—Germ. Edit.

[101] Two thousand six hundred according to App. I, 103, in which number, however, all the knights who perished in this war are included.—Germ. Ed.

[102] Cic. Cat. III. 6. § 14. On the other hand, Frontin. de colon. p. 112. Goes. Colonia Florentina deducta a III viris assignata lege Julia.—Germ. Ed.

[103] H. N. XIV. 8. 2?—Germ. Ed.

[104] This is evidently a slip of the memory, the passage of Asconius (in Pisonianam, p. 3, Orellii) running thus, *Magno*

opere me hæsitare confiteor, quid sit quare Cicero Placentiam municipium esse dicit. Video enim in annalibus eorum qui Punicum bellum scripserunt tradi, Placentiam deductam pridie Kal. Jun., primo anno eius belli, P. Cornelio Scipione, patre Africani prioris, Ti. Sempronio Longo Coss. &c.—Germ. Ed.

[105] Conf. vol. I, p. 523.

[106] The *Pontifex Maximus* was included among these.

[107] Dr. Schmitz has already remarked in vol. I, p. 416, of his version (published under the title of History of Rome from the first Punic War to the death of Constantine, by B. G. Niebuhr, in a series of lectures Lond. 1844), that this number does not rest upon any direct authority. Cic. *ad Att.* I, 14, 5, states the number of voters in the senate in a certain affair to have been about 415, fifteen having voted on one side, and on the other, *facile* 400; from which we may safely conclude that the sum total must have been larger. In the I. Maccab. 8, 15, at the end, therefore, of the sixth century, the number is mentioned to have been 320; yet when we consider the other statements which are made in that passage, we must not lay too much stress upon it.—Germ. Edit.

[108] In 1827 Niebuhr expressed himself on this point in the following manner:—

"That the result of his legislation could not have satisfied him, was in the very nature of things, and therefore he who had shed so much blood to get the government into his own hands, resigned the dictatorship two years after he had been appointed to it, as he saw the uselessness of his institutions, which he had established at the cost of so many atrocities. This is the most natural way of accounting for his resignation, which has been so much talked of: it was a mistake of very judicious people, to hunt out reasons for it which were too far-fetched."—Germ. Edit.

[109] The contradiction of this passage with that in vol. I. p. 469, in which Clitarchus is termed an *elegant* writer, seems to be accounted for by supposing that the expression "elegant" is in that place one of disparagement, referring

to Longin. c. 3 who calls him φλοιώδης καὶ φυσῶν. Of Sisenna, Cicero says in *Brutus* 64, *Hujus omnis facultas ex historia ipsius perspici potest, quæ, cum facile vincat omnes superiores, tum indicat tamen, quantum absit a summo, quamque hoc genus scriptionis nondum sit satis Latinis literis illustratum;* and *de Legg.* 1, 2.—*in historia puerile quoddam consectatur, ut unum Clitarchum, neque præterea quemquam de Græcis legisse videatur;* so that Niebuhr calls this *puerile,* this affected mannerism, the *horridum,* inasmuch as it so greatly *a summo abest.*—Germ. Ed.

[111] See Biographical Notices of (*Lebensnachrichten über*) B. G. Niebuhr II, p. 402.—Germ. Edit.

[112] A direct mention of the place is hardly to be found in Cicero; but in a general way he commends the Sabines as *severissimi homines, in Vatin.* 15, *ad Famil.* XV, 20.—Germ. Ed.

[113] Perhaps more correctly, Julius Salinator. Plutarch Sertor. c. 7.—Germ. Edit.

[114] *Histor.* III. in *Servius ad Virg.* Æn. I. 698.—Germ. Ed.

[115] It has been said that all the Roman gentile names, ended in *-ius;* but in names like Cæcina, Vibena, Porsena, and others, the termination *-na* remained, even after the clan had become Roman citizens. Ernesti, who had not perceived this, mistook Cæcina for a *cognomen,* and sought for the name of the clan; but the inscriptions confirm the fact of its being a gentile name.

[116] With the death of Sertorius, the lectures of 1826-7 are brought to a conclusion.—Germ. Ed.

[117] More correctly, *five.*—Germ. Ed.